CHICANOS

SOCIAL and PSYCHOLOGICAL PERSPECTIVES

CHICANOS

SOCIAL and PSYCHOLOGICAL PERSPECTIVES

CARROL A. HERNÁNDEZ

Department of Psychology, University of Washington,
Seattle, Washington

MARSHA J. HAUG

Department of Psychology, University of Washington,
Seattle, Washington

NATHANIEL N. WAGNER, Ph.D.

Professor and Director of Clinical Psychology Training,
University of Washington, Seattle, Washington

Photographs by Irwin Nash

SECOND EDITION

The C. V. Mosby Company

Saint Louis   1976

SECOND EDITION

Copyright © 1976 by The C. V. Mosby Company

All rights reserved. No part of this book may be reproduced
in any manner without written permission of the publisher.

Previous edition copyrighted 1971

Printed in the United States of America

Distributed in Great Britain by Henry Kimpton, London

Library of Congress Cataloging in Publication Data

Main entry under title:

Chicanos.

First edition published in 1971 compiled by
N. N. Wagner.
Bibliography: p.
Includes index.
1. Mexican Americans—Psychology—Addresses, essays,
lectures. 2. Mexican Americans—Social conditions—
Addresses, essays, lectures. I. Hernández, Carrol A.
II. Haug, Marsha J. III. Wagner, Nathaniel N.,
comp. Chicanos. IV. Nash, Irwin. [DNLM: 1. Emigration
and immigration. 2. Minority groups. 3. Prejudice.
4. Transients and migrants. E184.M5 H557c]
E184.M5W3   1976   301.45′16′872073   75-37769
ISBN 0-8016-5316-9

TS/VH/VH   9 8 7 6 5 4 3 2 1

CONTRIBUTORS

Murray Alpert, Ph.D.

Associate Professor of Psychiatry, New York University, School of Medicine, New York, N. Y.

Rodolfo Alvarez, Ph.D.

Associate Professor of Sociology, University of California, Los Angeles, Calif.

David Alvírez, Ph.D.

Assistant Professor of Sociology, University of New Mexico, Albuquerque, N. M.

Russell E. Ames, Jr., Ph.D.

Assistant Professor of Educational Psychology, Purdue University, Lafayette, Ind.

Edward Casavantes, Ph.D.

Associate Professor of Social Work and Ethnic Studies, California State University, Sacramento, Calif.

Anthony Gary Dworkin, Ph.D.

Assistant Professor of Sociology, University of Missouri, Columbia, Mo.

Robert B. Edgerton, Ph.D.

Associate Professor of Psychiatry, University of California, Neuropsychiatric Institute, Los Angeles, Calif.

Horacio Fabrega, Jr., M.D.

Associate Professor of Psychiatry and Anthropology, Michigan State University, College of Human Medicine, East Lansing, Mich.

Raymond T. Garza, Ph.D.

Assistant Professor of Psychology, University of California, Riverside, Calif.

Viktor Gecas, Ph.D.

Assistant Professor of Rural Sociology, Washington State University, Pullman, Wash.

Elena Gonzales, B.A.

Graduate Student in Clinical Psychology, University of Washington, Seattle, Wash.

Armando Gutierrez, Ph.D.

Assistant Professor of Government, University of Texas, Austin, Tex.

Herbert Hirsch, Ph.D.

Associate Professor of Government, University of Texas, Austin, Tex.

Quinton C. James, M.D.

Regional Chief, South Central Mental Health Services of Los Angeles County, Los Angeles, Calif.

Marvin Karno, M.D.

Associate Professor of Psychiatry, University of California, Neuropsychiatric Institute, Los Angeles, Calif.

Martin Kesselman, M.D.

Assistant Professor of Psychiatry, New York University, School of Medicine, New York, N. Y.

v

Harry H. L. Kitano, Ph.D.

Professor of Social Welfare and Sociology, University of California, Los Angeles, Calif.

Luis R. Marcos, M.D.

Clinical Instructor and Postdoctoral Fellow, Department of Psychiatry, State University of New York, Brooklyn, N. Y.

Cervando Martinez, M.D.

Assistant Professor of Psychiatry, University of Texas Health Science Center, San Antonio, Tex.

Charles G. McClintock, Ph.D.

Associate Professor of Psychology, University of California, Santa Barbara, Calif.

Mary Meeker, Ph.D.

Associate Professor of Educational Psychology, Loyola University, Los Angeles, Calif.

Robert Meeker, Ph.D.

Assistant Director, Center for Computor-Based Behavioral Studies, University of California, Los Angeles, Calif.

Jane R. Mercer, Ph.D.

Associate Professor of Sociology, University of California, Riverside, Calif.

Manuel Miranda, Ph.D.

Acting Associate Professor of Social Welfare, University of California, Los Angeles, Calif.

Armando Morales, D.S.W.

Assistant Professor of Psychiatry, University of California, Neuropsychiatric Institute, Los Angeles, Calif.

Nathan Murillo, Ph.D.

Associate Professor of Counseling and Psychology, California State University, Northridge, Calif.

Amado Padilla, Ph.D.

Associate Professor of Psychology, University of California, Los Angeles, Calif.

Eligio R. Padilla, Ph.D.

Assistant Professor of Psychiatry, University of California, Neuropsychiatric Institute, Los Angeles, Calif.

Norman Palley, B.A.

Los Angeles County Department of Mental Health, Los Angeles, Calif.

Dudley L. Poston, Jr., Ph.D.

Assistant Professor of Sociology, University of Texas, Austin, Tex.

Manuel Ramirez III, Ph.D.

Associate Professor of Psychology, University of California, Santa Cruz, Calif.

Rene A. Ruiz, Ph.D.

Professor of Psychology, University of Missouri, Kansas City, Mo.

†George I. Sanchez, Ph.D.

Formerly Director of the Center for International Education, University of Texas, Austin, Tex.

Leonel Urcuyo, M.D.

Staff Psychiatrist, New York University, School of Medicine, New York, N. Y.

Carole Ann Wallace, B.A.

Research Assistant, Department of Psychiatry, Michigan State University, College of Human Medicine, East Lansing, Mich.

Joe Yamamoto, M.D.

Professor of Psychiatry, University of Southern California, School of Medicine, Los Angeles, Calif.

---

†Deceased.

This volume is dedicated to
the development of scholarly excellence
in the area of oppressed and minority peoples
so that the injustices of neglect and
prejudice may be eradicated.

PREFACE

In the more than four years that have passed since the first edition, the research concerning Chicanos has increased significantly. This second edition has been reorganized to include some of this recent and pertinent research. As a part of this reorganization, however, major changes have occurred. The most significant of the changes (at least to us) has been an almost complete reemphasis of the introductory section. From articles offering a general discussion of group differences, prejudice, and discrimination, we have turned to several essays written by leading Chicano social scientists on various aspects of the Chicano experience.

As the first edition of this book was used for several courses, it quickly became obvious that the majority of students reading it came away from the experience with some factual knowledge about research findings on Chicanos. Unfortunately, however, very, very few came away with any intuitive "feel" for Chicanos and the Chicano experience in the United States. Very basic questions such as "What's the difference between Mexican-Americans and Chicanos?" or "Why don't Chicanos just learn English and be like everyone else?" were continually asked. In this new introductory section and the sections that follow we have attempted to provide some answers to these questions. To the extent that it is possible to answer these questions or to achieve that intuitive "feel" through scientific rather than literary, poetic, or philosophical writings, we hope that we have succeeded.

Actually, a major focus of the volume that we consciously tried not to change was the emphasis upon scientific and research writings as opposed to more easily read philosophical and personal essays. This is not to pass judgment as to which form is more important; anyone truly interested in the Chicano experience must become knowledgeable in, or at least acquainted with, both. One without the other inevitably results in an inadequate picture of the second largest minority group in the United States. Because of the focus we wished to retain, we were forced to turn down several creative, well-written, and philosophical manuscripts submitted by thoughtful Chicano authors. While we regretted not being able to include these works, we believed strongly that the major orientation and contribution of this particular volume had to be upon research findings about the Chicano. As much as possible we attempted to maintain a sense for Chicanos as a heterogeneous people, but we attempted to accomplish this through the various research studies. The literary and philosophical tracts we leave to other volumes and other authors, since this volume is intended for use in a college course in the social sciences.

In addition to a new introductory section and the continued emphasis upon more scientific works, this second edition has fewer sections than the original edition. Only three of the original seven sections remain—the introductory, personality, and mental health sections, and these three sections have been revised substantially. The sections previously labeled interethnic perceptions, sex roles and the family, Chicanos and the law, and Chicanos and the schools have been incorporated into the three revised sections and the two new sections—society and justice, and education and intellectual assessment. It is hoped that this basic reorganization will assist the reader in understanding the major issues developed in each section.

The final modification has been an increased emphasis upon mental health issues. In a very true sense, each of the preceding sections contributes to a foundation upon which the reader can build a better understanding of the often alien environment in which Chicanos must survive —both mentally and physically. Mental health is not a state of being, separate unto itself. All areas of an individual's functioning contribute to one's state of mental comfort or discomfort. For this reason the number of studies in the mental health unit has been doubled.

Unfortunately, some major areas of concern have not been included. There is no article in this volume dealing specifically with the relationship between Chicanos and the Church, although religion is a very strong influence in the life of most Chicanos. For those interested in this relationship, Cesar Chávez has an article in *El Grito* that examines some of the nuances of that relationship. The second area of neglect has been the role of the Chicana in the continuing struggle of the Chicano people. Nowhere were we able to find an article that we felt met our requirements of both sensitivity and knowledge. Rather than include an article of poor or secondary quality we chose not to include one at all. This lack of both quality and quantity of work is a sad statement about the researcher's view of the importance of the Chicana's role in the survival of the Chicano people.

In conclusion, then, it is obvious that this volume is not a comprehensive study of the Chicano people. It includes little, if any, about the literature, history, or varying philosophies of this group. Nevertheless, we are relatively content, for it was never our intention to create an all-inclusive volume. For that the reader must look elsewhere. What we have attempted is to acquaint the reader with some of the current sociological and psychological perspectives of Chicanos. There are many ways to try to reduce ill-founded prejudice and discrimination. The way we have chosen is through knowledge. If this volume aids some of its readers in questioning stereotypes and attitudes, then we have at least partly accomplished our goal. If it starts the reader on an ever greater quest for knowledge about the Chicano people, then we will have succeeded even beyond our hopes. (For those interested in this quest, there is an annotated bibliography at the end of this book.) It is hoped that this book will be a good beginning.

Carrol A. Hernández
Marsha J. Haug
Nathaniel N. Wagner

CONTENTS

PART FOUR
EDUCATION AND INTELLECTUAL ASSESSMENT

PART FIVE
MENTAL HEALTH

CHICANOS

SOCIAL and PSYCHOLOGICAL PERSPECTIVES

PART ONE
INTRODUCTORY SECTION

What is the essence of being Chicano? Sorting out what is unique in the experience of Mexican Americans from what they have in common with people in general, with other American minority groups, and with poor people is the task the writers in this section set for themselves.

Edward Casavantes dissects the common stereotypes of the Mexican American and distinguishes those characteristics that derive from the state of poverty from those rightly attributed to the culture of Mexico. He makes this well-taken point: "With rare exception, every time social scientists have studied 'Mexican Americans,' they have ended up describing *poor* Mexican Americans, . . . 'the quaint,' ignoring Mexican Americans who are middle class . . . (resulting in) the perpetuation of very damaging stereotypes. . . ." It is advisable to keep in mind the characteristics that constitute the "culture of poverty" in evaluating writings purporting to deal in essence with *mexicanismo,* and try to separate the stereotypes from the truth. But it should not be forgotten, either, that fully 30% to 40% of Chicanos do fall within the culture of poverty, and that this poverty and its concomitant factors form the bulk of the Chicanos' problems.

Nathan Murillo seems willing to accept (though with important reservations and qualifications) more of the stereotypes about Chicanos than Casavantes, who acknowledges only the Spanish language and some unnamed customs handed down from Mexico. There is a *grain* of truth (however small) in most stereotypes; intergroup differences do exist, but they are of a normative rather than absolute nature. The range of personality traits and behavior patterns is of course as wide among Chicanos as among Anglos, but the distribution in some cases is different. The "typical" Chicano is Catholic, the "average" Anglo, Protestant; yet one need not be Catholic to be considered Chicano, and

1

one may be devoutly Catholic and unquestionably Anglo. The average is a statistic, not a person, and if this is kept in mind, knowledge of such relative differences may be useful. The varying interpretations of the concept of courtesy cited by Murillo are a good example. Such attitudinal differences between Anglos and Chicanos have been the unrecognized cause of much misunderstanding and vague criticism of the Mexican family, as exemplified by Heller (1966) and Madsen (1964).

Mexican family relationships have been the object of more analysis, praise, and criticism than any other aspect of Mexican life—understandably so, since family ties are generally strong and highly valued by the individual. The family remains the single most important reference group for most individuals throughout life. The Mexican (and Mexican American) family has demonstrated a remarkable viability throughout the years and throughout a variety of social conditions. The fact of such stability should dispel any myth of uniformity, rigidity, or pathology in Chicano family structure. Any institution so characterized could obviously not endure the tumultuous changes that have rocked both Mexican and American society in the last

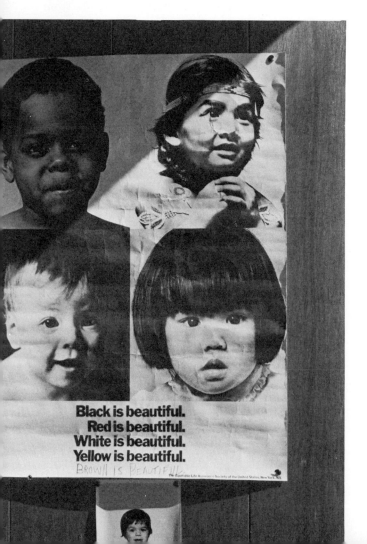

century. The family, like other facets of the culture, is a
dynamic historical entity, and each family unit is to some
extent unique, as is its situation.

Murillo outlines some of the problems and assets of the
Chicano family today, particularly with respect to the
changing role of women and the conflict between certain
Anglo and Mexican modes of interaction. His essay is particularly laudable because, firstly, it focuses on Mexican
Americans (far too often, wholesale generalizations have
been made from anthropological studies done in Mexico,
which, whatever their merit, do not address the situation
of those living in an Anglo-dominated society); and secondly, it highlights the well-adjusted, normal majority
rather than the pathological extremes that so fascinate
most anthropological and psychoanalytically oriented writers. If one were to judge by their representation in the literature, one would likely conclude that the chronically depressed, self-denying, overly submissive woman (like the
wife of Oscar Lewis's "Pedro Martinez"), the manipu-
lative, man-hating mother who warps her children emotionally, and the passive-dependent male who overcompen-
sates for his feelings of weakness and inferiority with
exaggerated masculine behaviors, were the rule rather
than the exception (see Maccoby, 1967). On the contrary,
as Murillo remarks, anyone familiar with Mexico's tumultuous history "must find it difficult to believe that submissiveness is a cultural characteristic of the Mexican"—of
either sex. (For those whose knowledge of Mexican history
is faulty, Turner's [1968] book, *The Dynamic of Mexican
Nationalism,* is recommended. It includes an especially
good chapter on the role of women in the Revolución de
1910 and subsequent feminist legislation and social
progress.) Chicanos are actively struggling with the question of sex roles and other issues that confront the modern
family in much the same way that Anglos are; but as Sutherland (1970), a Chicana feminist, observes, in their determination to preserve the great satisfactions and security
they obtain within the family, Chicanos are taking their
own distinctive path toward liberation.

Much is worth preserving and emulating in the Chicano
way of life. The mutual respect, affection, sense of responsibility, and present-time orientation characteristic of Chicano families has been shown to be a particularly adaptive
atmosphere in which to raise children; Goodman and
Beman (1970), for example, found that *barrio* children
manifested significantly better personal adjustment than
Anglo and Negro children in similarly bleak economic circumstances. Murillo's point is well-taken that "much of
our Anglo society's psychotherapy is aimed at developing
or rekindling a *here* and *now* time orientation in the client
as a means to improved mental health"—not to mention
conjoint family therapists' efforts to instill into their client
families the kind of warmth, mutual regard, and cohe-
siveness that characterize Chicano family structure. In a
different vein, Romano-V. (1970) notes that, "as a popula-

tion whose antecedents are Mexican, the bulk of Chicano existence has been oriented to a symbiotic residence within ecosystems. For in Mexico, unlike the United States, no plant or animal has been rendered extinct in its five hundred year history. Thus Chicano history has for centuries practiced what only today is becoming a concern of modern science for the conservation of natural resources and a balance of nature. In other words, what in ignorance and crudeness has been called the Mexican *traditional subjugation to nature* by Saunders, Edmunson, Kluckhohn, Heller, Samora, and many other social scientists, in reality has been a conscious philosophy for the maintenance of ecological balance in an ecosystem."

The final two articles in this section deal with the relations between the generations of Mexican Americans in light of historical influences and the emergence of the "Chicano generation." Alvarez discusses the unique historical experience of Mexican Americans, created as a people by military conquest of a part of Mexico by the United States. In this respect their situation is more comparable to the French Canadians' than to that of any of our immigrant groups. The Chicanos were "there first"; they had an established culture, economy, and way of life with roots in their environs; the Anglos were the immigrants. There the similarity ends, however, for Chicanos were in the pe-

culiar position after the conquest of being able, through geographical proximity, to maintain family and cultural ties with the mother country. This served both to retard the assimilation (read: cultural annihilation) of the *mexicanos* into the dominant society and to obscure somewhat the extent of Anglo racism from their view. Economic and political oppression of both subtle and not-so-subtle varieties have prevented Chicanos from even testing the barriers to equality in any substantial number until recently, and effectively isolated those who attempted to break out of the lower caste position so that their experience did not become part of the "collective consciousness" (that is, a shared and consensually validated frustration). Clearly, however, the Mexican Americans of previous generations have not been "sleeping," as has frequently and insultingly been implied, but have been striving to the limits of their resources to improve the lot of their people and laying the groundwork for the current, more visible struggle of the "Chicano generation."

The mutually-enhancing relationship between self-esteem and political activism is illustrated by Gutierrez and Hirsch in their study of Crystal City, Texas. Here, where Chicanos first succeeded in wresting political control of their own community from the hands of the Anglo minority, the investigators found that young Chicanos who

had been instrumental in bringing about the takeover and were now being educated in their native tongue and about their cultural heritage, manifested high hopes for their future, an impressive degree of political awareness and involvement, and a strong sense of identity and self-determination. This contrasts strongly with the "typical" findings of alienation and apathy (which some have dubbed "social science fiction!") and brings to mind the adage, "Nothing succeeds like success." Cultural pride made the transformation of Crystal City possible, and in turn this achievement further strengthened Chicano consciousness and self-esteem, setting the stage for even greater political and social accomplishments, and so on. We most certainly, as Gutierrez and Hirsch speculate, have not heard the last from the Chicano movement; and for this both Mexican Americans and Anglo Americans can be glad. As Alvarez observes, "The introspectiveness of the Chicano generation is leading to new insights. . . . The threat of cultural extinction has led the Chicanos to deep introspection as to what distinguishes him both from Mexicans in Mexico and from 'Anglos' in the United States. This introspection has led to a deep appreciation for the positive aspects of each culture and a creative use of our inheritance in facing the future." We share Murillo's hope "that the Anglo will also participate in this historical process by meeting *his* challenge of getting off his ethnocentric ego trip sufficiently to learn, understand, and explore *with* the Chicano more beneficial ways of living together based on mutual respect and equal opportunity . . . through a mutual understanding and acceptance of individual and cultural differences [we] can only profit and man can at last come closer to his highest ideals of achieving the maximum benefits of what life has to offer for all."

REFERENCES

Goodman, M. E., & Beman, A. Child's-eye-views of life in an urban barrio. In Helm, J. (Ed.), *Spanish-speaking people in the United States.* Proceedings of the 1968 Annual Spring Meeting of the American Ethnological Society. Seattle: University of Washington Press, 1970.

Heller, C. S. *Mexican American youth: Forgotten youth at the crossroads.* New York: Random House, 1966.

Lewis, O. *Pedro Martinez: A Mexican peasant and his family.* New York: Vintage Books, 1964.

Maccoby, M. On Mexican national character. *Annals of the American Academy of Political and Social Science,* 1967, *370,* 63-73.

Madsen, W. *The Mexican-Americans of south Texas.* New York: Holt, Rinehart & Winston, 1964.

Romano-V., O. Social science, objectivity, and the Chicanos. *El Grito,* 1970, *4*(1), 4-16.

Sutherland, E. Colonized women: The Chicana. In Morgan, R. (Ed.), *Sisterhood is powerful.* New York: Vintage Books, 1970.

Turner, F. C. *The dynamic of Mexican nationalism.* Chapel Hill: University of North Carolina Press, 1968.

CHAPTER 1 PRIDE AND PREJUDICE: A MEXICAN AMERICAN DILEMMA

EDWARD CASAVANTES

Lately, there has been increasing discussion about the "ethnic pride" of minority groups, including the Mexican American. Such discussions, however, are sometimes handicapped because of confusion about what it is that makes a person a member of an ethnic group—whether it is his culture, his national origin, his language, his skin coloration, or some combination of these factors.

The confusion is particularly pronounced in discussions about the Mexican American. For example, can one be middle class and still be called a Mexican American? Or can one be an intellectual and still be a Mexican American? The answer to both these questions is, of course, yes but an accurate ethnic definition of a Mexican American has been clouded because of the wide acceptance of a wide range of stereotypes that project a false image of what it is that constitutes being Mexican American.

Basically, there are three sets of qualities, or attributes—often hard to define—associated with being a Mexican American. The first set is not true at all; the second is true, in that it does describe the essence of the Mexican American; and the third is true in a limited sense, insofar as it does describe many Mexican Americans, but has really nothing to do with their being Mexican American.

With rare exception, every time social scientists have studied "Mexican Americans," they have ended up describing *poor* Mexican Americans, not Mexican Americans as they exist *in toto.* These social scientists have chosen to study that segment of the Chicano (an expression probably derived from "Mexicano," currently being used to designate the Mexican American) population that Ralph Guzman refers to as "the quaint," ignoring Mexican Americans who are middle class. The net result of this extraordinary scientific oversight is the perpetuation of very damaging stereotypes of the Mexican American.

The chart that appears on page 11 shows those qualities which have been invalidly attributed to Mexican Americans as part of their ethnicity.

In reality, as the title of the chart indicates, the attributes are actually those of people in poverty but these regularly cut across ethnic lines.

The first item says that, in general, Mexican Americans spend a larger proportion of their socialization time with relatives and with other people living nearby than do individuals from the middle class. And, indeed, a certain proportion of Mexican Americans do possess this attribute. Two, Mexican Americans are said not to generally join voluntary associations, which include educational, fraternal, church, and political associations. (Fortunately, though, the Mexican American is increasingly learning to join political organizations.)

Three, Mexican Americans are said to prefer the old and the familiar. They are

From Civil Rights Digest 3:22-27, Winter, 1970.

9

reluctant to engage in new situations or to form new social relationships. They appear to be especially hesitant to initiate social interactions with strangers. Four suggests that they generally demonstrate an anti-intellectual attitude and have little admiration for writers, intellectuals, artists, college professors, and the like. Thus, Mexican Americans are seen as demonstrating a lack of behavioral support for the school activities of their children.

Five, the male of the species is said to demonstrate manliness, "machismo." "Machismo" comes from the word "macho," which simply means "male." The average Mexican American male is supposed to demonstrate a great deal of "machismo" instead of, for instance, intellectualism or interest in the arts. Men who show "machismo" are alleged to brag a great deal about their male conquests, and to regularly refuse to do womanly things such as dishwashing, cooking, diaper-changing, or minding the children.

Six, Mexican Americans are often said to use physical force to settle arguments or to punish disobedient children.

Seven, Mexican Americans have been described as being unable to postpone gratification. Most are said to live on a day-to-day basis and few make plans or provisions for long-range activities.

Lastly, the Mexican American is said to be very fatalistic in his view of the world, feeling that he has very little control over nature, over institutions, over people, or over events.

As I stated earlier, *while these eight attributes have been used to characterize Mexican Americans, they are really characteristic of people living in poverty,* in the lowest socioeconomic level. In this context they do have validity. The danger lies in assigning these attributes as the unique possession of one ethnic group —as has been done with the Mexican American—instead of viewing them in their proper light, as the products of the "Culture of Poverty," a phrase borrowed from Oscar Lewis.

By "Culture" in the phrase "Culture of Poverty," Lewis means, in part, the ready-made set of behavioral solutions for everyday problems that continually emerge: a style of life, a way of thinking, a series of

attitudes and beliefs which emerge when an individual is forced to get along in his everyday activities without money. He does this by a unique and different way of using people. "Using" is not meant in a derogatory negative sense, but rather utilizing them. The reason is simple: *If you don't have money, you have to have people.* They simply do what they can to help each other. To give of themselves to each other, to lend emotional support, to help physically, this is the poor person's "money." Consequently, when poor Mexican Americans, or for that matter poor blacks or poor Puerto Ricans, don't have money, generally they must spend a larger portion of their time with relatives and other people living nearby than do middle class people.

Similarly, the poor generally don't join voluntary associations. The reason for this is probably wrapped up with the whole business of hopelessness which will be discussed in detail later. Thus poor Mexican Americans feel that joining an association will not do any good, because they have learned to live with hopelessness. In the past few years, however, Mexican Americans, as well as other ethnic groups, have increasingly been joining action groups when they have found that at times it does pay off.

Because they have had a poor education—thus a narrow and limited exposure to the world and its experiences—many seem to prefer the old and the familiar, rather than striking off in new directions, with new dimensions and new ideas. And, they don't like to form new social relationships, probably for the identical reasons that the more educated person sometimes feels awkward when walking into a completely new situation. Only the poor have many more such instances.

Poor people evidence anti-intellectualism in part because they haven't been well educated. People in poverty settings typically have no more than an eighth grade education, and quite often even less. It would be unusual for a man to be an intellectual without having had a relatively good exposure to "book learning". True, many poor have read a great number of books. But, in the main, the large portion are non-intellectual or anti-intellectual.

CHARACTEROLOGIC OR INTERPERSONAL STYLES
Attributes of most people living in the culture of poverty

1. Their life within the context of an extended family incorporates a *larger proportion* of available time (than is true of middle and upper class individuals) in interaction with relatives and with other people living nearby.
2. They are non-joiners of voluntary associations, including fraternal, church-related, and political associations.
3. They have a preference for the old and the familiar, demonstrated by a reluctance to engage in new situations, or to form new social relationships, especially to initiate interactions with strangers.
4. They demonstrate a marked anti-intellectualism, which expresses itself in little admiration for intellectuals, professors, writers, artists, the ballet, symphonies, etc., as well as in lack of support for schools or for the school activities of their children.
5. Males demonstrate "machismo." This is seen as opposite behavior to being intellectual or engaging in such activities as the ballet. Males who demonstrate "machismo" brag a great deal about their male conquests, and refuse to engage in any behavior which is associated with femininity, such as diaper-changing, dishwashing, cooking, etc.
6. There is a great deal of use of physical force, for example, to settle arguments or in the use of physical punishment with disobedient children.
7. They appear unable to postpone gratification. The tendency to live on a day-to-day basis looms extremely prevalent, and few provisions are made for long-range activities.
8. They are extremely fatalistic in their view of the world, feeling that they have very little control over nature, over institutions, or over events.

Adapted from: Cohen, Albert K., and Hodges, Harold M., Characteristics of the Lower-Blue-Collar Class.

Consequently, they don't have the feeling that school is really that necessary for success in life. Certainly a high proportion will not see a college degree as necessary for success.

The males demonstrate manliness, "machismo," perhaps as an overcompensation. *A man is his work.* But what kind of work does a man who lives in poverty have? Poor work, if any. He does not often have a job that he can be genuinely proud of; he does not have a vocation. Thus, he does not have a full identity. A man is supposed to be a working man, one who provides for his family, a protector, a giver of care and sustenance. Instead, the poor man has a low-paying job, or a half-time job, or maybe no job at all. Few men can live comfortably with the feeling of not being a good provider, and consequently, they often overcompensate and by this demonstrate that they nevertheless are strong and powerful. Therefore, they show excessive "machismo." This is probably what leads to the refusal to have anything to do with things that are "womanly."

What's wrong with "machismo," with being "macho?" There's nothing terribly wrong with it. It's only in the exaggeration, in the male demonstrating too much of a good thing, in the excess, that this becomes a dysfunctional thing. Perhaps dysfunctional "machismo" is best defined in terms of the motivation. If it is a greatly exaggerated overcompensation for feeling inadequate, and the overcompensation takes the form of excessive fighting, drinking, or bragging about conquests, then it is a dysfunctional "machismo."

Inability to delay gratification is due, at least in part, to realizing the fact that if you don't have money, it is very difficult to adequately plan for the future. How can you plan for the future when you don't know what's going to happen tomorrow? When you don't even know if you will have a job? Even if a poor man wanted to plan for the future, and he had a relatively steady job, it is usually not a well-paying one. Thus, he would have few provisions—that is, tangible financial provisions—for long-range planning of activities. So then, it becomes a day-to-day existence, but not necessarily because of some perverse quality in poor people, but because, in the past, planning and its attendant postponement of immediate gratification of needs has been experienced as futile.

Fighting in order to settle arguments, or to punish disobedient children, probably comes about partly as a function of the same business associated with being "muy macho," which in turn stems, at least in large measure, from the many frustrations associated with a man's lack of ability to hold a job.

Fatalism is a basic feeling, attitude, or belief that does affect—and may be very damaging to—people living in the culture of poverty. If you had lost the game many times, if you had never been able to make headway, if you had never been able to get a good job and hold it, if you had planned for a lot of things that never came true, I suspect you would lose hope too. This is regularly what happens to a man who comes from a poverty home. He simply has stopped trying because it has not done him —and others he has seen—a great deal of good to have tried.

The eight qualities just outlined are then basically the qualities or attributes of people from the culture of poverty, not the culture of Mexico. These same qualities have been used to describe blacks, American Indians, and Puerto Ricans.

From a combination of these stereotypes have arisen some totally false attributes of the Mexican American. And these stereotypes do not escape even the Mexican American himself. The following is a statement made by a Mexican American writer:

The Mexicano, or mestizo, a racial amalgamation of resigned stolid Indians and lighthearted Spaniards, has based his romanticism on the reality of the present and its relation to the past. The future is attacked with a fatalism, an indefinite term, mañana, which expresses a remoteness missing from 'tomorrow.' He lives an improvised, spontaneous existence. He never puts off for tomorrow what can be enjoyed only today. He is not lazy, but he works only enough to support his meager needs.

What then are the *real* qualities of being a Mexican American? Or, to put it another way, what constitutes the second set of attributes noted at the beginning of this article, those that accurately describe the essence of being Mexican American?

One, they have come or their parents or grandparents have come from Mexico (or from Spain in the case of the Hispano of northern New Mexico and southern Colorado) and brought with them many customs and many traditions. Secondly, they speak Spanish and many have a noticeable accent. These two qualities alone, I feel, comprise the major portion of the essence of being Chicano or Mexican American.

On another level, but also within the valid set of attributes, we know that the vast majority of Mexican Americans is Catholic. Of course, as is true of any group, insofar as it practices a given religion, much of its behavior is influenced by that religion. So, much of the behavior of the Mexican American is allied with his Catholicism. A simple example of this might be the "Día de Santo," the Saint's Day, where a small feast is planned to honor the Saint on whose day the youngster was born. It is very much like a birthday feast.

Lastly, in the group of five attributes, many Mexican Americans have darker skin and hair, and thus they are easily distinguishable. Many have what sociologists call "high visibility."

Here are in review—in my mind anyway—the true qualities or attributes of most Mexican Americans: They have come from Mexico, or perhaps from Spain via Mexico; they speak Spanish, many with an accent; they are Catholic; and, many have dark skin and hair. These are the things that a "true Chicano," a "real Mexican" must possess. These attributes are the things that make him Mexican.

Viewing three of these from a different perspective, however, we can see that you don't have to be a Catholic to be a Chicano; even less so, have darker skin, because dark skin is not a criterion for being Mexican, although many Mexicans have it. More essence comes from the first two characteristics: that their ancestors came —with their many customs and traditions —from Mexico and Spain and that they spoke Spanish.

Is it not the customs and language that make most people a particular people? If you are of Greek descent and you share Greek customs and speak Greek, then you can be said to be a Greek American. If you are Chinese, and you share Chinese customs and speak Chinese, then you are a

Chinese American. Likewise, should a Mexican American identify himself as being Mexican American, the essential qualities that he must have are the language and customs that he has brought, or his forefathers have brought, from Mexico: *that is his heritage.* Some of the more *tangible* items from this heritage are reflected in such things as the Mexican music that Mexican Americans love so dearly, and obviously, Mexican food.

The third and final set of attributes are those that are true for the majority of Mexican Americans, but only in a limited sense. The first of these is that perhaps 80 percent of their five to six million live in the five Southwestern States of Texas, New Mexico, Colorado, Arizona, and California. The second is that the average Mexican American (over age 25) can be described as having an educational level of less than 8 years. Now mind you, that says *average,* which really means that roughly 50 percent have even less than an eighth grade education, an appalling situation. The third is that between 30 and 40 percent of the families earn less than about $3,500 per year and thus are seen to be living in the culture of poverty.

With that I conclude the third of three different types of attributes of the Mexican American. The first was a set of false attributes usually ascribed to him because he is poor and/or because he is perhaps from a rural locale. The second group has to do with his national origin, and this is the set of true attributes: that his parents—with their culture and customs—come from Mexico, that he speaks Spanish, that he is Catholic, and that he is dark. This set usually does define Mexican. The third set of attributes is potentially irrelevant. It describes many Mexican Americans, that's true. However, a black man could live in one of the five Southwestern States and be poorly educated and be living in the culture of poverty. These characteristics have little to do with ethnicity or national origin.

Perhaps we can now come to some important conclusions. One of them is that it is poverty, much more than ethnicity, that seems to account for so many of the "failures" of Mexican American children in the classrooms; and of their fathers' "failure" in vocational endeavors. "Fail-

ures," not because they are black or brown, but because they are so badly educated and so poor.

While the Mexican American cannot erase prejudice overnight, a great deal can be done to diminish the effect and impact of prejudice by helping the Mexican Americans become well educated and achieve adequate employment.

For it is lack of education with its attendant poverty that helps keep Mexican Americans (and other ethnic groups) in the impossible situation we see today.

It is clear that the main element which acts as a barrier to the full development of the Mexican American is prejudice. Countless instances of both gross and subtle discrimination have been documented. See, for example, "The Mexican American," U.S. Commission on Civil Rights, 1968; "Civil Rights in Texas," U.S. Commission on Civil Rights, Feb. 1970; "Hearing Before the U.S. Commission on Civil Rights: San Antonio Texas, Dec. 9-14, 1968."

Some of this prejudice arises directly out of the acting-out of felt stereotypes such as those we have been trying to help destroy in this discussion. Other discriminatory practices are simply the result of obvious racist attitudes. When some or both of these are found in our schools, and deter or impede the adequate education of Mexican American children, forceful and decisive steps *must* be taken to eliminate them. For it is the school that offers the single best path out of poverty for the vast majority of Mexican Americans.

While racism and prejudice have no place in any part of our country, the practice is especially contemptible in American schools, for it is these very institutions that, with "forked tongue," *teach* the story of democracy and equal opportunity and then *act out* patterns of individual and wholesale discrimination.

Secondly, prejudice and discrimination in the schools are especially contemptible because they communicate to a child— that is, to an as yet not fully developed organism—feelings that suggest to him he is inferior, a notion that is false. Both common sense and some very recent highly sophisticated social science investigations thoroughly document the fact that the *na-*

tive capacity of the Mexican American child is fully equal to that of anyone else.

We also need to constantly stress to the individual Mexican American that he can make it; that many competent Chicanos have come from the ghettos, have come from small farms, from migrant camps; that he, too, has a good chance. Further, he needs to know that chances for success in life are becoming increasingly more open to him.

We must work to improve the self-image of the Mexican American so that neither he nor those he encounters act out a negative self-fulfilling prophecy.

It is clear, then, that there is literally nothing wrong with the Mexican American, except that he is economically poor and poorly educated.

Thus, it is also totally clear that, if the Mexican American is to develop his true potentialities, all barriers to his development must be erased.

The Mexican Americans' Ethnic Pride, of which we spoke at the very beginning, is totally and completely legitimate, for we are confident that being Mexican American is something of which we can be proud. We need only to banish our poverty and our ignorance.

If prejudice and discrimination stand in our forward thrust toward those ends, then we will need to take action against that prejudice and discrimination.

CHAPTER 2 THE MEXICAN AMERICAN FAMILY

NATHAN MURILLO

I was asked to talk on the subject of the Mexican American family. I find it neither possible nor desirable to separate the Mexican American either as an individual or as a family unit from his history, cultural heritage, sociological, or psychological context. However it seems desirable to focus more on certain aspects of the Mexican American family which have received, to my knowledge, relatively little attention. Therefore, I will attempt to describe and discuss today some intercultural conflicts and dynamics, as they apply to the diversity of people found under the rubric of Mexican American and particularly as they relate to the family.

Those of you who are interested in a more purely sociological view of the Mexican American family can readily find numerous sources of factual data showing conclusively that the Mexican American ranks at the bottom or near the bottom on nearly every measure of socioeconomic success that has been utilized by the experts. A recent book by Galarza, Gallegos, and Samora entitled *Mexican Americans in the Southwest* (1969) contains data based primarily on the 1960 United States census. The book is a report of a two-year study during which the authors traveled throughout the United States and Mexico studying economic, social, political, educa-

tional, and other factors influencing the Mexican American. Briefly, these are some of their findings: the Mexican American population in the United States is estimated to be between five and six million people. From one third to one half of the Mexican Americans in the Southwest live below the official level of poverty or immediately above it. Most are manual workers earning only the lowest wages. Educational opportunities have been so restricted that this ethnic group is some three to four years or more behind the educational attainment of the general society. At present more than 80 percent of the Mexican American population is urbanized. This last is contrary to the popular belief most Mexican Americans are farm workers.

Important as this information may be, it fails completely to provide much basis for a humanistic understanding of the Mexican American people in their daily lives. For a more vital perspective and a more compassionate understanding of this large, diverse group of people one must delve further into their cultural heritage and history. The more one does this, the more obvious it becomes that there is no real way to arrive at significant universals or generalizations regarding the Mexican American family as it exists in this ethnic group. The reality is that there is no Mexican American family "type." Instead there are literally thousands of Mexican American families, all differing significantly from one another along a variety of dimensions. There are significant regional, historical, political, socioeconomic, acculturation, and assimilation factors, for ex-

Paper presented at the Mexican American Seminars, Stanford University, Stanford California, April 3-4, 1970.

Grateful acknowledgement is given to Margarita C. Corral for her assistance in preparing this paper.

15

ample, which result in a multitude of family patterns of living and of coping with each other and with their Anglo environment. More precisely, there are families that are poor and a few that are wealthy; there are families where Spanish is the exclusive language spoken in the home and others in which it is never spoken. There are families who trace their ancestry back to their Spanish forefathers and others who trace their ancestry back to their Mayan, Zapotec, Toltec, or Aztec forefathers. Some families were living on the land which is now the southwestern part of the United States before the Pilgrims landed at Plymouth Rock while others have immigrated to the United States only in recent years.

Some of this diversity among the Mexican American people is reflected in the variety of names by which they have been known. At various times and in various places the Mexican American has been labeled Latino, Hispano, Spanish American, American of Spanish descent, and more recently (with increasing frequency and growing pride) Chicano. This last term has changed its meaning considerably in the past few years. It used to be primarily descriptive, but now it stands for a whole new orientation and a psychological identification with the *movemiento* which is working to improve conditions for all Latinos in this country. In sum, there is no stereotype Mexican American family pattern based on one unique traditional culture.

In Oscar Lewis's well known book *Five Families* (1959) he presents a sample cross section of families in Mexico—from a small peasant village in the country, a slum tenement in Mexico City, a new working-class housing development, and an upper-class residential district. At this time I would like to quote briefly from the introduction to that book:

> Although each family presented here is unique in a little world of its own, each in its own way reflects something of the changing Mexican culture and must therefore be read against the background of recent Mexican history.

I believe this statement could apply equally well to the Mexican American family. It is essential to maintain this type of perspective when consideration is given to a large diverse people as they continue to adjust to changing conditions.

In an essay on the distortion of Mexican American history, Romano (1968) bitterly assails the concept of traditional culture with respect to the Mexican American. He makes the particular point that traditional culture is a passive concept incorrectly and destructively applied to human beings in process who have survived primarily through their ability to grow, change and adapt to different times, places and circumstances. With specific reference to the Mexican American, Romano objects to their treatment by sociologists, anthropologists, and historians as an ahistoric people. As a result he says the Mexican American has never been seen through Anglo eyes as a participant in history or as a generator of the historical process. To partially correct this distortion Romano gives several examples of activism on the part of Mexican Americans in the Southwest over a period of years. Romano insists that to correct the distortion of Mexican American history it is necessary to adopt a historical culture and an intellectual historical view of Mexican Americans in place of the stereotype static concepts of a traditional culture and the nonintellectual Mexican American.

As a psychologist I believe that only a process-change orientation is applicable to human beings *if* there is a desire to understand them realistically as they live and express themselves through the dynamics of their behavior. I can only concur with Romano that a historical perspective *is* important in understanding others. Static concepts have little relevancy to the dynamic processes of living.

Although I agree with this basic thesis, I find it only creates more difficulty for me to present some understanding of the values and conflicts within and concerning Mexican American families. I find myself on the horns of a dilemma. On one hand there is the desire to present an accurate view of Mexican American families, about which one cannot in reality generalize because of the many significant differences among them. On the other hand is the necessity, based partly on practicality, to present a somewhat traditional cultural view of the Mexican American family, which may have little or no relationship to reality.

To compound the problem I feel it important to make clear that there are other relevant variables such as hierarchy of individual needs, developmental and maturational factors, and personality styles which enter into and frequently overshadow the more general social-cultural values. In other words, not only do historical and cultural factors affect interpersonal patterns of adjustment but also personal needs and personality styles play significant roles. It is not surprising to find that conflicts of values between an individual and his family may be just as great as between one family member's cultural identification and a different cultural tradition with which he may have contact. To again quote from Oscar Lewis:

Whole family studies bridged the gap between the conceptual extremes of culture at one pole and the individual at the other; we see both culture and personality as they are inter-related in real life.

This is the perspective I would like to maintain in addition to the historical heritage of the Mexican American family.

How can one describe a traditional Mexican American family when there is no uniform pattern? In an effort to solve this problem I have tried to temper my description of the "traditional" Mexican American family by describing it also in the context of some comparative cultural value systems and frequent areas of conflict among these. I will go further, however, and make explicit that the values discussed must be viewed from a probabilistic approach. That is, every value I attribute to a Mexican American person or family should be understood basically in terms of there being a greater chance or probability that the Mexican American, as compared with the Anglo, will think and behave in accordance with that value. Obviously, if my earlier words have any meaning, in the final analysis one must come to know and accept the uniqueness of the individual or of a specific family. Many Mexican Americans are not only bilingual but also bicultural, and it is very worthwhile to ascertain the special blending of cultures one may encounter in a person or family in order to acquire a realistic understanding.

I will introduce the Mexican American family by describing a few probable cultural value differences between Mexican Americans and the Anglos. Next I will talk about some concepts specifically related to the family. Following this I will note some of the conflicts and dynamics of these values in relationship to the Anglo society. Finally I will turn open the meeting for discussion with comments or questions from the floor.

The cultural differences between the Mexican American and the Anglo can be viewed in terms of differences in mental set or orientations, style, or "naturalness" in behavior. In many respects Latin values are more clearly defined and behavioral patterns are more closely adhered to than is common in the Anglo culture. This clarity of conceptualization implies no lack of variety, complexity, or richness of experience. On the contrary, I believe, a clear focus tends often to provide a basis for a more relevant and enriched experience for the individual. One is not so often left confused and searching for his place in life when recognizable guidelines are available. Thus the individual can experience life sooner and perhaps more fully. The Latin culture seems to provide more emotional security and sense of belonging to its members.

Let us now examine one cultural difference as an example: attitudes toward material things. In the Anglo society values stemming from the Puritan view tend to emphasize work as a form of responsibility leading for the most part to rewards of a tangible nature. The Anglo world is described sometimes as divided into two categories: those of work and of play. The *responsible* individual is the one who works first so that he can later enjoy his recreation with or among his material gains. However, a vicious cycle may be formed because recreation often then becomes an obligation for the purpose of enabling the individual to go back and work more effectively and with greater energy than before. The Mexican American is likely to have a different orientation. To him material objects are usually necessity things and not ends in themselves. In contrast to the Puritan ethic, work is viewed as a necessity for survival but not as a value in itself. Much higher value is assigned to other life activities in the Mexican culture. It is through physical and mental well-being and through an ability to experience, in response to environment, emotional feelings and to express these to one another and share them that one experiences the greatest rewards and satisfactions in life. By comparison, any pursuit of material things by the Mexican American through work and the accumulation of wealth are likely to suffer. To the Mexican American it is much more valuable to experience things directly through intellectual awareness and through emotional experiences rather than indirectly through past accomplishments and accumulation of wealth. For the Mexican American, social status and prestige are more likely to derive from an ability to experience things in this kind of spiritually direct way and to share such knowledge and feelings with others. The philosopher, poet, musician, and artist are more often revered in this culture than the businessman or financier.

The Anglo's tendency to judge others largely in terms of the absence or presence of material comforts which he values so highly may cause him to perceive the Mexican American as "culturally deprived." This ethnocentric attitude on the part of the Anglo, which implies that his standards are the only "right" ones, usually evokes ridicule and resentment from the Mexican American. The Mexican American has only to remember that long before the first crude Anglo frontiersman came chopping his way through the forest many of his own forefathers lived on haciendas in the Southwest, where life was as civilized as the European of the time. Latin art and music flourish everywhere. One can glimpse this for himself today by going where Chicano students, for example, congregate. Music is always heard and colorful murals surround. By contrast other areas seem dull and lifeless.

There appears to be a common tendency for the Anglo to live in a future or extended time orientation, whereas the Mexican American is more likely to live and experience life more completely in the present.

This difference in time orientation may be related to several factors; for example, value differences stemming from differences in religious ethics such as the Protestant and the Catholic or in socioeconomic factors. For an individual from the lower socioeconomic portion of our society, especially if he is brown or black, a limited time orientation may result from immediate survival needs and from restrictions on upward mobility due to realistic inequality of opportunity for education or advancement. However, for the Mexican American at least another concept might also come into play. From his cultural heritage he may retain some belief in the concept of the "limited good." This Indian idea says in effect that there is only so much good in the world and therefore only so much good is possible in any one person's life. It matters not how industrious one is for he will get no more than his share of good during his lifetime. A wise person will therefore not expend his energies unnecessarily but will accept life as it comes, enjoying the maximum each day has to offer. Whatever reasons there may be for a difference in time orientation between Anglo and Chicano I cannot say. I can only note that today much of our Anglo society's psychotherapy is aimed at developing or rekindling a *here* and *now* time orientation in the client as a means to improved mental health.

One effect of this time value difference is noteworthy. In the Anglo culture, being responsible is equated with being present for an appointment at a previously agreed upon time. After all, time is money. The Chicano, however, is not likely to be as locked in to the clock as his Anglo counterpart. Since his concept of responsibility is based on other values such as attending to the immediate needs of his family or friends, he may not arrive for an appointment on time. Yet in his eyes he is as responsible as the punctual Anglo.

There is one area in which the Anglo and the Mexican American are likely to be markedly disparate. This is the area of manners, courtesy, inter-personal relations—call it what you will. The Anglo is taught to value openness, frankness, and directness. He is much more likely to express himself simply, briefly, and frequently bluntly. The traditional Latin approach requires the use of much diplomacy and tactfulness when communicating with another individual. Concern and respect for another's feelings dictate that a screen always be provided behind which a man may preserve his dignity. By the way, there is available in English a book by one of Mexico's leading writers, Octavio Paz, which has as a major theme the many masks from behind which the Mexican faces life. The title of the book is *The Labyrinth of Solitude.*

The Mexican's manner of expression is likely to be elaborate and indirect, since he often also takes pride in the art of verbal expression. Often his aim is to make the personal relationship at least appear harmonious, since he respects the other's individuality. This does not mean, however, that he is evasive or deceitful. To him it is simply a matter of courtesy and one attains effective communication by hypothetically placing himself in the situation, by suggestion, or by talking about a make-believe situation. Taking this into account, one can well imagine the impossibility of attempting psychotherapy with more traditional Mexican Americans by utilizing the currently popular technique of confrontation.

The Mexican American often finds himself in difficulty if he disagrees with an Anglo's point of view. To him, direct argument or contradiction appears rude and disrespectful. On the surface he may seem agreeable, manners dictating that he not reveal his genuine opinion openly unless he knows the other well and unless he can take time to tactfully differ. The Anglo who is not aware of this may falsely assume that basic agreement has been reached and perhaps even that the Mexican American is rather submissive. Such an error in judgment often leads to later disappointment when supposed contracts are not carried out. As for submissiveness, anyone who is even casually familiar with Mexican history with its many wars, revolutions, and counter-revolutions must find it difficult to believe that submissiveness is a cultural characteristic of the Mexican. The concept of courtesy, therefore, often causes misunderstandings between Anglo and Latin.

A related characteristic of the Anglo in particular is likely to cause problems with the Mexican American. Anglo Americans have a style of kidding one another, partly as a means of expressing some feeling that might be hurtful to another person if expressed differently. This characteristic is frequently quite offensive to the Mexican American, who sees it as a severe put down and is likely to respond sharply and negatively to kidding. To him it is rude and depreciating. It is sometimes difficult to understand fully the Latin's sensitivity to criticism. Apart from a realistic reaction to prejudice and discrimination in this country, there seems to be a high degree of vulnerability to almost any kind of criticism on the part of Latins everywhere.

It may be related to another probable characteristic one encounters frequently among the Mexican American people, which is a sensateness or high degree of sensitivity to the environment. Apparently much more than the Anglo American, the Mexican American utilizes his full range of physiological senses to experience things about him. He is more likely to want to touch, taste, smell, feel, or be close to an object or person on which his attention is focused. This phenomenon appears in many ways. The Latin love for sounds, action, bright colors, and even spicy food is well recognized. In contrast to the Mexican American, the Anglo often seems to be cold, distant, and lacking in sensitivities.

At this time I would like to discuss more specifically some traditional Mexican American family values and patterns. I hope this will serve mainly as a point of departure for beginning to understand the many combinations and blends of culture that constitute today's Mexican American family patterns.

For the Chicano, the family is likely to be the single most important social unit in life. It is usually at the core of his thinking and behavior and is the center from which his view of the rest of the world extends. Even with respect to identification the Chicano *self* is likely to take second place after the family. For example, an individual is seen first as a member of the Ruiz or Mendoza family before he is seen as Juan or Jose—that is, before he obtains his more personal acceptance. Thus to a significant extent the individual Chicano may view himself much of the time as an agent or representative of his family. In many respects this means that he must be careful of his behavior lest his actions somehow reflect adversely on his family bringing them dishonor or disgrace.

The family maintains its position of prominence within the psychological life space of the Chicano individual, I believe, primarily by virtue of its ability to provide emotional and material security. A Chicano in need of emotional support, guidance, food, or money expects and is expected to turn to his family first in order to have such needs met. Only in unusual circumstances, dire need, or when there is no alternative will a Chicano or his family attempt to seek help from others. This often occurs at great expense to the pride and dignity of both the individual and the family. This is perhaps one reason why it is so difficult to get individuals or families to seek professional help for medical and emotional problems. As an illustrative case, I once was called to see a Mexican American woman in a hospital where she had been taken because of a so-called psychotic break. She had been in the hospital for about one week and did not seem to be responding to treatment. It so happened she spoke no English and none of the staff in attendance spoke Spanish. After conversing with her a bit I realized that she was quite concerned about her second son who was then 17 years old. She had been worried about this boy for many years, insisting that something was wrong with him as he did not behave normally. However, her husband refused to believe that the boy was anything other than stupid, clumsy, and lazy. As her son grew older, her anguish grew because of the increasing difficulties the son had in adjusting to normal activities. Finally she became so distraught she was taken to the hospital where I saw her. All of this time she could not go against her husband and seek help for her son, nor could she talk to her husband because of his refusal to listen. I promised to talk to the husband and see what I could do. After some discussion, I was able to persuade the father to allow his son to come in for an evaluation. He could accept this only because he wished his wife to get better and I assured him I thought seeing the son would make the

mother feel better. The son was evaluated and some mild organic condition was uncovered. The mother's "psychosis" disappeared within a day or so. A plan of treatment was arranged for the boy and was begun, but after a short while he dropped out. The father still could not accept the fact that his son might need outside help and I am sure this is why the boy stopped coming in for treatment even though he was eager for aid. Apparently, it was too much of a threat to the father's self-esteem.

The strength of the family, resting as it does on the foundation of providing security to its members, is sometimes expressed through a sharing of material things with other relatives even when there might be precious little to meet its own immediate needs. This sometimes causes Anglos bewilderment and provokes them to criticism when there is a lack of understanding of this aspect of the Chicano family feeling. This is especially true with some welfare workers who are trying to help a family make ends meet and discover that the family is sharing what they have with others outside the immediate home environment.

It is possible that a family may sever all relations with one of its members if that individual through his behavior brings shame or dishonor to it. This behavior can only be understood in the light of the importance and value attributed to family unity and identification in the Mexican American culture. Here again one may encounter a situation in which a son or daughter has gotten into trouble and the family refuses to cooperate with the authorities toward rehabilitation of the person because the individual has brought dishonor to the family, which then turns its back on the deviant one.

Within the Chicano or Mexican American concept of family there are two sub concepts. These are the *nuclear* family, consisting of husband, wife, and children, and the *extended* family, which encompasses grandparents, uncles, aunts, and cousins. Due to the patrilineal factor, relatives on the father's side of the family may be considered more important than those from the mother's side. In addition to these members, the extended family concept also includes compadres who are the god-parents of the children. For each child there may be a different set of compadres. The relationship between parents and compadres is very similar to that between the parents and other adult relatives where there is mutual respect and interchange of help and advice. Among extended family members there is often much com-munication, visiting, sharing, and close-ness of relationship. Such family members are expected to call upon one another and help one another whenever there is a need.

The interpersonal relations among parents and children who constitute the nuclear family are usually dictated by clearly defined patterns of deference.

According to Rubel (1966), who did one of the several anthropological studies of Mexican American families, the pattern that predominates is stated: "The elder order the younger and the men the women." This establishes two dimensions around which the interpersonal patterns within the family are usually organized. The first is respect and obedience to elders and the second is male dominance. The description of the family pattern that follows is based largely on Rubel's work.

The husband and father is the autocratic head of the household. He tends to remain aloof and independent from the rest of the family. Few decisions can be made with-out his approval or knowledge. He is free to come and go as he pleases without ex-planation to or questions by other family members. In essence the father represents authority within the family. All other fam-ily members are expected to be respectful of him and to accede to his will or direc-tion. An important part of his concept of *machismo* or maleness, however, is that of using his authority within the family in a just and fair manner. Should he misuse his authority, he will lose respect within the community.

In relating to his children the father fre-quently serves as the disciplinarian. He as-sumes responsibility for the behavior of the family members in *or* outside of the home. Misbehavior by another family member is a direct reflection on the father even though he might not have been present at the time of the misconduct.

During their earlier years the father is often permissive, warm, and close to the children. This changes significantly as each child reaches the onset of puberty. At this time the father's behavior toward his children becomes much more reserved, au-thoritarian, and demanding of respect. In Rubel's terms there is a discontinuity of af-fective relationship between the father and the children as they enter puberty.

The wife-mother is supposed to be com-pletely devoted to her husband and chil-dren. Her role is to serve the needs of her husband, support his actions and deci-sions, and take care of the home and chil-dren. In substance she represents the nur-turent aspects of the family's life. Although she is usually highly respected and revered, her personal needs are con-sidered to be secondary to those of the other family members. Her life tends to re-volve around her family and a few close friends. There is usually a close continuing relationship between mother and children, which perpetuates throughout her life. In contrast to the father and his relationship to the children, the mother continues to be close and warm, serving and nurturing even when her children are grown, mar-ried, and have children of their own. Rela-tionships between mothers and daughters and other female relatives are usually especially close, since the female is sup-posed to have relatively few contacts with others outside the family and so they fre-quently become the confidantes of one an-other.

During the early years of growing up the home is usually child centered. Both parents tend to be permissive and indul-gent with the younger children, sometimes to the point of spoiling them. However, even at the earlier ages children are not permitted to be frivolous or disrespectful within the home. Children receive training in responsibility, even at the earliest stages of development. They are often assigned tasks or responsibilities according to their age and ability, which they are expected to assume. This may take the form of car-ing for younger brothers or sisters, doing errands, taking a job to help finance the family's needs, or some similar activities. Whatever the responsibilities assigned the children, they are real and usually neces-sary for the welfare of the family. Therefore a feeling of importance as a family member and interdependence are developed from an early age onward. Much of the individual's self-esteem is related to how he perceives and others perceive him carrying out his assigned family responsibilities.

Among the children there is often less sibling rivalry than in Anglo families— due, perhaps, to the status each receives from age, sex, and family obligation. Children are taught to share, cooperate, and work together for the good of all family members. Boys are especially directed to look after and protect their sisters outside of the immediate home environment. This may be a brother's responsibility even when his sister is several years older.

Differences in patterns of behavior between male and female children are taught implicitly and explicitly from infancy. The boy is taught how to think and act like a man and the girl is taught her feminine role. However, at the onset of adolescence the difference in patterns of behavior between boys and girls becomes even more markedly apparent. The girl is likely to remain much closer to the home, to be protected and guarded in her contacts with others beyond the family, so as to preserve her femininity and innocence. Through her relationships with her mother and other female relatives she is prepared for the role of wife and mother. On the other hand the adolescent male, following the model of his father, is given much more freedom to go and come as he chooses and is encouraged to gain much worldly knowledge and experience outside the home in preparation for the time when he will assume the role of husband and father. During this period of development the young male is likely to join with others of his age in informal social groups known as *palomillas*. Through such association he gains knowledge and experience in holding his own with other males. The *palomilla* often affords the adolescent opportunities to develop and to demonstrate his machismo to his peers. Thus he begins to develop a reputation centered on skill, knowledge, experience, and ability, from which his social status and prestige in the community is eventually derived.

Perhaps it is now time to examine a few of the conflicts aroused in the Mexican American by virtue of his cultural pluralism.

The importance of the family to a Chicano and the close interpersonal ties that exist among family members, including those of the extended family, are not often appreciated in the Anglo society. To the Chicano, family needs and demands have highest priority. If his help is required by the family, he may temporarily forego job, school, or any other activity that might prevent him from meeting his family obligation. His actions in so doing may inadvertently affect the behavior of other family members. Let us look at a possible situation in order to more clearly illustrate this point. A mother who has a sick child has an appointment with a doctor. Since the mother speaks no English and since her husband has to work, a son is delegated the responsibility to serve as translator between his mother and the doctor. In order to do this he must absent himself from school. An older sister who also attends the same school is required to absent herself also, since her brother will not be there to look after her or protect her if the need should arise. This illustration was taken from an interesting film entitled "The Forgotten Family" that depicts the problems encountered by a poor Mexican American family living in an Anglo society.

The matter of courtesy and good manners may also cause important problems. An example is shown in the above-mentioned film when a Chicano youth is serving as translator between the doctor and his mother. The doctor tells the mother that she should not have waited so long to obtain medical attention for the sick child. However, the boy serving as translator finds it impossible to convey such a message to his mother for fear he might appear to her as rude and disrespectful. At the same time, he can say nothing to the doctor who is an authority figure. Therefore in the film he deliberately misinterprets to his mother what the doctor has said and in so trying to escape his difficult position fails to communicate some important medical information.

In another area, sometimes an insensitive or impatient Anglo is likely to misunderstand the hesitancy of a Mexican American woman or a Chicano youth with whom he is dealing to make decisions. Frequently women and children are not accustomed to making decisions without the prior knowledge and approval of their husband and father. It is often necessary for them to first get the father's permission before they are able to accept or agree to whatever is under consideration.

For the Chicano child there are frequent conflicts between the values that he learns at home and those he is taught in school. The most clear contradiction is between the authoritarian structure in the home and the more democratic ideals taught in school. Not only is this confusing to the child but it is threatening to the parents. Contrary to what many Anglos believe, education is highly valued among the Chicanos. Yet the education that the child receives in the Anglo school tends to break down the family unity which is the basis for security in the Mexican American culture. Part of the feeling experienced by parents is expressed in the following words taken from the epic poem "I am Joaquin," by Rodolfo Gonzales:

I shed tears of anguish
As I see my children disappear
Behind the shroud of mediocrity
Never to look back to remember me.
I am Joaquin.

Anglo schools tend to make Chicano children foreigners to their own parents. I sometimes wonder what would happen if Anglo children were required to speak only Spanish in school and were taught distinctly different values from those of their parents, especially if the parental values were viewed as "wrong" by the school thereby instilling shame and guilt in the children. The matter of identification is also important here. In our society most teachers are female. The Chicano male child frequently finds it hard to relate to a woman who behaves so differently from what he has learned to expect. His teacher is just the opposite from what a woman should be according to his cultural standards. For example, she is authoritarian instead of nurturing, and is businesslike instead of warm. To him she sometimes appears to be parodying a man, and he may find it hard to take her seriously.

Another factor that contributes substantially to problems and conflicts among Chicanos and between Chicanos and Anglos is that of language. In the schools and at work the Chicano is often ridiculed or embarrassed for not speaking correct English or for speaking with a "foreign accent." This despite the fact that Spanish was the first official language of the State of California.

The Chicano often senses a feeling of frustration and failure at his inability or difficulty in communicating to the Anglo his thoughts and feelings. The English that the Chicano has learned, compared to the Anglo's, is often acquired through a much more limited language experiential background and with relatively little practice. Yet, he is often expected to speak as fluently as the Anglo and is belittled when he cannot. The reverse situation often occurs with Chicanos who speak little or no Spanish. Since he is usually easily identifiable through physical appearance as Chicano, he may be embarrassed when others expect him to be proficient in Spanish. Often students in school are criticized in English class for the incorrect use of that language. When they arrive at their Spanish class, they are again criticized for their lack of fluency or grammatical expertness in that language. Needless to say such experiences do little to enhance one's self-esteem. Neither does the name "change" that frequently occurs when the young Chicano enters the Anglo school. Often "Juanito" becomes "John" and "María" becomes "Mary," leading to confusion of identification and often to negative self-attitudes. Presently I am seeing in therapy several college students who are very much concerned about their lack of proficiency in English. They are afraid to answer questions in class for fear of being laughed at by other students and teachers. Also they are reluctant to meet or make new acquaintances for similar reasons. Obviously this fear is partly symptomatic of additional problems but it remains a primary focus of concern for them, reinforced every day to some extent by reality experiences. One Chicano student who speaks no Spanish but is very Indian in his physical appearance told me of his initial reaction when he first realized he was of Mexican ancestry. He told his mother he was going to cut his arms so that all of the Mexican blood would run out and he would no longer be ashamed.

Once at least I observed a reversal of the tendency to Anglicize Spanish names in school. I had occasion to visit a Head Start class in East Los Angeles where the pre-dominance of the population is Chicano. It was somewhat amusing to hear a group of 4- and 5-year old Chicanitos reciting the nursery rhyme "María had a little lamb."

There is presently much confusion and conflict among Chicanos, as well as Anglos, as to the role of the woman in society. There are fewer and fewer women who are willing to accept the traditional role assigned to them according to traditional values. Chicanas are struggling for greater equality not only in the Anglo society but also in comparison to the Mexican American male. The Chicana has the difficult task of gaining for herself more flexibility in carrying out a greater variety of activities that traditionally have been denied her in the Mexican American culture. In her efforts to do this she runs the risk of diluting and of losing the many distinctive feminine qualities that make her so attractive to the male. The old concept of male-female roles in Chicano society is requiring a painful examination and reevaluation of what is important and what is less important in the functional roles between man and woman. Another case in point: At the college I am counseling a young Chicano couple in which the boy is a highly intelligent graduate student and the girl is a senior at the college. They are engaged to be married. However, at this time they are having a dispute because the boy wants his future wife to relate and behave in the traditional manner and she of course is opposing this. It remains to be seen how this difficulty will be resolved.

With increasing equalitarian contact between Chicanos and Anglos the chances for intermarriage between individuals of these different ethnic backgrounds rapidly increase. The understanding, acceptance, or adjustment to couples and families where intermarriage has taken place presents yet another area of difficulty where conflicts need be resolved. It poses one more problem to individuals and families in cultural transition. There is one Chicano I see who is torn between his affections for an attractive, wealthy Anglo girl and loyalty to his family and cultural heritage. So upset is he that he cannot focus on his studies and is seriously considering dropping out of school and going away so as to escape his immediate dilemma. This is despite the economic hardship he and his family have endured to maintain him in school till now and the sense of dishonor he would feel if he left.

Perhaps the most detrimental effect of all, resulting from attempts to live in a bicultural world, is the confusion and loss of self-identification that frequently occurs. One of the greatest challenges of the growing, developing individual is that of finding himself, or knowing what he is and who he is: the well-known "identity crisis." This task, which ordinarily reaches its greatest significance during adolescence, is not often easy to accomplish under usual circumstances. However, the problem can be greatly magnified for the bicultural youth who on almost every side finds himself and his values in conflict. He need only look at himself and his Anglo counterpart to notice the differences in skin color, speech, manner of behaving, neighborhoods, and economic position. It is no wonder that he may at times be confused or temporarily lose his sense of identity. Again I would like to quote a passage from the poem "I am Joaquin," which I feel beautifully expresses the Chicano's situation. I think it significant that the passage I am about to quote forms the opening of this poem.

I am Joaquin,
Lost in a world of confusion,
Caught up in a world of a
　　Gringo society,
Confused by the rules,
Scorned by attitudes,
Suppressed by manipulations,
And destroyed by modern society.
My fathers
　　　　Have lost the economic battle
And won
　　　　The struggle of cultural survival.
And now!
　　　I must choose
　　　　Between
　　　The paradox of
Victory of the spirit,
Despite physical hunger
　　　　Or
　　　To exist in the grasp
Of American social neurosis,
Sterilization of the soul
　　　　And a full stomach.

Some of the consequences of such conflicts are not too difficult to predict. There are likely to be sharp increases in the level of frustration and anger, perhaps with inappropriate displacements; there is likely to be a high level of anxiety, insecurity, and mistrust; and there may be confusion, alienation, and withdrawal from society. It should not be surprising to find a defiant or aggressive posture in many Chicanos, for their spiritual (if not physical) survival is at stake. It would seem to me that from a mental health point of view at least such behavior would be considered healthy and appropriate.

Taking a longer-range look at the situation, what might be some of the options open to the Chicano individual? For one thing he might cling to the past and attempt to withdraw within his cultural cloak but this results in a kind of spiritual suicide, since life is process and change. One cannot long cling to the past without dying, at least emotionally, and the Chicano loves life too much to give it up in this manner. For another he may attempt to fashion a compromise between his Mexican American and his Anglo American values. By so doing he is likely to end up with neither, having lost the essence of both. A third alternative perhaps is to try and assimilate himself into the larger Anglo society. This often fails because as he turns his back on his Mexican heritage he may find the doors to the Anglo society barred against him because of discrimination and prejudices.

Finally, there is a fourth alternative for the Chicano, which I believe offers him the greatest potentiality for achieving a satisfying life in this country. Instead of clinging to the past, compromising his principles, or frustrating himself in an attempt to be assimilated in the Anglo society, I think he will come to realize his creative potential for developing his own unique identity; that he will bridge the credibility gap between the Anglo's stereotyped image of the Mexican and his own knowledge of himself as a potent historical force for change. At the same time he is beginning to synthesize the cultural differences between Anglo and Chicano and to utilize the generation gap between his parents and himself as a steppingstone toward the development of a Chicano nationalism, such as his mestizo forefathers did when they sought and eventually evolved a Mexican nationalism from their Spanish and Indian heritage.

In conclusion I would like to state my faith in the Chicano and his ability to meet this great challenge. It is my hope that the Anglo will also participate in this historical process by meeting *his* challenge of getting off his ethnocentric ego trip sufficiently to learn, understand, and explore *with* the Chicano more beneficial ways of living together based on mutual respect and equal opportunity. My belief in man is such that I think he can learn to cooperate rather than compete with one another; that through a mutual understanding and acceptance of individual and cultural differences one can only profit and man can at last come closer to his highest ideals of achieving the maximum benefits of what life has to offer for all.

REFERENCES

Galarza, Ernesto; Gallegos, Herman; Samora, Julian. Mexican Americans in the Southwest. Santa Barbara; McNally & Loftin, Publishers, 1969.

Gonzales, Rodolfo: I Am Joaquin, 1967.

Lewis, Oscar. Five Families. New York: Basic Books, Inc., Publishers, 1959.

Paz, Octavio. The Labyrinth of Solitude. New York, Grove Press, Inc. 1961.

Romano, Octavio Ignacio. The Anthropology and Sociology of the Mexican Americans: The Distortion of Mexican American History. El Grito, Vol. II, No. 1, 1968.

Rubel, Arthur J. Across the Tracks, Austin: University of Texas Press, 1966.

The Forgotten Family. National Educational Media, Inc.

CHAPTER 3 THE MILITANT CHALLENGE TO THE AMERICAN ETHOS: "CHICANOS" AND "MEXICAN AMERICANS"[1]

ARMANDO GUTIÉRREZ
HERBERT HIRSCH

If history is a fabrication of the past out of the accepted myths of the present, then the history of the Chicano has been misinterpreted. Commonly treated as a docile, "sleepy," minority, the history of the Chicano has in fact been a history of political turbulence and political oppression. They have been latently and manifestly oppressed. While scholars seem reluctant to brand as violence the oppression foisted upon a sub-group by the dominant culture, that oppression is nonetheless a form of systemic violence. Controlling the systemic political roles and, therefore, the legitimate use of violence, the Anglo dominated state has systematically repressed any manifest stirrings of Chicano consciousness—even in areas where Chicanos are a numerical majority. This manifest oppression is exemplified by state action of the type which has made the Texas Rangers famous. Founded in 1835 with the purpose of handling the "Mexican problem," the Rangers have been used as an internal police force to "put down" any indigenous stirrings of overt rebellion. In the late 1800's, for example, there was a saying in South Texas that, "Every Texas Ranger has some Mexican blood. He has it on his boots."[2] As late as 1966 a Chicana passes on a story concerning the melon strike of Rio Grande City, Texas as told her by an eye witness.

When they saw the guns, the men (Chicanos attending a UFWOC meeting) put their hands in the air. They thought the Rangers—especially Captain Alee—were drunk. They were told to lay on the floor. They (the Rangers) were cursing them the whole time, saying they were going to kill the bastards. Then they proceeded to kick Maddaleno (Dimas, a young Chicano who allegedly committed the crime of yelling "viva la huelga" to a Ranger's face) and smashed the back of his head with the shotgun barrel. He is in the hospital in a critical condition, with a broken rib, concussion, blood clot near the spine.[3]

Latent oppression is harder to conceptualize and even more difficult to confront in the realm of political action. The his-

From Social Science Quarterly, 1973, pp. 830-845.

[1]We wish to thank Professor David Garza and the Government 370K students who spent their time helping us design the questionnaire and gather the data.

[2]Stan Steiner, *La Raza: The Mexican Americans* (New York: Harper & Row, 1969), pp. 360-377.

[3]See Arthur J. Rubel, *Across the Tracks: Mexican-Americans in a Texas City* (Austin: University of Texas Press, 1966) for some vivid personal accounts of the vigilante actions of the Texas Rangers. Also see W. P. Webb, *The Texas Rangers* (Boston: Houghton Mifflin Co., 1935).

toric effects of uni-lingual and uni-cultural education—while the policy itself is pursued through vigorous political action—are felt in less overtly political ways. The consequence of such a policy for the Chicano results in the destruction of the culture coupled with the concomitant destruction of individual identity. This identity crisis forced upon a subcultural people by the Anglo dominated state has severe political implications.[4] We know, for example, that an individual's sense of self-esteem is related to the way in which he views the larger world. In a political context, a person with a high sense of self-esteem, i.e., a strong sense of identity, is more likely to be interested and involved in political activity.[5] It was not, for example, until the blacks first began to organize and develop a sense of identity as a black in a white dominated society that they could begin to engage in effective, collective political action. Latent oppression is further manifested through the myth of cultural pluralism.[6] As perpetuated in the United States it would have subcultural peoples believe that it is the "right" of all peoples to engage in political activity. In fact, cultural pluralism exists on only one level. There are, of course, numerous cultural groups residing within the territorial boundaries of this country. Yet, this is not what is meant by cultural pluralism—or at least this is not what the rhetoric tells us. The melting pot concept reigns supreme. All

peoples, it states, have equal access to the resources necessary for collective political action and, therefore, all have an equal opportunity to manifest their desires through participation in the systemically defined channels of political action. The predominant pattern, we submit, has been one of cultural domination. This domination destroys identity and inculcates the most repressive of nonconscious ideologies.[7] Racism, as with political oppression may be both latently and manifestly displayed. It is manifest in the case of the white bigot blowing up school buses or aggressing against young blacks on their way to a previously all white school, or through the use of the Texas Rangers to quell strikes. It is latent in the case of the good liberal, i.e., "some of my best friends. . . ." It is even more latent and oppressive in its nonconscious form; when one culture succeeds in socializing another to the extent that the other culture (usually a subculture) believes in its own inferiority and incapacity for political action.[8] Thus we have a Mexican American who states, "Most Latins don't know how to think politically. We complain and complain about what is wrong but very few of us speak up and state exactly what we want. We need to shout our demands instead of whining about our grievances."[9] The latent oppression of which we earlier spoke is manifested in precisely this way. The Anglo dominated state has succeeded in inculcating a form of self-directed racism, or in our terms, weak self-identity. Latent oppression involves less cost to the dominant culture than manifest oppression. Every time the dominant culture is forced to resort to

[4]Robert L. Derbyshire, "Adolescent Identity Crisis in Urban Mexican-Americans in East Los Angeles," in Eugene B. Brady, ed., *Minority Group Adolescents in the United States* (Baltimore: The Williams and Wilkins Co., 1968), pp. 73-110.

[5]Morris Rosenberg, *Society and the Adolescent Self-Image* (Princeton: Princeton University Press, 1965), pp. 256-260. The literature on self-esteem is voluminous. For a review of some of the literature on internal and external control, see Julian B. Rotter, "External Control and Internal Control," *Psychology Today*, 5 (June, 1971), pp. 37-42+. Also see the bibliography to this article.

[6]Octavio Ignacio Romano-V, "The Anthropology and Sociology of the Mexican Americans," in Octavio Ignacio Romano-V, ed., *Voices: Readings from El Grito* (Berkeley, Calif.: Quinto Sol Publications, Inc.), pp. 26-39.

[7]Daryl J. Bem, *Beliefs, Attitudes and Human Affairs* (Belmont, Calif.: Brooks/Cole Publishing Co., 1970), pp. 89-99, defines a nonconscious ideology as "a set of beliefs and attitudes which he accepts implicitly but which remains outside his awareness because alternative conceptions of the world remain unimagined," p. 89.

[8]See Louis Knowles and Kenneth Prewitt, *Institutional Racism in America* (Englewood Cliffs, N.J.: Prentice-Hall, 1969).

[9]William Madsen, *Mexican Americans of South Texas* (New York: Holt, Rinehart and Winston, 1964), p. 110.

arms to put down an indigenous uprising it expends certain valuable resources. It is much more efficient, i.e., involves less cost, if the dominant culture can succeed in socializing large numbers of its subcultural citizenry (and for that matter dominant cultural citizenry) to believe not only that they are inferior and therefore must blindly and obediently defer to that dominant leadership, but that the subcultural members are themselves part and parcel of that dominant culture, that they are, in other words, Anglos. Thus, political activity is constrained by the Chicano's very perception of his own identity. This study seeks to examine the influence of racial self-identity upon social and political perceptions and on the implications of these for political activity.[10]

CULTURAL AND HISTORICAL SETTING

Crystal City, Texas occupies, from our perspective, a particularly important position in the history of the Chicano movement. It is the first community in which a majority which has previously been repressed by the state-wide dominant Anglo society has succeeded in turning systemically sanctioned politics to its advantage and has finally become politically what it has always been numerically—a "real majority." Thus we seek to investigate in this paper the effect of political liberation upon the political awareness of Chicano youth in one South Texas community.

The political implications of this investigation are profound. If the Chicano movement is to continue to grow it must politically socialize its young with a strong sense of "Chicano" identity. This study is a preliminary investigation to ascertain at this point in time whether this is in fact occurring.

---

[10]Our analysis is, of course, constrained because we are unable to make before and after comparisons. Since we were unable to get access to the Crystal City schools until after Chicanos dominated the school board we are unable to say how much of the process we are investigating is the direct result of that political action.

Crystal City

For the traveler destined for the Gulf Coast, Crystal City would probably be remembered (if at all) for the imposing sign on its outskirts proclaiming the city as the "Spinach capital of the world" and for the Popeye the Sailor statue in the city's square. This small city of 10,000 has only one other distinctive feature. For Chicanos from the West Coast to the Gulf Coast the mention of Crystal City is often accompanied by a raised fist and ringing "vivas." It is here that the Chicano movement has achieved its most significant success. It is to Crystal City that Chicanos throughout the United States look for that glimmer of inspiration which keeps the movement growing.

For a long time Crystal City was much like any other South Texas community. With a four to one proportion of Chicanos to Anglos, the city's government had traditionally been run by the economically dominant Anglos. The schools were no different. As late as 1970 the School Board was made up of five Anglos and two Mexican Americans. The faculty of the school system had some 97 Anglos and only 30 Mexican Americans—this in a setting in which Chicanos constituted some 86 percent of the total school population. To be sure, the Mexican Americans of Crystal City had "taken over" the city once before, in 1963. Control was short-lived, however, and the Anglos quickly re-established their control.

The groundswell began with the 1970 elections for school cheerleaders, which were traditionally chosen by the Anglo-dominated faculty. Given this impetus, and with a phenomenal amount of organization, Chicanos were able to take over the city and the school district virtually overnight. The changes which have occurred since this takeover in the spring of 1970 have been staggering. In the year following the takeover, a bilingual education program was instituted for grades 1, 2, and 3. Although no official or unofficial policy was implemented to reduce the number of Anglos in the schools, the number of Anglos in the schools (both as students and as teachers) was cut in half. Later (for the 1971-1972 school year) the Anglo student population had diminished to the unbelievable figure of 18. Anglo teachers were few; administrators fewer. Finally, Chicanos had taken over not only numerically but also spiritually. Classes were conducted largely in Spanish. Chicano culture and heritage were taught freely. Emiliano Zapata's name was heard more often than George Washington's.

At the time of the survey used in this study (May, 1971), Crystal City was in the middle of a metamorphosis that will continue to affect its citizens for years to come. The Chicanos of Crystal City seemed to have taken to heart the words of José Angel Gutiérrez, later to be elected School Board president: ". . . Mexicanos need to be in control of their destiny. They need to make their own decisions. We need to make the decisions that are going to affect our brothers and maybe our children. We have been complacent for too long." In the middle of this situation our survey was administered.

We originally expected that the effects of the Chicano political successes would not yet be completely internalized by our respondents. Hence, we thought that Chicanos would still score low on such scales as self-esteem and political knowledge.[11] After all, these Chicanos (grades 7 through 12) had spent more than half their lives in the schools as they had been run before the takeover. If one is to believe much of the political socialization literature, basic attitudes would have been formed much earlier. It was not, we thought, reasonable

to expect the changes which had taken place (even as dramatic as they were) to undo the "fruit" of 12 to 18 years of exposure to Anglo domination. Moreover, the influence of the larger Anglo society could not be completely kept out. Radio, television, newspapers, and magazines continued to present to the Chicano the same messages as before. While there are Spanish language radio and television networks and periodicals, the influence from the "outside" could hardly be expected to cease or be altogether mitigated. Our expectation, therefore, based on the limited amount of work previously done on the Chicano,[12] was to find low self-esteem scores and other characteristics normally attributed to subcultural groups. At the other extreme, there were some who felt that the unique place of Crystal City in the socio-historical map of the Mexican American people would have turned the previous expectations completely around. For the "grito" of Crystal City had been cultural pride. Tired of shuffling about at the feet of the "Magnificent Seven syndrome," the Crystal City Chicano had left the place reserved for him by Anglo society (asleep under the cactus, of course) and not only set about reversing the power structure of that community but had actually pulled it off. The Chicano, contrary to popular belief, had long been "awake," but now he was finally able to use systemic politics to assert himself. Would not such a dramatic physical change (from white to brown councilmen, teachers, administrators) cause great spiritual changes? Would not this change be manifested in the minds of the students? For it was the students themselves who had precipitated the stir. They had led the boycotting of classes. They had worked night and day to get the Raza

---

[11]For studies using these variables in other cultures see: Dean Jaros, Herbert Hirsch, and Frederick J. Fleron, Jr., "The Malevolent Leader: Political Socialization in an American Sub-Culture," *American Political Science Review*, 62 (June, 1968), pp. 564-575; Herbert Hirsch, *Poverty and Politicization: Political Socialization in an American Sub-Culture* (New York: The Free Press, 1971). There has been a recent increase in the number of good articles on the political socialization of blacks. See, for example, Edward Greenberg, "Children and Government: A Comparison Across Racial Lines," *Midwest Journal of Political Science*, 14 (May, 1970), pp. 249-275; and Schley R. Lyons, "The Political Socialization of Ghetto Children: Efficacy and Cynicism," *Journal of Politics*, 32 (May, 1970), pp. 288-304.

[12]Derbyshire, "Adolescent Identity Crisis"; Madsen, *Mexican Americans of South Texas*; Celia S. Heller, *Mexican American Youth: Forgotten Youth at the Crossroads* (New York: Random House, 1966); Anthony Dworkin, "Stereotypes and Self-Images Held by Native-Born and Foreign-Born Mexican-Americans," in John H. Burma, ed., *Mexican-Americans in the United States* (Cambridge, Mass.: Schenkman Publishing Co., 1970), pp. 397-409.

Unida party slate elected to the local offices. Therefore, it seemed equally logical that attitudinal changes would be manifested in the students. Importantly, it had not been the high school seniors, but the juniors and sophomores, who had led the "uprising." These people, of course, were still in the school when the survey was given. Expectations of high self-esteem, knowledge, etc. also seemed warranted.

METHODS
The sample

The team of researchers gave questionnaires to all pupils in grades 7 through 12 (786 students). We have no reason to suspect an unusually high or low absentee rate on the day the survey was administered. As a result of hostility and language difficulties, we ended up with a total sample of 726.

This sample consisted of 54 percent males and 46 percent females. In approximately 86 percent of the homes the father was present. An important breakdown which was not as clear as we might have hoped was that between migrants and non-migrants. By the time of the survey most migrants had already gone "up North." Even so, based on the children's place of birth and/or places lived, we determined that some 51 percent were or had been in the migrant stream. Yet, when we tried to use migrant status as a control variable the sample size decreased to 164 and was not useful due to the number of zero cells in the resulting tables.

Regarding the education of the parents, the sample substantiated the general pattern throughout the Rio Grande Valley.[13] The modal category for parents' education was that of grade school education. Some 37.8 percent of the students' fathers and 36.1 percent of their mothers had completed grade school. The next largest category were those with no education. The fathers in this group made up 22.3 percent of the sample while the mothers constituted 23.5 percent. Only 6.7 percent of all the students' parents had completed col-

---

[13]United States Commission on Civil Rights, *Mexican-American Study Report #1: Ethnic Isolation of Mexican Americans in the Public Schools of the Southwest* (Washington, D.C.: U.S. Government Printing Office, 1971).

lege. The majority (69.4 percent) of the sample did not know their parents' combined income. Of those reporting, 16.0 percent reported their parents' annual income as below $2,999. Of these over 40 percent ranked below the $1,000 category. Only 2.2 percent of the students reported their parents' yearly income as greater than $10,000. Parents' occupation was distributed similar to income. Most students did not know parents' exact occupation, or did not answer the question, making it impossible to use either income or occupation as control variables. Finally, the question was posed to the students as to what language was first learned in the home. Spanish ranked as the first language in 78.9 percent of the cases. This, of course, concurs with the fact that at the time of the sample Chicanos made up 86 percent of the total school population.

The questionnaire

One of the first questions to arise when the study under consideration was conceived was that concerning the applicability of standard questionnaire methods to Chicanos. The cultural and linguistic problems seemed of paramount importance. Therefore, the help of students in a Mexican American politics course was enlisted. Many of these students were Chicanos and after a painstakingly long process of suggestion, discussion, compromise, and deletion the final version of the survey offered a combination of both standard measures (political cynicism scale, faith in people scale, etc.) and some original and highly insightful categories applicable to Chicanos alone (part of the questionnaire was taken only by Mexican Americans). Thus, the students were asked to identify such terms as huelga, Cesar Chavez, Chicano, etc. In addition, questions were asked regarding family loyalty and ties. In categories regarding party preference, La Raza Unida party was included. Even with these precautionary measures, some of the students (particularly the seventh graders) seemed to have some difficulty in comprehending the meaning of various questions. Nevertheless, the authors are convinced that the final product offers a uniquely insightful look at the socialization of Chicanos amidst the turmoil of political change at the community level.

Chicano consciousness

A distinction which is at the base of our hypotheses, regards that made between those students who classify themselves as "Chicanos" as opposed to such terms as "Mexican Americans," "Latin Americans," and "Spanish Americans." In recent years the term "Chicano" (a derivative of Mexicano) has come to gain wide acceptance throughout the Southwest among those Spanish-speaking who wish to retain their culture and language amidst a society which discourages it. To be sure, many Mexican Americans not only do not identify with the term, but also regard it as degrading. But to the "militant" (be they young or old) Spanish-speaking the term signifies a unique identity and feeling which only one who has suffered the consequences of being Mexican can know. Not only is the term one which the Chicano has created himself but also one which often confounds the Anglo. For most Anglos do not know its origin, its meaning, or its correct pronunciation. Instead, Anglos have been most comfortable with such "acceptable" terms as Latin Americans or, more recently, Mexican Americans. Use of the term "Chicano," much like the refusal to anglicize one's name from Juan to John, is thus in some ways an act of defiance. It signifies a pride in one's culture, heritage and language. If Anglos want to know something about this culture and its customs, they will have to do it on Chicano terms.

Because of the voltage of the term it thus seemed particularly important to make a distinction between those who preferred the other more acceptable terms and those who preferred "Chicano." Of those reporting, 48.9 percent (253) called themselves "Chicanos" while slightly less, 47 percent (212) preferred the term "Mexican American." The rest of the categories yielded a small number of responses. The significance of the distinction between self-identification as a "Chicano" or a "Mexican American" is, as noted above, our particular focus.[14] Thus, we are interested in the social and political awareness (some might

wish to call it "consciousness") of the Chicano. The questions we seek to illuminate are: What is a "Chicano"? How does he view certain selected aspects of his social and political world? Finally, what are the consequences for political action of any differences in political perspective?

FINDINGS
The social world of the Chicano student

The link explicated earlier between self-identity and social and political perspectives of the Chicano should manifest itself in self perceptions of the possibility for the Chicano child to achieve success in the society at large. Hence, the student's perception of his social world could be expected to differ according to his own self identification as a "Chicano" or a "Mexican American." While our data are not comprehensive, they do focus on selected aspects of achievement orientation and perceptions as to the possibility of realizing these desires.

Students were asked to respond to items reflecting the rhetoric of the open society. Thus, Table 1 illustrates interesting findings.

Table 1. Self identification and perceptions of success

		Percent	
		Mexican American	Chicano
"Anyone can achieve his goal in life by hard work."			
Agree	1	51.0	52.6
	2	19.2	16.5
	3	16.7	13.9
	4	7.6	7.8
Disagree	5	5.5	9.1
Total Percent (N)		100.0(198)	99.9[a](230)
		$X^2 = 2.83$, gamma = .01	
"Do you think you have the same chance to succeed in life as anyone else?"			
Yes		76.7	76.7
No		23.3	23.3
Total Percent (N)		100.0(202)	100.0(236)
		$X^2 = .00$, gamma = .001	

[a]Percent does not equal 100 due to rounding.

[14]Alfredo Cuellar, "Perspective on Politics," in Joan W. Moore, *Mexican Americans* (Englewood Cliffs, N.J.: Prentice-Hall, 1970), pp. 137-156.

There are absolutely no significant differences between "Chicanos" and "Mexican Americans" in their acceptance of this portion of the American ethos. Even those whom we expected to demonstrate greater awareness of the barriers imposed against non-white people believe that hard work will lead to success and that they have the same chance to succeed that is offered to "everyone else." The Crystal City students seem to have internalized the "American dream." Like Horatio Alger, they view the United States ". . . as a 'land of promise' where golden opportunities beckon to able and ambitious men without regard to their original station in life."[15] There are a number of possible interpretations that one could place on these findings. It is possible that the Crystal City students believe that they (the individual respondents) will work hard and therefore achieve success while others who do not work as hard have less of a chance. This strikes us as similar to some perceptions of why people remain poor. They are poor because they do not work hard. If they did they could pull themselves up by their own effort. It is also possible that the responses are ego-defensive. That is, the "Chicanos" and "Mexican Americans" have to maintain their belief in the possibility of success in order to hang on to some sense of self-identity. A third alternative is related to the very special circumstances within Crystal City. If they could gain control of Crystal City after years of being ruled, then hard work can lead to success. However, when one travels outside the limited boundaries of Crystal City itself one's chances in the larger society necessarily begin to decrease. While we cannot substantiate any of these hypothetical conclusions, we do find, as we begin to inquire further, that aspirations and hopes for success remain high. Thus, fully 78 percent of Mexican Americans and 77 percent of Chicano identifiers believe they will at least graduate from high school. Again, this is possibly related to the special circumstances within Crystal City where the schools have, as noted previously, begun to reflect the culture of the

Chicano. Yet, their aspirations remain high when we examine further educational hopes.

Crystal City does not contain a college or a university. Despite this, 85 percent of the Mexican American identifiers and 81 percent of the Chicano identifiers want to attend college and 73 percent of the Mexican American identifiers and 72 percent of the Chicano identifiers believe that they will in fact have the opportunity to do so. That these findings persist despite the economic and cultural barriers mitigating against the possibility that they will be able to attend college attests to the power of the "American dream."

The persistence of this perception in the face of overwhelming empirical evidence to the contrary, we hypothesize, leads to heightened rather than lowered political consciousness. To aspire and then have one's aspirations shattered on the sharp realities of everyday life can have, at the very least, two consequences. First, it could lead to frustration, alienation and withdrawal, or, second, it could lead to frustration, alienation and heightened activity and consciousness. Given the Crystal City context we hypothesize that the more militant identifiers will move in the latter direction because they will be better able, as their sense of themselves as Chicanos develops, to see the holes in the dream. Their perceptions of political reality should be more realistic and they should demonstrate a greater willingness to undertake political action.

The political world of the Chicano student

The tentacles of the dominant ethos extend beyond social perceptions and are intimately interwoven into the world of politics. Yet, it is an over-simplification to draw a hard and fast line between the two. Political values overlap in important areas with social values. For example, the rhetoric of equal opportunity tells us not only that all have an equal chance for success in the society—defined, of course, in economic terms—but also that all are equal before the law. We asked a series of questions to ascertain whether there were significant differences between "Chicano" and "Mexican American" identifiers in

---

[15]Ely Chinoy, *Automobile Workers and The American Dream* (Garden City, N.Y.: Doubleday & Company, 1955), p. 1.

Table 2. Self identification and equality before the law

	Percent	
	Mexican American	Chicano
"In the United States, a person, no matter who he is, is always considered innocent before the law, until proven guilty."		
Agree 1	46.5	37.4
2	19.2	14.8
3	18.7	17.8
4	9.6	11.7
Disagree 5	6.0	18.3
Total Percent (N)	100.0(198)	100.0(230)

$X^2 = 16.39$, P < .01, gamma = .23, P < .005

"If you are poor or not white, you can never achieve freedom in America."		
Agree 1	11.6	18.4
2	10.6	9.6
3	19.1	18.0
4	11.0	16.7
Disagree 5	47.7	37.3
Total Percent (N)	100.0(199)	100.0(228)

$X^2 = 8.58$, gamma = −.15, P < .02

"If a person has enough money, he can buy his way out of any trouble."		
Agree 1	20.7	29.9
2	12.6	16.7
3	21.2	16.2
4	13.6	11.5
Disagree 5	31.8	25.6
Total Percent (N)	99.9[a](198)	99.9[a](234)

$X^2 = 7.66$, gamma = −.17, P < .01

[a]Percent does not equal 100 due to rounding.

Table 3. Self identification and selected political attitudes

	Percent	
	Mexican American	Chicano
Civil Liberties Score		
Low	30.8	18.7
High	69.2	81.3
Total Percent (N)	100.0(172)	100.0(214)

$X^2 = 7.66$, P < .01; gamma = .32, P < .002

Political Cynicism		
Low	1.5	1.7
Medium	48.5	34.6
High	50.0	63.7
Total Percent (N)	100.0(204)	100.0(237)

$X^2 = 8.81$, P < .02; gamma = .26, P < .002

this regard. Table 2 demonstrates that there are. Students who identify themselves as Chicanos are much more likely to disagree with the classic conceptualization of the United States' system of justice. They do not believe that a person is always "innocent until proven guilty."

Chicanos are more likely to agree that, "If you are poor or not white, you can never achieve freedom in America." Similarly, they are more likely to believe that, "If a person has enough money he can buy his way out of trouble." While cynical, this is a more realistic perception of the Chicano's contact with the dominant judicial system. He is beginning to perceive that there is a gap between rhetoric and practice. The Chicano, in other words, is probably less likely to unquestionably accept the pronouncements of the Anglo society. He may be experiencing a heightening of his political consciousness.

If this hypothesis is accurate, the trend should continue to appear in measures of selected political attitudes. Table 3 does show the continuation of this pattern—and the differences between the two groups are statistically significant. Chicanos score higher on civil liberties and political cynicism than do Mexican Americans. The higher political cynicism of the Chicano is related to the cynical perceptions of the judicial process. The higher civil liberties score is not inconsistent. Heightened political consciousness should lead one to place more rather than less emphasis upon civil liberties. If one has been discriminated against all one's life, then one can easily learn the value of a civil libertarian outlook. How else could a minority ever have the potential to mobilize their resources?

The items contained in the civil liberties scale used in this study concentrate on the right of unapproved of individuals to speak out or to hold public office—in other words, to attempt to mobilize their resources. Members of minority groups with high political consciousness are able to see the need for the maintenance of such liberties.

Having established, at this point in time, that there is a trend in the direction of heightened political awareness on the part of students who identify themselves as "Chicanos," we must inquire what the possible behavioral implications of this trend are. Are students who identify as "Chicano" more likely to be willing to engage in the more militant forms of political action? The data in Table 4 suggest that they are. Asked to respond to a series of questions regarding the necessity of changing "our form of government" and means to bring these changes about, Chicano students show up as more favorably disposed toward the use of collective political action.

For example, Chicano students are more likely than Mexican American students to agree that "the best way to handle problems is to band together." Moreover, fully 30 percent of the Chicano respondents disagree with the statement that "there is no sense in forming a third party" while only 16 percent of the Mexican American students feel the same way. Chicanos are also more likely to approve of the use of public marches or demonstrations (38 percent to 22 percent for Mexican Americans) and are less likely to condemn the use of violence as a political instrument.

In short, the pattern remains. Students who identify themselves as "Chicanos" are more likely to approve of and, by extension, engage in collective political action. In order to achieve a more comprehensive picture of the likelihood of action we administered a series of story completion or "semi-projective"[16] tests to the same group

---

[16]The tests we devised were based upon the work of Greenstein and Tarrow. See Fred I. Greenstein and Sidney Tarrow, *Political Orientations of Children: The Use of a Semi-Projective Technique in Three Nations* (Beverly Hills, Calif.: Sage Publications, 1970).

Table 4. Racial identification and the use of collective action

| | Percent | |
	Mexican American	Chicano
"The best way to handle problems is to band together with people like yourself to help each other out."		
Agree 1	41.2	49.6
2	32.2	24.3
3	17.6	13.5
4	6.0	5.6
Disagree 5	3.0	7.0
Total Percent (N)	100.0(199)	100.0(230)
	$X^2 = 8.39$; gamma $= -.08$	
"There is no sense in forming a third party to get new laws passed."		
Agree 1	16.9	15.4
2	21.0	22.0
3	32.8	20.7
4	12.8	12.3
Disagree 5	16.5	29.5
Total Percent (N)	100.0(195)	99.9[a](227)
	$X^2 = 13.75$; $P < .01$; gamma $= .13$; $P < .03$	
"The best way to get government officials to do something is to organize a public demonstration or march."		
Agree 1	22.5	37.6
2	18.0	20.5
3	34.5	26.6
4	11.0	7.9
Disagree 5	14.0	7.4
Total Percent (N)	100.0(200)	100.0(229)
	$X^2 = 15.98$; $P < .01$; gamma $= -.28$; $P < .001$	
"No matter how bad things may get, one should have faith in our government and never resort to violence."		
Agree 1	32.1	22.1
2	19.4	20.4
3	27.6	20.4
4	10.7	18.1
Disagree 5	10.2	19.0
Total Percent (N)	100.0(196)	100.0(226)
	$X^2 = 15.69$; $P = .01$; gamma $= .22$; $P < .001$	

[a]Percent does not equal 100 due to rounding.

of students. We used three similar stories[17] involving encounters between the police and another person. The stories read the same except that in the first story the culprit was Juan Gonzalez, in the second he was called John Grant, and in the third Beulah Johnson. The purpose of such tests is to allow the respondents to project their own feelings into the contrived situation. In this particular case we hypothesized that students who identified themselves as "Chicanos" would project much more militant emotions into the story than would students who called themselves "Mexican Americans." We were not disappointed for the results provided corroboration of the data previously presented. Thus, following the coding method originated by Greenstein and Tarrow, we separated the responses into three separate dimensions: Initial definition of the situation, outcome of the episode, and norms governing the encounter.

"Chicano" students were more likely to define the situation with regard to the encounter between Juan Gonzalez and the police as involving racial discrimination than were the Mexican American students (16 percent of the Chicano respondents and 6 percent of the Mexican American respondents perceived racial discrimination). On the other hand, 26 percent of the Mexican American students replied simply that the police were doing their job, while only 12 percent of the Chicano stu-

---

[17]The directions and stories read as follows: In answering the following questions you will have to use your imagination. This is not a test and there are no right or wrong answers. You will read the beginning of a story, and then you can finish it in any way you want. Simply imagine how the story would end. Do you understand? It is up to you to decide how to finish the stories and it doesn't matter what answers you give.
1. Juan Gonzalez was driving to work one morning. Since he was late he drove faster than the speed limit. A policeman stopped him. FINISH THE STORY.
2. John Grant was driving. . . .
3. Beulah Johnson was driving. . . .
(We originally conceived that Beulah Johnson would be perceived as a black woman. Most of our respondents, however, simply perceived the sexual dimension.)

dents responded in this vein. It is evident that students who identify themselves as "Chicano" are more suspicious of the authority structure of the Anglo society. They are more likely to perceive the subtle institutional forms of discrimination and racism than are students who identify as "Mexican Americans."

When we turn our attention to the respondents' projections regarding the "outcome of the episode" we find a similar pattern. While a large percentage of both types of identifiers perceive the Chicano as being punished (74 percent of the Mexican American students and 83 percent of the Chicano students) the trend is more evident when the stimulus on the story is shifted from Juan Gonzalez to John Grant. In the case where the Anglo is stopped by the police 46 percent of the Mexican American identifiers finished the story by having the officer give a ticket to Mr. Grant, while only 29 percent of the Chicano identifiers answered in this way. Students who identify as Chicanos are again less likely to accept the equality before the law argument. They perceive that a white person who is stopped by the police is less likely to be punished than a Chicano. Further evidence can be found in the fact that when the stimulus is shifted to Beulah Johnson 52 percent of the Mexican Americans see the woman as being punished while only 32 percent of the Chicano identifiers noted the same phenomena. As we noted earlier, most of the respondents did not perceive Beulah Johnson as a black woman—they only perceived the sexual dimension. The higher political cynicism or realism of the Chicano identifiers is reflected in that they are more likely to believe that a woman will have a greater chance to get away with speeding than a Chicano. They have, in other words, a less idealized conception of the role of the police. Call it cynicism or a realistic appraisal of the American ethos. Whatever the label, students who are in the process of developing their identity as "Chicano" are more likely to perceive the existence of discrimination.

The last dimension analyzed dealt with the students' projection of norms governing the episode. Again we find Chicano identifiers as more likely to perceive "racial inequality" in the case of Juan Gonza-

Table 5. Self identification and fine imposed in story completion

	Percent	
	Mexican American	Chicano
Higher fine for Mexican	37.4	63.6
Higher fine for Anglo	2.6	1.4
Higher fine for Woman	7.0	2.9
All same	37.4	24.3
No fine	15.6	7.8
Total Percent (N)	100.0(115)	100.0(140)

$X^2 = 18.03; P < .01;$
gamma $= -.40; P < .001$

lez than Mexican American identifiers (18 percent of Chicano identifiers as compared to no Mexican American identifiers). Moreover, in the John Grant story Chicano students tended to project that the "Anglo is above the law" (17 percent as compared to 8 percent of Mexican American students). The results of the semi-projective tests are best summarized by the perception of who gets fined. As Table 5 demonstrates, students who identify themselves as "Chicano" are more likely to project a higher fine for Juan Gonzalez than for John Grant or Beulah Johnson. They are also less likely than Mexican American identifiers to project an equal fine for all of those stopped by the police. In conclusion, the results of the semi-projective tests corroborate our earlier data on political orientations. Students who identify themselves as Chicanos are more likely to perceive inequality and to project these perceptions in their answers. They are, in other words, more acutely aware of the subtle institutional forms of discrimination and they are more likely to be willing to take direct action to bring about political change.

CONCLUSION

While our data do not enable us to make before and after comparisons between students who self identify as "Chicano" or "Mexican American," we have been able to provide a preliminary description of the differing levels of political consciousness at this point in time.

While the Chicano students of Crystal City do not differ from those who self identify as Mexican American in their perceptions of the American dream, particularly regarding their own possibility for success in this society, the results on the political dimension do form a defineable trend. Crystal City students who self identify as "Chicano" tend to have a higher level of political consciousness than students who self identify as "Mexican Americans."

This higher level of political awareness if manifested by Chicano identifiers in that they are much less likely to unquestioningly accept the usual cliches regarding equality before the law and justice in America. Their level of political cynicism is higher than that of Mexican American identifiers and so are their civil liberties scores. Chicano students, moreover, express greater readiness to engage in the various forms of collective political action, i.e., marches, demonstrations and the formation of third parties, and they are less likely to reject the use of violence to achieve political ends. Chicano identifiers, as noted in the results from the semi-projective tests, are more likely to be sensitive to the more subtle institutional forms of discrimination. In other words, Chicano identifiers no longer feel that they are at the mercy of their environment. They have begun to develop a sense of identity and a sense that they can control their environment—especially their political environment.

These findings have, it seems to us, important historical-political consequences. If the heightened Chicano consciousness manifested by self-identification as a "Chicano" is a result of the political success of La Raza Unida party in Crystal City, then as Chicanos tend to consolidate their gains, as their successes extend outward into realms other than the political, their social consciousness should also undergo radical revision. Moreover, the continued success should tend to decrease the number of students who identify themselves as "Mexican Americans." This decrease should then manifest itself in further developing the level of political consciousness among Crystal City Chicanos.

Implications such as these extend beyond the territorial boundaries of Crystal

City. As Chicanos begin to experience political success in other parts of the country their sense of identity will probably undergo a process comparable to that which we have seen in Crystal City. A strong sense of self leading one to identify oneself strongly with one's cultural-racial group will increase the number of Chicano identifiers and will, therefore, steadily increase political awareness. This awareness should then result in greater political activity. In other words, we have not heard the last from the Chicano movement—we may only have seen the beginning.

CHAPTER 4 THE PSYCHO-HISTORICAL AND SOCIOECONOMIC DEVELOPMENT OF THE CHICANO COMMUNITY IN THE UNITED STATES[1]

RODOLFO ALVAREZ

The closest approximation to objective knowledge can be gained from the confrontation of honestly different perspectives that subsume the same or related sets of facts. What is presented in this paper is a marshalling of historical fact from a perspective not traditionally taken into account in scholarly discourse on Mexican Americans. The objective is to confront the reality of Mexican American society as we have experienced it and from that basis to generate hypotheses for future multidisciplinary research in this area. For this purpose we identify four historical periods and describe the climate of opinion within the generation of Mexican Americans that numerically dominates the period. What I mean by a "generation" is that a critical number of persons, in a broad but delimited age group, had more or less the same socialization experiences because they lived at a particular time under more or less the same constraints imposed by a dominant United States society. Each generation reflects a different state of collective consciousness concerning its relationship to the larger society; psycho-historical differences related to, if not induced by, the economic system.

We begin our analysis with the assertion that, *as a people,* Mexican Americans are a creation of the imperial conquest of one nation by another through military force. Our people were thrown into a new set of circumstances, and began to evolve new modes of thought and action in order to survive, making Mexican American culture different from the culture of Mexicans in Mexico. Because we live in different circumstances we have evolved different cultural modes; just as we are neither identical to "Anglos" in the United States nor to Mexicans in Mexico, we, nevertheless, incorporate into our own ethos much from both societies. This is because we respond to problems of existence that confront us in unique ways, distinct from the way in which Anglos and Mexicans experience them.

How, then, did we pass from being a sovereign people into a state of being compatriots with the newly arrived Anglo settlers, coming mostly from the southern United States, and, finally, into the condition of becoming a conquered people—a charter minority on our own land?

The coming of the Spaniards to Mexico began the development of a mestizo people which has come to be the largest category

From Social Science Quarterly, 1973, pp. 920-942.

[1]This paper is an extension of the ideas developed by the author in: Rodolfo Alvarez, "The Unique Psycho-Historical Experience of the Mexican American People," *Social Science Quarterly,* 52 (June, 1971), pp. 15-29. I am indebted to Reynaldo Flores Macias and Victor Velasquez for extensive editorial and research assistance.

of Mexican society. The mestizo is the embodiment of biological, cultural and social heterogeneity. This sector of Mexican society was already numerically ascendant by the time Mexico gained its independence from Spain. Sovereign Mexico continued more or less the identical colonization patterns that had been developed by Spain by sending a cadre of soldiers, missionaries, and settlers to establish a mission and presidio where Indians were brought in and "Christianized."[2] Once the Indians were socialized to the peculiar mixture of Indian and Hispanic-Western cultural patterns which constituted the mestizo adaptation to the locale, they were granted tracts of land, which they cultivated to support themselves in trade with the central settlement, and through that, with the larger society with its center in Mexico City.[3] As the settlement grew and prospered, new outposts were developed further and further out into the provinces. Thus, Mexican society, like the Spanish society before it, was after *land* and *souls* in its development of the territories over which it held sovereignty.[4] The Indian quickly was subjugated into the lowest stratum of society to do the heaviest and most undesirable work at the least cost possible—although biologically "pure," but fully acculturated Indians frequently entered the dominant mestizo society. They also tended to marry settlers coming north from central Mexico to seek their fortunes.[5] Light and dark skinned alike were "Mexican."

What is of historic significance here is that in the early 1800's, particularly on the land now called Texas, this imperialistic system came into direct conflict with another;[6] that sponsored by England which resulted in the creation of the United States of America. Both systems set out aggressively to induce the economic development of the area. However, while the Hispanic system sought economic development through the acquisition of *land* and *souls,* the Anglo system that had been established on the northern Atlantic seaboard was one of acquiring *land, but not souls.*[7] An Indian could not have been elected president of the United States as Don Benito Juarez was in Mexico. Rather, the Indian was "pushed back" as the European settlement progressed.[8] He had to be either manifestly cooperative in getting out of the way (and later into reservations), or be exterminated. The new society in the United States was, therefore, a great deal more homogeneous than in Mexico since it was fundamentally a European adaptation to the new land and not in any way a mixture of Indian and European elements.

It should be said here, without wanting to overemphasize, that there is some evidence from correspondence between Thomas Jefferson and James Monroe that these and other key figures in the United States had intended to take the Southwest long before U.S. settlers started moving into Texas.[9] Insofar as the stage was not yet set for this final move, the coming of United States citizens into Texas was a case study in peaceful cooperation between peoples with fundamentally different ideological perspectives. The Anglo settlers initially and publicly made the minimal necessary assertions of loyalty to Mexico—despite the fact that they did not live up to the letter of the settlement contracts[10] which called for them to become Mexican citizens and Roman Catholic.[11]

[2]Wayne Moquin and Charles Van Doren, *A Documentary History of the Mexican American* (New York: Bantam Books, 1972), pp.2-3.

[3]George L. Rives, *The United States and Mexico, 1821-1848* (New York: Scribner's Sons, 1913), Vol. II, p. 29.

[4]*Ibid.,* pp. 24-25.

[5]Herbert L. Priestly, *The Coming of the White Man, 1492-1848* (New York: Macmillan, 1929).

[6]Samuel Harmon Lowrie, *Culture Conflict in Texas, 1821-1835* (New York: AMS Press, Inc., 1967).

[7]Eugene C. Barker, *Mexico and Texas, 1821-1835* (Dallas: P. L. Turner Co., 1928), p. 72. Also, Edward H. Spicer, *Cycles of Conquest: The Impact of Spain, Mexico, and the United States on the Indians of the Southwest, 1533-1960* (Tucson: University of Arizona Press, 1962), pp. 279-367.

[8]Priestly, *Coming of the White Man,* pp. 220-221.

[9]Rives, *United States and Mexico,* pp. 23-24.

[10]Lowrie, *Culture Conflict,* p. 52.

[11]Antonio Lopez de Santa Ana, *et al., The Mexican Side of the Texas Revolution, 1836* (Dallas: P. L. Turner Co., 1928), p. 307.

This cooperative experience lasted until approximately 1830-35. During this time Texas was being rapidly settled by Mexicans moving north ("rapidly," considering their form of colonization). Also, some Europeans, a few of them Roman Catholic, arrived in Galveston and settled throughout the territory.[12] Others, in a stream that was ultimately to become the majority, came from the southern region of the United States.[13] I call this the cooperative experience because there is historical evidence that all of these people, regardless of their point of origin, cooperated relatively well with each other. The frontier was sufficiently rugged that all needed each other's help and ideas in order to survive. Because everyone was given title to generous amounts of land, there was no struggle over land, which was the capital that they all sought. This period may be characterized as one in which every group could, apparently, optimize accomplishment of its objectives. The Mexican government needed to settle the area to secure its claim over the land and to reap the economic gain from its productivity; the settlers, whatever their origin (Indian, mestizo, European, or Anglo) came to develop their own personal economic assets. Because the country was so biologically and culturally heterogeneous, the question of how to develop a stable functioning society was crucial, once the break with Spain had been accomplished. During this period, some Anglo filibustering (insurrectionist activity in a foreign country) did take place. However, there is evidence that other Anglo groups were instrumental in helping to put these activities down. The *general* tone of the times was that of intercultural cooperation. Each group learned from the others as they applied their resources to the economic development of the area.

Somewhere around 1835 began what I call the "revolutionary experience." This was a revolutionary experience, in the usual sense of the term, only toward the end of this phase, as was perhaps inevitable given widespread territorial ambitions in the United States (subsequently labeled "manifest destiny" by historians of the period). The conflict was exacerbated by an ideological struggle within Mexican society between federalists and centralists. These political philosophies, while based to a considerable degree on economic self-interest of the partisans of either faction, also embodied widely divergent views on the nature of man himself.

The centralists were for administrative control over all Mexican territory by the governing elite in Mexico City. The federalists, on the other hand, were idealists trying to implement in Mexico the noble political principles of the rights of man as enunciated by the United States Constitution (after which the federalist constitution of 1824 was modeled) and by French political theorists of the Enlightenment. They were for egalitarianism in practice within a culturally and racially heterogeneous society, and not only in principle within a relatively racially and culturally homogeneous society, as in the United States. The centralists were skeptical of the possibility of self-government by a heterogeneous population, the major proportion of whom they considered inferior culturally, especially so because a poor country, such as Mexico, could not invest sufficient resources to educate the masses, who were mostly Indian.[14]

It appeared to the majority of settlers in Texas—Mexicans, as well as others—that federalism would provide the best economic outcome for them. The province of Texas became a stronghold of federalism,[15] and the majority decided to remain loyal to the federalist Mexican constitution of 1824. Santa Ana by this time had switched his ideological stance from federalism to centralism and had taken control of the central government in Mexico City. His reaction to events in Texas was to send troops to discipline the dissident province.

[12]George Conclin, *A New History of Texas; and a History of the Mexican War* (Cincinnati: District Court of Ohio, 1847), p. 150.
[13]Barker, *Mexico and Texas.*
[14]Benjamin Keen, *Readings in Latin American Civilization: 1492 to Present* (2nd ed.; Boston: Houghton Mifflin Co., 1967), pp. 165-166.
[15]Joseph M. Nance, *After San Jacinto: The Texas-Mexican Frontier, 1836-42* (Austin: University of Texas Press, 1963), pp. 172, 142-251.

However, the poorly professionalized army acted badly in Texas and alienated much of the populace by the unnecessary spilling of blood. The fact that many of these settlers came from the slaveholding South probably did not make relations with Mexicans, whom they considered inferior, easier. Heightened sentiment led to hostile actions and a revolution was started. The upshot was that Santa Ana personally came to command the army that was to put down the revolution and was himself defeated. Once the chief executive and the army of the sovereign country of Mexico were defeated, there was no real pressure for the dissident province to remain a loyal entity within the mother country—even though many of the settlers had set out originally simply to attain a federalist rather than a centralist government in Mexico. Furthermore, when the fighting broke out, adventurers and fortune seekers poured from the United States into Texas to participate in the fight. Evidence that these people, as well as their friends and relatives who remained behind, had a great sense of their "manifest destiny" to acquire more land for the United States,[16] is abundant and is illustrated by the fact that from as far away as Cincinnati, Ohio, came contributions of cannons and supplies as soon as it appeared that separating Texas from Mexico was a possibility.[17] Once hostilities began and these people began to pour in, the federalists loyal to Mexico were outnumbered and full-blown independence from Mexico was declared. When Santa Ana was ultimately defeated, it was still not clear that Mexico would be incapable of reassembling an army and returning to discipline the dissident province. The extreme biological and cultural heterogeneity which characterized Mexico then (as it does today) was one of the bases of Mexico's difficulty in self-government.[18]

The depth of Mexico's internal disarray became apparent soon enough. Texas was absorbed into the United States, provoking armed conflict with Mexico. If Mexico had not been able to discipline Texas, it certainly was no match for the well trained and well equipped U.S. Army backed by a *relatively* homogeneous society. By 1848 Mexico had lost approximately 50 percent of its territory. It appears that perhaps Santa Ana may have personally profited by Mexico's disarray.[19] With the signing of the Treaty of Guadalupe Hidalgo,[20] the Mexican American people were created *as a people:* Mexican by birth, language and culture; United States citizens by the might of arms.

THE CREATION GENERATION

Following incorporation of the Southwest into the United States in the mid-1800's there developed the experience of economic subjugation, followed by race and ethnic prejudice.[21]

Mexico . . . simply had to accept the best deal possible under the circumstances of military defeat; that deal meant that Mexico lost any respect it might have had in the eyes of the Mexicans living on the lands annexed by the United States. This rapid change must, certainly, have given them a different social-psychological view of self than they had prior to the break. The break and annexation meant that they were now citizens of the United States, but surely they could not have changed their language and culture overnight merely because their lands were now the sovereign property of the United States; thus they maintained their "Mexicanness." Because their cultural ties were to Mexico, they were, in effect, "Mexicans" in the United States. As the number of "Americans" in the region increased, "Mexicans" became an ever smaller proportion of the population. They were . . . a minority. They thought, spoke, dressed, acted, and had all of the anatomical characteristics of the defeated Mexicans. In fact, were they not still "Mexicans" from the point of view of "Americans" even though they were United

[16]Ramon Eduardo Ruiz, *The Mexican War: Was it Manifest Destiny?* (New York-Holt, Rinehart and Winston, 1963).

[17]Seymour V. Connor, *Texas: A History* (New York: Crowell Co., 1971).

[18]Leopoldo Zea, *The Latin American Mind* (Norman: University of Oklahoma Press, 1963). Also, Daniel Cosio Villegas, *American Extremes* (Austin: University of Texas Press, 1964).

[19]Santa Ana, *The Mexican Side.*

[20]Mexico and the United States, *El Tratado de Guadalupe Hidalgo, 1848* (Sacramento: Telefact Foundation, 1968).

[21]Edward E. Hale, *How to Conquer Texas Before They Conquer Us* (Boston: Redding and Co., March 17, 1845), p. 8.

States citizens by virtue of the military defeat and treaties that gave sovereignty to the United States? For all of these reasons and more, the "Mexican" minority could be viewed as the deviants onto whom all manner of aggressions could be displaced whenever the Calvinistic desire for material acquisition was in the least frustrated.[22]

It is the psycho-historical experience of a rapid and clear break with the culture of the parent country, and subsequent subjugation against the will of the particular population under analysis—all of this taking place on what the indigenous population considered to be its "own" land—that makes the experience of Mexican Americans different from all other ethnic populations that migrated to this country in the nineteenth and twentieth centuries.

All of the factors necessary for the development of race prejudice against Mexicans, now Mexican Americans, were present after 1836 in Texas. Any bloody war will engender very deeply felt animosity between contending factions. Furthermore, in order to kill, without feelings of remorse, it may be necessary to define the enemy as being sub-human and worthy of being killed. In the case of the fight between centralist and federalist forces in Texas it should be noted that the centralist army was almost exclusively Mexican, having been recruited deep in Mexico and brought north by Santa Ana.[23] The federalist forces in the province of Texas, on the other hand, were a mixture of Mexican, European, and U.S. settlers.[24] However, once the centralist forces were defeated, the hatred toward them, that had now become a hatred of Mexico and Mexicans, could easily be displaced onto settlers who in every respect could be said to be Mexicans, even though they had been federalists and had fought for Texas independence.

Second, since most of the settlers in Texas who came from the United States were from the slave-holding South, the idea of racial inferiority was not unknown to them and could easily be used to explain the hostile emotions they held toward the Mexicans, against whom they had just fought a winning fight.

A third factor making for the development of intense race prejudice against Mexican Americans was economic. Once Texas became independent it left the door open wide for massive migration from the United States. Title to the land had already been parceled out under Mexican sovereignty. Through legal and extra-legal means, the land was taken away from those provincial Mexicans, who as Texans had cooperated to try to give the province a measure of autonomy. These were the betrayed people, betrayed by their fellow Texans, once Texas became fully autonomous. By 1900 even those provincial Mexicans who had owned large tracts of land and who had held commanding social positions in Texas and throughout southwestern society had been reduced to a landless, subservient wage-earner class—with the advent of a new English language legal system, masses of English speaking, land hungry migrants, and strong anti-Mexican feelings—both by force of arms and through legal transactions backed up by force of arms.[25] Furthermore, it was the importation of race prejudice that created an impenetrable caste boundary between the dominant provincials of northern European backgroud and the provincial Mexicans. Once race prejudice was imported and accepted on a broad scale as an adequate explanation and justification for the lower caste condition of local "Mexicans," these attitudes could spread rapidly into the rest of the Southwest, when the United States acquired a large proportion of northern Mexico. The experience of socio-economic and political subjugation was repeated throughout the Southwest, with some variations for peculiar circumstances in specific areas, New Mexico in particular. Many of the distinctly Mexican

[22]Alverez, "Psycho-Historical Experience," pp. 19-20.

[23]George P. Garrison, *Texas: A Contest of Civilization* (Boston and New York: Houghton Mifflin Co., 1903), pp. 104-105.

[24]*Ibid.*, p. 105.

[25]Clark S. Knowlton has documented the procedure by which the lands were taken away from the newly become Mexican Americans in his "Culture Conflict and Natural Resources," in William Burch, *et al., Social Behavior, Natural Resources, and the Environment* (New York: Harper, 1972), pp. 109-145.

American attitudes throughout the country today stem from the subjugation experience of this period.

THE MIGRANT GENERATION

By 1900 the socioeconomic as well as political subservience of the Mexican American throughout the Southwest was well established. At the same time, the United States population was slowly becoming urbanized and was increasing *very rapidly* in size.[26] Instead of small farms and ranches that provided income for one family, agriculture was increasingly conducted on very large farms in order to grow massive quantities of food profitably. Despite the growing mechanization during this period (after 1900 and before World War II), the large farms and ranches of the Southwest required massive manual labor at certain periods in the growing season. Cheap Mexican labor was inexpensive and required much less care than the machines that were only then coming on the farms.

To provide the massive agricultural labor needed, recruiters were sent deep into Mexico to spread the word of higher wages on the large farms in the United States. Coincidently with this "pull," political upheavals in Mexico created a population "push." The resulting huge waves of migrants[27] coming north to work the fields give the name "Migrant Generation" to this period. Until the 1920's the migrant stream flowed north predominantly through Texas (where racial attitudes were imposed) and then beyond Texas to spread out over the agricultural region of the Great Lakes and western United States. It was not until after World War II that the migrant flow began to come predominantly through California. These people have been called "immigrants" by social scientists and by policy makers because they moved from one sovereign county to another. However true their "immigrant" status might have been *legally,* they were not immigrants either *sociologically* or *culturally* because of the peculiar psycho-historical experience of Mexican

Americans in the Southwest prior to 1900. Even those who eventually settled around the Great Lakes and later in the Northwest usually lived for a period of time in the Southwest where they were socialized into the cultural mode of the period.

There are at least four reasons why Mexicans arriving after 1900 but before World War II should be sociologically viewed as "migrants" who simply expanded the number of people who had more or less the same consciousness of lower caste status as those Mexican Americans who were here prior to 1900. First, the post-1900 waves of Mexican nationals coming into the United States did not come into a fresh social situation where they were meeting the host society for the first time. They did not arrive with the "freedom" to define themselves in the new society in accordance with their own wishes and aspirations. Not only were they denied the social-psychological process of "role taking" among the established higher status occupations, but demands and impositions of the dominant society were such that neither could they experiment with the process of "role making"; i.e., the creation of alternative but equal status occupations.[28] They did not arrive with the "freedom" that comes from having one's self-image and self-esteem determined almost exclusively from one presentation-of-self to strangers, where these strangers have no prior experience with which to question or invalidate the social claims being made by the performance.[29] Immigrants from other lands arrived in the United States, and their place in the social hierarchy was, in a sense, freshly negotiated according to what the group as a whole could do here.[30] The social situations that the post-1900 waves of Mexicans entering the United States encountered was very different from that of immigrants from other lands.

[26]Moquin and Van Doren, *A Documentary History*, p. 329.

[27]*Ibid.*

[28]Ralph Turner, "Role Taking: Process versus Conformity," in Arnold Rose, ed., *Human Behavior and Social Process* (Boston: Houghton Mifflin, 1962).

[29]Erving Goffman, *Presentation of Self in Everyday Life* (New York: Anchor Books, 1959).

[30]Harold Garfinkel, *Studies in Ethnomethodology* (Englewood Cliffs, N.J.: Prentice Hall, 1967).

Their experience upon entering the United States was predefined by the well established social position of pre-1900 Mexican Americans as a conquered people (politically, socially, culturally, economically, and in every other respect). They came to occupy the category closest to simple beasts of burden in the expanding regional economy.

The people coming from Mexico, in very large numbers after 1900 viewed themselves and were viewed by the dominant host society as the "same" as those Mexican Americans who had been living on the land long before,[31] during, and after the psycho-historical experience described above as resulting in the "Creation Generation." Before they came they knew they would find, and when they arrived they did find, a large, indigenous population with whom they had language, kinship, customs, and all manner of other genetic, social, cultural, and psychological aspects in common. The very interesting and highly peculiar circumstance in the case of the post-1900 migrant from Mexico is that he left a lower *class* status in Mexico to enter a lower *caste* status in the United States without being aware of it. The reasons he was unaware of it are multiple, reflecting the great network of characteristics in common with the people already here. The fact is that the vast majority of Mexican Americans never realized they were in a caste, as opposed to a class, category because they never tried to escape in any substantial numbers. The permeability of normative boundaries need never be an issue, so long as no one attempts to traverse them. Until World War II there existed a state of pluralistic ignorance between those few individuals and groups of Mexican Americans who tried to escape the caste and the majority of relatively unaware members of the Mexican American population. The state of development of mass communications probably prevented widespread knowledge across the Southwest of the many isolated incidents that took place during this period. When a critical proportion of Mexican Americans began to earn enough money to pay for their children's education and began to expect services that they saw non-Mexican American members of the society enjoying, they found out that they were not viewed just simply as members of a less affluent class, but, rather, as members of a despised caste. This was the critical test. If they had achieved skills and affluence in Mexico, race and ethnicity would have been no barrier to personal mobility into a higher socioeconomic class. It was the attempt to permeate the normative boundaries and the subsequent reaction by the larger society that brought out in the open the way they were perceived by the dominant host society. During the period designated as the "Migrant Generation," there were many isolated instances of great conflict between groups of Mexican Americans trying to alter their lower caste status, but they were locally overpowered, and a general state of acquiescence became the state of collective consciousness.

A second factor that characterized post-1900 incoming Mexicans as migrants rather than immigrants is that the land they came to was virtually identical to the land they left.[32] Today there is a sharp contrast between the terrain north and south of the border because of mechanization and irrigation for large scale industrialized farming on the United States side, and the same old water-starved flatland on the Mexican side. However, in the early period when the great waves of migrants came, the land was sufficiently similar to what they had left behind that it did not require a cognitive reorientation for them.

The fact that the land they came to was very similar, physically, to the land they left behind is very important because it had been part of Mexico. Thus, the post-1900 migrant from Mexico to the United States was not leaving land to which he had a deep identity-giving psychological relationship and going off to another, very different "foreign" land, to which he needed to develop another sort of identity-giving relation. The Irish immigrant, for example, experienced a great discontinuity between the land of origin and the land of destination. Furthermore, the na-

---

[31]Moquin and Van Doren, *A Documentary History,* p. 331.

[32]*Ibid.*

tion-state and the culture identified with the land to which he was going had never been part of the nation-state and culture he was leaving behind. When the Irish immigrant left "Ireland" to go to "America," there surely must have been a very clear psychic understanding that he was leaving behind a land to which he had a very special relationship that made him an "Irishman." The post-1900 migrant from Mexico need not have noticed any change. He was simply moving from one part of his identity-giving land to another. The work that he was to perform on the land of destination was identical to the work he performed on the land of origin.

A third set of factors that distinguished the Migrant Generation from immigrants from other countries involves the physical nature of the border that they had to cross to come into the United States. Over large distances the border between the United States and Mexico was never more than an imaginary line. Even in that part of Texas separated from Mexico by the Rio Grande, the natural obstacles are minimal. During much of the year people could simply walk across, and certainly at other times they could cross the river as any other river might be crossed. The amount of *time* that it takes to cross the border also affects the degree of anticipatory socialization that the person can engage in prior to arrival at his point of destination. The Irish immigrant spent the better part of *two weeks* crossing an enormous physical obstacle, the Atlantic Ocean. The great physical boundary separating his land of origin from his land of destination could not escape his notice. The time it took to traverse that boundary afforded the immigrant the opportunity gradually, but profoundly, to engage in serious contemplation that allowed him to significantly "disassociate" his identity from one nation-state and its culture and to engage in more or less effective anticipatory socialization for his new identity and new life in another nation-state and its culture. The point here is that the nature of the physical border (its overpowering size) and the time it took to traverse it made it virtually impossible for the immigrant not to be deeply conscious of the fact that he was entering a new society and therefore, a new place

within the structure of that society. This was not the case with the Mexican migrant.

A fourth set of factors distinguishing Mexicans of the Migrant Generation from immigrants from other countries is the nature of their activity in coming to this country. There is undoubtedly a significant psychic impact deriving from the degree to which the individual is a free and autonomous agent in determining the course of his own behavior. The greater the degree to which the individual perceives himself as self-determining, the less his behavior will precipitate a change of his already established identity. Conversely, the more the individual perceives (and his perceptions are validated) that his behavior is significantly determined by others, the greater will be the impact of that realization on his identity. The Irish immigrant, for example, had significant others affecting his behavior in such a way that he could not avoid considering the identity that he was rejecting and the one he was assuming. He had to ask for official permission to leave his country of origin, be physically conveyed across an ocean to enter a country he had had to obtain official permission to enter. Those actions forced him to consider his purpose in making the crossing, and whether he was prepared to abandon one identity for the other; whether he was prepared to pay the psychic price. The Mexican migrants, on the other hand, were "active agents," more or less in control of their own movement. They did not, in the early 1900's, have to ask anyone for permission to leave one country to enter the other. If they made their own personal decision to go, they simply went. There was no official transaction that in any way impinged on their collective self-identity. It took seven minutes to cross a river. The significance of the decision to swim or use the bridge is analogous to the modern-day decision either to walk downtown or to pay for a taxi—hardly an identity-making decision. It was not until the mid-1930's that the border was "closed," that is, when an official transaction was required to cross the border. By this time, however, such an enormous number of people had already crossed, and the Mexican American population, within the lower caste existing in the south-western United States, was so large that it did not matter in terms of the conceptual argument. The later migrant waves simply inflated the lower caste and took on its psychic orientation (i.e., its collective state of consciousness), despite the fact that by the official transaction they were made conscious that they were now in the sovereign territory of another nation-state. This was so because all other factors still applied, and, in addition, the impact of the large population into which they moved was overwhelming.

The post-1900 migrants came mainly to Texas and California. There they assumed the already established lower caste position we have described as a consequence of the prior established social structure. Socio-psychologically, the migrants, too, were a conquered people, both because the land of origin had been conquered by the United States and because the Mexican Americans, with whom they were completely commingled, had been treated as a lower caste of conquered people inside the now expanded version of the United States. As such, they were powerless appendages of the regional economy. Their manual labor was essential to the agricultural development of the area. But whenever the business cycle took a turn for the worse, they were easily forced to go back to Mexico;[33] they were forcibly deported. Their United-States-born children were deported right along with the parents. The deportation of Mexican Americans—United States citizens—was not uncommon, since to the U.S. Border Patrol, U.S. Immigration Service ("Migra"), and the Texas Rangers there frequently seemed little or no difference between Mexican Americans and Mexican nationals; they were all simply "Mexican."[34]

There is for Mexican Americans a very bitter irony in all of this. The irony is that the post-1900 migrants and the pre-1900 lower caste citizens of Mexican descent learned to live more or less comfortably with all of this largely because of their frame of reference. Both constantly com-

pared themselves to Mexican citizens in Mexico. That they should have Mexico as their cultural frame of reference is understandable. The irony is, however, that they never compared themselves to other minority groups in this country, possibly because of geographic isolation. The price the Mexican American had to pay in exchange for higher wages received for stoop labor in the fields and for lower status work in the cities was a pervasive, universal subjugation into a lower caste that came about silently and engulfed him, long before he became aware of it. He became aware of his lower caste, economically powerless position only when he (or his children) tried to break out of the caste and was forced to remain in it. By that time it was too late. He had learned to enjoy a higher wage than he would have had in Mexico and to accept a degrading lower caste position. His lower socioeconomic position in the United States was never salient in his mind.

THE MEXICAN AMERICAN GENERATION

Starting somewhere around the time of the Second World War, and increasing in importance up to the war in Vietnam, there has developed another state of collective consciousness which I call the "Mexican American Generation." This generation increasingly has turned its sense of cultural loyalty to the United States. As members of this generation were achieving maturity, they began to ask their parents:

What did Mexico ever do for you? You were poor and unwanted there. Your exodus reduced the unemployment rate and welfare problems that powerful economic elements in Mexico would have had to contend with, so they were happy to see you leave. You remained culturally loyal to the memory of Mexico, and you had dreams of returning to spend your dollars there. You sent money back to your family relations who remained in Mexico. Both of these acts of cultural loyalty on your part simply improved Mexico's dollar balance of payment. And what did Mexico do for you except help labor contractors and unscrupulous southwestern officials to further exploit you? I am an "American" who happens to be of Mexican descent. I am going to participate fully in this society because, like descendents of people from so many other lands,

---

[33] *Ibid.*

[34] Carey McWilliams, *North from Mexico* (New York: Greenwood Press, 1960).

I was born here, and my country will guarantee me all the rights and protections of a free and loyal citizen.[35]

What the members of the Mexican American generation did not realize was that, relative to the larger society, they were still just as economically dependent and powerless to affect the course of their own progress as the members of the older Migrant Generation. If the Migrant Generation had Mexicans in Mexico as their socioeconomic reference, the Mexican American Generation, in similar fashion, did not effectively compare its own achievements to those of the larger society, but to the achievements of the Migrant Generation. This comparison was a happy one for the Mexican American Generation. They could see that they were economically better off than their parents had ever been. They could see that they had achieved a few years of schooling while their parents had achieved virtually none.

What the Mexican American Generation did not realize was that their slight improvement in education, income, political efficacy, and social acceptance was an accomplishment only by virtue of comparison to the Migrant Generation which started with nothing. The Mexican American Generation was far behind the black population as the black population was behind the Anglo on every measure of social achievement; i.e., years of education achieved, political efficacy, annual income per family, etc. But these comparisons were rarely made during this period when Mexican Americans changed from being a predominantly rural population employed in agricultural stoop labor to an urban population employed predominantly in unskilled service occupations. Today, for example, approximately 83 percent of the Mexican American population lives in cities, even though in most instances the mass media still portrays Mexican Americans as rural stoop laborers. This was the period when the first relatively effective community protective organizations began to be formed. The organizing documents are so painfully patriotic as to demonstrate the conceptualized ambitions of the membership rather than their actual living experience.

The change of Mexican Americans from a rural to an urban population was precipitated by the rapid industrialization of agriculture that was brought about initially by the production requirements of World War II (and the simultaneous manpower drain required for the military) and was subsequently sustained and enhanced by the scientific and technological revolution that followed the war. Agriculture had increasingly been organized around big farms since 1900 in order to meet the demands of an expanding population. The massive production required by World War II in the absence of Mexican American labor— since the Mexican American population participated disproportionately in the war —led to the increasingly rapid conversion of agriculture to resemble the industrialized factory. During the initial phases of the war, much stoop labor was imported from Mexico,[36] but later this became less necessary because machines increasingly were filling the need for all but the most delicate agricultural picking jobs. The entire economic system reached the highest development of the ideals of industrialized society. Perhaps more money and somewhat better working conditions were to be found in cities, but that was not because of any gains on the part of Mexican Americans; it was rather because of the nature of urban living and industrial production of the post-World War II era of United States capitalism. Compared to the majority, the Mexican American still had no determinative input into the economic system. Lack of unions and lack of political effectiveness meant that the Mexican American was earning less than any other group for comparable work. Lack of education meant that the Mexican American did not have sufficient understanding of the nature of the society in which he lived and its economic system to even know that he was being treated unfairly. To the extent that he became conscious of his economically disadvantaged position, he was powerless to do anything about it.

[35]Alvarez, "Psycho-Historical Experience," pp. 24-25.

[36]Carey McWilliams, *Brothers Under the Skin* (Rev. ed.: Boston: Little, Brown and Co., 1964), p. 128.

At this point it is fair to ask: If the Mexican American Generation was so poorly educated, how did it ever get the training, skills, and general awareness of things to be able to move in large numbers from the fields to the cities and survive? Here, we have to introduce another statement about socioeconomic dependency. About the time of World War II when industrialization was beginning to be felt out in the fields, a substantial proportion of the Migrant Generation was nearing old age. Older people began to move to the cities to do the lighter work that was available there. At the same time, the young people were being moved into the war effort, young men to the military and young women to work in the war production industries and the skills and technical competency that young Mexican Americans acquired in the military were directly transferable to industrial employment in the cities after the war ended.[37]

Finally, the fact that they fought and saw their military friends and neighbors die in defense of the United States led Mexican Americans generally not to question their relative status in the economy and their lack of control over it. Little did they realize that everyone else was also experiencing both a real and an inflationary increase in economic standing; that other groups were experiencing a faster rate of economic increase because of their more effective direct participation in bringing it about. The Mexican American was only experiencing a kind of upward coasting with the general economy and was not directly influencing his own economic betterment. As a group, Mexican Americans remained at the bottom of the socioeconomic ladder.

Many Mexican Americans attempted to escape their caste-like status by leaving the Southwest to seek employment in the industrial centers of the mid-western Great Lakes region and in the cities of the Northwest.[38] Others went to California. A high degree of industrialization and a very heterogeneous population (religiously, ethnically, and politically) have always been the factors that attenuated discrimination against Mexican Americans in California. In fact, it is in California (and of course in the Midwest to a smaller extent) that the Mexican American first began to have the characteristics of a lower *class* population on a massive scale, as opposed to the lower *caste* experience. Of course, among the southwestern states on a smaller but widespread scale, the state of New Mexico seems to have come to a condition of class as compared to caste emphasis in a prolonged, gradual manner. This was perhaps due to the fact that the experience of the Migrant Generation never took place as intensely in New Mexico. The post-1900 immigrants came in large numbers to Texas early in the period and to California later (circa W.W. II).[39] However, New Mexico was essentially bypassed by the Migrant Generation. Furthermore, in New Mexico the experience of the Creation Generation was neither as severe nor as complete as it was in Texas and California. In New Mexico the Creation Generation experience did take place, but so-called Hispaños managed to retain some degree of political and economic control since they represented such a large percentage of the population—even with, or in spite of, all the extensive land swindles by invading Anglos.[40] Interestingly, the fact that the Mexicans in middle and northern New Mexico were never fully subjugated into a lower caste position is reflected in the linguistic labels they use to identify themselves. It may be argued that in order to differentiate themselves from those who had been subjugated into a lower caste,[41] the so-called Hispaños in New Mexico started calling themselves Spanish Americans some time around the First World War, despite the fact that their anatomical

---

[37]Matt S. Meier and Feliciano Rivera, *The Chicanos: A History of Mexican Americans* (New York: American Century Series, Hill and Wang, 1972), pp. 200-201.

[38]Moquin and Van Doren, *A Documentary History,* p. 402.

[39]Leo Grebler, *Mexican Immigration to the United States: The Record and its Implications* (Advance Report #2, Mexican American Study Project). Also, Manuel Gamio, *Mexican Immigration to the United States, 1883-* (Chicago: University of Chicago Press, 1930).

[40]Knowlton, "Culture Conflict."

[41]Moquin and Van Doren, p. 394.

features were those of Mexican mestizaje and did not resemble Spaniards. At that time, their previous geographic isolation began to be ended by large numbers of Anglos from Texas who came to settle in the southeastern part of the state of New Mexico. The Texans brought with them their generalized hatred of Mexicans and their view of them as lower caste untouchables. Thus, out of self-protection, New Mexicans started to call themselves Spanish Americans and to insist that they could trace their racial and ethnic origins to the original Spanish settlements in the area. The linguistic ruse worked so well that Mexican Americans in New Mexico came to believe their own rhetoric. The point to be made here is that this linguistic device was used by a large and isolated population that had not been fully subjugated into a lower caste to maintain in New Mexico the semblance of a class position. It is in New Mexico more than in any of the other southwestern states that Mexican Americans have participated in the society as people who have had the freedom and possibility of social mobility to become members of various social classes. They did this, however, at the price of altering their identity to make themselves acceptable to stronger economic, if not political, interests in the state. Today, however, the younger members of the post-World War II period are developing a new consciousness even in New Mexico. It is the current high school and college age offspring of the so-called Spanish Americans who are using the term Chicano and who are demanding documentation for the presumed historic culture links to Spain.[42] What they are finding—the greater links to Mexican and to Indian culture—is beginning to have an effect on their parents, many of whom are beginning to view themselves as Mexican Americans with some measure of pride.

Some of the tensions within the Mexican American community during this period of time could be explained in terms of the generalized attempts to be more like "Anglo" citizens. Those people who were themselves born in the United States had greater legitimation for their claims of loyalty to the United States and for their psy-

chic sense of security on the land. They in fact would, in various disingenuous ways, disassociate themselves from those whose claim to belonging could not be as well established; even parents or family elders who were born in Mexico and came over during the period described as the Migrant Generation would be viewed as somehow less legitimate. In the cities a slight distinction was made between the older Mexican Americans who now held stable working class and small entrepreneurial positions as compared to newly arrived migrants from Mexico who entered the urban unskilled labor pool. This, of course, increased the insecurity and decreased the willingness to engage in collective action among the members of the Migrant Generation. They were in a particularly insecure position psychically, economically, and in almost every other regard. They were rejected and mistreated by the dominant Anglo population and rebuffed (as somehow deserving of that mistreatment) by their offspring.

The Mexican American Generation purchased a sense of psychic "security" at a very heavy price. They managed to establish their claims as bona fide citizens of the United States in the eyes of only *one* of the social psychologically relevant populations: *themselves*. The dominant Anglo population never ceased to view them as part of the "inferior" general population of Mexican Americans. The Migrant Generation never fully believed that their offspring would be able to become "Anglos" in any but the most foolhardy dreams of aspiring youth. They had a very apt concept for what they saw in the younger person wanting to become an Anglo facsimile: "Mosca en leche!" The Mexican American who so vehemently proclaimed his United States citizenship and his equality with all citizens never realized that all of the comparisons by which he evaluated progress were faulty. Because of his psychic identification with the superordinate Anglo, he abandoned his own language and culture and considered himself personally superior to the economically subordinate Migrant Generation. The fact that he could see that he was somewhat better off educationally and economically than the Migrant Generation led the Mexican American of this

---

[42]Meier and Rivera, *The Chicanos*, pp. 270-272.

period to believe himself assimilated and accepted into the larger society. He did not fully realize that his self-perceived affluence and privileges existed only in comparison to the vast majority of Mexican Americans. He did not realize that for the same amount of native ability, education, personal motivation and actual performance, his Anglo counterpart was much more highly rewarded than he. He never made the observation that even when he achieved a higher education, he still remained at the bottom of the ladder in whatever area of economic endeavor he might be employed. Individuals, sometimes with the help of protective organizations, did bring some legal action against personal cases of discrimination. But despite a growing psychic security as citizens of the United States, they did not make effective collective comparisons. The greater security that the Mexican American Generation achieved was a falsely based sense of self-worth. To be sure, because a sizable proportion of the population managed to exist for several decades with a sense of self-worth, they could give birth to what will be called the Chicano Generation in the next section of this paper. However much the Mexican American Generation may have been discriminated against educationally and especially economically, they did achieve enough leisure and economic surplus so that their offspring did not begin from a hopeless disadvantage at birth. This extra measure of protection was perhaps the greatest indicator that the Mexican American Generation was now part of a class and not a caste system.

THE CHICANO GENERATION

In the late 1960's a new consciousness began to make itself felt among Mexican Americans. By this time the population was solidly urban and well entrenched as an indisputable part of the country's working underclass. Migration from Mexico had slowed and was predominantly to urban centers in the United States. Theories of racial inferiority were dying, not without sophisticated revivals, to be sure, but in general the country was beginning to accept the capacity of human populations given equal opportunities and re-

sources. Moreover, despite the ups and downs of the market-place, it was becoming clear to all that both technological sophistication and economic potential existed in sufficient abundance to erradicate abject poverty in the United States. These conditions had not existed in the Southwest with regard to the Mexican American population since that historical period immediately preceeding the Creation Generation.

The Chicano Generation is now comparing its fortunes with those of the dominant majority as well as with the fortunes of other minorities within the United States. This represents an awareness of our citizenship in a pluralistic society. It is perhaps early to be writing the history of the Chicano Generation, but already it is clear that we have gone through an initial phase and are now in a second phase. The first phase consisted of the realization that citizenship bestows upon those who can claim it many rights and protections traditionally denied to Mexican Americans. The second phase, only now achieving widespread penetration into the population's consciousness, is that citizenship also entails obligations and duties, which we have traditionally not been in a position to perform. These two perspectives are rapidly colliding with each other. The general mental health of the Chicano community is being severely buffeted by the change in comparative focus and the relative current inability to achieve measurable success according to the new standards.

The parameters of the Mexican American population had been slowly changing, until by the mid-1960's the bulk of the post-World War II baby boom had reached draftable age and now faced the prospect of military service in the war in Vietnam. As a cohort, these young Mexican Americans were the most affluent and socio-politically liberated ever. The bulk were the sons and daughters of urban working class parents. However, a small proportion were the offspring of small businessmen; and an even smaller proportion were the offspring of minor bureaucratic officials, semi-professionals, and professionals. Especially in these latter types of families, a strong sense of the benefits of educational certification and of the rights of citizenship had been developed. When the bulk of this cohort of young people reached draftable age, which is also the age when young people generally enter college, they made some extremely interesting and shocking discoveries, on which they were able to act because they had the leisure and resources to permit self-analysis and self-determining action.

Despite the fact that the Mexican American population has the highest school dropout rate of any ethnic population in the country, by the mid-1960's a larger proportion than ever before were finishing high school. These young people then faced three major alternative courses of action, all of them unsatisfactory. One course was to enter an urban-industrial labor force for which they were ill-prepared because a high school education is no longer as useful as in previous generations. And even for those positions for which a high school education is sufficient, they were ill-prepared because the high schools located in their neighborhoods were so inadequate compared to those in Anglo neighborhoods.[43] Moreover, persistent racial discrimination made it difficult to aspire to any but lower working class positions. Another course of action, which a disproportionate number of young men took, was to go into military service as a way to travel, gain salable skills, and assert one's citizenship, as so many Mexican Americans had done in the previous generation. But unlike the Mexican American going into the military of World War II, the young Chicano of the mid-1960's went into a highly professionalized military, the technical skills for which he found difficult to acquire because of his inadequate high school preparation. So instead of acquiring skills for the modern technical society into which he would eventually be released, he disproportionately joined the ranks of the foot soldier and was disproportionately on the war ca-

sualty list. A third course of action open to the young Mexican American leaving high school in the mid-1960's was to make application for and enter college. This alternative was unsatisfactory because colleges and universities were not prepared to accept more than the occasional few—and then only those who would be willing to abandon their ethnicity. Refusal to admit was, of course, based on assertions of incapacity or lack of preparation. The former has racist underpinnings, while the latter is class biased since poverty and the inferior schools in which Chicano youth were concentrated did not permit adequate preparation for college and eventual middle class certification.

No matter which course of action the bulk of the young people took they disproportionately faced dismal futures. The larger society in which this ethnic minority exists had become so technical, bureaucratized, and professionalized—in short, so *middle class*—that the strictly lower working class potential of the bulk of the Mexican American population was irrelevant to it. Faced with the prospect of almost total economic marginality, the Chicano Generation was the first generation since the Creation Generation to confront the prospect of large-scale failure—of, in effect, losing ground, of psychically accomplishing less than the Mexican American Generation. The low-skill, labor-intensive society into which the Migrant Generation broke from its caste-like condition and within which the Mexican American Generation had established a firm, but strictly lower working class status, was disappearing. The United States was now predominantly professionalized and middle class, with increasingly fewer labor-intensive requirements. It is in this relatively more limited context that the Chicano Generation came to have relatively higher aspirations.

With higher aspirations than any previous generation, with the prospect of a severe psychic decline compared to its parent generation, and now, because of its greater affluence and exposure, it had to compare itself to its youth counterpart in the dominant society. The broader exposure comes from many sources, including television and greater schooling in schools that, how-

---

[43]Herschel T. Manuel, *The Education of Mexican and Spanish Speaking Children in Texas* (Austin: University of Texas, 1930). Also, Thomas P. Clark, *Mexican Americans in School: A History of Educational Neglect* (New York: College Entrance Examination Board, 1970).

ever inferior, were better than those to which prior generations were even minimally exposed. The Chicano Generation very painfully began to ask of what value its United States citizenship was going to be. At this time a significantly large proportion of the black population of this country "revolted." That may well have been the spark that ignited the Chicano movement. The Mexican American Generation had asserted its United States citizenship with great pride, asserting a relationship between economic success and their complete "Angloization" which was now shown to be false. The Chicano Generation came to realize that it was even more acculturated than the previous generation, yet it did not have any realistic prospects of escaping its virtually complete lower and working class status. Its new consciousness came into being at a time when the Chicano Generation could hardly find any older role models with certified middle class status. Comparatively, for example, out of a population of twenty-four million there are 2,200 black persons who have earned Ph.D. degrees in all disciplines combined.[44] Among the eight million (approximately) Mexican Americans there are only 60 who have earned Ph.D. degrees, when a similar level of disadvantage would lead us to expect approximately 730. The number of Ph.D.'s in a population is used here as a sort of barometric indicator of the level and quality of technically trained and certified leadership available to a population within a predominantly middle class society. This is so because one can guess at the ratio of lawyers and doctors as well as master and bachelor degrees for each Ph.D. Thus, the Mexican American population which began to enter colleges and universities in noticeable numbers only as late as the mid-1960's is almost completely lacking in certification for middle class status.

Another indication of the lack of certified leadership that is self-consciously concerned with the welfare of the community is the lack of institutions of higher learning of, for, and by Chicanos. There are over 100 black institutions of higher learning (both privately and publicly supported, including colleges, universities, law schools and medical schools). As recently as five years ago there were no such institutions for Chicanos. Now there are a handful of schools that either have been created *ad hoc* or where a significant number of Chicanos have moved into administrative positions due to pressures from large Chicano student enrollments. The point here is that however inadequate the black schools may have been, compared to "white" schools, they provide the institutional foci within which a broad sector of the black population has been trained and certified for middle class status since prior to 1900. Mexican Americans could neither get into institutions of the dominant society, nor did we have our own alternate institutions. Thus, the difficulty of acquiring broad scale consciousness of the condition of our people is apparent, as is the insecure ethnic identification of the early few who entered "white" institutions.

The Chicano Generation has experienced the pain of social rejection in essentially the same fashion (in the abstract) that it was experienced by the Creation Generation. That is, having been ideologically prepared to expect egalitarian co-participation in the society in which it exists, it had instead been confronted with the practical fact of exclusion from the benefits of the society. Because it can no longer compare itself to its immediate predecessors (no matter what the quantity or quality of accomplishments of the Mexican American Generation), it has to compare itself to other groups in the larger society. Relative to them it is more disadvantaged than any other ethnic group, except the American Indian with whom it has much in common both culturally and biologically. Every new demographic analysis gives the Chicano Generation more evidence of relative deprivation,[45] which leads to the rise of a psychic sense of betrayal by the egalitarian ideology of the United States not unlike that experienced by the Creation Generation. Members of the Chicano Generation are therefore saying to the previous generation:

---

[44]Author's records, unpublished research.

[45]Leo Grebler, J. Moore, Ralph Guzman, *The Mexican-American People* (New York: Free Press, 1970).

So you are a loyal "American," willing to die for your country in the last three or four wars; what did your country ever do for you? If you are such an American, how come your country gives you less education even than other disadvantaged minorities, permits you only low status occupations, allows you to become a disproportionately large part of casualties in war, and socially rejects you from the most prestigious circles? As for me, I am a Chicano, I am rooted in this land, I am the creation of a unique psycho-historical experience. I trace part of my identity to Mexican culture and part to United States culture, but most importantly my identity is tied up with those contested lands called Aztlán! My most valid claim to existential reality is not the false pride and unrequited loyalty of either the Migrant Generation or the Mexican American Generation. Rather, I trace my beginnings to the original contest over the lands of Aztlán, to the more valid psycho-historical experience of the Creation Generation. I have a right to inter-marriage if it suits me, to economic achievement at all societal levels, and to my own measure of political self-determination within this society. I have a unique psycho-historical experience that I have a right to know about and to cultivate as part of my distinctive cultural heritage.[46]

The concerns of the Chicano Generation are those which predominantly plague the middle class: Sufficient leisure and affluence to contemplate the individual's origin and potential future, sufficient education and affluence to make it at least possible for the individual to have a noticeable impact on the course of his life's achievements, but not so rich an inheritance that the individual's prominence in society is virtually assured.[47] The Chicano Generation is the first sizable cohort in our history to come to the widespread realization that we can have a considerable measure of self-determination within the confines of this pluralistic society. Yet we are only at the threshold of this era and have hardly begun to legitimate our claims to effective self-determination, i.e., acquisition of professional-technical certification as well as establishment of relatively independent wealth. Our capacity to secure middle class entry for a sizable proportion of our population is threatened on two major fronts.

First, we are threatened by our redundancy or obsolescence at the bottom of the social structure. This has two dimensions: we cannot earn enough money to support a United States standard of living on laborer's wages; even if we were willing to do the few remaining back-breaking jobs, there would not be enough work to go around because these are being automated, and the few that are around will be taken over by cheap Mexican labor from Mexico, unless we organize factory and farmworkers effectively.[48] Thus, in a sense, the economic bottom of our community is falling away.

Second, we are threatened because just as the middle class sector of the larger society is getting ready to acknowledge our capacities and our right to full participation, we find that the major proportion of our population does not have the necessary credentials for entry—i.e., college, graduate and professional degrees. When large corporate organizations attempt to comply with federal equal employment regulations concerning the Spanish speaking population, they do not care whether the person they hire comes from a family that has been in the United States since 1828 or whether the person arrived yesterday from Mexico or some other Latin American country. The irony is that as discrimination disappears or is minimized, those who have historically suffered the most from it continue to suffer its after effects. This is so because as multi-national corporations have begun their training programs throughout Latin America, and especially in Mexico, a new technically skilled and educated middle class has been greatly expanded in those countries. Many of these persons begin to question why they should perform jobs in their home country at the going depressed salaries when they could come to the United States and receive higher salaries for the same work and participate in a generally higher standard of living. This, in effect, is part of the brain drain experienced by these

[46]Alvarez, "Psycho-Historical Experience," p. 25.

[47]George C. Homans, *Social Behavior: Its Elementary Forms* (New York: Harcourt Brace & World, 1961).

[48]Richard B. Craig, *The Bracero Program* (Austin: University of Texas Press, 1971).

countries from the point of view of their economy. From the point of view of the Chicano community, however, we experience it as being cut off at the pass. That is, just as the decline of prejudice and the increase in demand for middle class type positions might pull us up into the secure middle class, a new influx of people from another country comes into the United States economy above us. Because it would cost corporations more to develop Chicanos for these positions, and because we do not have a sufficiently aware and sufficiently powerful Chicano middle class to fight for the selection of Chicanos, and because of federal regulations which only call for Spanish surname people to fill jobs, without regard to place of origin, it is conceivable that the bulk of our population might become relegated into relatively unskilled working class positions. Thus, the plight of the urban Chicano in the 1970's is not only technically complicated (how do you acquire middle class expertise with working class resources), but psychically complex (how do you relate to urban middle class immigrants from Spanish speaking countries and to rapidly organizing rural Mexican Americans) at a time when the general economy of the United States appears to be in a state of contraction, making competition for positions severe. Unless we can deal creatively with these trends, we will remain at the bottom of the social structure. This, in spite of outmoded social theories that postulated that each wave of new immigrants would push the previous wave up in the socioeconomic structure.

The introspectiveness of the Chicano generation is leading to new insights. The psycho-historical links of the Chicano Generation with the Creation Generation are primarily those of collective support against a common diffuse and everywhere present danger. The threat of cultural extinction has led the Chicano to deep introspection as to what distinguishes him both from Mexicans in Mexico and from "Anglos" in the United States. This introspection has led to a deep appreciation for the positive aspects of each culture and a creative use of our inheritance in facing the future. The fight for self-definition is leading to a reanalysis of culture. For example, Anglo research has defined "machismo" as unidimensional male dominance, whereas, its multi-dimensional original meaning placed heavier emphases on personal dignity and personal sacrifice on behalf of the collectivity—i.e., family or community. This concern for the collectivity comes through again in the emphasis placed on "la familia" in activities within a Chicano movement perspective. The fight for professional and middle class certification is the fight for our collectivity to be heard. The objective is to produce enough certified professionals who can articulate and defend our peculiarly distinct culture in such a manner that educational and other institutions of the dominant society will have to be modified. Until we have our own certified savants, we will continue to be defined out of existence by outsiders insensitive to the internal dynamic of our own collectivity. The willingness to fight may be what will get us there. YA MERO!

PART TWO
SOCIETY AND JUSTICE

The following papers deal with the overt manifestations of prejudice against Chicanos in two of the most vital arenas of community life: the legal system and the world of work. The two are interrelated, as noted by the U.S. Commission on Civil Rights: false arrests result in innocent persons losing their jobs; police harrassment of addicts and others who are trying to rehabilitate themselves prevents them from holding onto jobs; organizational efforts aimed at bettering the lot of Mexican American workers are interfered with by police; and jailed Mexican Americans are economically exploited by farmers who secure their release by paying their fines—at a discount undisclosed to the worker—on condition that they work for the farmer until the original amount of the fine is paid off. Such practices were found to be appallingly common; and yet "indirect" costs like these are apparently not taken into account in the cost-of-prejudice figure produced by Poston & Alvirez, who based their estimate solely on non-farmworker, full-time wage earners. Since farmworkers and the underemployed, who comprise a large proportion of the Chicano population, are acknowledged by all to be at an even greater disadvantage, the true "cost" of being a Mexican American worker is undoubtedly much higher than $900 a year—an already staggering figure. (See Wright, 1965; Dunn, 1967; Steiner, 1969.)

The costs of legal inequities are not solely economic, of course. The toll in terms of self-esteem, mental health, family disruption, and the distrust and hatred generated between minority groups and the dominant group and its institutions is dreadful, and often sadly unnecessary. For example: putting aside police stupidity, mistakes, prejudice, and brutality, and the question of the frequencies of these—it has been found that certain legitimate law enforcement methods (such as frequent stop-and-search and motorized patrolling) and the mere presence of police can heighten tensions; preventive random raids in high-crime districts bring more innocent people into unpleasant contact with police; and it stands to reason that the greater the police concentration in an area, the greater the average amount of police-citizen contact (hence a greater chance for unpleasantness to occur) and the more likely it is that minor infractions of the law will be observed. Armando Morales (1970) illustrates this point with drunkenness and drunk driving arrest rates for East Los Angeles as compared to the West Valley area. He notes that, while the ratio of major crime to population is virtually identical in the two areas, the rate of drunkenness-related arrests is several times higher in the Chicano-dominated East Los Angeles area than in the overwhelmingly Anglo West Valley. Of vital importance is the fact that the drunkenness-related arrest rate is proportional to the ratio of officers employed in the two areas. He additionally cites an instance in which the police presence was increased in the West Valley area and the drunkenness arrest rate simultaneously skyrocketed.

Of even greater importance is data presented by Morales

(both in his *El Grito* essay and again in The Impact of Class Discrimination and White Racism on the Mental Health of Mexican-Americans, which appears later in this volume) concerning the relationship of mental health to the arrest rates for alcohol and drug abuse. The gross over-representation of Mexican Americans in alcohol and drug conviction statistics and their concomitant underrepresentation in mental hospitals and other mental health facilities attests to the *lack of availability of treatment* for alcoholism, addiction, and other mental health problems in the poor and Spanish-speaking communities. The poor get jailed for what the rich get medical and psychological help. Such inequity causes genuine and well-founded resentment while helping to sustain prejudices and unfavorable stereotypes concerning Mexican Americans.

Riots often represent the ultimate expression of both economic frustration and police-community misunderstanding, as the 1968 *Report of the National Advisory Commission on Civil Disorders* revealed in their study of the black communities of certain riot-torn cities. In his contribution to this section, Morales demonstrates the close similarity between the 1970 riots in East Los Angeles and the ghetto riots analyzed by the Kerner Commission. Obviously the recommendations of that commission for relieving the underlying causal conditions of the distur-

bances would be equally appropriate for East Los Angeles. But like most government-commissioned reports, this one has been largely ignored. As Morales points out, the law enforcement control approach seems to be the chosen solution despite the evidence that excessive use of police power is one of the determinants of such disturbances. When will we learn?

The police are by no means the sole offenders, though, as the courtroom transcript included here shows. Overt expressions of crass bigotry like Judge Gerald Chargin's are, of course, rare in the courts, but, nevertheless, are illustrative of what many feel are the unexpressed (and possibly unconscious) sentiments of not a few jurors, judges, lawyers, and police officers. This suspicion is aggravated and reinforced by the fact that juries are overwhelmingly WASP in composition. What exactly constitutes a trial by peers will no doubt remain an issue for some time to come, but when a juror remarks, as reported in the U.S. Civil Rights Commission report, that "No Mexican American is worth ten thousand dollars," you know you've been had!

An ironic epilogue to the Chargin incident: though Judge Chargin was censured and forced to retract and publicly apologize for his outburst, he was subsequently reelected in 1972. In 1966, running unopposed, Chargin had obtained 158,362 votes. In 1972, after being censured by his colleagues, he received 143,235 and his closest opponent received 71,079. No further comment is needed.

The final article in this part, by Padilla and Ruiz, explores prejudice and discrimination in a more conceptual, general fashion, and anticipates topics covered in greater detail in the remainder of this book. Perhaps the most valuable feature of this essay is the wealth of references to

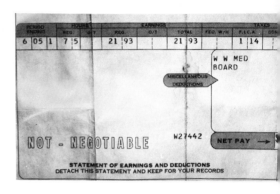

relevant studies of Chicanos that it contains, for most of
the major works on prejudice have slighted them. Gordon
Allport's *The Nature of Prejudice* remains the major theoretical work in this area and is recommended to those seeking a fuller treatment of the issue. It seems to be fairly
well established by now (Raab and Lipset, 1962) that the
foundation of prejudicial attitudes and intergroup tensions
lies in *behavior*—not the reverse—and that enforced non-
discrimination effectively extinguishes prejudice and hostility. This is surely a source of encouragement for those
actively engaged in the fight against injustices to all minorities. The recommendations at the end of the Padilla and
Ruiz article provide a well-reasoned program for future efforts to combat the effects of prejudice and discrimination,
with particular attention to the unique problems of the
Spanish-speaking minorities.

REFERENCES

Allport, G. *The nature of prejudice.* Garden City, N.Y.: Doubleday
  Anchor Books, 1958.
Dunn, J. G. *Delano: The story of the California grape strike.*
  New York: Farrar, Strauss & Giroux, 1967.
Morales, A. Mental and public health issues: The case of the Mexi-
  can American in Los Angeles. *El Grito,* 1970, *3*(2), 3-11.
Raab, E., & Lipset, S. M. The prejudiced society. In Raab, E. (Ed.),
  American race relations today. New York: Doubleday & Co.,
  Inc., 1962.
Report of the National Advisory Commission on Civil Disorders.
  Bantam Books, 1968, pp. 299-322.
Steiner, S. *La Raza: The Mexican Americans.* New York: Harper
  & Row, 1969.
Wright, D. *They harvest despair.* Boston: Beacon Press, 1965.

CHAPTER 5 JUDGE GERALD S. CHARGIN: A PUBLIC RECORD

IN THE SUPERIOR COURT OF THE STATE OF CALIFORNIA

IN AND FOR THE COUNTY OF SANTA CLARA

JUVENILE DIVISION

HONORABLE GERALD S. CHARGIN, Judge   Courtroom No.1

———

In the Matter of
(Name deleted),
a minor.
         No. 40331

———

STATEMENTS OF THE COURT

San Jose, California   September 2, 1969

———

APPEARANCES:

For the Minor: FRED LUCERO, ESQ., Deputy Public Defender

For the Probation Department: WILLIAM TAPOGNA, ESQ., Court Probation Officer

Official Court Reporter: SUSAN K. STRAHM, C.S.R.

September 2, 1969   10:25 a.m.

STATEMENTS OF THE COURT

The Court: There is some indication that you more or less didn't think that it was against the law or was improper. Haven't you had any moral training? Have you and your family gone to church?

The Minor: Yes, sir.

The Court: Don't you know that things like this are terribly wrong? This is one of the worst crimes that a person can commit. I just get so disgusted that I just figure what is the use? You are just an animal. You are lower than an animal. Even animals don't do that. You are pretty low.

JUDGE GERALD S. CHARGIN: A PUBLIC RECORD **63**

I don't know why your parents haven't been able to teach you anything or train you. Mexican people, after 13 years of age, it's perfectly all right to go out and act like an animal. It's not even right to do that to a stranger, let alone a member of your own family. I don't have much hope for you. You will probably end up in State's Prison before you are 25, and that's where you belong, anyhow. There is nothing much you can do.

I think you haven't got any moral principles. You won't acquire anything. Your parents won't teach you what is right or wrong and won't watch out.

Apparently, your sister is pregnant; is that right?

The Minor's Father: Yes.

The Court: It' a fine situation. How old is she?

The Minor's Mother: Fifteen.

The Court: Well, probably she will have a half a dozen children and three or four marriages before she is 18.

The County will have to take care of you. You are no particular good to anybody. We ought to send you out of the country—send you back to Mexico. You belong in prison for the rest of your life for doing things of this kind. You ought to commit suicide. That's what I think of people of this kind. You are lower than animals and haven't the right to live in organized society—just miserable, lousy, rotten people.

There is nothing we can do with you. You expect the County to take care of you. Maybe Hitler was right. The animals in our society probably ought to be destroyed because they have no right to live among human beings. If you refuse to act like a human being, then, you don't belong among the society of human beings.

Mr. Lucero: Your Honor, I don't think I can sit here and listen to that sort of thing.

The Court: You are going to have to listen to it because I consider this a very vulgar, rotten human being.

Mr. Lucero: The Court is indicting the whole Mexican group.

The Court: When they are 10 or 12 years of age, going out and having intercourse with anybody without any moral training—

they don't even understand the Ten Commandments. That's all. Apparently, they don't want to.

So if you want to act like that, the County has a system of taking care of them. They don't care about that. They have no personal self-respect.

Mr. Lucero: The Court ought to look at this youngster and deal with this youngster's case.

The Court: All right. That's what I am going to do. The family should be able to control this boy and the young girl.

Mr. Lucero: What appalls me is that the Court is saying that Hitler was right in genocide.

The Court: What are we going to do with the mad dogs of our society? Either we have to kill them or send them to an institution or place them out of the hands of good people because that's the theory—one of the theories of punishment is if they get to the position that they want to act like mad dogs, then, we have to separate them from our society.

Well, I will go along with the recommendation. You will learn in time or else you will have to pay for the penalty with the law because the law grinds slowly but exceedingly well. If you are going to be a law violator—you have to make up your mind whether you are going to observe the law or not. If you can't observe the law, then, you have to be put away.

STATE OF CALIFORNIA ⎫ ss.
COUNTY OF SANTA CLARA ⎭

I, SUSAN K. STRAHM, do hereby certify that the foregoing is a true and correct transcript of the STATEMENTS OF THE COURT had in the within-entitled action taken on the 2nd day of September, 1969; that I reported the same in stenotype, being the qualified and acting Official Court Reporter of the Superior Court of the State of California, in and for the County of Santa Clara, appointed to said Court, and thereafter had the same transcribed into typewriting as herein appears.

Dated: This 8th day of September, 1969.

SUSAN K. STRAHM, C.S.R.

CHAPTER 6 CHICANO-POLICE RIOTS*

ARMANDO MORALES

The title of this article implies that Chicanos have rioted *and* the police have rioted in East Los Angeles in 1970. Who started this violent confrontation between Chicanos and the police—or is it a confrontation between Chicanos and *white Anglo-Saxon* police? What were the underlying causes of the East Los Angeles January 1, August 29 and September 16, 1970, riots? A difficult, complex question indeed. Viewing the problems from a historical perspective one could say the conflict began when the Southwest Mexicans told the Anglos "Mi casa es su casa" (My home is your home) and the hospitable invitation was taken literally. The Anglo, a foreigner, conquered the native Mexican in his land and culture. But the Mexican, i.e. the Mexican American, really has not been conquered, as evidenced by the existence and persistence of his culture in the United States and the fact that he periodically asserts himself as a means of salvaging some of his dignity. Riots in this respect are a human, natural response for survival to a set of intolerable living conditions established by those in authority. The Mexican American, like the black man, merely conforms more often than not, to the *role* of a conquered person.

It is observed that in the East Los Angeles riots there are more similarities than differences in the prime, explosive mixture components that led to riots in 150 cities across the United States in 1967. Compar-

ing the U.S. Riot Commission Report findings and basic causes of the riots with the East Los Angeles situation proved to be a frightening experience. All that had to be substituted was the word "Mexican American" for "Negro" and "barrio" for "ghetto" in order for the conditions to be identical. The following is from the U.S. Riot Commission (Kerner) Report:

The record before this Commission reveals that the causes of recent racial disorders are imbedded in a massive tangle of issues and circumstances—social, economic, political, and psychological—which arise out of the historical pattern of Negro-white relations in America. . . . Of these, the most fundamental is the racial attitude and behavior of white Americans toward black Americans. Race prejudice has shaped our history decisively in the past; it now threatens to do so again. White racism is essentially responsible for the explosive mixture which has been accumulating in our cities since the end of World War II. . . .

The ghettos too often mean men and women without jobs, families without men, and schools where children are processed instead of educated, until they return to the street—to crime, to narcotics, to dependency on welfare, and to bitterness and resentment against society in general and white society in particular. . . . A climate that tends toward the approval and encouragement of violence as a form of protest has been created by white terrorism directed against nonviolent protest, including instances of abuse and even murder of some civil rights workers in the South; by the open defiance of law and federal authority by state and local officials resisting desegregation; and by some protest groups engaging in civil disobedience who turn their backs on nonviolence, go beyond the Constitutionally protected rights of petition and free assembly, and resort to violence to attempt to compel alteration of laws and policies with which they disagree. This condition has been

---

*This is a modified version of a chapter which appeared in "Ando sangrando" (I am bleeding): a study of Mexican American-police conflict and an analysis of the East Los Angeles 1970 riots, La Puente, Calif., 1972, Perspectiva Publications.

reinforced by a general erosion of respect for authority in American society and reduced effectiveness of social standards and community restraints on violence and crime. . . .

Finally, many Negroes have come to believe that they are being exploited politically and economically by the white "power structure." Negroes, like people in poverty everywhere, in fact lack the channels of communication, influence and appeal that traditionally have been available to ethnic minorities within the city and which enabled them—unburdened by color—to scale the walls of the white ghettos in an earlier era. The frustrations of powerlessness have led some to the conviction that there is no effective alternative to violence as a means of expression and redress, as a way of "moving the system." More generally, the result is alienation and hostility toward the institutions of law and government and the white society which controls them. . . .

These conditions have created a volatile mixture of attitude and beliefs which needs only a spark to ignite mass violence. . . . all the major outbursts of recent years were precipitated by routine arrests of Negroes for minor offenses by white police. But the police are not merely the spark. In discharge of their obligation to maintain order and insure public safety in the disruptive conditions of ghetto life, they are inevitably involved in sharper and more frequent conflicts with ghetto residents than with residents of other areas. Thus, to many Negroes police have come to symbolize white power, white racism and white repression. And the fact is that many police do reflect and express these white attitudes. The atmosphere of hostility and cynicism is reinforced by a widespread perception among Negroes of the existence of police brutality and corruption, and of a "double standard" of justice and protection—one for Negroes and one for whites.[1]

These therefore, are the ingredients that are frequently found in communities that have rioted. These ingredients have been (and still are) present in the Mexican American East Los Angeles community for many years.* The Riot Commission's find-

---

*See Leonard Pitt. The Decline of the Californios. (Los Angeles: University of California Press, 1966), p. 160. In his "Race war in Los Angeles" chapter, Pitt states: "Plainly, by 1854 the Spanish-speaking of Los Angeles felt oppressed by a double standard of justice such as some of them had previously experienced in the gold mines. One sees here in embryo resentments about 'Anglo justice' similar to those that have incited Mexican Americans in more recent times."

ings that channels of "communication, influence and appeal that traditionally have been available" to other ethnic minorities in the city which "enabled them—unburdened by color—to scale the walls of the white ghettos in an earlier era" does not hold true for American Indians and Mexican Americans. Even though the political, economic and education situation for blacks and Mexican Americans in Los Angeles is terrible compared to Anglo-Saxons, these conditions are even more acute for Mexican Americans than for blacks.

Accepting a preliminary, tentative observation (until that time when an official body makes a complete investigation of the three East Los Angeles riots) that the East Los Angeles community possesses those explosive ingredients found in other riot cities, a rough sketch of the East Los Angeles riots will be presented. Preceding these discussions, however, some comments on the general theory of riots will assist in better understanding the East Los Angeles riots. The Los Angeles zoot suit and Detroit riots of 1943 could have been described as "communal" riots, i.e. one ethnic-racial group fighting a different ethnic-racial group for a contested area. The riots of the 1960's have been described mostly as "commodity" riots—the riots were an outburst against property and retail establishments, including looting.[2] The business establishments were mainly owned by outside white proprietors. The deaths and casualties resulted mainly from the force used against the Negro population by police and National Guard units. In describing the natural history of commodity-type riots, two considerations have to be kept in mind: One, the style of intervention by the law enforcement officers has deeply influenced the anatomy of race riots in the United States.[3] The response of the police at the outbreak of commodity riots in various communities was very different, ranging from highly effective and professional behavior to weak and irresponsible action that exacerbated rioting and prolonged tension. Thus, points out Morris Janowitz, who had studied patterns of collective racial violence, "the stages of a riot are not pre-determined but reflect the pattern of intervention of law enforcement agencies."[4] The second consideration is that it is very difficult to assemble accurate documentation in order to describe the natural history of a riot—especially the behavior of rioters in a commodity riot. Janowitz further points out that from all sources, one conclusion emerges, namely the absence of organized conspiracy in commodity riots. The absence of organized conspiracy however, does not mean the absence of a pattern of events.[5]

Research studies of some 75 riots in the 1965-67 period demonstrate a pattern of events in these outbursts. The difference from one outburst to another involved the extent to which each one proceeded through the various stages of increased and intensified collective behavior. Commenting on the various stages, Janowitz states:

One is struck by the repeated reports of the carnival and happy-day spirit that pervades the early stages of a commodity riot. The new type of rioting is most likely to be set off by an incident involving the police in the ghetto where some actual or believed violation of accepted police practice has taken place. The very first phase is generally nasty and brutish: the police are stoned, crowds collect and tension mounts. The second stage is reached with the breaking of windows. Local social control breaks down and the population recognizes that a temporary opportunity for looting is available. The atmosphere changes quickly, and this is when positive enthusiasm is released. But all too briefly. If the crowds are not dispersed and order restored, the third stage of the riot is the transformation wrought by arson, firebombs, and sniper fire and the countermeasures taken by police and uniformed soldiers.[6]

The countermeasures employed by police deeply influence the course of rioting—even in some cases prolonging the period of reestablishing order. Too little response by law enforcement may escalate a riot as will an overreaction by police. There were wide differences in response patterns to early manifestations of disorder by local police in the 1960's riots. For example, the police commissioner of Detroit followed a loose policy in the early phase of the Detroit rioting, assuming that local civilian Negro leadership would contain the disorder. He had previous experience in which this approach worked effectively. Knowledge of the community and its leaders coupled with confidence in the leadership would seem to play an important part in this approach.

On the other hand, New York City and Chicago police have an operational code to intervene with that amount of force judged to be appropriate for early stages of the confrontation. The objective was to prevent the spread of disorder. The police took special steps to prevent routine police performance from developing into incidents that might provoke tension. Janowitz states:

If an incident became the focal point for tension and the collection of a crowd, the police responded early and in depth in order to prevent the second stage from actually expanding. Numerous police were sent to the scene or kept in reserve nearby. The police sought to operate by their sheer presence, not to provoke further counteraction. They sought to prevent the breaking of windows and the starting of looting that would set the stage for an escalated riot. If actual rioting threatened, one response was the early mobilization of local National Guard units and their ready reserve deployment in inner city garrisons. . . . Whereas the communal riot involved a confrontation between the white and the black community, the commodity riot, especially as it entered into the third and destructive phase, represents a confrontation between the black community and law enforcement officials of the larger society.[7]

If communal riots involve a confrontation between the black and white community, might not commodity riots of the 1960's actually represent a more sophisticated, advanced form of communal riots since most police are *white* and the targets for destruction are usually owned by *whites?* It might also be theorized that while the "race riots" of the 1940's primarily involved white *citizen* aggression toward ethnic minorities that were making economic progress in the war years, i.e., a threat to established political-economic equilibrium, the white citizen attitude of the 1940's is now being expressed *through* and *by* the white police and more important, *with the sanction of the dominant white society.* In this respect I would suggest that there is little difference between the communal and commodity riots as it involves ethnic minority groups. Hugh Davis Graham and Ted Robert Gurr conclude that resistance to undesirable change has been a more common source of collective violence in America than "revolutions of rising expectations."[8] They maintain that most ethnic and religious violence in American history has been retaliatory violence by groups "farther up the socioeconomic ladder who felt threatened by the prospect of the 'new immigrant' and the Negro getting both 'too big' and 'too close.'"[9] They also state that aggressive vigilantism has been a recurrent response of middle and working-class Americans to perceived threats by outsiders or lesser classes to their status, security and cultural integrity. The zoot-suit riots of the 1940's might be perceived in this manner. The armed forces "vigilantes" were envious of the zoot-suiter's freedom and threatened by his cultural style. The vigilante action was supported by a larger white community that was threatened by the Mexican American's progress in the war years.

Graham and Gurr assert that evidence in riots supports one basic principle: Force and violence can be successful techniques of social control and persuasion when they have extensive popular support. If they do not, they say, their advocacy and use are ultimately self-destructive, either as techniques of government or of opposition. They further remark:

The historical and contemporary evidence of the United States suggest that popular support tends to sanction violence in support of the status quo: the use of public violence to maintain public order, the use of private violence to maintain popular conceptions of social order when government cannot or will not. If these assertions are true—and not much evidence contradicts them—the prolonged use of force or violence to advance the interests of any segmental group may impede and quite possibly preclude reform.[10]

This observation appears questionable in light of the violent confrontation of demonstrators and police during the week of the Chicago Democratic National Convention of 1968. There appeared to be public support and a condoning of police violence against demonstrators by city officials and, even though there was published criticism, the city's response was to ignore the police violence.[11] Although there was more public support for the police violence than not, demonstrators today assume credit for

this having been an important turning point that resulted in greater Vietnam anti-war public support. It would appear important to analyze whether or not there was a loss of anti-war popular support to the Mexican American community following the August 29, 1970, riot.

A final factor to consider in the analysis of the East Los Angeles riots is the general response of the United States leadership to the riots reported in the Kerner Report. The Kerner report felt that the highest priority for national action was funds and legislation to deal with the social and economic problems of the black ghetto. Instead of social legislation and funds to improve the social conditions that were a basic cause of the riots, numerous laws against riots and rioters and an increase in penalties was the approach taken.[12] This trend was also seen in the National Institute of Municipal Law Officers published report on riots which includes a bibliography of over fifty articles, journals and reports that appeared after the Detroit riots of 1967, dealing with riot *control*.[13] In other words, the approach taken was to *control* the symptom rather than treat the *basic cause* of the symptom. This attitude was expressed into law on June 19, 1968 (Public Law 90-351) by the 90th Congress and became known as the Omnibus Crime Control and Safe Streets Act of 1968. The sum of $50,000,000 was appropriated for projects to improve and strengthen law enforcement. Part C, Section 301b, 6, provided for:

The organization, education, and training of regular law enforcement officers, special law enforcement units, and law enforcement reserve units for the prevention, detection, and control of riots and other violent civil disorders, including the acquisition of riot control equipment.[14]

Perhaps confirming that the law enforcement *control* approach did not resolve ethnic problems in the cities, Urban America, Inc., and The Urban Coalition reporting on America's racial crisis one year after the Kerner Report revealed that blacks and whites remained deeply divided in their perceptions and experiences of American society. In fact, blacks and whites were found to be a year closer to being two societies, increasingly separate and scarcely less equal. They stated: "Outright resistance to slum ghetto needs and demands intensified during the same months."[15]

Following in the footsteps of the "hardline" national trend and anticipating civil disorder in East Los Angeles, various city and county government and business leaders decided to build a $567,386 riot control center *in* East Los Angeles. Participating in the November 18, 1968, groundbreaking ceremonies were Roy Neshek, president of the Belvedere Rotary Club, John Espinosa, East Los Angeles realtor, Harry Rollett of the Southern California Edison Company, Sheriff Peter Pitchess, Art Chayra, president of the East Los Angeles Jay Cees, Robert Weber, industrialist, Manuel Veiga, Jr., of Veiga-Robinson Mortuary, Supervisor Ernest E. Debs, Whittier Congressman Chet Holifield, Bell Gardens Mayor William R. Irvine, City of Commerce Mayor Maurice H. Quigley, County Engineer John A. Lambie, Assemblyman Jack Fenton, Assemblyman Walter Karabian, and Judge Ben Vega. The East Los Angeles representatives were Espinosa, Veiga and Weber. The riot control center, named the "Special Enforcement Bureau," was financed by a joint-powers authority representing Los Angeles County, Bell Gardens (a predominantly middle-class, Anglo-Saxon resident community) and the City of Commerce (a predominantly Anglo-Saxon business community). The Special Enforcement Bureau was erected to "provide facilities adequate for law enforcement reserve personnel used to back-up regular field deputies in emergencies throughout East Los Angeles (a predominantly Mexican American community) and portions of the southeast area (a predominantly black community) of the County."[16]

There were angry rumors in the Mexican American community that the Special Enforcement Bureau was designed to be used against them and that it housed two armored tanks. At a United Mexican American Students police-community meeting held at California State College on Saturday, August 2, 1969, Captain Tom W. Pinkston of the East Los Angeles Sheriff's station admitted to me that they "only had one" armored tank at the riot control center.

Applying this "control the symptom" approach as a solution to a very complex problem may create additional problems. For example, society in general begins to believe that this is *the* answer to urban unrest as they have not been exposed to other approaches. Secondly, it may have a psychologically provoking effect to the urban areas where these "control" measures are implemented by law enforcement. These measures may also have the effect of communicating an *expectation* to the ethnic minority community which is internalized—particularly by the militant element in the community—thereby fulfilling the expectation, i.e., a self fulfilling prophesy. Finally, this approach may unintentionally give sanction to an irresponsible element in the police agency to "act out" their anger and hostility toward the minority community, feeling secure that if they do provoke the community into violence, there quickly will be sufficient *control force* available to quell the disturbance. The Urban Coalition and Urban America, Inc., drew a similar conclusion regarding police irresponsibility when they stated:

> Incidents involving the police continued (after the riots) to threaten the civil peace in the slums and ghettos. There was some evidence of a hardening of police attitudes and a weakening of traditional civil controls over their activities.[17]

This feeling is also expressed in the following statement which appeared in the East Los Angeles community *Eastside Sun* newspaper on Thursday, December 3, 1970:

Dear Editor,

The Congress of Mexican American Unity, supported by the National Moratorium Committee and the Barrio Defense Committee, has issued an urgent appeal to the people of Southern California to rally in defense of the beleaguered Mexican community. According to the Moratorium leaders, the Los Angeles Police Department in East Los Angeles "is engaged in a deliberate campaign of terror—of force and violence against the Mexican youth in the community. Beatings, arrests, and roustings are daily occurrences."

The young community leaders have compiled "a fact sheet of terror."

Wed. night, Nov. 11 some 15 police cars were parked half a block from the Moratorium headquarters. "They did not raid the headquarters because we had several law students and a reporter present observing the activities."

Fri. Nov. 13 at approximately 7:30 PM, six members of the Special Operations Conspiracy Squad of the Police Dept. entered the headquarters of the Moratorium Committee without knocking and without a search warrant. When asked for a search warrant, they pulled out their service revolvers and their leader said, "These are all the search warrants we need." They then proceeded to bully and terrorize the people in the building.

Sat. Nov. 14 at about 10:30 in the morning Ralph Flores was picked up as he was going to a drug store to purchase some medicine for his child. He was arrested, beaten, his life threatened, and then was released.

Sat. Nov. 14, some 30 members of the Los Angeles Police Department again raided the Moratorium headquarters. They assaulted the people there, and as a result, three youths, Antonio Uranda, Juan Reyes and Roberto Flores required medical attention. They were subsequently charged with "felonious assault on a police officer."

Three other young men, Ralph Ramirez, Sergio Robledo and Frank Martinez were charged with "interfering with a police officer."

Ralph Rodriguez, a young man crippled by spinal meningitis, was arrested on Wed., Nov. 18, questioned, "roughed up" and released.

Brown Beret Jesse Cevallos has been constantly harassed, his family threatened, and his own life is in danger.

It is the general feeling of some community leaders that the police department is deliberately attempting to foment rebellion as an excuse to enter the community on a "shoot-out basis." These community leaders, in a desperate attempt to forestall such action, are urgently appealing to the Anglo community throughout Southern California to come to the assistance of the Chicano people.

"Your voice, your word, your support against a program of genocide by officials sworn to 'law and order' is perhaps the only way to stop these growing assaults. We call upon all men and women of conscience to speak their mind now! End this organized terror campaign!"

> Esteban Torres
> Rosalio Munoz
> Rev. Antonio Hernandez
> Antonio Bernal
> Ralph Ramirez
> Celia Rodriguez
> Mauricio Terrazas
> Bert Corona
> Humberto Camacho
> Abe Tapia[18]

The above signatures represent a very responsible element of the Mexican American community. Torres is chairman of the 300 organization Congress of Mexican American Unity, and Tapia is state chairman of the Mexican American Political Association.

To recapitulate prior to examining the East Los Angeles riots, in analyzing the theory, history and experience of riots in America, the following circumstances seem to be present:

1. Social, economic, political and psychological oppression of the ethnic minority group.
2. White racism toward the ethnic minority group.
3. Ethnic minorities feel they are being politically and economically exploited by the white power structure.
4. Ethnic minorities lack influence and channels of communication.
5. Ethnic minorities are frustrated by a feeling of powerlessness.
6. There is alienation and hostility toward the institutions of law and government and the white society which controls them.
7. Major outbursts were precipitated by routine arrests of ethnic minorities by white police.
8. Police have come to symbolize white power, white racism and white repression to ethnic minorities.
9. There is a widespread perception among ethnic minorities of the existence of police brutality and corruption, and of a double standard of justice and protection—one for ethnic minorities and one for whites.
10. The riots of the 1960's have been mostly "commodity" riots.
11. Deaths and casualties resulted from the force used against ethnic minorities by police and National Guard units.
12. There is an absence of organized conspiracy by ethnic minorities in commodity riots.
13. A carnival and happy-day spirit pervades the early stages of a commodity riot.
14. The police are stoned, crowds collect and tension mounts in the first phase of the riot.
15. The second phase of the riot is characterized by loss of local social control, the breaking of windows and looting occurs.
16. The third stage is characterized by arson, firebombs, sniper fire and the countermeasures taken by police and uniformed soldiers.
17. Too little reaction or an overreaction by law enforcement may escalate a riot.
18. A flexible policy of minimum police intervention allowing the local civilian ethnic

minority leadership to contain the disorder has been effective.

19. Another mode of intervention by police is to use that amount of force judged to be appropriate for the early stages of confrontation in order to prevent the spread of disorder.

20. The third phase of the riots represents a confrontation between the ethnic minority community and law enforcement officials of the larger society.

21. Most ethnic minority violence in American history has been retaliatory violence by groups farther up the socioeconomic ladder who felt threatened by the ethnic minority getting both "too big" and "too close."

22. Force and violence can be successful techniques of social control and persuasion when they have extensive popular support.

23. The prolonged use of force or violence to advance the interests of any segmental group may impede and quite possibly preclude reform.

24. Nationally, an approach to *control* riots rather than treat the basic causes of riots was adopted.

25. Incidents involving the police continued after the riots to threaten the civil peace in the ethnic minority community. There was some evidence of a hardening of police attitudes and a weakening of traditional controls over their activities.

These twenty-five items will serve as a framework for a preliminary analysis of the three 1970 East Los Angeles riots. The data will be taken from three sources: newspapers, the California State Advisory Committee Report to the United States Commission on Civil Rights, and a few indepth interviews of witnesses.

The January 1, 1970, East Los Angeles Riot:

There was very little information available regarding this riot. The *Los Angeles Times* carried a very brief article on the incident on page three of the paper. The article reported that on January 1, 1970, about one hundred persons smashed windows and looted stores after New Year celebrations by a crowd of 5,000. It was labeled a major disturbance by police as it took law enforcement officers more than two hours to disperse the crowds. Damage occurred as forty-two storefront windows were shattered and some stores were looted along the mile-long Whittier Boulevard business district. Sheriff deputies arrested eleven persons on charges of looting

and resisting arrest.[19] The businesses are primarily owned by non-Spanish surnamed whites who do not live in the Mexican American community. Much more information is required to make an adequate analysis of the January 1, 1970, riot.

The August 29, 1970, East Los Angeles Riot:

Approximately 15,000 to 20,000 persons—mostly Mexican American—were in East Los Angeles on August 29 to attend a well-publicized National Chicano Moratorium March. The event was organized by Rosalio Munoz, former UCLA student body president, and supported in near unanimity by Mexican American organizations throughout the Southwest.

The Moratorium was to protest America's involvement in the war in Southeast Asia and, simultaneously, to decry the high percentage of Mexican American battle casualties, both wounded and killed in action. Moratorium leaders urged young Mexican Americans to resist military service abroad in favor of fighting for social justice at home. The Moratorium Committee had kept the police fully informed of its intentions and program. It provided monitors to accompany the marchers and maintain order.

The Los Angeles County Sheriffs were to clear the parade route and to direct traffic as necessary at cross streets. The sheriffs, being concerned by the influx of young Mexican American militants from all over the Southwest for the event and by reports of possible trouble from revolutionaries and other subversive groups, also made additional preparations to meet any situations that might develop.[20] No public announcement of any dangers from revolutionaries seeking a confrontation was made, and many of those who attended the event brought their entire families.

The marchers gathered in East Los Angeles' Belvedere Park and followed a scheduled parade route down East Third Street, Beverly Boulevard, Atlantic Boulevard, and Whittier Boulevard where it ended at Laguna Park. According to Sheriffs' reports, the marchers had traveled only five blocks when some deputies became targets for rocks and bottles. It was there, according to Sheriff Peter Pitchess, that marchers took over the entire width of the street, violating their parade permit which limited them to only one-half of it.

At 2:34 PM, a liquor store at 3812 Whittier Boulevard was looted and windows were broken and a second store was looted at 3:25 PM, according to the sheriff. Officers with riot guns were already stationed at street-corner barricades. It was at 3:10 PM that the sheriffs had decided to declare the situation "critical" and move in to disperse all crowds in the area. They used tear gas freely.

At the peak of the turmoil, a dozen fires burned out of control along Whittier Boulevard, and about 500 police and sheriff's deputies were involved. Sheriff Pitchess reported that 40 officers were injured in the melee and that 25 radio cars were damaged. A main battleground was Laguna Park, at the end of the parade route, where marchers had settled on the grass to listen to music and hear a series of speakers.[21]

Following a disturbance at the edge of the park, the sheriffs moved in with tear gas to disperse the entire crowd. It is this action and resultant incidents which have drawn most of the complaints from the community. Community members charge that the sheriffs overreacted and, in breaking up a peaceful assembly, turned on the panic and hostility. Citizens have complained by the dozens of unwarranted brutal treatment by the deputies. An exact toll of injured civilians is not yet known, but arrests during and following the confrontation exceeded 400.[22]

The above information was based upon the California State Advisory Committee's evaluation of information gathered by its members and by members of the United States Commission on Civil Rights Western Regional Field Office and the Commission's Office of General Counsel. The following witness account was taken from *La Raza,* a local East Los Angeles barrio newspaper:

The marchers proceeded peacefully down Atlantic Blvd., watched by curious people on the sidewalks who have not fully grasped what "Chicano Power" means. While marching on Whittier Blvd. near Eastern Ave., the marchers were hit with bottles from the overpass. The overpass is part of the Long Beach Freeway that

runs parallel to Eastern Ave., North and South. Some of the marchers were cut.

The march proceeded West on Whittier Blvd. It was a hot summer day and some of the marchers fainted along the way, but they were quickly taken care of by medical crews that were assigned to station wagons.

Two blocks before Laguna Park, a scuffle occurred between Sheriff's deputies and the marchers. No one seems to know how or why it started, but it was quickly quieted by the monitors.

It took almost one hour for all the marchers to file into Laguna Park, rest their tired aching feet, and find a place on the lawn. Many families began to open up their picnic baskets and have a late lunch. Others were searching for refreshments to cool off.

This is where the trouble started. Many Chicanos went to a liquor store to buy sodas and beer. The owner of the liquor store was swamped with business. He attempted to close his doors in order to deal with the customers inside. In fact, he succeeded in doing so.

The sheriff's station in East L.A. (where in the past two years six Chicanos have "supposedly" committed suicide) claims to have received a call from the owner asking for their assistance in calming the people coming into the store (the store owner denies calling the sheriff's station). The sheriffs responded to the call by sending more units into the area. Next they moved in numerous police units across the street from Laguna Park. Obviously, this drew the attention of some of the people in the park, especially since there were about 40 to 50 sheriff deputies standing behind their cars. The deputies then formed a parallel formation and with their billyclubs started advancing. No warnings about illegal assemblies or such. At that time, the Chicano Moratorium security personnel came in to keep peace and they would have been able to do so if the sheriff's deputies had gone back to their cars, but instead of retreating, they attacked not only the monitors, but the people who were peacefully hearing the speakers. They indiscriminately fired tear gas capsules into unaware crowds of Chicanos who were sitting on the grass. Shoes, purses and lost children on the field stood as symbols of the inhumanity expressed by the deputies.

As chaos ensued, children were lost from their parents, fathers who came to the front to defend their children were beaten, bloodied and arrested! Chicanos and Chicanas everywhere were crying in amazement over what they were seeing.

Men were kicked, struck in the chest and stomach and brutally beaten over the head. They were then dragged unconscious to awaiting police cars. Our people rallied time after time and pushed the perros back with stones and fists but sticks, stones and fists cannot stand against guns, clubs, and tear gas missiles. After an hour or two of fighting, the Metropolitan Police from Los Angeles City reinforced the sheriffs. The Metro Police are trained to deal with demonstrations. They hit first and ask questions later.

Men, women and children were indiscriminately tear-gassed. The fighting spread into the side street and spilled onto Whittier Blvd. A few police cars were set on fire but Chicanos paid dearly for it. The fighting spilled over onto Whittier Blvd. Store windows were broken and buildings set afire. The following night Wilmington erupted along Avalon Ave. Results: The same as in East Los Angeles, destruction in the business areas and numerous arrests.

That same night, four policemen were shot in the Chicano area, the Casa Blanca district of Riverside.

Now that most of the turmoil has stopped, many people are walking around as if in shock, with questioning expressions on their faces. The most interesting questions come from the Anglo community. Why did it happen? Why?

That question has been asked in numerous black ghettoes throughout the nation. Puerto Ricans have heard it in New York, and New Jersey and now that same question is being asked again in our Chicano communities. Why did it happen?[23]

In an official memorandum from Herbert L. Carter, executive director of the Los Angeles County Commission on Human Relations to the official county body's commissioners, the events of August 29th were described as follows:

On Saturday, August 29, three members of our staff observed and/or participated in the parade/rally. All agree that the march along East Third Street, Atlantic Boulevard, and Whittier Boulevard was peaceful, festive and non-violent, except that near the corner of Eastern Avenue at Whittier Boulevard, a young man threw a bottle at a parked partrol car. That young man was immediately reprimanded by parade monitors and was carefully watched throughout the remainder of the parade.

As the parade progressed westward on Whittier Boulevard toward Laguna Park and the culminating rally, persons along Whittier Boulevard were urged to join the march and many of them did. Although the festive atmosphere was maintained, cries of "Chicano Power" and "Viva La Raza" were now heard more frequently and forcefully.

When the parade participants reached Laguna Park, they were joined by perhaps 8,000 to 10,000 additional persons who had not participated in the march. Our staff estimated that the crowd then numbered 20,000 people, with perhaps 80 percent of them being under 25 years of age. The gathering at the park was, according to our staff consultants, peaceful. Although, admittedly, one could hardly see because of the masses of people in such a small area nor could one hear too well because the sound equipment was insufficient either in quality or quantity, the crowd was entertained by folk songs and dancing and was commended by Rosalio Munoz, Chairman of the Moratorium Committee, for their participation. It should be noted that although the predominant numbers of the rally were identifiable as Mexican American, the crowd also included Anglos and blacks in sizable numbers. Moreover, there were large numbers of teenagers and children.

At approximately 3 PM staff persons observed a considerable number of bottles (wine and other alcoholic beverages) in the park area and decided to leave since members of their families were present. As one staff person began to leave the park, he heard a siren of an approaching police vehicle. At this point, many of the people began to leave the entertainment area to see what was going on. The rally monitors, with the use of a loudspeaker, attempted to get the crowd to stay in the park and urged them not to move from that area. As our staff member began to observe what was going on on Whittier Boulevard (a number of police patrols had been called to a liquor store approximately a half block down the street) he noticed bottles being thrown at police vehicles on Whittier Boulevard. Shortly thereafter he heard the sound of many sirens and observed a large number of police cars converging on Whittier Boulevard and approaching Laguna Park. At this point, people were running all over the park in panic. Our staff person indicated that he was able to hear transmissions on the patrol car radios, but at no time did he hear a declaration on the part of law enforcement officials that the rally in Laguna Park had been declared an unlawful assembly. Our staff person reported that tear gas was dispensed toward the crowd, and inasmuch as he was affected by the tear gas, he proceeded to leave the park area. After crossing the street, he observed the scene one final time and noted that a number of police car windshields had been smashed, several people had been injured and destruction of properties along Whittier Boulevard was beginning to take place.

First of three fatalities attributed to the riot was Ruben Salazar, Los Angeles Times columnist and news director for Spanish language television station, KMEX.

Salazar had spent the day covering the moratorium and ensuing trouble. He had stopped at the Silver Dollar Cafe at 4945 Whittier Boulevard with another newsman when he was shot through the head by a tear gas missile fired by a member of the sheriff's department.

There are many conflicting stories surrounding the events which led up to his death.

An inquest into the death of Salazar is now being conducted by the county coroner. Mexican American groups who have been monitoring the inquest proceedings walked out twice, charging that the inquest was a "sham."

These recent happenings, plus the fact that Salazar was regarded as the Chicanos' most eloquent spokesman have raised doubts in the community which only an independent high-level investigation into all of the facts can resolve.[24]

Delfino Varela, a long-time East Los Angeles resident and professional social worker, presents his perception of "A Walk in the Sun" on August 29, 1970:

We strolled down the street, my brother-in-law, a niece, my wife, our one-year-old baby in his stroller and I. Behind us were but a few people, in front were thousands and thousands. All of us affirmed there were more thousands than we had ever seen, brothers-in-law, nieces, wives, husbands, and one-year-old babies in their strollers, all strolling together in the noonday sun.

The voice of a friend who fled Germany kept coming back, "Marches here are so sloppy," she said. "Everybody just strolls along and there's no rhythm to it. You should have seen our marches in Germany," she said.

I was glad we were a motley crew, all out of step and with no rhythm. They'll never goose-step this crowd into fascism, I thought, these thousands of nieces, cousins, brothers-in-law, aunts and uncles, and the one-year-old babies in their strollers, they're too undisciplined, too massive, too uncontrollable for any Hitler.

Behind the few people in back of us was the end of the long, long line of countless thousands, some say twenty-five, some thirty, and behind all this rode two black busses massively built of steel and rubber with white roofs. These motorized vultures followed close, and their insides were filled with walking vultures. This long, long line of children, women, boys, and girls was followed closely by these two black busses, and the creatures inside them waited tensely for the battle and their noses quivered as they smelled the blood of our women, men, nieces, aunts and uncles and the one-year-old babies in their strollers.

In three and a half miles the long, long line was at the park. A quiet modest park, but well suited for the brothers-in-law, nieces, wives, and the one-year-old babies in their strollers, and for their sodas, candies, balloons, buttons and picnic lunches. Today, this would be a people's park.

But the two black busses were close behind, and at the park they were joined by a third, full of armed men full of dislike for the brothers-in-law, wives, nieces, and for the one-year-old babies in their strollers. Without a word they formed across the street from the park in long and silent lines, soon to move across the street toward the people in the park.

We were leaving but were ordered back into the park and the northern exit facing the police was closed to us. Soon, around us we heard them coming, the men from the black, black busses, from the west, and in back of all the brothers-in-law, nieces, wives, and one-year-old babies in their strollers.

Swinging clubs they came, without a word just swinging clubs and throwing gas.

As we walked through the alleys, choking with the gas that was spread throughout the park and for several blocks away, I looked at my one-year-old baby in his stroller and his red and watery eyes. He seemed amazed, and looked in wonderment in all directions. He didn't know that men who come in big black busses threw things at little children to make them cry and run when they are in their strollers at the park.[25]

Dr. James S. Koopman, a physician at the UCLA School of Medicine's department of pediatrics, was a participant in the Moratorium march, along with his wife. He commented:

Everyone was assembled peacefully at Laguna Park. My wife and I sat on the grass amongst diverse people. Immediately around us were little children playing with a puppy, an older woman with a cane, a pregnant woman with a small baby and a family eating hamburgers and French fries. The program began and after two speeches a Puerto Rican rhythm group was providing entertainment. The first sign of any disturbance I saw was when some people in the distance began to stand up. The loudspeaker calmly assured us that nothing was happening and that we should sit down. Seconds later I saw a row of gold helmets marching across the park, forcing everyone toward the high fences. The exit was too small for everyone to leave quickly. I, along with everyone else, panicked. The terrible tragedies of human stampedes in the soccer stadiums of Peru and Argentina were uppermost in my mind.[26]

Sheriff's deputies responded to a "burglary in progress" call at the Green Mill liquor store (owner Morris Maroko denied making the call). The deputies responded with red lights flashing. A sheriff's spokesman said that the two units that arrived were met with "overwhelming resistance and more units responded."

One of the second wave of sheriff's units responding was a unit from the Special Enforcement Bureau, the specially trained anti-riot detail. Special Enforcement deputy Ray Baytos, 26, and his partner left their vehicle and were on the northwest section of the park at Whittier and Alma (the liquor store is a block away from Laguna park and cannot be seen from the park) when the two were assaulted by a group of people. Baytos was beaten with a large board, kicked, struck, his helmet taken and his revolver stripped from him, according to the Sheriff's Department. Then, two shots were fired at him from his own gun, both missing deputy Baytos. The incident was observed by other deputies and a radio call of extreme urgency went out for help. The participants were unaware of the Baytos incident. "The first sign of any disturbance I saw was when some people in the distance began to stand up," said Dr. Koopman.[27]

Attorney Toby Rothschild claims that the red lights and sirens of the oncoming deputies caused a crowd to gather at the northwest edge of the park. Parade monitors attempted to move the group back to the park and away from the deputies on Whittier Boulevard, Rothschild said. Rothschild further stated:

Most of them were turning and going back and the debris (being thrown) had stopped. Then there were sirens, and eight or ten (Sheriff's) cars and a bus arrived. The sirens attracted the entire group back. There was very little that could be done to stop people from either side from doing things. I did not hear any order to disperse.[28]

The Sheriff's Department claimed, however, that dispersal orders were given from several loud speakers on patrol cars surrounding the park. Sheriff Pitchess said that the decision to clear the park came after "a very thorough assessment of the situation."[29] The events flowed swiftly and the deputies formed their line. Skirmishes

broke out and then died down. A line of parade monitors linked arms between the deputies advancing from the north and the body of demonstrators on the south. The bombardment from missles reached an intense level and then died off. Many thought the rally would be allowed to continue. The monitors shouted "Get out of here, leave us alone," at the deputies.[30] This was followed by a long lull as monitors and deputies looked at each other across a narrow no-man's-land. Javier Gonzalo maintains that "After that interval, somebody flipped a finger or words were interchanged and then it really got nasty."[31] As startled demonstrators fled in panic, some in the crowd decided to fight the deputies. According to the Los Angeles Times, it was 2:50 PM when the Green Mill liquor store was crowded with customers and 3:25 PM when the first reports of looting reached the Sheriff's Department. At 3:36 PM a fire station at Eastern and Verona was under attack and the riot was under way.[32] The Mexican American–police confrontation at the park occurred at approximately 3:00 PM—*before* the riot began. Most minority group–police confrontations in other riots occurred *after* the riots were underway.

The September 16, 1970 East Los Angeles Riot:

For almost thirty years, the Mexican American community in Los Angeles has honored the anniversary of the Mexican Independence by having a parade. Because of the August 29, 1970, disturbance, there was much discussion about whether to hold the 16th of September parade. It was cancelled but a week before the 16th, it was decided after consultation with the Sheriff's Department, the Mexican Consul General and the sponsors to hold the parade with the help of the monitors.[33] The sponsors wanted to take the crowd to East Los Angeles College Stadium for speeches and an opportunity to give vent to emotions there, instead of in the streets. A representative of Sheriff Pitchess told the Board of Trustees of the Los Angeles Community Colleges—the group that had the authority to make the decision—that the sheriff "had no objection to the use of the stadium, and it might have advantages."[34] But the conservative majority of the board voted 4 to

3 against allowing the Mexican American groups to use the college stadium. Esteban Torres, executive director of the Congress of Mexican American Unity, who sought the permit, then said his group would seek a Superior Court order to force the board to allow holding a rally at the school. Torres felt that it would have been disastrous to end the parade at Belvedere Park rather than the college stadium because: "There are no real facilities there for speakers. Our biggest concern is the security of the area. I understand there is a sheriff's substation in the park."[35] On Wednesday, September 16, the College Board of Trustees' decision was upheld when Superior Court Judge Richard Schauer denied a restraining order that would have allowed the parade participants the use of the college stadium.[36]

At 5:15 PM, the parade began. The following is a newspaper account of the parade preceding the disturbances:

A Marine Corps color guard carrying the flags of the United States and Mexico stepped out smartly. Behind them were carloads of politicians and public officials, a traditional part of Independence Day parades. Then charros—Mexican cowboys—on spirited horses, and pretty girls on decorated floats. Interspersed were organizational groups, but many appeared militant in nature. The first carried the banner of the National Chicano Moratorium Committee, the organization which staged the parade and rally that turned into violence Aug. 29. Originally numbering about 200, their ranks swelled as the parade proceeded along First to Gage Avenue, then north to Brooklyn Avenue and eastward toward the (Belvedere) park. Spectators dashed from the sidewalks to join the line and shout the chants of "Chicano Power," and "Raza si, guerra no" (people yes, war no). In front of them marched a somber line of green-sashed members of the Congress of Mexican American Unity, which had earlier distributed hundreds of lapel buttons stating "Non-Violence Sept. 16."[37]

The first deviation from the original plan of the parade, according to the Los Angeles Times, came when the marchers bypassed Belvedere Park, the intended end of the route, and continued to the college. There had been some general movement to disperse once the marchers reached the stadium parking lot and monitors and deputies alike appeared relieved. By that time,

several hundred of the unofficially estimated 150,000 persons who had lined the parade route began to join the more militant elements among the marchers. The first sign of violence came at 7:10 PM, a few minutes before the parade officially ended. The last marching group, predominantly teen-agers and militant youths, reportedly began throwing rocks and eggs at reserve deputies who were riding motorcycles, policing the end of the event. The deputies sought shelter behind parked cars. A second call was received moments later when Monterey Park police said they were facing a hostile, rock-throwing mob at the corner of Floral Ave. and Collegian Way, near the college campus. Shortly afterward, windshields of three sheriff's patrol cars were smashed, a truck and a Los Angeles Department of Parks and Recreation Trailer was reported afire at Belvedere Park, and rocks shattered windows at the Constitution Savings and Loan Co., 1200 W. Riggin Street. Other shops were smashed and looted at the Atlantic Square Shopping Center, a liquor store and an electrical supply store were looted, and Monterey Park police asked Los Angeles police for aid. Instead, they were reinforced by the Sheriff's Department. Deputies reported that attempts to burn the college administration building were unsuccessful, but the sound of smashing glass and shots continued for several hours.[38] More than 100 persons were injured and three persons—one a sheriff's deputy—were shot. At least 68 persons were arrested. In all, 64 peace officers were injured, 45 sheriff's deputies and 19 Monterey Park officers. Sheriff Pitchess said that bullets fired from the crowd wounded two civilians and a deputy. Pitchess said his officers fired no shots. Chief Holladay of the Monterey Park police said his officers fired no shots. Two attorneys acting as observers, who asked not to be identified, told the Los Angeles Times that they didn't see how monitor Raymond Hernandez could have been shot by deputy sheriffs. One of the attorneys said he didn't see the deputies fire at all. The other said the deputies did fire in the direction of flashes and says there were either firecrackers or shots from the direction of the park—a block to the east of the intersection of Brooklyn and Mednik Avenues. Victim Raymond Hernandez, however, disagreed with the testimony of the attorney observers. Hernandez stated:

It had just gotten dark and we were moving the crowd back, pushing them back. All of a sudden to my right side I heard four shots. I turned around and saw deputies aiming their rifles straight ahead—not into the air, but straight ahead, down, in my direction. I said "Don't shoot! Don't shoot!" But they fired again and I got hit. They were firing like a firing squad.[39]

Hernandez said he was facing the deputies when he was shot and saw them fire their weapons.[40] Serious allegations against the Sheriff's Department such as these make an impartial investigation of the disturbance mandatory.

An in-depth witness report was given me by Luis Oropeza, currently a graduate student at the University of Southern California School of Social Work. Oropeza was a parade monitor and what makes his statement particularly significant is that he also tells of his experience of being arrested and placed in jail. His statement is as follows:

Here is my account of the events as I witnessed them on September 16, 1970, in East Los Angeles. I arrived at Rowan and Brooklyn at about 5:30 PM to catch the tail end of the parade. The streets were lined with people who seemed in a festive mood. Many of the people were women and children. The sheriffs and LAPD were manning the parade. The sheriffs seemed to outnumber the LAPD. However many LAPD were without guns, there were many previously plain cars that appeared to have been marked with "to protect and serve" emblems just for this occasion. Another noticeable fact was that the sheriffs were not standing at intersections as on August 29 (the Moratorium march) but were standing on the sidewalk behind the crowd watching the parade.

As we marched to Belvedere Park, many marchers began to turn into the park; others ahead of me were turning around and returning to the park area. However, several hundred were continuing toward Atlantic Boulevard. As we passed the street which leads to the ELA Stadium, I saw about two hundred people on this street and I heard shouts to this crowd, telling them to turn around. The group that had been carrying a picture of Ruben Salazar marched up the ELA College steps and placed the picture on the roof connecting the admissions building and student center. The crowd was very excited and I had very definite fears about the possibility of the beginning of a riot.

After the picture had been placed on the roof, the crowd moved quickly toward Atlantic Boulevard and within a minute or two, someone threw a rock through Constitutional Savings Bank. The violence grew quickly and without my realizing it, as I was making efforts to help control the violence, a line of the Monterey Park Police was forming across Atlantic Boulevard. There were approximately two or three hundred Chicanos confronting the police with a fairly steady flow of rocks and bottles. However, out of these hundred, only about fifteen or twenty were actually coming forward sporadically to throw something.

I went back to the police line and spoke with a Monterey Park Officer with double bars on his lapels who seemed to be in charge. I asked him not to move in and to send a car to contact our security people so they could come to the "front line." He refused and told me to speak to the sheriffs of whom there were now a few. I could not see anyone in charge but the sheriff I approached said they could not help, that they had been called to assist and the Monterey Park Police were in charge. I reapproached the officer in charge who seemed to be making some effort to contact our people; however I now feel I misinterpreted his behavior since we never received any kind of major help from the Belvedere Park area. The main difficulty in controlling the crowd was the fact that those few of us who were trying for some reason were not maintaining a strong line. Also the few throwing things would dash out then dash into the crowd to hide.

I approached the police several times trying to reassure them we could control and move back the crowd, asking them to be patient warning of escalation if they moved in. I was told I had a few minutes several times, but whether or not the police were actually allowing extra time or were adhering to a previously agreed to schedule or time limit, I'm still not sure. I heard two comments made by different officers. A sheriff apparently in charge turned to the officers behind him and said (in reference to the hail of rocks) "All right, just keep cool." I heard another officer say angrily "we're going to kick some Chicano ass." By this time the sheriffs had completely taken over the riot control. Suddenly, without any warning or command to disperse, tear gas was fired into the crowd and the police moved forward. The confrontation lines moved back to directly in front of East L. A. College, where a small fire was started. I started to help put out the fire when I felt a club in my back and hear an officer tell me angrily to move out. I remarked impatiently that I had done nothing. Suddenly he said, "I saw you throw a rock (turning to another officer); didn't you see him throw a rock?"

The officer responded, "Yea, I saw him." I was put into a car hurriedly without being handcuffed. A few minutes later two younger Chicanos were put in the car with me. I then heard an officer outside the car say in reference to me "What's he doing in there, he's not even handcuffed." The response from another officer, "I don't know, someone just threw him in there." The second officer got into the car next to me and I commented that the police had been "sorta" cool. He said that it was pretty hard to keep your cool. Although the other two were handcuffed I remained free all the way to the sheriff's station. On the way, one of the officers warned us not to fool around, and pointing the handle of a metal flashlight at us said that we should remember that in the car, "there are no witnesses."

We got to the sheriff's station at Belvedere Park where the preliminary booking was made. The officers seemed to be in a rather lighthearted mood. The officer who led me through the booking said that he had been the arresting officer, when actually he had not. He stated the charge as a 415, disturbing the peace, and also stated there was no evidence for the charge. I later felt that this officer had tried to do me a favor. He could have made the charge anything he liked. There was a small incident at the sheriff's station. One of the fellows arrested with me seemed slightly irritated by the fact that he was arrested for nothing and was receiving the generally gruff treatment the officers were showing. We were all leaning on a patrol car and for no other reason than this fellow's irritation, ordered angrily and demanded that he not only lean against the car, but over it. After I had been booked, a vinyl cord was clamped around my crossed wrists. I was then taken to a large bus where an officer seemed to be severe without any kind of provocation on our part. With a strongly severe expression he ordered us to "Get to the back of the bus, the last seat and sit your ass down and don't get up." There were two other younger boys in the bus directly behind the cab. They appeared to be slightly loaded and not to have been connected with the riot. There was some loud talking and remarks made to the police outside, especially as the group became larger. The officer in charge of the bus came in and told us to shut up "or we'll throw some tear gas in here and see how funny you laugh then."

I remember looking at my watch at the time of my arrest. It was about 8:00 PM. As I mentioned before, we had been tied with vinyl cords. They were tied tightly enough to cause pain continuously. I could not move my hands without increasing the pain, so that there was no position that eased the pain, only made it worse. Gradually my hands began to swell and feel numb and it became difficult to move my fingers. We made some attempts to loosen each others cords with our teeth, but it was impossible as well as being extremely painful.

Several of the people in the bus had been beaten by the police. I can remember seven of these. All of them came in without any kind of first aid. The blood was still streaming down their faces in four of the cases. One had a bleeding nose and face; another had blood trickling from his inner ear. One person had blood in three large patches on his head. Blood was running from the side of his head down his neck. One of the last who came in was really in bad shape. The right side of his face was swollen, he had a black eye and it was difficult to make out his features because of the large amount of blood on the left side of his face. Two other guys came in and showed evidence of body injury. One was limping and the other had large welts on his arms from a nightstick. All these people were tied like the rest of us, and apparently had not even been allowed to even treat themselves. The general response of the group on the bus was light, even light-hearted. There were some angry and vulgar remarks, but at no time did anyone get even close to getting out of hand. There were several comments made by a few of us to keep the action cool. The two younger fellows at the front were standing up occasionally and the officer in charge became increasingly hard with them. The times they did stand they were searching for matches for cigarettes.

While we were still in the station, we saw a small car drive up with a Mexican flag attached to the roof. A few young Chicanos got out and glanced at us, but turned away disinterestedly. Six of them got into the car to leave. When they got back in, one of them took off the flag, laughed and waved it mockingly. The sheriffs around joined in the laughter and the car drove away. We remained on the bus with the windows closed until we had about twenty-five people on board. We then took off, left the one girl on the bus (who had been kept in a special booth toward the front) at Sibyl Brand and we continued to the L. A. County Jail, the "new county."

We arrived at the county and were all hauled into a cell with bars on all four sides, a cage. The sheriffs surrounding the cell looked at all of us in the way one looks at a strange animal at the zoo. Their faces seemed to say "Wow, look at the Chicanos from the East LA riot." The two young kids who had been sitting at the front of the bus were then brought in. One of them made a movement with his shoulder to show he did not want to be pushed. Immediately a signal was given and five sheriffs entered the cell. Even after there was no struggle and while five officers were holding the boys the bus officer with a vengeful expression on his face took an arm of one of the boys and bent it further behind his back. They were then grabbed fiercely by all five officers even though they had long since stopped struggling, and even appeared dazed, were dragged along the floor from the cell and taken through a door. The cage was opened and those with any wounds were superficially looked at by a man in a white uniform. They were never touched by this man, even for purposes of inspection, nor were they asked any questions about their condition.

We were moved into a cell where we were searched by sheriffs who wore surgical gloves. The next step was a waiting room where we were allowed to make phone calls, and go to the rest room. Small tags were stapled to our clothing to identify it. We moved into a room in which we disrobed, were inspected for any surface infection or disease, showered, sprayed and finally given our "blues." As my pockets were being searched, my belongings were thrown back for me to catch. During this whole procedure we were ordered about in a way similar to boot camp. The whole attitude of the officers seemed contemptuous of us; they avoided looking at us directly or touching us, giving the definite impression that we were beneath contempt. We did nothing to provoke this attitude. The officers seemed to carry this attitude around with them permanently. We were finally given permission to take two sandwiches, one of baloney, and one of cheese (one slice in each, no dressing) and one cup of coffee without cream or sugar, and we went into "the tank." The tank was littered with uneaten sandwiches and orange peels. There was garbage all over the floor. Two men had cleared away a space next to the garbage cans and were trying to sleep. There were no telephones in the tank, but there was a sign saying that if you had no change, you would not be given any by trustee or officer. There were only a few benches; many of us had to clear away garbage to sit on the floor. I had been arrested at 8:00 PM; it was now 11:30.

We were finally led from the tank and taken for an X-ray. Most of our time was spent waiting. While we were waiting for a blood sample to be taken from us a man in white uniform asked if there were any medical complaints. He looked at one of us. He asked the person to bend his head down and from six inches away without touching his head said that it was okay. The blood sample was taken. Instead of the elastic band around our arms we were told to hold our upper arm. We were finally taken to our cells. By the time I got to my cell it was 3:00 AM. It's

significant that even though we arrived at the county at 11:00 and the cell assignment is made almost immediately after getting out of the "cage," we did not finally get to our bed until four hours later. The whole booking process, even for the group of us, should not have taken much more than an hour. It seems as if a great deal of pointless waiting is put into the process. I arrived at my cell and tried to sleep but could not because of the noise. At 4:00 AM I was called from my cell to talk to a lawyer from the National Chicano Moratorium Committee who had come to see me. I was then taken back to my cell and shortly after 5:00 AM we went to breakfast (scrambled eggs, potatoes, bread, applesauce, jelly, coffee) which was better than I thought it would be. However we were forced to eat hurriedly since we were allotted a limited amount of time per table. We were ordered to leave whether we were finished or not. We ate with only a single spoon.

I spent the next day in jail, and was impressed by the friendliness of the people in the cells. I was also impressed by the fact that I was there for disturbing the peace with those who had been convicted of various felonies and some who were merely there on warrants for neglecting traffic citations. At approximately 2:00 PM I was released from my cell and taken to the release room. After waiting three hours, it took fifteen minutes for me to change and be given my possessions. Again, there was much pointless waiting. At 5:30, I walked out. It was then I was told by my brother who was waiting for me that he was told I had left my cell at 10:30 that morning. He was told at 12:00 to go to lunch and when he returned at 1:00 I would be out. Several other people told me of speaking to authorities by phone and the information they were given did not fit my experience. My conclusion was that the people who gave out information either did not know my actual situation or knew it and gave wrong information to pacify my relatives and friends who were anxious about my welfare.

A Preliminary Analysis of The ELA Riots:

In the following preliminary analysis of the East Los Angeles riots of 1970, there are certain problems in the data that prohibit one from reaching definite conclusions because of outright contradictions in many of the witness statements—monitor Hernandez stating that he saw the deputies shoot him and Sheriff Pitchess denying that his deputies fired—that would require intensive legal investigations to get at the true facts. Rather than deal with specific, minute facts, I have presented some information regarding the East Los Angeles riots in order to place them in a conceptual framework based on prior riot experience as seen in the United States. In this way one can better understand the underlying dynamics of riots and be in a better position to predict and more important, hopefully *prevent* future collective violence that involves Mexican Americans and the police. The following Riot Analysis Framework represents an adapted version of the twenty-five circumstances and conditions (mentioned earlier) found in the riots of the 1960's.

DISCUSSION

From this information, it is seen that the three ELA riot circumstances were very similar to those situations found in the U.S. riots in the 1960's. The core ingredients for riots as seen in the first nine items were practically identical. However, not much can be concluded regarding the natural history of the 1-1-70 ELA riot because of the lack of information. The little information that is available, however, indicates that the 1-1-70 riot fits the pattern of a commodity riot in that it took place in a business district and the outburst was primarily directed at retail establishments —not the police. Although the 8-29 riot could be labeled a commodity riot because of the burning of business establishments on Whittier Boulevard, it still had some elements that would support it being labeled a *communal* riot due to three factors: (1) there was a severe Mexican American–Anglo Saxon (police) physical confrontation at the park *before* the riots; (2) there was a battle over the park, i.e., a "turf"; and (3) it all occurred *in* the Mexican American community. The statement "Get out of here, leave us alone," shouted by the monitors (in-group) defined the social situation thereby placing the police in the "out-group" category. The subsequent commodity-type behavior could be seen as *displaced anger* provoked by the Sheriff's deputies. In this context, James P. Comer in explaining the dynamics of black and white violence states:

A black student was ordered off the lawn at his predominantly white college campus by a white policeman. To be a man—a black man—he had to hit the policeman, a symbol of oppression. But it was a 'minor incident' and to avoid difficulty he had to hold back. In fury, rage and confusion he smashed his arm through a plate-glass window a few minutes later. Such feeling occasionally results in a loss of control after 'trigger incidents' (reflecting white superiority and black helplessness) with attendant burning of property. With a breakdown in personal control, blacks, employed and unemployed, loot and plunder the 'symbolic enemy.' Such reactions on the part of oppressed groups have been reported throughout human history.[41]

Within the above context, it would seem that the Sheriff's Department, by moving in on the unsuspecting audience, panicked and "triggered" the crowd into fight and flight action. The physical power and the tear gas of the deputies apparently overwhelmed the crowd (reflecting Anglo-Saxon superiority and Mexican American helplessness) to the degree that they displaced their anger onto Whittier Boulevard.

The September 16th disturbance appeared to be even more of a communal riot than the August 29th incident. Evidence to support this observation is seen in the fact that most of the violence was directed at the police. The result was that a very large number of police were injured. Furthermore, it appears that the Sheriff's Department initially cooperated with the sponsoring agencies by allowing them to use Mexican American citizen monitors to police the parade. While the 1-1-70 incident appeared to be a spontaneous commodity riot explosion, and the 8-29 disturbance a *displaced anger* response to an overreaction by the Sheriff's Department, the 9-16 disorder appeared to reflect retaliatory behavior by militant youth toward the police for their aggressive actions against Mexican Americans on August 29.

There is no evidence to support, or not support that a white "backlash" occurred following the 1-1-70 disturbance. In fact, not too many citizens are even aware that the incident occurred. While there is evidence to show that a white backlash occurred following the riots of the 1960's, this did not appear to happen following the 8-29-70 ELA riot. In fact, there appeared to have developed greater cohesion in the

RIOT ANALYSIS FRAMEWORK

Circumstance-condition found in 1960's riots	ELA 1-1-70 Riot	ELA 8-29-70 Riot	ELA 9-16-70 Riot	
1. Socio-economic, political & psychological oppression	yes	yes	yes	yes
2. Evidence of racism	yes	yes	yes	yes
3. Feeling of exploitation	yes	yes	yes	yes
4. Lack influence and communication means	yes	yes	yes	yes
5. Feeling of powerlessness	yes	yes	yes	yes
6. Hostility toward law and government	yes	yes	yes	yes
7. Outburst precipitated by routine arrest	yes	no	in part	no
8. Police symbolized white power	yes	yes	yes	yes
9. Perception of police brutality and double standard of justice	yes	yes	yes	yes
10. a. Commodity riot	yes	yes	yes	no
b. Communal riot	no	no	in part	yes
11. a. Deaths resulted from police force	yes	no deaths	yes(2)	no deaths
b. Injuries resulted from police force	yes	?	yes	yes
c. Police injuries	yes	?	yes	yes
12. Absence of organized conspiracy	yes	yes	yes	yes
13. Carnival spirit prior to riot	yes	yes	yes	yes
14. 1st phase: police stoned, crowds collect, tension mounts	yes	no	yes	yes
15. 2nd phase: breaking of windows and looting	yes	yes	yes	yes
16. 3rd phase:				
a. Arson, firebombs	yes	no	yes	yes
b. Police countermeasures	yes	no	yes	yes
17. Police escalate riot by:				
a. Too little reaction	yes	?	no	no
b. Overreaction	yes	no	yes	no
18. Local citizens allowed to handle disorder; minimum police intervention approach	yes	no	no	yes
19. Preventive appropriate police force approach	yes	?	no	yes
20. 3rd phase of riot a minority group-police confrontation	yes	?	all three phases yes	yes
21. Retaliatory violence for minority getting "too big"*	?	?	?	?
22. Force and violence can be successful social control technique*	?	?	?	?
23. Minority group use of violence may preclude reform* (backlash)	yes	no	no	?
24. Control of riots rather than treating basic cause of riots was adopted	yes	yes	yes	yes
25. Evidence of a hardening police attitude toward minority group and weakening of controls over police behavior	yes	yes	yes	yes
Total: "Yes" 27	14	22	22	
"No" 1	9	4	5	
"?" 2	7	2	3	
"In Part" 0	0	2	0	

*Items 21, 22 and 23 represent theoretical propositions or hypothetical statements rather than circumstances, conditions or behavior observed in the U.S. 1960's riots.

Mexican American community and a general support from the broader white community. This undoubtedly was a reason for the impressive public turnout for the September 16th parade.

Item 25 concerns abrasive police practices that occurred *after the riots* threatening "the civil peace in the slums and ghettos," and a "hardening of police attitudes and a weakening of traditional civil controls over their activities."[42] This is very much dangerously so in the Mexican American East Los Angeles community. Might this not be a form of "white backlash"? If it does not stop, it is because the dominant society *wishes that it not stop!*

As this piece goes to press, the Los Angeles community witnessed a fourth riot involving Chicanos and the police as on January 9, 1971, the Los Angeles Police Department dispersed a crowd of about 1,000 Chicano Moratorium demonstrators at the department's Parker Center headquarters. The Chicanos were protesting the brutality of the police in their transactions with barrio residents in the Chicano community. Forty-two persons (some injured) were arrested in the clash which was followed by a brief spree of window breaking in the downtown Los Angeles shopping area.[43] LAPD Chief Edward Davis blamed "swimming pool Communists" and Brown Berets "sophisticated in Bolshevik tactics" for the disturbance. Viewing the Chicano demonstration as child-like and hence applying a paternalistic solution to the problem, Chief Davis warned Mexican American parents that "they're (Communists) using the young Mexican Americans as prison fodder. And I suggest that the parents put a stop to it."[44] As a means of attempting to clarify the viewpoint of the Chicano Moratorium Committee which has scheduled another demonstration for January 31, 1971, the following letter was submitted to the Los Angeles Times for publication:

Dear Editor,

We, of the Chicano Moratorium Committee are writing to you in response to your plea for some social facts to understand the strained situation between Chicanos and the police. The current conflict between Chicanos and the police is a political confrontation that historically has its roots in the mid 1800's when another police government body—the U.S. Army—forcibly took the land away from the Mexicans in this area. Subsequent brutal acts by border patrol and immigration law enforcement officers frequently leading to reciprocal violent defensive reactions by Mexicans made the situation more acute. The deportation of 312,000 persons of Spanish-surname—many American citizens—by Immigration law enforcement officials during the Great Depression for political-economic reasons, further strained and intensified the anger of people of Mexican descent toward the law and law enforcement.

Denying the Mexican American population in Los Angeles protection from rioting vigilante servicemen during the 1943 "Zoot Suit" riots, raised further doubts in Mexican Americans as to who it actually was that the police were there to "protect and serve." Labeling the riots "Zoot Suit" only served to reveal the racist motivations of the press by applying a historically permanent label that implied "the Mexicans did it," thereby simultaneously protecting the servicemen from public ridicule. The Sheriff's Department Captain Ayers "biological basis" racist report to the county grand jury during this period—that people of Mexican descent were biologically prone to criminal behavior—further intensified public racist attitudes toward Mexican Americans which also had the effect of permitting more aggressive police behavior toward a "biological crime prone" population. The report was commended as an "intelligent statement" by LAPD Chief Horral. Subsequently in 1960, Chief Parker revealed his racist attitudes toward Mexican Americans (and absorbed by LAPD) when he said that Mexican Americans were like "wild Indians from the mountains of Mexico," and that genes had to be considered when discussing the "Mexican problem." And today, a new label "Communists" is being applied to Mexican Americans by Chief Davis to discourage Mexican American protest while simultaneously eliciting public support for police violence.

It has been a Chicano experience that when he has attempted to peacefully protest against the educational institutions that produce an excessively high Chicano student drop-out rate; the wealthy Catholic Church that has milked the Chicano of his meager financial resources with no reciprocal benefits; and the U.S. involvement in the Vietnam war which has resulted in a severe overrepresentation of Chicano deaths—in effect depriving the Chicano community of its future youth resource—these efforts have always been met with police initiated political violence. In this respect the police have been given and have adopted, a sentry role to protect and serve these institutions that are gradually socially and psychologically destroying a class of people with a rich, proud heritage and tradition. Chicanos, by day and night, are reminded of their low status in society by a sentry helicopter that was not a "called-for" service by the Chicano community. The Chicano lives in a totalitarian-like atmosphere within a broader Los Angeles community that is comfortably (with the exception of the black community) functioning as a democracy. Being a population group numbering close to a million people in this area, we have no city or county elected Mexican American political representative to assist us with our problems. Our behavior can only be seen as a normal response to an abnormal condition created by those in political power.

The police brutality that occurs ten to twenty times a month in East Los Angeles again communicates to us our worth to the broader society that does not seem to care. We have not received federal protection against this abuse since the law was initially enacted in 1872. We desperately wish to be a part of this society but your powerful sentry repeatedly sends us away bleeding. We are now directly protesting against the sentry. But it is not only the day to day police brutality that we have experienced for numerous decades that gravely concerns us, but

rather a far more severe problem that our society isn't even aware of, and that is that the police are increasingly becoming a more powerful, political force in our increasingly less free democratic society. The recent Skolnick Report to the National Commission on the Causes and Prevention of Violence warned that "the ranks of law enforcement have become an ultraconservative social force which shrilly protests positive change." The Report also concluded that the increasing police militancy is hostile to the aspirations of dissident groups in society and that the police view protesters as a danger to our American political system. Although this is a national report, the situation is identical in Los Angeles as confirmed not only by our experience, but by the recent UCLA Report of the 5-5-70 student-police confrontation which stated that "police attack was discriminatory, focusing on minority group members and long hairs."

Rather than calling off our protests and return to a life of fear under police totalitarian aggression, we have to continue to protest for survival purposes. If Chicanos lose their right to protest in society because of police political violence, you likewise are losing your freedom in America. In this respect our insistence of the right to protest guarantees the right of *all* people in America to protest. If we allow police violence to intimidate us, it is really the broader society that is victimized![45]

Sincerely,
Rosalio Munoz,
Chicano Moratorium Committee
Los Angeles

REFERENCES AND NOTES

1. Report of the National Advisory Commission on Civil Disorders. (New York: Bantam Books, 1968), p. 206.
2. Hugh Davis Graham and Ted Robert Gurr. Violence In America: Historical and Comparative Perspectives. (New York: Bantam Books, 1969), p. 420.
3. Ibid., p. 418.
4. Ibid., p. 419.
5. Ibid.
6. Ibid., p. 420.
7. Ibid., p. 421.
8. Ibid., p. 805.
9. Ibid.
10. Ibid., pp. 813-814.
11. Daniel Walker. Rights In Conflict. (New York: Signet Books, 1968), p. 3.
12. Richard A. Chikota and Michael C. Moran. Riot in the Cities. (Rutherford: Fairleigh Dickinson University Press, 1970), p. 107.
13. Ibid.
14. Public Law 90-351, 90th Congress, H.R. 5037, June 19, 1968, Omnibus Crime Control and Safe Streets Act of 1968, Part C, Section 301, pp. 2-3.
15. Urban America, Inc., and The Urban Coalition. One Year Later. (New York: Frederick A. Praeger, publishers, 1969), p. 115.
16. Belvedere Citizen, Thursday, November 21, 1968, p. 1.
17. One Year Later, p. 115.
18. Eastside Sun, Thursday, December 3, 1970, p. 1.
19. Los Angeles Times, Part I, Friday, January 2, 1970, p. 3.
20. "Police-Community Relations In East Los Angeles, California," A Report of the California State Advisory Committee to the United States Commission on Civil Rights, October, 1970, p. 14.
21. Ibid., p. 15.
22. Ibid., p. 16.

23. La Raza, El Barrio Communications Project, P.O. Box 31004, Los Angeles, p. 2.
24. "Police-Community Relations," p. 18.
25. Delfino Varela. "A Walk in the Sun." Regeneracion, Volume 1, No. 6, 1970, p. 6.
26. Los Angeles Times, Wednesday, September 16, 1970, Part I, p. 25.
27. Ibid.
28. Ibid.
29. Ibid.
30. Ibid.
31. Ibid.
32. Ibid.
33. Los Angeles Times, Thursday, September 17, 1970, Part I, p. 26.
34. Los Angeles Times, Wednesday, September 16, 1970, Part I, p. 3.
35. Ibid.
36. Los Angeles Times, Thursday, September 17, 1970, Part I, p. 3.
37. Los Angeles Herald-Examiner, Thursday, September 17, 1970, p. A-6.
38. Los Angeles Times, Thursday, September 17, 1970, Part I, p. 3.
39. Los Angeles Times, Friday, September 18, 1970, Part I, p. 30.
40. Ibid.
41. James P. Comer. Violence in America, pp. 460-461.
42. One Year Later, p. 114.
43. Los Angeles Times, Wednesday, January 27, 1971, Part I, p. 19.
44. Los Angeles Times, Friday, January 15, 1971, Part I, p. 1.
45. The letter in its original form was obtained from Mr. Munoz. The edited version of the letter was published by the Los Angeles Times on Saturday, January 23, 1971, Part II, p. 4. The editor, Anthony Day, edited out comments about Chief Horral, Chief Parker, Chief Davis and practically all of paragraph four. This form of editing does not allow the general reader to have sufficient information upon which to make a more intelligent evaluation of the police-Chicano conflict. Although perhaps not intended, the effect is one of eliciting more support for the police which then might tend to escalate the conflict.

CHAPTER 7 MEXICAN AMERICANS AND THE ADMINISTRATION OF JUSTICE IN THE SOUTHWEST: SUMMARY OF A REPORT OF THE UNITED STATES COMMISSION ON CIVIL RIGHTS, 1970

INTRODUCTION

The U.S. Commission on Civil Rights undertook its study of *Mexican Americans and the Administration of Justice in the Southwest* on the basis of allegations that this second largest minority group in the country was being denied equal protection of the laws. Its purpose was to determine what, if any, factual basis existed for such allegations.

The Commission's investigations were made in Arizona, California, Colorado, New Mexico, and Texas where nearly four of the five million Mexican Americans in this country live. Its extensive staff research and field work in these States were supported by the findings at a Commission hearing in San Antonio, Texas in 1968, by a meeting of the Texas State Advisory Committee to the U.S. Commission on Civil Rights in 1967, by meetings of the California and New Mexico State Advisory Committees to the Commission in 1968, and by a questionnaire sent to 793 selected law enforcement agencies in the five States. The questionnaire sought to determine the respondents methods of recruitment and selection of officers, the extent to which they employed Mexican Americans, their officer training and assignment policies, and general information on police-community relations. In addition, the California Rural Legal Assistance, Inc. (CRLA) conducted a study for the Commission on service by Mexican Americans on grand juries in selected California counties.

The investigation covered the gamut of all categories of persons concerned—law enforcement officers, probation officers, prosecuting attorneys, judges, public defenders, attorneys in private practice, leaders of Mexican American organizations, and private citizens who alleged that they had experienced, or been witness to, discriminatory treatment.

Out of their words emerged a bleak picture of biased treatment that Mexican Americans receive from law enforcement agencies in the Southwest. It ranges from verbal abuse to violent beatings; from unwarranted arrests to improper use of bail; from underrepresentation in law enforcement agencies and juries to lack of serious inquiry into these allegations at all levels of government. Discriminatory treatment of Mexican Americans was not confined to a particular age group; juveniles as well as adults were treated with the same lack of sensitivity. The Commission found that this had brought about an attitude of distrust, fear, and hostility on the part of the Mexican American community toward the agencies of law enforcement, a situation aggravated by the inability of a large segment of the Spanish-speaking Mexican American community to communicate with law enforcement representatives who understand only English.

SOCIOLOGICAL DATA

(See Introduction to Report, which includes historical background)

The Mexican Americans living in Arizona, California, Colorado, New Mexico, and Texas constitute the largest cultural minority in the Southwest. According to the 1960 census, they numbered three and one-half million persons. Nationally, they numbered in excess of five million according to a U.S. Census estimate of November 1969. Approximately 85 percent of these persons were born in the United States, more than half of them children of native-born parents. Hence, they are not recent immigrants.

Mexican Americans in the Southwest are, for the most part, poor. More than half of the rural Spanish surnamed families, or 54 percent, and almost one-third of the urban Spanish surnamed families, or 31 percent, have annual incomes of less than $3,000, a figure below the poverty line.

They are burdened with a high incidence of unemployment. Those who can find work are generally limited to the unskilled categories of labor.

The educational attainment of the Mexican American falls substantially below that of the rest of the population in the region.

Mexican Americans are leaving the agricultural rural environment in increasing numbers. According to 1960 census figures, 70 percent of the Spanish surnamed population lived in urban areas. Here ethnic discrimination and low socioeconomic status restrict them to identifiable neighborhoods referred to as "barrios", the ghettos of Anglo*-oriented cities.

Many problems of social, cultural, and economic adjustment face the Mexican American in the Southwest. Of these, his relationship with law enforcement agencies in the administration of justice is among the foremost.

---

*The term Anglo is used throughout the report, as it is used throughout the Southwest, to refer to white persons who are not Mexican Americans or members of other Spanish surnamed groups. It has no derogatory connotations in the Southwest or in the Report or in this Summary.

TREATMENT OF MEXICAN AMERICANS

(Chapter 1 of the Report)

The Commission's investigations found widespread discrimination against Mexican Americans by law enforcement officials which ranged from verbal abuse to actual physical violence. Evidence shows that it is a fact of the Mexican American's life to be subjected to unduly harsh treatment by police, to be frequently arrested on insufficient grounds, to receive harassment and penalties disproportionately severe compared to those imposed on Anglos for the same acts.

The most extreme allegations of brutality came from residents of small towns where the consensus was that such incidents were not unusual. According to one Mexican American lawyer practicing in south Texas, conditions have not changed with the years and law enforcement officers are still determined to suppress any attempts to challenge abuses of their authority by Mexican Americans. He said:

And they think they have a right to. They think laws are made for them to use as they like. . . . And when you stand up and speak for your rights . . . they think that you're infringing on their rights. . . .

A businessman, a life-long resident of a California town, related to members of that State's Advisory Committee that he had been beaten by local police in 1963. He told them that, while having a soft drink at a bar, three policemen had told him to come outside for a talk. Since there were many migrant workers at that time in the town—whose normal Mexican American population was 20 percent—he thought they had made a mistake and told them "they were barking up the wrong tree." At that, he said, one of the officers called him "just another smart Mexican" threw him down, kicked him, handcuffed him, squeezed him into a car, and took him to jail where he was charged with drunkenness. He was later acquitted without difficulty. However, it took great effort to find a lawyer willing to bring a civil suit against police officers. Recovery was finally obtained against one of them. But, the man recalled as he told the story to the Committee:

In the process of trying to get me in they kicked me and kicked me and kicked me and I would get up and I said: 'Why are you doing this to me' . . . and they would say: 'Get in there, you damn Mexican.'

Widespread evidence compiled since the 1967 meeting of the Texas State Advisory Committee in Starr County reveals that this is neither an isolated nor unique instance of treatment Mexican Americans in the Southwest receive from law enforcement agencies. Many experiences were described to the Commission which exemplified what Mexican Americans allege to be common use of discriminatory, excessive police force against them.

A 13-year-old Mexican American boy in Los Angeles was severely beaten by three policemen in connection with an arrest for alleged burglary. According to the boy's mother, she was called at 1:30 a.m. by an officer who told her that her son had been arrested the preceding evening and had fallen and injured his head. The officer assured her the boy had sustained only a slight cut and there was nothing to worry about. As a result, she said she did not at first believe the boy when he said he had been beaten.

On the morning after the arrest, however, profuse bleeding from the head made it necessary for him to be taken to the hospital. There it was discovered that he already had 40 stitches in his head put in the previous night at the same hospital where the officers had taken him between the time of his arrest and their call to his mother. According to the son and several witnesses, the stitches were required because of the severity of the beating inflicted by the officers.

Some incidents reported to the Commission were so severe that they had resulted in the death of the victim. These generally involved cases in which resistance to arrest or attempt to escape from police custody had been made. Here, again, Mexican Americans have asserted that such vicious force would not have been used against an Anglo under similar circumstances.

Such an episode happened in Stanton, California. Two young men enroute home late one night were stopped, questioned, and searched by a police officer. The officer reportedly gave no reason for his ac-

tions but said he was going to take them to jail because they lacked identification. At that point, it was reported, one of the men, an 18-year-old, started to run away from the officer. A police car cruising at the scene stopped and an officer who saw the youth running fired his revolver and killed him. The officer was prosecuted on a charge of involuntary manslaughter but the case was dismissed after the prosecution presented its case.

A similar incident in Alpine, Texas was described to the Commission. According to reports of local residents, a police officer was chasing the car of a 16-year-old Mexican American in order to get information from him about his brother. The officer, it was reported, had a reputation for being rough and abusive and had, in the past, been accused of harassing the young man's brother and other Mexican Americans.

The chase ended when the boy stopped his car and fled on foot. The pursuing officer shot him once—fatally. A police investigation resulted in filing a charge of murder without malice against the officer and an indictment by the local grand jury. As of August 1969, the case had not come to trial.

The Commission heard numerous similar allegations that law enforcement officers in Albuquerque, Austin, Denver, El Paso, Los Angeles, San Antonio, and Tucson and in smaller communities in the Southwest also used excessive force against Mexican Americans. Although the Commission could not establish the validity of each of the complaints, their prevalence, as revealed by Commission investigations, indicates the existence of an overwhelming problem in human relations that calls for immediate corrective action.

OTHER FORMS OF ABUSE
(Chapter 1 of the Report)

Evidence was found that indicated the double standard of police activity has had a significant impact in alienating Mexican Americans from law enforcement officers. Nowhere is this more apparent than in police relations with juveniles.

Among the frequent allegations of discriminatory treatment against Mexican American young people, the Commission heard the following: that Anglo juvenile offenders were generally released without charge and put into custody of their parents while their Mexican American peers, charged with the same offense, were jailed or sent to a reformatory.

In Silver City, New Mexico, a 16-year-old boy, arrested for truancy, was jailed. According to his mother, the school principal and the probation officer reportedly offered the boy his choice of going to the State reformatory, joining the Job Corps, or leaving the State. "They do this for Spanish-speaking people, they give them this kind of choices. To Anglos, it is just a matter of going to their parents and solving this between them. That is the way it's done for one group and done differently for another," the mother observed. But this incident was something of an exception; usually officials do not bother to notify Mexican American parents when their children are arrested.

". . . whether engaged in delinquent activities or not, whether members of delinquent gangs or not, Mexican American boys in general perceive getting into trouble with the police as a natural state of affairs and staying out of trouble as a stroke of fortune."

This statement, based on extensive interviews with Mexican American youths in Los Angeles by Celia Heller, author of *Mexican American Youth: Forgotten Youth at the Crossroads,* reflects the frequency of arrests on "suspicion" and of dragnet "stop and frisk" practices in Mexican American neighborhoods. Such police practices have a particularly adverse effect on young people and prove especially disturbing to Mexican Americans, formerly addicts, who are on probation or parole and are trying to hold a job and reestablish themselves in the community.

Federal probation officers in Albuquerque reported that police often deliberately inform employers of the records of their employees who are former addicts. Alternatively, they arrest the parolee for investigation and detain him, with the result that he misses several days' work and loses his job.

In rural areas, Mexican Americans, especially migrant workers, find it difficult to obtain police protection when they need it. In urban areas, Mexican Americans feel the police are in the barrio to "keep them in line" not to protect them. Consequently, as a Los Angeles resident explained: "People do not see the police as protector. They prefer to seek a relative's help rather than risk an officer's suspicions."

INTERFERENCE WITH MEXICAN AMERICAN ORGANIZATIONAL EFFORTS
(Chapter 2 of the Report)

Law enforcement officers in the Southwest have blatantly interferred with Mexican American organizational efforts to improve the conditions of their lives.

This was vividly illustrated in a series of incidents in northern New Mexico in June 1967 which culminated in the so-called "Tierra Amarilla" raid.

On June 3, 1967 a meeting of the Alianza Federal de Mercedes, an organization more commonly known as the "Alianza" and established to improve the status of Mexican Americans in the Southwest, had been called in Coyote, a northern New Mexico town. A number of Mexican Americans have charged that Alfonso Sanchez, then district attorney for the First Judicial District of New Mexico who had jurisdiction over that section of the State, and other law enforcement officers had used all their resources to discourage and intimidate members from attending the meeting. Meanwhile, sheriffs' deputies and police were stopping cars enroute to the gathering place and handing out notes warning against attendance.

On June 2 and 3 Sanchez allegedly ordered the arrest of 11 officers of the Alianza. Some were arrested and taken to the courthouse in Tierra Amarilla for arraignment. At that point a group of armed Mexican Americans attempted a "Citizens' arrest" of the district attorney to prevent further arrests among their ranks. Violence flared, two law enforcement officers were wounded, and the invaders fled, reportedly taking two other officers with them as hostages.

Meanwhile, large numbers of Mexican Americans had been traveling to the meeting for several days from all parts of the State. On June 5, soon after the shooting in Tierra Amarilla, armed policemen—

sheriffs, State troopers, and National Guardsmen—surrounded the picnic grounds where the meeting was to be held and reportedly kept men, women, and children by force for more than 24 hours without shelter or drinking water. According to reports, there was no indication that more than a few of these victims had even been aware of the shooting at Tierra Amarilla.

A married couple gave the following account of this incident. "At the barbeque State police came and asked us to come out into the open and were told to sit on the floor which at the time was completely muddy and we did so. We were searched and during this time we couldn't go to the restroom and my wife was threatened by a State policeman that he would shoot her if she went to pick up a little child from the house near the camping site. We were not allowed to go to the outhouse if we were not accompanied by a guard. We were relased at the end of 24-hours." During their detention, approximately 80 armed State police, augmented by about 450 National Guardsmen, surrounded those gathered for the Alianza meeting. They were taken from the picnic facilities for interrogation but allowed to return at night where they found that all their food, left unattended by their abrupt departure, had burned and there was no food or water to be had.

Another man who had attended a gathering at Canjilon reported that policemen had put rifles behind his back and he was made to sit down for questioning. "They kept me and my 5-year-old son until the next day and we didn't have any drinking water or for cooking, so we had to drink water from a dirty water hole 'cause they wouldn't let us move. When I returned home . . .my boss had seen my picture on TV or in the news. He called me a criminal and said we were criminals and he fired me from my job. My son still is very scared and he cries every time he sees a policeman."

In southern Texas, the attitudes of Mexican Americans toward police interference were more intensely hostile and fearful than in any other area. These feelings were most acutely expressed against the Texas Rangers. In testimony before a Commission hearing, a Pharr, Texas farm

worker said: "Many people hate them, many people are afraid. . . . They will be hit or kicked. . . ." A Mexican American doctor from McAllen, Texas, said that he is afraid to be alone on the highway if there is a Ranger around. The extent of this fear is indicated by the fact that the mother of a State senator—Senator Joe Bernal of San Antonio—gave a party to celebrate her son's safe return from Starr County, where Senator Bernal had had an angry encounter with Captain A. Y. Allee of the Rangers. This was during a period from 1966 to 1967 when attempts by the United Farm Workers Organizing Committee (UFWOC) to organize Mexican American farm workers in Starr County led to harassment of the union organizers by the Texas Rangers. The Texas State Advisory Committee to the Commission found that the Texas Rangers had encouraged farm workers to cross picket lines, and stated that the harassment and intimidation by Rangers of UFWOC members, organizers, and sympathizers "gave the appearance of [the Rangers] being in sympathy with the growers and packers rather than the impartiality usually expected of law enforcement officers."

Thus, the Commission found that actual experience of injustice has formed the attitudes of Mexican Americans toward the police. Unhappy and biased contacts with law enforcement officials usually represent the norm for the average Mexican American citizen in his encounters with the law.

INADEQUACY OF REMEDIES
(Chapters 3 and 4 of the Report)

In the Southwest, administrative and judicial remedies for illegal police acts are inadequate to provide prompt and fair redress. In most southwestern cities the only body to which complaints of malpractice by law enforcement officers can be addressed is the local law enforcement agency itself. The fact that complaints must be lodged with the organization to which the accused officer belongs discourages already discouraged minority group members who have grievances from complaining.

In response to public pressure, some cities in the Southwest have established independent or quasi-independent police review boards; however, the effectiveness of these has been limited.

Redress against illegal police acts is worsened by the shortage of lawyers who will undertake to engage in law practices which include bringing suits against the police. The following apology heard by a victim of police brutality who was seeking a lawyer is typical: "I'm sorry, I can't do nothing about it because I've got to live here in this town and I am going to make bad relations if I do this."

Although most civil actions against policemen are brought under a Federal statute which makes liable any person acting under color of law who deprives any other citizen of his rights, privileges, and immunities under the Constitution, few cases based on police misconduct are brought to court. As of 1968, only two such cases had been brought by Mexican Americans and only one had been won by a Mexican American in California.

Criminal litigation on the basis of police brutality is rare. There are few reports of successful local prosecution of law enforcement officers for illegal actions against Mexican American citizens in the five States. In two cases where local authorities sought to prosecute the officer for homicide, each was dismissed by the judge after presentation of the prosecution's case.

Instances of police retaliation against complainants indicate that to pursue any remedy against police abuse may be dangerous to Mexican Americans. A Texas lawyer in advising a complainant said, " ' . . . you understand that beyond doubt there is going to be reprisals. You have to be a man of a lot of intestinal fortitude to take a witness stand in the man's town and tell what he had done to you. If you are willing to do this, well, I have the willingness and ability to go in and help you, because I'm not afraid.' And many times they never come back . . . and, really, you can't blame them. There are a lot of reprisals in these little towns."

Federal remedies have not been utilized commensurately with the authority they possess to effectively combat discriminatory action by law enforcement officials.

The Federal Bureau of Investigation conducts preliminary investigations of apparent violations of the United States Code (18 U.S.C. § 241 and 242). An investigation normally includes interviews with the victim, with the law enforcement officer who is the subject of the complaint, with some, but not necessarily all, of the witnesses, a check of medical records or reports, arrest records or reports, and photographs of the victim if the injury is recent and visible. The standard for initiating a prosecution is based on whether or not a violation can be proved. According to the Department of Justice, the probability of success in court is not a criterion.

Between January 1, 1965 and March 31, 1969, the Department of Justice received 256 complaints of police abuse from Spanish surnamed persons in the five States. The Commission examined 100 of these cases. During that period of time, only two prosecutions had been brought based on Mexican American complaints. In only one instance had a full investigation been made.

The Department of Justice reported that where action was not taken on a complaint, there usually was a question as to whether the police officers had used excessive force or whether the complainant resisted arrest. The Department reported that it required independent evidence that was not available. The Commission was of the opinion that more prosecutions could have been brought. In many cases, according to the Commission's findings, witnesses to the incident or persons who could testify about the complaint where physical abuse was involved, would have been accessible had they ever been sought out.

JURY EXCLUSION
(Chapter 5 of the Report)

The Commission found obvious and widespread underrepresentation of Mexican Americans on grand and petit juries in State courts in many areas of the Southwest.

To qualify as a juror, all of the five States require a minimum age of 21 years and residency of varying lengths. All of them disqualify for jury service persons convicted of felonies. Arizona, California, and Colorado require ability to speak and understand English. Texas requires jurors to be able to read and write English. New Mexico, alone, by statute does not require jurors to speak or understand English. All of the States except Colorado require jurors to be of sound mind, a requirement to which Texas and Arizona add that of "good moral character."

Generally, juries are selected from lists of eligible jurors compiled by jury commissioners appointed for that purpose. No mandatory statutory direction is given as to the source of names to be included in the list, except in Texas where, in specified populous counties, jury lists have to be compiled from tax lists.

Two factors assure that few Mexican Americans will serve on juries in the Southwest. One is the paucity of Mexican Americans in the pool of eligible jurors who make up the venire list, the group from which jury members are selected; the other is the existence of the peremptory challenge, the statutory right of the prosecutor or defense attorney in a criminal case to challenge a limited number of prospective (petit) jurors without giving reason for his action.

"It turns out to be a game trying to get your Mexican American juror on as the district attorney tries to get him off," said a Mexican American lawyer who practices in Los Angeles.

It is only recently that Mexican Americans have appeared on grand juries in Texas and they appear only in token numbers. In California, a study of 20 counties by the California Rural Legal Assistance, Inc. revealed that the percentage of Spanish surnamed grand jurors over a period of 8 to 12 years was significantly less than the Spanish surnamed percentage of the counties' population.

The alleged language barrier is an ubiquitous reason given to explain the dearth of Spanish surnamed grand jurors in the Southwest. But according to the 1960 census, Spanish surnamed persons over 25 years of age in the Southwest had completed 7.1 median years of schooling and, therefore, have at least a working grasp of the English language. This tends to dispel the argument that Mexican Americans are ineligible for jury service because of language disability.

Since, for the most part, Mexican Americans are in a low-income bracket, the argument is often advanced that grand jury service imposes an untenable financial burden on them. In Los Angeles, it appears unlikely that only four Mexican Americans earned incomes during the 12-year period [of the CRLA study] sufficient to enable them to serve on grand juries.

In a central Texas court, all of the jury commissioners queried in connection with a lawsuit to reform grand juries stated they selected individuals whom they knew personally. In addition, each said he knew whom he would select before the commissioners met as a body.

All of the judges questioned claimed that they had not deliberately avoided nominating Mexican Americans. Most, however, seemed wholly unaware of any obligation to select a cross section of the community for jury duty.

The Federal Jury Selection and Service Act of 1968 eliminated the "keyman system," by which the Federal jury commissioner conferred with persons in the community he considered knowledgeable to ask them to select potential jurors.

Under this act individuals are deemed eligible for jury service in Federal courts if they: possess U.S. citizenship; are at least 21 years of age; fulfill local residency requirements; have the ability to speak English and to read and write it sufficiently well to fill out a juror qualification form. Those receiving the questionnaires are selected at random from voter registration lists or lists of persons actually voting. However, most States juries are still selected by the "keyman system."

The underrepresentation of Mexican Americans on juries breeds a lack of confidence in the impartiality of judgments and reenforces the feeling of bias held by the jury. Defendants often plead guilty to avoid any prejudices by the court.

In civil suits, the property and life of a Mexican American is considered to be worth less than an Anglo's. A Texas attorney reported that "insurance company adjusters had told him an injured or dead Mexcian [American] isn't worth as much as an injured or dead Anglo." To give an example, the trial of a civil suit involving a Mexican American resulted in a hung jury because one juror said that "No Mexican American is worth ten thousand dollars."

The Commission found that grand and petit juries in the Southwest do not represent a proportionate amount of the Mexican American population of the region. Discriminatory factors, such as the wide discretion vested in officials with the duty of choosing juries and use of the peremptory challenge to strike Mexican Americans from the potential jury lists, play a significant role in creating this unrepresentative situation.

BAIL

(Chapter 6 of the Report)

All five Southwestern States guarantee the right to bail in their respective constitutions before conviction on noncapital cases. They also forbid excessive bail. The Commission's findings revealed that local officials in the Southwest abuse their discretion in imposing excessive bail or withholding the right to it altogether.

As an example, included in the information gathered by the Texas State Advisory Committee at its 1967 meeting were data presented by a staff organizer for the United Farm Workers Organizing Committee (UFWOC) who reported that he had been arrested during the organization's 1966-67 strike for allegedly threatening the life of a Texas Ranger. His bail was set at $2,000, the maximum fine for the offense. Later that day a well known, wealthy landowner from Starr County agreed to sign a property bond for his release. Local officials, however, refused to accept it, despite the credentials of the Starr County resident and demanded copies of his tax records to prove he owned enough property to cover the bond. As a result, the organizer remained in jail from the time of his arrest on a Friday afternoon until the following Monday because the necessary proof could not be obtained at the closed county courthouse until then.

Many Mexican Americans do not fare as well. Bail is often beyond the amount the fine or penalty would be if charges were proven. The man who cannot afford this must, therefore, remain in jail until trial.

In some cases, when bail is unavailable, Mexican Americans are held for several days while the district attorney's office determines whether or not charges are to be filed. During this period the men being held are questioned and an investigation is conducted but they are not eligible for release on bail. In many cases, the district attorney's office decides to release the person rather than file an information charging him with an offense.

In some parts of the Southwest, complaints were made that law enforcement officers had not made it sufficiently clear to Mexican American defendants that their initial judicial appearance was not the trial itself and they had not been found guilty of a crime. As a result, many defendants did not show up for trial, forfeited their bail, and, thus, established a criminal record in addition to leaving themselves open to arrest in the future for failure to appear at trial.

An investigator for the Alamosa County District Attorney's office in the San Luis Valley, a poor rural district in southern Colorado, told a staff interviewer that Mexican American defendants are encouraged not to appear at trial and to forfeit their bail. He disclosed another and even more distressing problem resembling involuntary servitude or peonage, which is a violation of Federal law.

Sometimes, he said, during the harvest season, local farmers pay the fines of jailed Mexican Americans on condition that the men work for the farmer until the fine is paid off. In such instances, he explained, the police magistrate gives the farmer a "discount" which reduces the fine. This fact is not communicated to the Mexican American who, unknowingly, works out the time representing the original amount.

In Denver, Los Angeles, and Phoenix, an alternative to the traditional cash bail system is being used. This means that the defendant is released on his own recognizance under a promise to return to trial.

Release of the defendant on his own recognizance has had mixed success. It has made possible the release of persons who cannot afford bail but who, after a brief investigation, are considered to be good risks to return for trial.

This system has been established in Los Angeles and Phoenix although, in the latter city, a superior court probation officer and an attorney declared that Mexican Americans could not benefit from it as easily as Anglos. In Artesia, New Mexico, a Mexican American, long a resident of the area, was refused such release when he was arrested for drunken and reckless driving and he did not achieve it until a Commission attorney spoke with the justice of the peace. In Denver an undersheriff reported the new system of release by personal recognizance had worked well. Only 5 percent of the defendants had failed to return for trial. He added, however, that in his opinion standards applied to each defendant seeking release on his own recognizance were too rigid.

Commission investigators found that, almost without exception, the system of bail in the Southwest is frequently used more severely against Mexican Americans than against Anglos and becomes another form of discrimination.

REPRESENTATION BY COUNSEL
(Chapter 7 of the Report)

A sizable proportion of both rural and urban Spanish surnamed families in the Southwest live on incomes of less than $3,000 per year. This, obviously, means they cannot afford private counsel in either civil or criminal matters. In misdemeanor cases, court-appointed counsel is not available except in California and, as a result, Mexican Americans appearing in lower-level courts are subject to injustices. Poor quality of legal representation is the rule and not the exception even in cases where court-appointed counsel is required. Some parts of the Southwest house large concentrations of poor Mexican Americans but maintain no legal aid programs to assist indigents in civil matters.

Most of the small communities and rural areas of the Southwest have rejected federally assisted programs because local conservative elements have labeled them as "socialistic."

Public defenders are often overworked and court-appointed attorneys are sometimes unconcerned, inexperienced, or both. Most of the 650 Mexican American attorneys in the Southwest practice in the cities but, even here, Mexican Americans are underrepresented in the legal profession. The number of Mexican American lawyers in small communities and rural areas is far fewer. Some programs, notably the Mexican American Legal Defense and Educational Fund (MALDEF) are in process of helping train Mexican American lawyers. To compound the present problem, attorneys in the Southwest are sometimes reluctant to accept Mexican Americans as clients because their cases are controversial or are not sufficiently rewarding financially.

ATTITUDES OF MEXICAN AMERICANS TOWARD THE COURTS
(Chapter 8 of the Report)

Because of their dismal experiences with the courts, many Mexican Americans are distrustful of them and are convinced that, being insensitive to Mexican American culture and background, they are insensitive to the current needs of the Mexican American. These hostile feelings are most apparent in northern New Mexico where descendants of the Spanish settlers have lost their land and, thus, their means of livelihood, often through the legal system imposed on them by the Anglos who settled on their own territory.

The feeling that law is being used to create and perpetuate injustice has led to a conflict of crisis dimensions in northern New Mexico where tension between local residents and the Forest Service is high, difficulties are encountered in enforcing the law, and the people have no confidence in the courts.

In northern New Mexico the director of a development program commented to the Commission that: "It seems that if we are going to have justice, then we must also develop the kind of sensitivity we need for the values of the people to whom the justice is being directed."

ROLE OF LANGUAGE DIFFERENCES
(Chapter 9 of the Report)

Although many Mexican Americans in the Southwest are bilingual, a great many others know little or no English and are, consequently, handicapped by a language disability in their relations with law enforcement officers or in courtroom proceedings. Even simple contacts in these surroundings can escalate into serious situations but very few law enforcement agencies have made an effort to provide their officers with instruction in conversational Spanish.

English is the language most often used in the courtrooms of the Southwestern States but of the five, only California and Colorado make it mandatory to do so although few judges in that area speak Spanish.

This creates additional difficulties for the Mexican American who may know enough English to "get by" but cannot be articulate about complicated legal matters. An illustration of this is found in the case of a husband and wife who were declared to be unfit parents based on a complaint filed by the local welfare department of Silver City, New Mexico. Lacking legal counsel and unable to describe their situation adequately, the parents had to see three of their children removed from their custody. Their supply of English was simply not equal to the demands of the court and of justice.

Similar difficulties in communication with probation and parole officers limit the Mexican American's opportunity to be placed on probation or parole instead of in jail and can create obstacles toward getting him his freedom. Often parolees cannot understand their rights and, thus, are deprived of them.

Lack of adequate interpreters creates still another obstacle toward equitable treatment in the courtroom for Mexican Americans. New Mexico is unique among the five Southwestern States in clearly establishing the right to interpretation. But the use of qualified interpreters is not widespread in the courts of the Southwest. Often makeshift arrangements are made and even in cases where professioal interpreters are used, members of the Mexican American community have criticized them as being improperly trained or unskilled to work as court interpreters.

A defendant's rights to have an interpreter provided for him has received relatively little attention in the Federal courts. To date there have been no Federal court decisions on whether a non-English speaking defendant in a criminal case in a State court has a constitutional right to have an interpreter appointed.

PARTICIPATION IN AGENCIES OF LAW ENFORCEMENT AND JUSTICE
(Chapters 10–11 of the Report)

Private citizens and public officials, including judges, lawyers, and probation officers, expressed to the Commission their belief that the fear which many Mexican Americans feel toward law enforcement agencies could be dispelled by increasing the number of Mexican American law enforcement officers at all levels of authority. At present, these are significantly lacking.

The majority of the law enforcement agencies which responded to the Commission questionnaire indicated that they had made no particular effort to recruit Mexican Americans in the last 2 years. They cited their educational and physical fitness standards as being probable deterrents to Mexican American applicants. But the Commission feels that the agencies' failures to initiate recruitment programs particularly designed to attract and stimulate the Mexican American into this area of work is a major factor in his lack of representation in law enforcement bodies.

The larger the city, the poorer the record. Only nine agencies indicated that they sponsored a recruiting program in local Spanish language newspapers and only 16 agencies reported using local radio and television stations for recruitment purposes.

In testimony before the Commission hearing in San Antonio, the director of the Texas Department of Public Safety stated that only 38 Mexican patrolmen were employed in the department. He admitted the figure was arrived at by classifying uniformed officers serving in the drivers' licenses service and the motor vehicle inspection service as "patrolmen."

Failure to employ more Mexican Americans in this area has patently created additional problems in police-community relations and has further weakened the slender confidence of the Mexican American in the American law enforcement system.

The situation is aggravated by the shortage of Mexican American judges and prosecutors. Of the 58 Federal district judges, only two are Spanish surnamed. Nine hundred and sixty-one judges are serving on State courts in the five States. Of these,

32, or 3.0 percent, are Spanish surnamed.

Of the 590 State district attorneys and public prosecutors and their assistants, only 20, or slightly more than 3 percent, are Spanish surnamed.

Similar inequities exist in Federal agencies serving the five Southwest States. Despite the Government's long-established policy of equal employment opportunity and its recent positive emphasis on it, Department of Justice statistics at the time of the study showed that out of a total of 6,079 employees, 448 or 7.36 percent, were Mexican American. For the most part, these employees held lower grade jobs. Two and a half percent were in junior supervisory and junior executive grades but in the executive and higher supervisory grades only nine of the 1,068 employees—about one-third of 1 percent—were Mexican American. Mexican Americans constituted only three of the top 772 FBI employees in these States and only six of the 196 top grade employees in the Bureau of Immigration and Naturalization.

The Commission's research has disclosed that a great abyss separates the Mexican American and the Anglo communities in the five Southwest States it studied. On the one hand, it found that the Mexican American community felt itself intimidated and, based on personal experience of harassment, had become hostile to law enforcement agencies. On the other hand, it found that the Anglo community, which traditionally has regarded the Mexican American people and culture as inferior, has treated them with indifference and disrespect.

Nowhere are these inimical attitudes more pronounced nor do more damage to both communities than in the administration of justice. Understanding and comprehensive steps must be taken to close the abyss and create a just society for all American citizens in the Southwestern part of the Nation.

FINDINGS
(As They Appear in Report)
1. Police misconduct

There is evidence of widespread patterns of police misconduct against Mexican Americans in the Southwest. Such patterns include:

(a) incidents of excessive police violence against Mexican Americans;
(b) discriminatory treatment of juveniles by law enforcement officers;
(c) discourtesy toward Mexican Americans;
(d) discriminatory enforcement of motor vehicle ordinances;
(e) excessive use of arrests for "investigation" and of "stop and frisk";
(f) interference with attempts to rehabilitate former narcotics addicts.

2. Inadequate protection

Complaints also were heard that police protection in Mexican American neighborhoods was inadequate in comparison to that in other neighborhoods.

3. Interference with Mexican American organizational efforts

In several instances law enforcement officers interfered with Mexican American organizational efforts aimed at improving the conditions of Mexican Americans in the Southwest.

4. Inadequacy of local remedies for police malpractice

Remedies for police malpractice in the Southwest were inadequate. For example:

(a) in most Southwestern cities the only places where individuals can file complaints against the police are the police departments themselves. Internal grievance procedures did not result in adequate remedies for police malpractice;
(b) some cities in the Southwest have established independent or quasi-independent police review boards but these have not provided effective relief to complainants;
(c) civil litigation by Mexican Americans against police officers accused of civil rights violations is infrequent;
(d) there are few instances of successful local prosecutions of police officers for unlawful acts toward Mexican Americans;
(e) there have been instances of retaliation against Mexican Americans who complained about law enforcement officers to the local police department or to the FBI.

5. Federal remedies

(a) Agents of the Federal Bureau of Investigation have often failed to interview important witnesses in cases of alleged violation of 18 U.S.C. 242 or interviewed such witnesses in a perfunctory and hostile manner.

(b) More aggressive efforts to implement 18 U.S.C. 242 by the Department of Justice are needed.

6. Underrepresentation of Mexican Americans on juries

There is serious and widespread underrepresentation of Mexican Americans on grand and petit State juries in the Southwest. The Commission found that:

(a) neither lack of knowledge of the English language nor low-incomes of Mexican Americans can explain the wide disparities between the Mexican American percentage of the population and their representation on juries;

(b) judges or jury commissioners frequently do not make affirmative efforts to obtain a representative cross section of the community for jury service;

(c) the peremptory challenge is used frequently both by prosecutors and defendants' lawyers to remove Mexican Americans from petit jury venires.

The underrepresentation of Mexican Americans on grand and petit juries results in distrust by Mexican Americans of the impartiality of verdicts.

7. Bail

Local officials in the Southwest abuse their discretion in the following ways:

(a) in setting excessive bail to punish Mexican Americans rather than to guarantee their appearance for trial;

(b) in failing to give Mexican American defendants an opportunity to be released until long after they were taken into custody;

(c) by applying unduly rigid standards for release of Mexican Americans on their own recognizance where such release is authorized.

In many parts of the Southwest, Mexican American defendants are hindered in their attempts to gain release from custody before trial because they cannot afford the cost of bail under the traditional bail system.

8. Counsel

There are serious gaps in legal representation for Mexican Americans in the Southwest. For example:

(a) the lack of appointed counsel in misdemeanor cases results in serious injustices to indigent Mexican American defendants;

(b) even in felony cases, where counsel must be provided for indigent defendants, there were many complaints that appointed counsel often was inadequate;

(c) where public defender's offices are available to indigent criminal defendants, they frequently did not have enough lawyers or other staff members to adequately represent all their clients, many of whom are Mexican Americans;

(d) in parts of the Southwest there are not enough attorneys to provide legal assistance to indigent Mexican Americans involved in civil matters;

(e) many lawyers in the Southwest will not handle cases for Mexican American plaintiffs or defendants because they are controversial or not sufficiently rewarding financially;

(f) despite the enormous need for lawyers fluent in Spanish and willing to handle cases for Mexican American clients, there are very few Mexican American lawyers in the Southwest.

9. Attitudes toward the courts

Mexican Americans in the Southwest distrust the courts and think they are insensitive to their background, culture, and language. The alienation of Mexican Americans from the courts and the traditional Anglo-American legal system is particularly pronounced in northern New Mexico.

10. Language disability

Many Mexican Americans in the Southwest have a language disability that seriously interferes with their relations with agencies and individuals responsible for the administration of justice. The Commission found:

(a) there are instances where the inability to communicate with police officers has resulted in the unnecessary aggravation of routine situations and has created serious law enforcement problems;

(b) Mexican Americans are disadvantaged in criminal cases because they cannot understand the charges against them nor the proceedings in the courtroom;

(c) in many cases Mexican American plaintiffs or defendants have difficulty communicating with their lawyers, which hampers preparation of their cases;

(d) language disability also adversely affects the relations of some Mexican Americans with probation and parole officers.

11. Interpreters

Interpreters are not readily available in many Southwestern courtrooms:

(a) in the lower courts, when interpreters were made available, they are often untrained and unqualified;

(b) in the higher courts, where qualified interpreters were more readily available, there has been criticism of the standards of their selection and training and skills.

12. Employment by law enforcement agencies

Employment of Mexican Americans by law enforcement agencies throughout the five Southwestern States does not reflect the population patterns of these areas. The Commission found that:

(a) neither police departments, sheriffs' offices, nor State law enforcement agencies employ Mexican Americans in significant numbers;

(b) State and local law enforcement agencies in the Southwest do not have programs of affirmative recruitment which would attract more Mexican American employees;

(c) failure to employ more Mexican Americans creates problems in law enforcement, including problems in police-community relations.

13. Courts and prosecutors

Other agencies in charge of the administration of justice—courts, district attorneys' offices, and the Department of Justice—also have significantly fewer Mexican American employees than the proportion of Mexican Americans in the general population.

RECOMMENDATIONS
Law enforcement
(As They Appear in Report)

Recommendation 1—Federal civil actions. The Commission recommends that Congress enact legislation authorizing civil actions by the Attorney General against law enforcement officers and agencies to enjoin patterns of discriminatory treatment as well as interference with lawful organizational efforts of minorities in furtherance of their civil rights.

Recommendation 2—Municipal liability. The Commission recommends that Congress amend 42 U.S.C. § 1983, which provides Federal civil remedies for police malpractice, to make the governmental bodies who employ officers jointly liable with those officers who deprive persons of their civil rights.

Recommendation 3—Improved Federal investigations. The Commission recommends that the Department of Justice review and reivse its procedures for ascertaining whether there have been violations of 18 U.S.C. 241, 18 U.S.C. 242, and Title I of the Civil Rights Act of 1968, the statutes which impose criminal penalties for misconduct of police officers toward citizens. Such measures should include:

(a) the requirements of a full, rather than merely a preliminary, investigation by the Federal Bureau of Investigation in a higher percentage of cases before a decision is made that a complaint lacks prosecutive merit;

(b) increased supervision of the Bureau's investigative practices, including more frequent reinvestigation of complaints by the Department's attorneys.

Recommendaton 4—Federal enforcement program. The Commission recommends that the Civil Rights Division increase the manpower available for prosecuting violations of 18 U.S.C. 241 and 242 by law enforcement officials, including:

(a) the hiring of a number of criminal lawyers specializing in prosecution and

(b) the establishment of a unit of independent investigators.

Recommendation 5—State remedies. The Commission recommends that States take steps to control and lessen the injuries to individual rights created by police abuse of authority. Such steps should include administrative procedures for rapid and adequate compensation of claims for injuries suffered through police malpractices.

Recommendation 6—Local remedies. The Commission recommends that internal complaint procedures of police departments be handled by independent agencies or boards within the departments with an independent investigative staff and the power to recommend appropriate disciplinary action against officers guilty of misconduct. A complainant should have a right to be present at the hearings of such agencies or boards and be represented by counsel who may cross-examine witnesses.

Juries

Recommendation 1—Federal legislation relating to State juries. The Commission recommends that Congress enact legislation to ensure that no person be excluded from service as a grand or petit juror on State juries on account of race, color, religion, sex, national origin, or economic status. This statute should require the revision of State jury selection systems, substituting random selection of jurors on the basis of objective and comprehensive lists, such as voter registration lists or actual voting lists, for keyman systems or other systems vesting undue discretion in judges, jury commissioners, or clerks. The Federal statute should also:

(a) require State courts to keep records of jury selection by race and major ethnic categories, including Spanish surname. Such records also should include the race and major ethnic category of jurors peremptorily challenged;

(b) require State courts, where representative panels result in an unrepresentative jury because members of a group are eliminated by English language disability, to call a proportionately larger number of persons from that group as veniremen, to ensure a fair chance of a representative jury;

(c) require the State to increase the pay of jurors and shorten the terms of grand juries, to facilitate service by poor people.

Bail

Recommendation 1—Bail reform. The Commission recommends that the States should enact bail reform legislation designed to ensure that indigent defendants will not be unfairly detained in jail until trial because they are unable to afford the traditional cash bail.

Recommendation 2—Prompt proceedings. All persons should be brought before a judicial officer to be charged and given an opportunity to seek release on bail or on their own recognizance without unnecessary delay.

Representation by counsel

Recommendation 1—Legal assistance. Legal assistance should be made available to every indigent defendant immediately after his arrest in all criminal cases arising in State and local courts regardless of the nature of the charge.

In order to implement this recommendation, the State should establish statewide systems of legal representation for defendants in all criminal cases.

Recommendation 2—Legal services programs. Congress should amend the Economic Opportunity Act of 1964 to repeal the provision which prohibits Legal Services Programs (LSP) funded by the Office of Economic Opportunity (OEO) from representing defendants in criminal cases.

Recommendation 3—Training programs for Mexican American lawyers. Congress should substantially increase the funds available to the Office of Economic Opportunity (OEO) for programs designed to help law schools recruit and train Mexican American law students.

Language disability and inequality before the law

Recommendation 1—Interpreters. The States in the Southwest should establish programs for the recruitment, training, and employment of court interpreters to be used in areas where there are large concentrations of Mexican Americans.

Recommendation 2—Bilingual personnel

(a) State and local governments in the Southwest should establish programs for training in coversational Spanish for those individuals responsible for the administration of justice in areas of the

Southwest where there are large concentrations of Mexican Americans.

(b) Bilingual capability in Spanish and English should be recognized by Federal, State, and local agencies responsible for the administration of justice as a special qualification for employment in areas of the Southwest where there are large concentrations of Mexican Americans.

Participation

Recommendation 1—Affirmative recruitment program. The Commission recommends that State and local law enforcement agencies establish:

(a) affirmative recruitment programs specially designed to increase the number of Mexican American law enforcement personnel;

(b) training programs to increase the ability of Mexican Americans and other minority persons employed by law enforcement agencies to obtain promotions to supervisory positions.

Recommendation 2—Qualifications. Law enforcement agencies shoud review their qualifications for appointment and eliminate those which may not be job-related and which may tend to discriminate against Mexican American applicants.

Recommendation 3—Judges. The President of the United States and the Governors of the five Southwestern States of Arizona, California, Colorado, New Mexico, and Texas should use their powers to appoint qualified Mexican American attorneys to the Federal and State courts.

Recommendation 4—Department of Justice. The Department of Justice, including the Federal Bureau of Investigation, should take affirmative action under its continuing equal employment opportunity program both to hire additional Mexican Americans in the Southwest and particularly to train and promote their present Southwestern Mexican American employees into supervisory and professional level positions. The Civil Service Commission should review and evaluate the equal employment opportunity of the Department of Justice to ensure that this program will:

. . . provide the maximum feasible opportunity to employees to enhance their skills so they may perform at their highest potential and advance in accordance with their abilities. . . .

CHAPTER 8 ON THE COST OF BEING A MEXICAN AMERICAN WORKER[1]

DUDLEY L. POSTON, Jr.
DAVID ALVÍREZ

There is a substantial amount of evidence suggesting definite income differences between Mexican Americans and Anglos. Among males 14 years of age and older in 1959, for example, Mexican American income as a percent of Anglo income varied from a high of 73 percent in California to a low of 49 percent in Texas.[2] By 1969 some progress had been made, but Mexican American income still varied between 81 percent of Anglo income in Arizona and California to 65 percent in Texas.[3]

Necessarily, part of the difference between Mexican American and Anglo income is due to educational and occupational differences,[4] since on the whole Mexican Americans show much lower levels of educational attainment and are more concentrated in the manual occupations, particularly those requiring few skills.[5] However, it is doubtful that all of the income differential owes to compositional factors; there is evidence, both direct and indirect, that Mexican Americans suffer discrimination in the labor market, and this is reflected in the amounts of income they receive. For instance, when compared with Anglos, Mexican Americans have higher rates of unemployment and underemployment, and thus tend to be underrepresented in certain industries and most unions (where wage scales generally are higher). They are also underrepresented in many of the better paying occupations, and in federal and state government as well.[6]

From Social Science Quarterly, 1973, 697-709.

[1]Revision of a paper presented at the annual meetings of the Society for the Study of Social Problems, New Orleans, Louisiana, August, 1972. The authors are grateful for financial, programming and clerical support from the Population Research Center, the University of Texas at Austin. We also thank Harley L. Browning and Frank D. Bean for helpful comments on an earlier draft of the paper.

[2]Harley L. Browning and S. Dale McLemore, *A Statistical Profile of the Spanish-Surname Population of Texas* (Austin: Bureau of Business Research, The University of Texas, 1964), p. 61.

[3]U.S. Bureau of the Census, *Census of Population: 1970. General Social and Economic Characteristics,* Final Report PC(1)-C 4, *Arizona,* C 6, *California,* C 45, *Texas* (Washington, D.C.: U.S. Government Printing Office, 1972).

[4]Walter Fogel, *Mexican Americans in Southwest Labor Markets* (Mexican-American Study Project, Advance Report 10, Graduate School of Business Administration, University of California, Los Angeles, October, 1967).

[5]U.S. Commission on Civil Rights, *Hearing Held in San Antonio, Texas, December 9-14, 1968* (Washington, D.C.: U.S. Government Printing Office, 1968), p. 785.

[6]*Ibid.*, pp. 786-787, 790-791, 1056-1058, 1073-1083, 1105-1117; see also Alfred J. Hernandez, "Civil Service and the Mexican American," in John H. Burma, ed., *Mexican Americans in the United States* (Cambridge, Mass.: Schenkman Publishing Company, 1970), pp. 171-179.

To what extent then are income differences between Mexican American and Anglos males due to educational and occupational differences, and to what extent are they due to minority status? The central purpose of this paper is to examine the cost of being a Mexican American male worker[7] after taking into consideration the differentials in occupation and education. Since the samples of Mexican American and Anglo males to be examined will be similar with respect to other relevant socioeconomic and demographic characteristics any income difference remaining will be interpreted as evidence of discrimination against Mexican Americans.

The methodology to be employed here is similar to that used by Siegel[8] in an investigation of income differences between black and white male workers. After removing the structural effects of education, occupation and region, he concluded that the cost of being a Negro worker was slightly in excess of a thousand dollars per year. Although our sample design is not the same as Siegel's, whenever possible, comparisons will be made throughout this analysis between Siegel's findings and ours.

DATA AND METHODS
Data

The data reported in this analysis were taken from the 1960 1/100 Public Use Sample compiled by the U.S. Bureau of the Census.[9] This data source provides detailed information for one percent of all individuals enumerated by the census in 1960, data previously available only in the form of aggregate tabulations. The accessibility of these data for a sample of individuals permits analyses heretofore not possible with a data base from the Bureau of the Census.

Spanish surname data

An analysis based on 1960 census data investigating income differences between Mexican American and Anglo male workers is to a certain degree handicapped by the quality of the Mexican American data. Mexican Americans *per se* were not enumerated in the 1960 census; instead they were identified on an ex post facto basis by the Bureau of the Census as "white persons of Spanish surname." Coders were instructed to classify a person as Spanish only if the name appeared on a list of about 7,000 Spanish surnames, a list compiled by the Immigration and Naturalization Serivce. Although this approach has been considered by some as preferable to the earlier Census practice of "having the enumerators identify persons in terms of race or of the use of the mother tongue,"[10] there are nonetheless certain limitations with the use of Spanish surnames.

The most important of course is the imperfect correspondence between Mexican Americans and persons of Spanish sur-

---

[7]This analysis focuses on males, rather than on males and females combined because of earlier evidence showing rather large income disparities between the sexes. Without a control for sex, the ethnic comparisons would be nowhere as clear. Cf. Dudley L. Poston, Jr., "On the Cost of Being a Female Worker," a paper presented at the annual meetings of the Southwestern Social Science Association, San Antonio, Texas, March, 1972.

[8]Paul M. Siegel, "On the Cost of Being a Negro," *Sociological Inquiry*, 35 (Winter, 1965), pp. 41-57. Fogel, *Mexican Americans in Southwest Labor Markets*, looked also at Mexican American and Anglo income differences but did not control for education and occupation simultaneously.

[9]U.S. Bureau of the Census, *One In a 100: A Public Use Sample of Basic Records from the 1960 Census*, Description and Technical Documentation (Washington, D.C.: U.S. Government Printing Office, March 16, 1971). In defense of an analysis which by time of publication is based on data more than 13 years old, we only note that the 1970 Public Use Sample tapes were not yet available when this analysis was written. The authors will undertake, however, a re-examination of the findings contained here with the 1970 data in early 1973, and the results from the two time periods will be compared.

[10]Browning and McLemore, *A Statistical Profile of the Spanish-Surname Population of Texas*, p. 2.

name. Theoretically, the use of surnames could either over- or under-enumerate the actual number of Mexican Americans in the population. But most do agree that the net result is under-enumeration.[11]

This is an important consideration in the interpretation of analyses involving Spanish surname data, since "white persons of Spanish surname" does not correspond precisely with Mexican American persons. However, our purpose here is not one of providing an accurate population count of Mexican Americans, but rather is a statistical comparison of income differences between Mexican American and Anglo males. Despite the fact that deficiencies in the Spanish surname data are present, we do not anticipate that improved data would greatly alter the analyses to be presented below.

Sample constraints

In selecting the sample of Mexican American and Anglo males, we decided to employ only those who were full-time workers, between the ages of 20 and 40, in predominantly urban occupations, and residing in one of the five southwestern states of Arizona, California, Colorado, New Mexico and Texas. Let us examine each of these constraints in turn.

An investigation of income differences between any two groups is very much dependent upon the distribution of full- versus part-time workers in each group. There is evidence in 1960 of proportionately greater part-time work among Mexican American heads of families than among Anglo heads.[12] And since incomes are usually less for part-time than for full-time workers, a comparison of average incomes between Mexican Americans and Anglos would exaggerate income differences. Accordingly, only fulltime workers from the two ethnic groups were allowed to enter the sample.

There are certain methodological problems in the identification of full-time workers, since a question of this nature is not asked directly by the census enumerator. We thus included in the sample those Mexican American and Anglo males who both (1) worked 40 or more weeks in 1959, and (2) worked 35 or more hours in the week preceding April 1, 1960, the date of the census enumeration. The obvious assumption here is that those who worked a full week during the week preceding the census enumeration were also working 35 or more hours in the 40 or more weeks they worked in 1959. This is the closest one can get to the full-time variable with data from the decennial census.

The second constraint placed on the sample of male workers was that of age; only those between the ages of 20 and 40 were included. (By allowing only Mexican Americans and Anglo males of these ages into the sample, it is felt the two groups would be more comparable than if no age limitations were imposed.) These age restrictions permitted the inclusion of a larger portion of native-born Mexican Americans than would have been the case if all males between the ages of 20 and 64 were included. Among Mexican Americans between the ages 20 to 39, 16.4 percent were foreign born, while among Mexican American men 40 to 64 years of age, 38.5 percent were foreign born.[13] Had all ages been included, the Mexican American component would have consisted of a larger proportion of foreign born persons with both little or no formal eductation and rather substantial language and cultural handicaps. Because of their inferior occupational and education positions,[14] income differences between the Anglo and Mexican American workers would have

---

[11]*Ibid.,* p. 3. Also see José Hernández, Leo Estrada and David Alvírez, "Census Data and the Problem of Conceptually Defining the Mexican American Population," *Social Science Quarterly,* this issue.

[12]Browning and McLemore, *A Statistical Profile of the Spanish-Surname Population of Texas,* p. 39.

[13]U.S. Bureau of the Census, *U.S. Census of Population: 1960,* Subject Reports, *Persons of Spanish Surname,* Final Report PC(2)-1B (Washington, D.C.: U.S. Government Printing Office, 1963), Table 2.

[14]On the socioeconomic characteristics of these older Mexican American workers, see Leo Grebler, Joan W. Moore and Ralph C. Guzman, *The Mexican American People: The Nation's Second Largest Minority* (New York: The Free Press, 1970), p. 219.

been greatly inflated if we included the older Mexican Americans.

Second, by not including persons beyond age 40 in the sample, only those workers who began work during and after World War II are examined. This is important because of the evidence that World War II was a turning point for Mexican Americans in terms of reduced discrimination, and increased economic and educational opportunities.[15] During and following the war many jobs were made available for the first time to Mexican Americans. And in terms of education, one post-war development was a major reduction of "separate but equal" schools in the southwest, thus resulting in higher quality education for Mexican Americans.[16] Finally, Mexican American veterans, more so than Anglos, have profitted from their experiences in the military service in terms of better jobs, higher incomes and increased educational opportunities.[17] In sum, this post-war cohort of Mexican Americans is quite different from preceding cohorts, if only in terms of decreased cultural barriers and increased socioeconomic status, and should thus be a better one to compare with Anglos in a study of income differentials. Any income difference between these two ethnic groups exclusive of compositional factors can more clearly be attributed to discrimination.

A third constraint imposed on the sample is the selection of the predominantly urban occupations. Farmers and farm managers, and farm laborers and foremen were excluded because of the well-documented findings on the economic retardation of

Mexican Americans in rural farm areas.[18] It is in the rural occupations that the greatest economic disparities exist. Since the proportionate representation for Mexican Americans was twice as great as the Anglos in these occupations in 1960,[19] including the agricultural occupations would have inflated even more the income differentials between the two ethnic groups.

Finally, the sample of male workers has a regional control. Only those workers from the five southwestern states are included. To a certain degree this constraint was forced upon us since 1960 Spanish surname data were available only for residents of these states. This is not a problem insofar as the Mexican American population is concerned because the greatest number of Mexican Americans (an estimated 87 percent in 1960)[20] reside in the Southwest. But in terms of the Anglo population we had two alternatives: take only those from the Southwest or use the entire United States sample. We decided in favor of the former since there are definite regional differences in terms of wages, dollar value, and possible hiring practices. A comparison of Mexican Americans from the Southwest with Anglos from the entire nation might very well be confounded by regional differences.[21]

The restrictions or constraints imposed on the sample of Mexican American and Anglo workers just described not only make the two ethnic groups more comparable with respect to the relevant demo-

[15]*Ibid.*, pp. 201, 302.

[16]Thomas P. Carter, *Mexican Americans in School: A History of Educational Neglect* (New York: College Entrance Examination Board, 1970), pp. 67-70.

[17]Whereas research has demonstrated that among Anglos, veterans are at a disadvantage socioeconomically with nonveterans, the opposite occurs among Mexican Americans. See James C. Miller, III and Robert Tollison, "The Implicit Tax on Reluctant Military Recruits," *Social Science Quarterly,* 51 (March, 1971), pp. 924-931, and Harley L. Browning, Sally C. Lopreato, and Dudley L. Poston, Jr., "Income and Veteran Status: Variations among Ethnic Groups," *American Sociological Review,* 38 (Feb. 1973), forthcoming.

[18]Irene B. Taeuber, "Migration and Transformation: Spanish Surname Populations and Puerto Ricans," *Population Index,* 32 (Jan., 1966), p. 13.

[19]Browning and McLemore, *Statistical Profile of the Spanish Surname Population of Texas,* p. 41.

[20]Grebler, *et al., Mexican American People,* p. 15.

[21]Although there may be important differences among the five southwestern states, sample size restrictions did not permit comparisons between or within states. However, since the position of Mexican Americans relative to Anglos is probably better in California than in Texas, we would predict that income differentials between the two groups would be underestimated in Texas and overestimated in California, with the other three states falling somewhere in between.

graphic and socioeconomic characteristics, but they also work to decrease the income differences between the two groups.

FINDINGS

We examine first the average incomes of Mexican American and Anglo full-time male workers at various levels of educational attainment for each of eight occupational categories.[22] Anglo-Mexican American income differences are then analyzed at each level of educational attainment, but after the effects of occupational composition have been removed. Finally, the analysis turns to the overall income differences between the two ethnic groups after eliminating the effects of both education and occupation. These findings should suggest the cost of being a Mexican American.

In Figures 1 through 8 are plotted for each occupational category the relationships between educational attainment and average income. The Mexican American curves are represented by dashed lines with solid lines indicating the curves for Anglos.[23]

---

[22]Since so few males are found in the occupational category of private household workers, this occupational group was also deleted from the analysis.

[23]In constructing these 8 scatter diagrams we followed Siegel's procedures and grouped the educational data accordingly:

0-7 years of school completed	6
8 years of school completed	8
1-3 years of high school completed	10
4 years of high school completed	12
1-3 years of college completed	14
4 or more years of college completed	16

We note with Siegel that the "use of these scores may slightly distort the observed relationship between education and income, especially at the extremes. However, it is unlikely that knowlege of the exact mean years of school completed . . . (by ethnic group) for the educational groupings used would alter any of the conclusions drawn here." See his "On the Cost of Being a Negro," p. 47. In addition, entries are not shown on the scatter diagrams if they represent averages based on less than 10 sample cases. Since a 1/100 sample was used, we did not report an income average for an occupation by education group if the total number of workers in the group was less than 1,000.

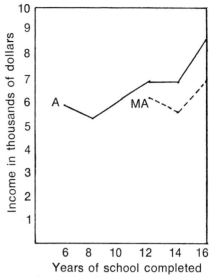

Fig. 1. Professional, technical, and kindred workers.

An overall pattern emerges after examining these eight figures. With only one exception, Anglo workers show higher average incomes than Mexican Americans in every occupational group and at every level of educational attainment. Figure 1, for example, notes that Mexican American professionals with two years of college earn on the average less than Anglo professionals with only two years of high school. Further, Mexican Americans with four or more years of college show average incomes nearly $1,600 less than Anglos of the same occupation and education.

The income differences between Mexican Americans and Anglos among managers, officials and proprietors (Figure 2) are even more striking. At every level of educational attainment, save one,[24] the average income of Anglo managers is at least $1,200 more than Mexican American managers, and in the case of those workers with 1-3 years of college, the differential is $2,700. Of all the occupational categories, it is among the managers that the largest income differences exist between

---

[24]Among managers with 1-3 years of high school, Mexican Americans report a higher average income than Anglos. Presumably the higher average for Mexican Americans is due to two of the 14 workers in this category reporting incomes of $21,500 and $15,500 respectively.

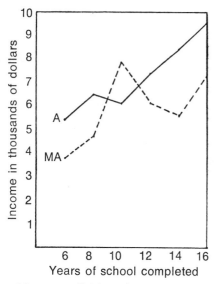

Fig. 2. Managers, officials, and proprietors.

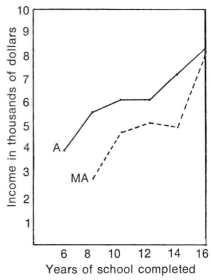

Fig. 4. Sales workers.

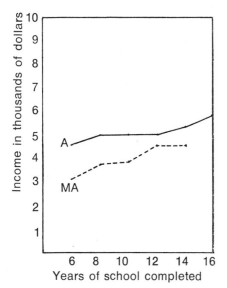

Fig. 3. Clerical and kindred workers.

the two ethnic groups. Similar results have been found in comparisons between white and black workers.[25] Apparently, minority

[25] See Siegel's "On the Cost of Being a Negro," p. 48. In another examination comparing income differences between male and female workers, the managerial category once again contained the greatest overall differences. Cf. Poston, "On the Cost of Being a Female Worker."

group members have been relegated to those proprietor-positions characterized by substantially lower pay. This barrier to a certain degree is reflecting in what Siegel has called the "etiquette of retail relationships." Presumably Mexican Americans are denied access to those higher paying managerial positions in which they would hold supervisory power over Anglos, and thus engage in small-scale retail activity.

Substantial differences also exist among clerical workers (Figure 3) and sales workers (Figure 4), although in this latter occupation we see for the first time a tendency for Mexican American incomes to approximate more closely those of the Anglos with increasing education. Whereas among sales workers with only an elementary education, Anglos report average incomes nearly $3,000 greater than those reported by Mexican Americans, the difference is reduced to $300 among those with four or more years of college.

Among craftsmen (Figure 5), operatives (Figure 6), and service workers (Figure 7) the average income difference at each level of education varies only slightly between $800 and $1,000, but in all cases, the advantage is in favor of the Anglos. Observe as well that in these three occupational groups, although the average incomes reported by Mexican American males do increase somewhat with increas-

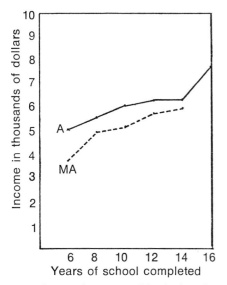

Fig. 5. Craftsmen, foremen, and kindred workers.

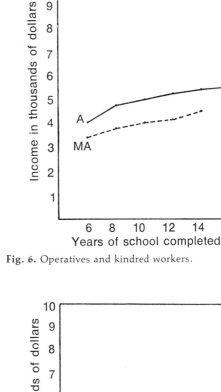

Fig. 6. Operatives and kindred workers.

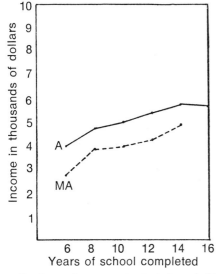

Fig. 7. Service workers, except private household.

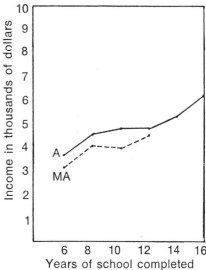

Fig. 8. Laborers.

ing education, the differences between their incomes and those of the Anglos remain constant to a great degree over most levels of educational attainment.

Finally, among Mexican American and Anglo laborers (Figure 8), the income differences are at their lowest, ranging from no more than $600 for workers with 1-3 years of high school to less than $300 for those with high school educations. But then the fact that Mexican Americans and

Anglos are the closest in terms of income in this occupational group has already been suggested elsewhere.[26] The same general results were also found between white and black males, although the income differences were slightly larger than those reported in Figure 8.[27]

---

[26]Grebler, *et al., Mexican American People,* pp. 230, 234.

[27]Siegel, "On the Cost of Being a Negro," p. 49.

We turn at this point to Anglo-Mexican American income differentiation as it varies by levels of educational attainment, but here the compositional effects of occupation will be excluded. This is necessary because of earlier evidence on the differences between the occupational structures of Anglos and Mexican Americans.[28] Had we merely summarized the income differences over all occupations, one could argue that the gross Anglo-Mexican American income differences at the various levels of education could be due to the differences in the occupational distributions of Anglos and Mexican Americans.

These compositional effects of occupation are easily removed by decomposing the difference between Anglo and Mexican American incomes at each educational level into two terms: one expresses the total difference attributable to Anglo-Mexican American differences in occupational composition ("the mean income difference attributable to composition"), and the other represents the difference due to Anglo-Mexican American income differences specific to occupation ("the mean income difference net of composition").[29]

Table 1 presents the results of the decomposition process. Whereas the average Mexican American income advances with increasing education (column 1), the mean difference between Anglo and Mexican American income (column 2) fluctuates in an almost curvilinear fashion with educational attainment. The differences are the greatest at the highest and lowest levels of education, and the least at the mid-levels. But when these mean differences are decomposed into the two components mentioned above, the second portion (column 4) represents the income differences exclusive of the effects of the different occupational structures of the two ethnic groups. Stated in another way, if Anglos and Mexican Americans had identical occupational distributions, differences would still exist between their incomes.

Inspecting these differences, it appears that the disparity between Anglo and Mexican American incomes increases with education. For instance, among workers with 8 years of education, there is an $800 difference in favor of the Anglos, but this differential increases to over $1,200 for those with 4 or more years of college. As Grebler, *et al.* have noted, the fact "that more education fails to improve the income position of Mexican Americans in proportion to that of the majority is a matter of considerable social significance."[30]

However, it is possible to interpret these data in yet another way with somewhat different results. We suggest that *relative* rather than *absolute* income differences between the two ethnic groups be examined. As an example, observe the absolute income differences in column 4 for those

---

[28]Browning and McLemore, *Statistical Profile of the Spanish Surname Population of Texas,* p. 41.

[29]If we let M represent mean income of Anglo males and m represent mean income of Mexican American males, the gross mean differences may be represented by

$$(1) \quad M - m = \sum_i N_i M_i - \sum_i n_i m_i,$$

where N_i represents the proportion of Anglos in the ith occupation, and n_i and m_i represent the corresponding proportions and mean incomes for Mexican Americans. We expand (1) to

$$(2) \quad M - m = \sum_i N_i M_i + \sum_i n_i M_i - \sum_i n_i M_i - \sum_i n_i m_i$$

This formula may be regrouped and rewritten as

$$(3) \quad M - m = \sum_i n_i (M_i - m_i) + \sum_i M_i (N_i - n_i).$$

The first term on the right side of (3) is the sum over all Mexican Americans of the Anglo–Mexican American mean income differences within each occupation. The second term of (3) is that portion of the gross differences due to occupational composition. This methodology is adapted from Siegel, "On the Cost of Being a Negro," p. 54; see also Evelyn M. Kitagawa, "Components of a Difference Between Two Rates," *Journal of the American Statistical Association,* 50 (Dec., 1955), pp. 1168-1194.

[30]Grebler, *et al., Mexican-American People,* p. 196.

Table 1. Decomposition of mean differences between Anglo and Mexican American income in 1959 specific to educational groups

Years of school completed	Mean Mexican American income (1)	Mean difference in Anglo–Mexican American income (2)	Mean income difference attributable to occupational composition (3)	Mean income difference net of composition (4)	Percent relative income difference (4)/(1) (5)
Elementary 0-7 years	$3,363	$1,279	$300	$ 979	29.1
Elementary 8 years	4,249	995	204	791	18.6
High school 1-3 years	4,573	996	167	829	18.1
High school 4 years	5,001	1,058	298	760	15.2
College 1-3 years	5,202	1,453	238	1,215	23.4
College 4 years or more	7,207	1,251	12	1,239	17.2

with 1-3 years of college and those with 4 years or more. These differences ($1,215 and $1,239 respectively) are not that different from each other in absolute terms. However, coupling these with the mean Mexican American incomes in column 1, it is clear that a difference of $1,215 between Anglos and Mexican Americans when the mean Mexican American income is $5,202 (column 1) is substantially greater in relative terms than a similar difference of $1,239 when the mean Mexican American income is $7,207. The entries in column 5 reflect in percentage terms the increased amount of relative income earned by Anglo workers over Mexican Americans at each level of educational attainment after controlling for occupational distributions.

Rather than indicating a positive relationship between the disparity in Anglo–Mexican American income and education as was the case with absolute income, the relative income data suggest an oppopsite interpretation. For the most part the relative income differences between the two ethnic groups decrease with increasing education. Among workers with less than an eighth grade education, Anglos report average incomes nearly 30 percent greater than the means reported by Mexican Americans, exclusive of occupational differences between the two groups. This difference, however, declines to about 17 percent for those with 4 or more years of college. Clearly, the relationship between education and income differentiation depends to a large extent upon the manner by which income differences are measured.

The final part of the analysis goes one step farther than the previous one: here we examine the income differences between the ethnic groups exclusive of the compositional effects of both education and occupation. The methodology employed is merely an extension of the decomposition equation discussed above; education was added as an additional compositional variable.

The total income difference in 1959 between Anglo and Mexican American full-time male workers between the ages of 20 and 40 in the predominantly urban occupations residing in one of the five southwestern states was $2,050. Of this total difference $1,141 are attributable to the different occupational and educational distributions of Anglos and Mexican Americans. The remaining portion of the difference, $909, can be attributed to minority membership. Recall that this $900 differential results after assuming statistically that the two ethnic groups have the same occupational and educational distributions. Further, the difference does not result from the fact that when compared with Anglos, the Mexican American workforce is characterized by a proportionately greater number of part-time workers, more agricultural employees, and a more sizeable number of foreign-born workers since the sample was defined in such a way that workers with the above characteristics were excluded. Accordingly, in that all relevant socioeconomic and demographic characteristics of Anglo and Mexican American workers were controlled or held constant, we have reason to believe that the $900 differential remaining is mainly, if not exclusively, the result of membership in a minority group. On the average Mexican Americans may attribute a full $900 of the difference between their incomes and those of the Anglos as due to their being Mexican American.

DISCUSSION AND CONCLUSION

To place our findings in comparative context, we might ask whether the Mexican American—Anglo income differences are similar to black—white differences. There has been some work on this latter comparison, but one study in particular deserves mention: we refer here to the analysis mentioned earlier by Siegel[31] in which after controlling for the compositional effects of occupation and education,[32] the cost of being a Negro was found to be approximately $1,000.

At first glance it appears that the Negro worker is slightly more disadvantaged than the Mexican American in terms of income comparisons with Anglos, since our study shows an Anglo-Mexican American differential of a little more than $900. However, Siegel employed *all* white and Negro workers in his analysis, and, as a consequence, part-time and agricultural workers were among those included. Yet the black labor force (as is true of Mexican Americans) is also more characterized by part-time workers and agricultural employees than is the white labor force;[33] accordingly we suggest that had Siegel included only the full-time, nonagricultural workers, the cost of being a Negro would probably have been at least $100 less than that reported. Presumably, Mexican Americans show about the same income disparity vis-à-vis the majority ethnic group as would a comparable sample of black workers. A confirmation of this hypothesis, however, must await further empirical test.

Another matter to be addressed concerns the possibility that some portion of the reported $900 cost of being a Mexican American is due to differences in the detailed occupations held by Mexican Americans and Anglos. Since we have used only the broad occupational categories, the ethnic distribution within a category is probably not the same. For instance, in the craftsmen category, the electricians, engravers, plumbers, opticians, jewelers, and other better paying craftsmen occupations are probably more often held by Anglos, with Mexican Americans more frequently occupying such craftsmen positions as blacksmiths, excavating operators, mechanics, paperhangers, etc. This and other dissimilar ethnic distributions within the categories, one might argue, would "explain away" the overall income difference between the two ethnic groups.

Siegel confronted this question in his analysis, and our response to a certain degree reflects his arguments. For instance, we suggested earlier that at certain levels of education Mexican Americans may be prohibited from obtaining precisely the same jobs as Anglos for a number of reasons, one of which has been referred to as the "etiquette of retail relationships." Another reason would be the existence of numerous barriers prohibiting Mexican Americans from entering the more skilled trades, especially those governed by discriminatory unions.

We suggest that invoking the detailed occupation argument as a reason for all,

[31]Siegel, "On the Cost of Being a Negro," pp. 46-57.

[32]Since Siegel included blacks and whites from all states, he also employed a regional control for South-nonSouth; see *Ibid.*, p. 46.

[33]Herman P. Miller, *Income Distribution in the United States* (A 1960 Census Monograph) (Washington, D.C.: U.S. Government Printing Office, 1966), p. 157.

or part of the $900 cost of being a Mexican American does not mean that the discrimination cause may be excluded. For in many cases it is because of discrimination, whatever its degree of subtlety, that Mexican Americans and Anglos do not hold exactly the same detailed jobs within a particular broad occupational category.

The income differences discussed earlier thus do not necessarily reflect differences in pay between Mexican Americans and Anglos for *precisely* the same type of work and educational training. With Siegel we note that "various features of the social organization of the relations between the ... [two ethnic groups] may also play a role in accounting for the differentials."[34] But whatever the final explanation of the differences, it is clear that among male workers of the same general level of employment, Anglos report average incomes greater than those of Mexican Americans

with the same level of educational attainment.

We end with a note of caution. While it is true that the major inference of this study is one in which ethnic-based discrimination is argued as the principal cause for the $900 difference between Anglo and Mexican American income, this statement applies only to full-time workers, between the ages of 20 and 40, in the predominantly urban occupations, residing in the Southwest in 1960. The extent to which discrimination has an impact in the income differences among *all* workers of these ethnic groups must necessarily remain an empirical question for the present time. However, among these workers examined here, Mexican Americans are denied access to the same income structure when compared to their Anglo counterparts, and this occurs because of their minority group membership. Mexican Americans earn less because they are Mexican Americans, not Anglos.

---

[34]Siegel, "On the Cost of Being a Negro," p. 48.

CHAPTER 9 PREJUDICE AND DISCRIMINATION

AMADO M. PADILLA
RENE A. RUIZ

Because this is a complex area of research with literature stemming from many different disciplines, we shall begin by defining key terms. *Prejudice* is here defined as the belief maintained by a large segment of the dominant society that the Spanish speaking, Spanish surnamed (SSSS) possess a pattern of negatively valued traits. Such belief systems may develop out of personal contact with the SSSS, but, most commonly, prejudice toward others is learned from contact with prejudiced people. This review of the literature will show that the SSSS have long been victims of prejudice.

The second term is *discrimination,* defined here as the effects of prejudice. The U.S. census reports and other surveys indicate a history of reduced family incomes, poor health care, inadequate nutrition, inferior education, underemployment, and general sociopolitical impotence. These are all indices of discrimination. At several places in this review we have made the point that continued socioeconomic depression of this type is conducive to psychological stress.

In a later section of this chapter we shall summarize literature describing the psychological *responses* of the victims of prejudice and discrimination. First, we shall make some theoretical observations on the origins of prejudice.

From Latino Mental Health: A Review of the Literature; Rockville, Maryland; National Institute of Mental Health, pp. 117-134.

ORIGINS OF PREJUDICE

The cause of antipathy of one group toward another probably antedates Neanderthal Man but is undiscernible from recorded history. Of greater relevance to this review, data are unavailable that would explain the origin of prejudice directed toward the SSSS residents of the United States. Nevertheless, some insight into this process is found in Allport's (1958) work, Senter and Hawley (1945-1946) and Cota-Robles de Suarez (1971). In very general terms, people tend to perceive "differences" (i.e., "they" are different from "us") as negative and unfavorable. Furthermore, when there is any kind of "power conflict," whether political, social, or economic, these differences tend to become exaggerated and are perceived as even more negative and unfavorable. Presumably, this process began when the Anglo and SSSS cultures first came in contact with each other in what is today the southwestern United States.

Spanish-speaking people colonized the Southwest more than 350 years ago. Some of the villages in northern New Mexico were founded in 1598. A century later Spanish settlements were made in Texas, and almost two centuries later, in California. Thus, at the point of original contact, the SSSS owned the land and exercised politico-military power. The SSSS were "different" from the invading Anglos in terms of language, history, culture, religion, customs, and length of residence. Since corroborative data are impossible to generate we are speculating that as Anglos expanded the size of the area under their dominion they became increasingly convinced of their "right" to own, cultivate, and exploit the lands which had been wrested from the "inferior" inhabitants (for an analysis of this see Merk 1963). It became easier and easier for the invaders to perceive the indigenous inhabitants as inferior culturally, economically, and intellectually as more and more land was expropriated. The rights of the indigenous inhabitants became increasingly less important. Today the SSSS's plight of poverty, lack of education, and inadequate health care is cited as evidence of inferior status.

Unfortunately, such processes tend to be self-perpetuating and ultimately demonstrate their own validity in a tautological fashion. After all, if people are "inferior," they don't warrant the expenditure required for an adequate education; if people are poorly educated, they will hold menial positions with low incomes. When family finances are restricted and schools are of poor quality, children will tend to "drop out" early and seek gainful employment, however humble, to supplement family income. And, of course, there is the ultimate non sequitor: If people are poorly educated and menially employed, they are obviously "inferior," and their children don't want or need adequate schools.

Data exist indicating that the perception of ethnic differences begins fairly early. Johnson (1950) studied onset of prejudicial attitudes of Spanish-American and Anglo children toward each other. Findings are complex, but basically, the Spanish American appears to develop prejudicial attitudes at about 4 years of age and the Anglos earlier. Anglos appeared *more* prejudicial and their attitude of "superiority" increased gradually with age—it was most prominent at age 12 (the oldest group of subjects). In the following section, we examine research illuminating the *nature* of the prejudices directed against the SSSS.

NATURE OF PREJUDICE

Despite the historical fact that this country was founded on the principle of equality among people, an abundance of data exists to indicate that the greater society has held, and continues to hold, a series of discriminatory attitudes toward various ethnic, racial, and cultural groups. The most obvious historical facts which support this assertion include genocidal policies directed toward native Americans, the introduction of black slavery to the Americas, and land expropriation from the SSSS which accompanied the expansion of the western frontier. Demographic data from blacks, Indians, and the SSSS comprise more "subtle" indices: higher infant mortality rates, decreased longevity among adults, and all the other morbid characteristics of ethnic-minority-group poor in the United States. We shall concentrate first on the most blatant indices of majority-group prejudice toward the SSSS.

An article by Simmons (1961) presents data from a small community in south Texas with a population estimated as 56 percent Mexican American. The choice of geographic region may have some potentiating effect upon the *intensity* of attitudes held by Anglos toward Mexican Americans, but other articles (cited below) suggest they are fairly representative in terms of *content*. Simmons' analysis of this community indicates the "upper" social class is exclusively Anglo and the "lower" social-class group is primarily Mexican American. The "middle" class includes a few Mexican Americans who appear to have earned this status by virtue of their talents as bilingual salesmen. Simmons offers three explanations for this phenomenon of socioeconomic stratification on an ethnic basis: (1) many recent Mexican immigrants are unfamiliar with Anglo culture and cannot assimilate readily; (2) Mexican Americans tend to live together in self-enforced isolation; and (3) negative attitudes and discriminatory practices are directed toward the SSSS. Considering the questionable validity of the first two "explanations," let us investigate the third in more detail.

According to Simmons, at the philosophical level, the typical Anglo adheres to "ideals of the essential dignity of the individual and of certain inalienable rights to freedom, justice and equal opportunity" (p. 288). In reality, however, these constitutional rights are granted only to a "high-type" Mexican (quotation marks in original). A member of the SSSS group is accorded "high-type" status by meeting three Anglo criteria: "occupational achievement . . . wealth . . . and command of Anglo ways" (p. 288). Even becoming a "high type," however, does not ensure acceptance into the majority culture because some Anglos do not believe that "Mexican Americans will be ultimately assimilated" (p. 289). This belief, held by "most Anglo-Americans" is based on the "assumption that Mexican Americans are essentially inferior" (p. 289). This "inferiority," according to Simmons' analysis of attitudes held by the majority of Anglos, is based on a "stereotype" of Mexican Americans as physically unclean with tendencies toward drunkenness and other criminal behavior. Further, the Mexican American is identified with menial labor, but as a worker he is considered improvident, undependable, childlike, and indolent. Possessing attitudes such as these, the Anglo-Americans feel justified in their practices of exclusion. But as Simmons points out, even the intended favorable features of the stereotype reinforce the Anglo's notion that Mexicans belong in a subordinate status. For example, Simmons states,

> Among those [traits] usually meant to be complimentary are the beliefs that all Mexicans are musical and always ready for a fiesta, that they are very "romantic" rather than "realistic" (which may have unfavorable overtones as well), and that they love flowers and plants and can grow them under the most adverse conditions. Although each of these beliefs may have a modicum of truth, it may be noted that they can reinforce Anglo-American images of Mexicans as childlike and irresponsible since they support the notion that Mexicans are capable only of subordinate status. [p. 292]

(The *effects* of these prejudicial attitudes upon the lives of the SSSS will be elaborated in a succeeding section.)

If these prejudices seem extreme or unrepresentative, consider the corroborative evidence gathered by Pinkney (1963). Attitudes toward Mexican and Negro Americans were elicited from 319 native-born, white residents of a western city. Six questions were directed at "local policy." For example, the question eliciting highest agreement indicates that 76 percent of the respondent group "approved . . . of Mexicans . . . being hired as

department store sales clerks." Least approved (46 percent) was "living in mixed neighborhoods." If these data are alarming, consider those dealing with "equal rights." Only 36 percent of the respondents indicated that Mexican Americans should have "the right to . . . live with other Americans."

The reader is reminded that these data are considered fairly representative of national attitudes. There is no comment which can further illuminate the observation that a significantly large percentage of this sample was willing to abrogate the constitutional rights of fellow Americans on the basis of minority group membership. Now let's turn to less obvious indications of racial prejudice.

Bogardus (1943-1944) presents a fairly dispassionate discussion entitled "Gangs of Mexican American Youth." He describes the tailoring of the "zoot suit," the origin of the label "Pachuco," and examines the causes of riots that occurred in the early 1940's. From the vantage point of a retrospective view of 30 years, however, his arguments are outlandish and patronizing. He notes that "they like to carry knives" (p. 58) and laments that "gang warfare is aggravated by the use of liquor, poisonous liquor, and sometimes by the smoking of marijuana cigarettes . . . which may drive their victims literally mad with hallucinations" (p. 59). He talks about intellectual retardation due to "inbreeding," but concedes that "not all are born bad" (p. 59). He supports the claim that the Nazi party may be indirectly responsible for the Pachuco riots (remember this was World War II), but pontificates that police and sailors cannot solve social problems by beating people (see especially p. 63).

Another article was presented to the scientific community around the same time by Humphrey (1945). He describes "stereotypes" formed by Detroit social workers of Mexican-American youth in relatively favorable terms such as *modest, courteous, gentle, docile,* and *reticent.* He identifies "types" of youngsters who are respectful toward parental authority, work, and other Mexican-American friends. Although this kind of personality trait identification is benign in and of itself, Humphrey goes on to explain social upheavals such as the Los Angeles "zoot suit" riots in a manner implicitly detrimental to Mexican Americans. He does not "blame" Mexican-American youth for these events, but neither does he mention the roles played by roving bands of sailors and police in instigating and maintaining this particular conflict. Neither he nor Bogardus identify the highly inflammatory role played by local newspapers during that crisis period (see McWilliams 1968). An excellent summary of McWilliams' analysis of the role played by the press in the "zoot suit" riots can be found in Marden and Meyer (1968), who state:

> Whipped up by the press, which warned that the Mexicans were about to riot with broken bottles as weapons and would beat sailors' brains out with hammers, the excitement erupted and two days of really serious rioting occurred, involving soldiers, sailors, and civilians, who invaded motion picture houses, stopped trolley cars, and beat up the Mexicans they found, as well as a few Filipinos and Negroes. At midnight on June 7 the military authorities declared Los Angeles out of bounds for military personnel. The order immediately slowed down the riot. On June 8 the mayor stated that "sooner or later it will blow over," and the chief of police announced the situation "cleared up." However, rioting went on for two more days. Editorials and statements to the press lamented the fact that the servicemen were called off before they were able to complete the job. The district attorney of an outlying county stated that "zoot suits are an open indication of subversive character." And the Los Angeles City Council adopted a resolution making the wearing of zoot suits a misdemeanor [p. 143]

A more recent article by Martinez (1969) describes how Mexicans and Mexican Americans are portrayed in newspapers, magazines, and on television. He cites ads which portray the SSSS as "overweight . . . always sleeping . . . stinking." Morales (1971) concurs that American advertising portrays SSSS unfavorably. Both authors agree that ads which demean the SSSS serve to convince the majority group of their "white superiority" and simultaneously possess the potential to make members of the minority group uncertain of their status. It requires a great deal of personal confidence and pride in cultural heritage to resist concerted propaganda

that one is a member of an "inferior" group.

Let us turn to older research to examine the prejudicial attitudes of educators. West (1936) submitted a list of "pupil traits" to 72 Anglo and 60 Spanish-American teachers from rural towns in New Mexico. All taught classes that included both Anglo and Spanish-American students. Basically, Anglo-American teachers acceded Anglo student superiority on 17 of 21 traits, approximately twice as often as Spanish-American teachers rated students of their own ethnicity as superior. Furthermore, Spanish-American teachers saw "no difference" between Anglo and Spanish-American students approximately 50 percent of the time; whereas, only 27.4 percent of the Anglo teachers chose this response option. Approximately 35 years ago, then, both Anglo and Spanish-American teachers were perceiving Anglo students as somehow "superior" to SSSS students. The implication is clear that these evaluations were subsequently communicated in terms of attitudes of ethnic superiority and inferiority. One can only speculate on the adverse effect such negative propaganda must have had upon motivation for continued education and preparation for better employment among the oppressed group.

A more recent study by Werner and Evans (1968) serves to illustrate how school systems preserve negative attitudes toward the SSSS. Using 40 Mexican-American boys and girls as subjects, ages 4 and 5, the authors studied preference for dolls of light and dark skin color following the method originated by the Clarks in 1939. Upon beginning school, these children stopped grouping dolls by sex and size and began to group by skin color. In general, white dolls were "good," and dark dolls were "bad." Following exposure to school, Mexican Americans identified with the white, "good" dolls. This study *tends* to imply that dark-skinned children were conditioned as a result of their school experience to evaluate dolls as "bad" which most resembled their own skin color. Unfortunately, we must be cautious about generalizing from this study because the authors used "Negro dolls [with] black hair and brown skin" (p. 1041) to represent Mexican Americans even while acknowledging that these people have "a wide range of skin color" (p. 1040).

Bloombaum, Yamamoto, and James (1968) report data highly relevant at this point. Half-hour interviews were conducted with 16 practicing psychotherapists to investigate attitudes toward Mexican Americans, Negroes, Japanese Americans, Chinese Americans, and Jews. Basically, 22.6 percent of all responses were scored as "culturally stereotypic" in terms of "imputations of superstitiousness, changeability in impulse, grasp of abstract ideas, and distinction between illusion and facts" (p. 99). The authors report that Mexican Americans are "most frequently the objects of such stereotypes, with Negroes, Jews, Chinese Americans, and Japanese Americans following, in that order" (p. 99). To measure the extent to which psychotherapists maintained "social distance" between themselves and minority-group members, they were asked to rank preference for marriage partners on the basis of race. Negroes were "least preferred," Mexican Americans were intermediate, and Jews were "most preferred." The major conclusions which emerge are that even psychotherapists are prejudicial toward Mexican Americans and that these prejudices reflect closely the unfavorable beliefs held by the greater society.

A partial summary of inferences drawn from studies reviewed thus far: There is a lengthy history of prejudice directed against the SSSS in the United States. Prejudice is sometimes expressed overtly (e.g., data from Simmons 1961 and Pinkney 1963) but sometimes is expressed with some degree of subtlety (e.g., see articles published in scientific journals by Bogardus 1943-1944; and by Humphrey 1945). Even psychotherapists involved in the delivery of mental health services reveal negative prejudices toward certain minority group members which resemble those found in the general population (Bloombaum, Yamamoto, and James 1968). Finally, and most alarming, we find evidence that the schools and advertising media are actively involved in the dissemination of prejudices which support the myth of "white superiority" by degrading the SSSS (Martinez 1969, Morales 1971,

and Werner and Evans 1968). At this point, let us turn to the question of what happens to minority group members against whom the majority group holds antagonistic prejudices.

To support the notion that discrimination for the SSSS worsens with length of time in the United States, we can turn to findings reported by Siegel (1957). In this investigation, Siegel found that as length of stay in Philadelphia increased for Puerto Ricans, so did the frequency of mention of "discrimination" as what was liked *least* about Philadelphia. Responses to a Social Distance Scale, for instance, showed that slightly less than half of the 209 Puerto Ricans said that continental Americans willingly admit them to their streets as neighbors; about one-fourth said that continental Americans admit Puerto Ricans to their clubs as personal friends or to close kinship by marriage. Moreover, 44 percent answered in the affirmative to the question, "Do you think that continental Americans would like to exclude Puerto Ricans from this country?" Finally, unemployment was listed as one of the greatest problems encountered after leaving Puerto Rico; and, among those who were employed, a great disparity was noted between level of job aspiration and actual level of job achievement.

EFFECTS OF DISCRIMINATION

Up to now, we have only hinted at how the lives of the SSSS have been influenced adversely by majority-group prejudices. Here we shall become more explicit. Discrimination against the SSSS results in *economic* deprivation such as unemployment, underrepresentation in professions and technical occupations, and lower wages, to mention only a few. Discrimination in *justice* results in police harassment, inadequate legal aid and protection, exclusion from jury service, and so on. The relatively small number of SSSS legislators or appointed governmental representatives are illustrations of discrimination in *politics*. *Educational* discrimination results in inadequate school supplies, inferior buildings, poorly trained teachers and a low mean years of school attendance. These general conclusions may be inferred from any recent report of the U.S. census or from some of the several surveys reporting demographic data relevant to the SSSS.

Katzman (1971) summarizes data from Mexican Americans and Puerto Ricans (as well as other minority-group members) showing differences in occupation, income, employment, and labor force participation. A number of authors describe much more specific effects among the SSSS as a result of prejudice and discrimination. Cota-Robles de Suarez (1971) discusses a number of sociopsychological factors (to be presented below). Meadow and Bronson (1969) report increased psychopathology and Ulibarri (1971) describes attitudinal changes generally considered to be maladaptive.

RESPONSES TO PREJUDICE AND DISCRIMINATION

A number of authors agree that the SSSS experience adverse psychological reactions to prejudice and discrimination. Cota-Robles de Suarez (1971) identifies these responses: obsessive concern with negative implications of ethnicity, denial of ethnic group membership, withdrawal, passivity, clowning, self-hatred, aggression against one's group, and group solidarity. Although these labels are self-explanatory, we shall examine a few in greater detail to provide better understanding of these behaviors and how they interact.

These behaviors may be experienced as either pleasant or unpleasant, depending in part upon whether or not they are successful in reducing stress. For example, "clowning" would probably be experienced as pleasant because of attendant social popularity combined with stress reduction. Withdrawal, on the other hand, is more unpredictable in its effect because it may take so many forms—e.g., social isolation, dropping out of school, or expatriation. Many of these reactions to prejudice may be adaptive since they reduce stress and preserve the psychological well-being of the person. For example, it may be adaptive for a SSSS student to terminate inferior education when its continuation would have no discernible effect upon the probability of better employment or increased income.

Several authors agree with the contention of Cota-Robles de Suarez (1971) that the SSSS experience "self-hatred" in response to prejudice and discrimination. Sommers (1964) presents anecdotal evidence in support of this premise. She describes the psychiatric case history of a young Mexican-American male who experiences guilt and a depreciated self-image when he rejects his own subculture in a vain attempt to play the role of an "All-American Boy." Research data confirming this thesis are presented by Petersen and Ramirez (1971). Their subjects were Negro, Mexican-American and Anglo-American school children in the fifth to eighth grades. They responded to one measure of "real self" and another of "ideal self" to test the hypothesis that the greatest "disparity" (or dissatisfaction with self) would be found among minority subjects. Further confirmation was provided by an item analysis of the self-ratings which revealed that minority-group subjects significantly described themselves in depreciatory terms such as "dull," "lazy," "stubborn," and "unfair."

Working in another area of research, Dworkin (1965) reports data supporting the premise that the SSSS experience low self-esteem. He compared attitudes of native-born and foreign-born Mexican Americans (NBMA and FBMA) toward Anglos and toward themselves. He predicted that the FBMA who comes to the United States seeking economic advancement would have favorable attitudes toward Anglos and self because he is "optimistic" concerning future success. The NBMA, on the other hand, has a lifetime of unpleasant experience with the majority group. He has noted the numerous advantages enjoyed by Anglos relative to his own position. As a result of this relative disadvantage, the NBMA develops a strong, negative stereotype of Anglos and an unfavorable self-image. Inspection of Table 1 indicates that 11 of the 12 self-images of the NBMA may be considered as negative, while only "proud" can be regarded to be positive. On the other hand, 10 of the 12 self-images of the FBMA may be considered to be positive, while only "short, fat, and dark" and "field workers" may be regarded as negative.

Table 1. Self-images held by native-born and foreign-born Mexican Americans[1]

Native-born Mexican American		Foreign-born Mexican American	
Words most frequently agreed to	Percent	Words most frequently agreed to	Percent
Emotional	100	Proud	100
Unscientific	94	Religious	100
Authoritarian	92	Strong family ties	100
Materialistic	92		
Old-fashioned	88	Athletic	98
Poor and of a low social class	86	Gregarious	96
		Friendly	96
Uneducated or poorly educated	84	Happy	94
		Field workers	90
Short, fat, and dark	84	Racially tolerant	88
		Short, fat, and dark	84
Little care for education	82	Practical	80
Mistrusted	78	Well adjusted	76
Proud	78		
Lazy, indifferent, and unambitious	78		

[1] Adapted from Dworkin (1965).

The studies which follow are very interesting since they lead to different, and sometimes opposite, conclusions than earlier reports. One study by Hishiki (1969), for example, found less favorable "self" and "ideal-self" concepts among California Mexican-American sixth-grade girls than among a comparable group of Georgia non-Mexican-American subjects. Closer examination of other reported data, however, reveal more and larger correlations between self-concept and academic achievement among Mexican-American girls than among the other group of subjects. Furthermore, a majority of subjects in both groups expect "to go to college" even though the Mexican-American children obtain mean IQ scores lower than 100 and academic achievement scores 2 years below grade level. These latter two findings suggest that at least some of the Mexican-American girls have the personal confidence or "self-esteem" to perform well in school and to anticipate and plan for higher education.

An informal paper by Carter (1968) argues strenuously against the thesis that Mexican-American students have negative self-concepts. Although his data-collection procedures and measuring instruments are described somewhat casually, he indicates that parents, students, teachers, and administrators of seventh-grade, eighth-grade and high school students in a geographic area that was 65 percent Mexican American were interviewed and tested. His conclusion warrants quotation:

Nothing supported the belief that Mexican American students saw themselves more negatively than the "Anglo" students. However, it was very obvious that teachers and administrators believed them to be inferior and to conclude they saw themselves that way. [p. 218]

Further confirmation of this conclusion stems from a self-concept questionnaire administered to 190 Mexican-American and 98 Anglo high school ninth-graders. No significant differences were found, although, "In some cases, the Mexican Americans had a slightly larger percentage rating themselves on the positive extreme" (p. 218).

Two related papers dealing with person perception among minority-group school children yield data bearing directly upon the self-concept and self-esteem among Mexican Americans. In one (Rice, Ruiz, and Padilla, in press), Anglo, black, and Chicano preschool and third-grade school children were presented with photographs of young Anglo, black, and Chicano men. Subjects were asked a series of eight questions designed to test their ability to correctly identify the three photographs in terms of ethnic or racial membership and to state a preference for one of the three. Three significant findings were revealed by the data. First, preschool subjects could discriminate between photographs of the Anglo and black males, but they could not differentiate the Anglo from the Chicano. Second, preschool Anglo children reliably *preferred* photographs of their own group, while black and Chicano children did not indicate any preference. Finally, third-grade subjects of all ethnicities were able to discriminate between Anglo, black, and Chicano male photographs. Of major importance, however, is the finding that *only* the Chicano children displayed a strong preference for their own ethnic group. These data are interpreted as reflecting a significant degree of pride in group, heritage, and self.

The second study (Padilla, Ruiz, and Rice 1973), employed a total of 658 second-, fourth-, and sixth-grade Anglo, black, and Chicano children. Stimulus photographs were of children of all three ethnicities and of approximately the same age as the subjects. Male subjects were presented with six photographs of male children and females with six female photographs. The task for subjects was to respond to a series of 43 questions designed to measure the ability to make an accurate discrimination, to state a preference, and to predict future occupation by selecting one of the six pictures. In general, accuracy of discrimination increased with grade level as expected. Only one of three Anglos in the sixth grade indicated they would "most like to be" like a member of their own ethnicity, while 81 percent of the Chicano boys and 58 percent of the Chicano girls selected a photograph of a Chicano child in response to this question. In choosing a "friend," only about 20 percent of the Anglos chose a member of their own group, whereas 75 percent of the Chicano boys and 53 percent of the Chicano girls selected a photograph of a child of their ethnicity. Again, these data are interpreted as indicating a strong preference for one's own ethnicity among Chicanos, which in turn, carries a strong connotation for enhanced self-esteem.

A recent article by Peñalosa (1970) is relevant here. Peñalosa identified a number of events which support the inference that Mexican Americans are undergoing a process of enhanced self-esteem. He makes the point, for example, that the use of the term "Chicano (is) . . . a mark of ethnic pride . . . chosen by members of the group itself" (p. 47). As corroborative evidence, he cites a current resurgence of interest in the culture of Mexico, the development of institutes of Chicano studies at a number of colleges and universities, the increase in artistic and cultural works emanating from the barrios, enhanced social influence and political power (e.g., through appointed office), and the forma-tion of numerous university student organizations (e.g., United Mexican-American Students and *Movimiento Estudiantil Chicano de Aztlan*).

Basically, we agree with the interpretation by Penalosa that events based on enhanced ethnic pride tend to increase self-esteem. Although objective data are unavailable, we are suggesting that one might examine the Chicano and Puerto Rican *movimientos* for answers. It is obvious that the SSSS are beginning to insist upon the full exercise of their human, legal, social, and economic rights. Although this insistence is probably in response to prejudice from the majority group to some degree, it does not necessarily follow that striving for freedom is based on low self-esteem. On the contrary, it seems much more reasonable to assume that assertive insistence upon one's rights is predicated on a conviction of personal worth.

FUTURE NEEDS AND RECOMMENDATIONS

All human rights of the SSSS must be guaranteed if the democratic ideals of American society are to be preserved. This means that the SSSS must be free to exercise their legal, political, social, and economic rights without interference from any type of governmental or educational representative. To provide only two examples, teachers must respect their pupils, and police must cease harassment. Rhetoric, however well-intentioned, will never resolve this type of social problem. Let us therefore move to proposals for programs of investigative research and social action which might reduce the effects of prejudice and discrimination.

Prejudice and discrimination feed upon each other. Majority-group members tend to perceive the SSSS as inferior *because* the SSSS are poor, unemployed, uneducated, and politically weak. These attitudes will change in a positive direction as conditions of economic impoverishment and political impotence are alleviated. These comments should not be misconstrued as a sentimental appeal that we all begin to practice "brotherly love." What is being suggested is that a better society can be established with enforcement of existing legislation guaranteeing public education and nondiscriminatory hiring practices.

A related recommendation is the formation of a study commission to determine how best to educate representatives of society who deal officially with the SSSS. Possibly, crash programs in SSSS culture, designed for specific occupational groups (e.g., teachers and police), might minimize disruption. A related recommendation is consideration of some form of "intense encounter" between SSSS and officials, especially in geographic areas with histories of conflict. Educational units, such as departments of Chicano and Puerto Rican studies, could conceivably provide the necessary administrative structure and faculty.

The efficiency of these programs will depend in part on the nature of the information the American public is receiving about the SSSS. The news media must discontinue the practice of demeaning the SSSS, if these kinds of social-action programs are to be successful. The goal of greater participation in American society by the SSSS can be achieved, but only if there is respect for human dignity and only if the dominant society recognizes that the SSSS are proud of their heritage and will strongly resist "deculturation."

Research can contribute in several ways. One is to evaluate the success of the preceding recommendations. Research techniques can be applied to determine what type of educational program will be most successful in altering prejudice among, for example, Anglo police officers stationed in barrio areas or teachers working in schools with high percentages of SSSS students.

More knowledge is needed concerning personality development among the SSSS. We know that some individuals respond to the stress of discrimination with very adaptive coping mechanisms, but others do the opposite. Why? What assets and liabilities underlie these two responses? Can "coping with discrimination" be taught like other skills? Answers to questions such as these can make obvious contributions to our knowledge of personality development, as well as help to create a better society.

We know much too little about self-esteem among the SSSS. Additional and con-

tinued research on the self-concept among the SSSS, a *motivational* construct, should be supported. We are uncertain whether the SSSS have typically "positive" or "negative" self-images. We do believe, however, that any child, whether SSSS or not, who is convinced he cannot succeed at school, on the job, or in life, will probably perform below potential, fail, or drop out. Thus, we support research on the various facets of self-concept as a means of ultimately understanding the effects of stress and how coping mechanisms are acquired and employed by the SSSS.

Several related points merit inclusion here. If the proposed research on self-concept indicates ameliorative programs would be helpful (e.g., "build confidence"), then, of course, these should be implemented. It should be noted that the role of the school is crucial. The SSSS may lack self-confidence within the school system because of low achievement and/or negative attitudes from teachers. Should this prove to be the case, then these ameliorative programs might best be conducted within the schools themselves. Remedial educational programs could be combined with some variation of counseling sessions designed to enhance self-esteem. It goes without saying, of course, that teacher attitudes erosive to student esteem must be corrected in one way or another. The point has been made before in several sections that the schools must fulfill the purposes for which they were created.

One of the papers cited indicated that a significant percentage of Anglo-Americans appear willing to abrogate the civil rights of others on the basis of race or ethnicity. We recognize that research is a long-term commitment and that the research programs outlined here cannot immediately and directly modify the kinds of attitudes implied by the findings reviewed. On the other hand, collection and dissemination of this type of information seems to possess the potential of alerting concerned citizens of the dangers involved in some social attitudes held by some Americans.

REFERENCES

Allport, G. W. *The Nature of Prejudice.* Cambridge, Mass.: Addison-Wesley, 1954.

Bloombaum, Milton; Yamamoto, Joe; and James, Quinton. Cultural stereotyping among psychotherapists. *Journal of Counseling and Clinical Psychology,* **32**(1):99, 1968.

Bogardus, Emory S. Gangs of Mexican-American youth. *Sociology and Social Research,* **28**:55-66, 1943-1944.

Carter, Thomas P. The negative self concept of Mexican American students. *School and Society,* **96**(2306):207-209, 1968.

Cota-Robles de Suarez, Cecilia. Skin color as a factor of racial identification and preference of young Chicano children. *Aztlan,* **2**(1):107-150, 1971.

Dworkin, Anthony G. Stereotypes and self images held by native-born and foreign-born Mexican-Americans. *Sociology and Social Research,* **49**(2):214-224, 1965.

Hishiki, Patricia C. Self concepts of sixth grade girls of Mexican-American descent. *California Journal of Educational Research,* **20**(2):56-62, 1969.

Humphrey, Norman D. The stereotype and the social types of Mexican-American youths. *Journal of Social Psychology,* **22**(1):69-78, 1945.

Johnson, Granville B. The origin and development of the Spanish attitude toward the Anglo and the Anglo attitude toward the Spanish. *Journal of Educational Psychology,* **41**(7):428-439, 1950.

Marden, C. F., and Meyer, G. *Minorities in American Society.* New York: American Book Company, 1968.

Martinez, Thomas M. Advertising and racism: The case of the Mexican American. *El Grito,* **2**(3):3-13, 1969.

McWilliams, C. *North from Mexico: The Spanish Speaking People of the United States.* New York: Greenwood Press, 1968.

Meadow, Arnold, and Bronson, Louise. Religious affiliation and psychopathology in a Mexican-American population. *Journal of Abnormal Psychology,* **74**(2):177-180, 1969.

Merk, F. *Manifest Destiny and Mission in American History: A Reinterpretation.* New York: Vintage Books, 1963.

Morales, Armando. The collective preconscious and racism. *Social Casework,* **52**(5):283-293, 1971.

Padilla, A. M.; Ruiz, R. A.; and Rice, A. "Perception of Self and Future Achievement Among Children of Different Ethnic Backgrounds." Unpublished manuscript, 1973.

Peñalosa, Fernando. Recent changes among the Chicanos. *Sociology and Social Research,* **55**(1):47-52, 1970.

Petersen, Barbara, and Ramirez, Manuel, III. Real ideal self disparity in Negro and Mexican-American children. *Psychology,* **8**(3):22-28, 1971.

Pinkney, Alphonso. Prejudice toward Mexican and Negro Americans: A Comparison. *Phylon,* **24**(4):353-359, 1963.

Rice, A. S.; Ruiz, R. A.; and Padilla, A. M. Person perception, self-identity, and ethnic group preference in Anglo, black, and Chicano preschool and third grade children. *Journal of Cross-Cultural Research,* in press.

Senter, Donovan, and Hawley, Florence. The grammar school as the basic acculturating influence for native New Mexicans. *Social Forces,* **24**(4):398-407, 1945-1946.

Siegel, Arthur I. The social adjustments of Puerto Ricans in Philadelphia. *Journal of Social Psychology,* **46**(1):99-110, 1957.

Simmons, Ozzie G. The mutual images and expectations of Anglo-Americans and Mexican-Americans. *Daedalus,* **90**(2):286-299, 1961.

Sommers, Vita S. The impact of dual cultural membership on identity. *Psychiatry,* **27**(4):332-344, 1964.

Ulibarri, Horacio. Social and attitudinal characteristics of Spanish-speaking migrant and ex-migrant workers in the Southwest. In: Wagner, Nathaniel N., and Haug, Marsha, J., eds. *Chicanos Social and Psychological Perspectives.* Saint Louis: The C. V. Mosby Company, 1971, pp. 164-170.

Werner, Norma E., and Evans, Idella M. Perception of prejudice in Mexican-American preschool children. *Perceptual and Motor Skills,* **27**(3):1039-1046, 1968.

West, Guy A. Race attitudes among teachers in the Southwest. *Journal of Abnormal and Social Psychology,* **31**(3):331-337, 1936.

PART THREE

PERSONALITY STUDIES

Personality trait constructs have been a focus of controversy within psychology for decades. Though laymen almost universally conceptualize other people (and themselves) in terms of seemingly enduring personality traits, psychologists are divided as to whether traits even exist. At one extreme are those who believe that there are a finite number of human traits determinable through a combination of semantics and mathematics; at the opposite pole are the diehard behaviorists who insist all behavior is controlled by environmental circumstances (past and present); and somewhere in between are those who concede that some people (but not all) manifest trait-like consistency in some (but not all) situations. The argument goes on endlessly, and seems to produce more heat than light. Strangely enough, however, the debate seems always to focus on the attributions made to *individuals,* ignoring the equally common practice of characterizing *groups.* If the stereotyping of an *individual* is questionable, consider how much graver the error in labelling an entire minority group, whose variability is likely to be many times greater, and then predicating social policy on the label. Yet this is precisely what happens, again and again. To make matters worse, as Amado Padilla observes, psychologists have tended to accept wholesale the value-laden, imprecise characterizations set forth (in terms of psychology) and to add insult to injury by trying to prove they are true without ever looking closely at the concepts themselves. Most such concepts (like "dependency" and "subjugation to nature") do not hold up at all well under scrutiny.

One very interesting and illuminating fact about the stereotypes applied to Mexican Americans (and other minority groups) is that *they are practically identical to the stereotypes applied to women:* dependency, being instead of doing ("passivity"), subjugation to nature ("anatomy is

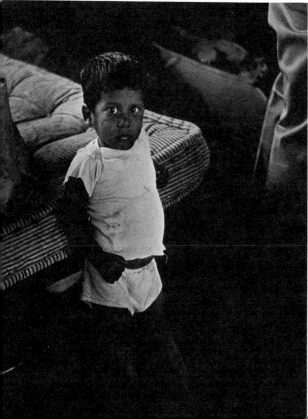

destiny"), lack of achievement orientation, emotionality, religiosity, and so on, right on down to love of music and flowers. It almost seems as if the white males who dominate in the social sciences (as they do in the larger society) have a single notion of "otherness" that they apply to all non-whites and non-males. In that they are both subordinate groups, women and ethnic minorities doubtless do have much in common; but these commonalities are usually viewed as innate characteristics rather than possible responses to oppression. Also, McClintock's cautionary note stressing the variability of behavior within groups and the overlap in behavior between groups is sound advice that is regularly ignored in treatises on women and minorities.

One of the sanest discussions of this whole problem is to be found in Maccoby and Jacklin (1974). They make the important point that, while between-group differences (of a relative frequency and degree nature) do appear, some at a very early age, they are *not* so major or so all-pervasive as to constitute broad, generalized traits like "dependency," or other such vague concepts. Garza and Ames's findings on locus of control are a perfect illustration: even a seemingly straightforward construct like I-E (internal-external locus of control) must be broken down into situational components to be meaningfully applied. One's habitual behavior in one situation may reflect internal control, whereas given a different set of cues one becomes an "externalizer." Even more important is Maccoby and Jack-

lin's conclusion that, despite their divergent "natural tendencies," *all children learn things—including the use of various "cognitive styles"—in exactly the same way:* the same laws of learning, the same developmental sequences apply to all. Thus a competitive child can learn to cooperate, a "nonanalytic" thinker can develop visual-spatial skills, and the like, given adequate motivation and opportunity. (The nightmarish corollary to this theorem is that given the "right" set of conditions, that is, a hostile, discriminating society, competent, self-respecting individuals can "learn" in a matter of months to devalue themselves, their accomplishments, their beliefs, their potential, and their fellow human beings, as Gecas and Dworkin both so chillingly demonstrate.) The aim of all education should be to accurately assess each child's starting point on each separate skill and to develop those skills, whatever their original level, to the extent that the individual can be *flexible,* choosing from a *range* of behaviors whichever one is most appropriate to the moment. If personality studies have any value, it lies in alerting us to the variability of human behavior patterns, which must be taken into account in planning social services responsive to the needs of all.

REFERENCE

Maccoby, E. E., & Jacklin, C. N. *The psychology of sex differences.* Palo Alto: Stanford University Press, 1974.

CHAPTER 10 DEVELOPMENT OF SOCIAL MOTIVES IN ANGLO-AMERICAN AND MEXICAN-AMERICAN CHILDREN[1]

CHARLES G. McCLINTOCK[2]

The choice behaviors of second-, fourth-, and sixth-grade Mexican-American and Anglo-American children in a maximizing difference game were compared. All of the subjects received information about own and other's choices after each trial, as well as own and other's cumulative point scores across 100 plays of the game. The results clearly indicated the following: (a) For both cultural groups, competitive choice behavior became more dominant with increments in grade level; (b) the Anglo-American children sampled were more competitive at each grade level than the Mexican-American children sampled; and (c) for all cultural and grade groups, competitive choices increased over trial blocks. The increase in competitive responding as a function of grade was interpreted in terms of developmental theory of achievement motivation set forth by Veroff. Some educational implications of differences between Anglo-and Mexican-American children were noted, as well as some cautionary statements concerning the interpretation of cross-cultural data.

The present study is concerned with the development of social motives in two cultural groups within the United States, namely, the majority Anglo-American middle-class culture and the minority Chicano (Mexican-American) lower-middle-class and upper-lower class culture. The study is one in a series of investigations that focus on cultural differences and similarities in the development of social mo-

tives (McClintock, 1972b; McClintock & Nuttin, 1969).

The theory of social motivation that underlies the present investigation is outlined elsewhere (McClintock, 1972a; Messick & McClintock, 1968). This conceptualization asserts that decision-making behavior in situations of social interdependence, namely, in settings where own and other's outcomes are a function of both own and other's behaviors, is determined by the goals (motives) of the participants and by the strategies (instrumental acts) they employ to achieve these goals. In a series of studies employing non-zero-sum games that provide decision makers an opportunity to express various goals in situations of social interdependence, three major motives have been repeatedly observed: (a) maximization of own gain (individualism), (b) maximization of joint gain (cooperation), and (c) maximization of relative gain (competition).

From Journal of Personality and Social Psychology **29**(3):348-354, 1974. Copyright 1974 by the American Psychological Association. Reprinted by permission.

[1]The research reported here was principally supported by Grant R01 HD03258 from the National Institute of Child Health and Human Development and secondarily by Grant GS3061 from the National Science Foundation.

[2]Requests for reprints should be sent to Charles G. McClintock, Department of Psychology, University of California, Santa Barbara, California 93106.

The present investigation is concerned with ascertaining whether motivational differences exist between Anglo- and Mexican-American samples of children in the second, fourth, and sixth grades. Previous studies have indicated that changes in the relative dominance of the preceding motives as a function of age are similar across a number of cultures, namely, as children become older they increasingly make choices that indicate they are more strongly motivated to maximize relative rather than own or joint gain (McClintock, 1972b). Further, these studies indicate that the rate of this developmental change varies between cultures.

Thus, the present study seeks to extend these prior findings by comparing two cultural groups within the United States. Discerning whether differences in motivational orientation exist between these two groups is relevant not only for extending our description and understanding of the etiology and development of social motives, but may also have implications for evaluating an educational system that serves both Mexican-American and Anglo-American students. To date, considerable attention has been given to the assessment of cognitive and intellectual skills in various ethnic groups (see, e.g., Lesser, Fifer, & Clock, 1965), and a number of investigations have been made of progress in the school system as a function of the ethnic distribution of students in classrooms (see, e.g., Coleman, Campbell, Hobson, McFarland, Mood, Weinfold, & York, 1966), but little research has been undertaken to ascertain whether systematic differences in social motivation exist between ethnic student populations. Should such differences be obtained, one might then begin to systematically explore whether the types of learning environments provided in schools are more or less effective, given differences in the relative dominance of various motives.

Several studies conducted by Madsen and collaborators (Kagan & Madsen, 1971; Madsen & Shapira, 1970) indicate that differences exist between the cooperative and competitive orientation of Mexican-American and Anglo-American children and that these may vary as a function of age level. In the first of these studies, the investigators reported that seven–nine-year-old Mexican-American children behave less competitively and hence more successfully in a task requiring coordination to achieve a goal than Anglo-American or Black-American children of comparable ages. In the second study, the researchers reported that in a task requiring one of the players to "step aside" in order for the other to win on a given trial and to take turns over time for both to win, differences in instructional orientation, age, and culture produced different levels of cooperation. It was found that (a) an "I" orientation produced less cooperation than a "we" one; (b) four–five-year-olds were more cooperative than seven–nine-year-olds; and (c) seven–nine-year-old Mexican-American children were more cooperative than Anglo-Americans of the same age. In other studies with Mexican children, these researchers have found that both Mexican and American children display increasing competition with age, but Mexican children, particularly those that live in rural areas, are significantly less competitive than American children of comparable ages (Kagan & Madsen, 1972; Madsen, 1971).

Given the prior cross-cultural research findings, we would anticipate that one would observe an increase in relative gain or competitive choices as a function of age or grade level for both Anglo- and Mexican-American children. Furthermore, given the prior results of Madsen and collaborators, we would anticipate that at all age levels Mexican-American children would be less relative gain oriented (competitive) than their Anglo-American counterparts.

METHOD

Subjects

The subjects were 108 Mexican-American and 108 Anglo-American children equally distributed across three grade levels: second, fourth, and sixth. The Anglo-American children were all males, and hence for the game task, there were 18 male dyads tested at each grade level. The Mexican-American population included both male and female dyads: for the second grade, there were 11 male and 7 female dyads; for the fourth, 11 male and 7 female dyads; and for the sixth, 13 male and 5 female dyads. The use of male dyads and female dyads in the Mexican-American sample was necessitated by restriction in the number of male subjects available. In the Results section, we examine whether the sex of dyads had a measurable effect on the dominance of competitive choice behavior.

The samples above included only subjects whose behavior during a pretest indicated that they understood the implications of the various choices in the experimental task. The experimenters working with the Mexican-American children came from a similar background and provided instructions in English, Spanish, or both depending on the language facility of the children. Dyads were selected so as to minimize the inclusion of close friends in the same pair. The socioeconomic status of the Mexican-American and Anglo-American samples was not matched, and hence this variable remained uncontrolled. The possible implications of this source of noncontrol are considered in the Discussion section of the present article.

The task

The task employed was a maximizing difference game that was instrumented for children. The matrix structure of the game is given in Figure 1. As indicated in this figure, a cooperative choice (A_1 or B_1) permits both own and joint gain maximization in any given trial or across any series of trials, whereas a competitive response (A_2 or B_2) permits relative gain maximization. The responses are defined cooperative and competitive insofar as an A_1 or B_1 choice provides the other with reinforcement (points), whereas an A_2 or B_2 response impedes the other from achieving points and hence guarantees that the other cannot obtain more points than self.

A schematic picture of the experimental choice and display apparatus for the present study is presented in Figure 2. Each child had his own choice and display apparatus that included four rectilinear boxes with the four possible outcomes attending the two choices of the subject and the two of the other player. Outcome lights in the center of each box displayed which outcomes had attended the players' joint choices. The light came on only after both children had completed making their choices. The choices themselves were made by pushing one of two buttons labeled left and right in Figure 2. A series of lines running from the buttons to the various rectilinear boxes indicated what point outcome attended the various combinations of button choices. A red start signal or light indicated the beginning of each trial. Hence, on each trial each subject pushed one of his two buttons after the start signal came on. After both had chosen, a light came on in that rectangular box that indicated the outcome of their joint choices, and the subject could see how

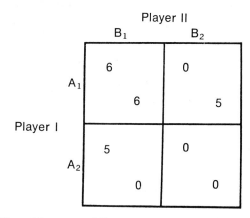

Fig. 1. Maximizing difference game matrix. (Outcome for Player I is in upper left corner of each column.)

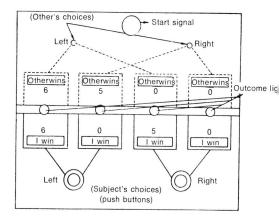

Fig. 2. Maximizing difference game apparatus.

many points he had obtained on the trial and how many the other player had obtained. Dyads played the game for 100 trials.

In addition to trial by trial information regarding own and other's outcomes, a digital display system (comparable to a basketball game scoreboard) was updated after each trial to display both the player's own total cumulative score and that of the other player. A parallel display system was designed to help second graders evaluate their own and the other player's cumulative scores should they have difficulty understanding numerical (digital) point totals. Buttons corresponding in number to each subject's payoffs were inserted after each trial into a series of calibrated transparent glass tubes. The subjects could then visually compare through time how many buttons they each had in their respective tubes. Finally, a screen prevented the subjects from seeing one another, and they were requested not to communicate with one another during the game.

General procedures

For both Anglo-American and Mexican-American children, pairs of subjects were taken from classes to an experimental trailer for testing. Very detailed instructions were given to the children together on the nature of the task, and both played a number of demonstration trials. In these trials, the children had to indicate successfully what choice they and the other player would have to make in order to produce each of the four possible outcomes as displayed in the four rectilinear boxes on the display board. If the children could not, the situation was explained again, and they were tested again. In addition, the two cumulative scoring systems were explained and illustrated. (Phenomenological data collected on other populations using the same apparatus indicates that the task is readily understood by most children in the second, fourth, and sixth grades.) No specific goals were given children regarding what outcomes they should attempt to achieve during the game. They were merely informed that they were playing a game in which it was possible to obtain points.

RESULTS

Given the motivational structure of the maximizing difference game, the overall analysis of game choices are presented in terms of the number of maximizing relative gain or competitive choices. In this game an own or joint gain orientation should lead to a cooperative choice, a relative gain to a competitive one. Figure 3 presents the mean proportion of relative or competitive choices for the three grade levels for Anglo-American and Mexican-American dyads and for male dyads and female dyads within the Mexican-American sample. Because the relationship between both Mexican-American male dyads and female dyads and the Anglo-American dyads was comparable, the Mexican-American data were collapsed across sex of dyad, and an analysis of variance was computed with culture and grade as between-dyad factors, and trials as a within- or repeated-measures factor.

As indicated in Table 1, all three main effects were significant. Anglo-American children were more competitive than were Mexican-American; competition increased as a function of age level; and choices tended to become more competitive as the game progressed.

There was no Grade × Culture interaction, reflecting the almost linear increase within both cultures in competitive

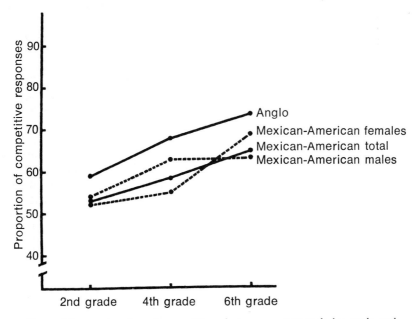

Fig. 3. Mean proportion of competitive choices over 100 trials by grade and culture. (The Anglo-American sample was 18 male dyads per grade. The Mexican-American sample was 11 male dyads and 7 female dyads in the second and fourth grades and 13 male dyads and 5 female dyads in the sixth grade.)

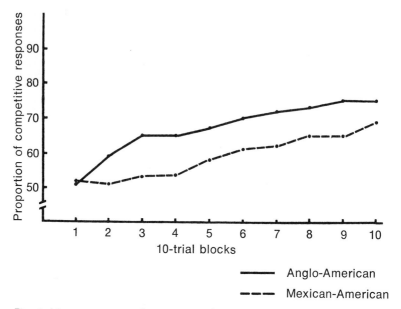

Fig. 4. Mean proportion of competitive choices by 10-trial blocks for Anglo-American and Mexican-American second, fourth, and sixth graders.

Table 1. Analysis of variance of competitive choices: Culture × Grade × Trials

Source	MS	df	F
Between			
Culture (A)	710.53	1	10.50***
Grade (B)	630.45	2	9.32**
A × B	11.74	2	.17
Error	67.66	102	
Within			
Trials (C)	206.47	9	52.68***
A × C	12.84	9	3.28***
B × C	10.04	18	2.56***
A × B × C	6.57	18	1.68*
Error	3.92	918	

* $p < .05$.
** $p < .01$.
*** $p < .001$.

responding as a function of trade level. The significant trial effect, which reflected an increase in competitive choices through the course of the game, is apparent in Figure 4. This figure also indicates that the significant Trial × Culture interaction derived from the fact that the Mexican-American population showed a slower rate of increase in competitive responding in the early trial blocks. The significant Trial × Grade interaction reflected the more rapid increase in competitive responding across trials in sixth as compared to fourth as compared to second grade. The triple interaction, though significant, was small in magnitude and hence is not interpreted here. Thus, the analysis of variance and Figures 3 and 4 indicate that as hypothesized, for both cultural groups there was an increase in choices based on relative gain motivation as a function of age and that at each grade level, Anglo-American children were more competitive than Mexican-American children.

DISCUSSION

As in prior studies using the maximizing difference game with children at various age levels and from differing cultural backgrounds, we have observed an increasing level of competitive or relative gain motivation as a function of age. Because of the structure of the maximizing difference game, it is difficult to ascertain what motives lead to higher cooperative responding in the younger children—whether it is predominantly consideration of own gain maximization or joint gain maximization that leads to the A_1 and B_1

choices depicted in Figure 1. Preliminary findings from an ongoing study of nursery school children would seem to indicate that very young children are concerned principally with own gain maximization, behaving more like the "rational economic man" model of man than their older counterparts.

Both the present and prior studies on the development of cooperative and competitive behaviors, as well as the motives that give rise to them, have been principally descriptive in nature. However, the major findings of these studies are consistent with a conceptual model of the development of achievement motivation proposed by Veroff (1969). Veroff distinguished *autonomous* from *social* achievement, noting that the first implies establishing and evaluating goals in terms of some internalized personal standard and that the second implies social comparison and establishment of a relative standard of performance. He went on to argue that in very young children, especially those younger than five or six, the child is egocentric and does not use others' outcomes as a basis of evaluating his own. In terms of our definitional system, we would characterize a child of this age as predominantly own gain oriented.

Veroff argued that with further socialization by parents and the schools, the child enters a second developmental phase of achievement motivation, a social comparison stage. He notes, "Social comparison does not necessarily mean aggressive competition, but it often does. Furthermore, successful social comparison does not have to mean social approval, but it often does [1969, p. 47]." In effect, in terms of our motivational scheme, one would anticipate during the social comparison stage an increase in relative gain or competitive behavior, particularly in situations where outcomes are mutually determined and where an opportunity for comparison of outcomes exists. And indeed this is what we have observed repeatedly across various cultures.

Veroff finally asserted that there is a third possible stage in the development of achievement motivation, a final "mature" orientation to achievement, namely, some form of integration between autonomous

(individualistic or own gain) and social comparison (competitive or relative gain) strivings. We have no direct evidence on this latter stage except that we have observed in several of the cultures where we have data for both sixth-grade and university students that the latter make fewer relative and more own gain choices than the former in comparable settings of outcome interdependence.

One implication of the observed differences in the rate of development of competitive responding between Anglo- and Mexican-American children can be noted. Given the strong likelihood that American primary schools both shape and use competitive motives to promote and reward academic achievement and performance, one can ask whether Mexican-American children may not be ontogenetically out of phase with the educational system of the majority culture. If this should obtain, then a society concerned with improving the effectiveness of its educational programs is confronted with several alternative courses of action. It may establish separate institutions or programs that effectively take into account the normative rate of development of social motives in minority children. It may attempt to influence the development of the motivational orientations of minority children to correspond with the majority and maintain those educational programs designed to serve such motives. Or, conversely, it may attempt to modify the motivational orientations of the majority to correspond to the minority and revise its educational programs accordingly—a somewhat unlikely course of action.

In conclusion, several limitations of the present investigation are noted. First, the comparison of Anglo- and Mexican-American children suffers from the usual lack of control on possible variables other than cultural background that might be responsible for the observed differences. We did not, for example, attempt to control on either the socioeconomic status of the families of the children or on individual intelligence. In terms of the socioeconomic status characteristics of the two samples, each is fairly typical of the majority of Anglo-American and Mexican-American families in this society, and the findings representative in this sense. In effect, our Anglo-American children were drawn principally from middle-class families, our Mexican-American children from lower- and lower-middle-class families. Further studies are obviously required to establish whether socioeconomic status is a major contributor to the obtained differences or whether other variables such as differences in cultural norms account for them. It might be noted that in previous studies large variations in competitive choice behavior have been found between cultures even when systematic attempts have been made to control for socio-economic status (McClintock, 1972b). In terms of intelligence, it remains problematic as to whether appropriate measures exist to make meaningful comparisons or establish adequate controls across two samples whose cultures vary and where one group comes from a monolingual background and the other principally from a bilingual background.

A second limitation of the present investigation is characteristic of most comparative research. Namely, in order to measure differences between diverse groups in a meaningful way, it is first necessary to establish commonality of process and measurement. In the present study, several means were employed to establish comparable tasks and measures across both grades and cultures. However, no single study is likely to assure commonality with certainty.

Finally, a cautionary note should be introduced regarding the interpretation of the observed differences between culture and grade levels. In making such comparisons, one typically summarizes one's observations in terms of averages or means. It is important, particularly in cross-cultural research, to stress that there is variability of behavior within groups and an overlap in behavior between groups. Failure to recognize variability often leads to simplified assertions that contribute to stereotyping of the attributes or the behaviors of members of groups.

REFERENCES

Coleman, J. S., Campbell, E. Q., Hobson, C. J., McFarland, J., Mood, A. M., Weinfold, F. D., & York, R. L. *Equality of opportunity.* Washington, D.C.: U.S. Government Printing Office, 1966.

Kagan, S., & Madsen, M. C. Cooperation and competition of Mexican, Mexican-American, and Anglo-American children of two ages under four instructional sets. *Developmental Psychology,* 1971, **5**, 32-39.

Kagan, S., & Madsen, M. C. Rivalry in Anglo-American and Mexican children of two ages. *Journal of Personality and Social Psychology,* 1972, **24**, 214-220.

Lesser, G. H., Fifer, G., & Clock, D. H. Mental abilities of children from different social class and cultural groups. *Monographs of the Society of Research in Child Development,* 1965, **30**(4, Serial No. 102).

Madsen, M. C. Development and cross-cultural differences in the cooperative and competitive behavior of young children. *Journal of Cross-Cultural Psychology,* 1971, **2**, 365-371.

Madsen, M. C., & Shapira, A. Cooperative and competitive behavior of urban Afro-American, Anglo-American, Mexican-American, and Mexican village children. *Developmental Psychology,* 1970, **3**, 16-20.

McClintock, C. G. Game behavior and social motivation in interpersonal settings. In C. McClintock (Ed.), *Experimental social psychology.* New York: Holt, Rinehart & Winston, 1972 (a).

McClintock, C. G. Social motivation—A set of propositions. *Behavioral Science,* 1972, **17**, 438-454. (b)

McClintock, C. G., & Nuttin, J. M., Jr. Development of competitive game behavior in children across two cultures. *Journal of Experimental Social Psychology,* 1969, **5**, 203-218.

Messick, D. M., & McClintock, C. G. Motivational bases of choice in experimental games. *Journal of Experimental Social Psychology,* 1968, **4**, 1-25.

Veroff, J. Social comparison and the development of achievement. In C. Smith (Ed.), *Achievement related motives in children.* New York: Russell Sage Foundation, 1969.

CHAPTER 11 A COMPARISON OF CHICANOS AND ANGLOS ON LOCUS OF CONTROL[1]

RAYMOND T. GARZA
RUSSELL E. AMES, Jr.

Studies have shown that perceived locus of control can be affected by cultural background (Parsons, Schneider, & Hansen, 1970; Reitz and Groff, 1972; Tin-Yee Hsieh, Skyhut, & Lotsof, 1969). A couple of studies have indirectly dealt with the locus of control orientation of Mexican-Americans. A study comparing Anglo- and Mexican-American eighth grade students on personality traits and academic achievement suggested that Mexican-Americans are less internal than Anglo-Americans (Rogers, 1972). Using an unpublished instrument to assess locus of control, Stone and Ruiz (1971) found no differences between Anglos and Mexican-Americans on internality.

What would be the expected locus of control orientation of Chicanos on the basis of their cultural characteristics? Some have argued that fatalism is a predominant Mexican-American cultural characteristic, while others have contended that fatalism is a function of socioeconomic background. Justin (1970) suggested that, compared to their Anglo peers, Mexican-Americans are lacking in feelings of personal control. While comparing American and Mexican-American value orientations, Cabrera (1964) mentioned attitudes of fatalism as being a cultural characteristic of

[1]Paper presented at the forty-sixth annual convention of the Midwestern Psychological Association, Chicago, Illinois, May, 1974.

Mexican-Americans. Casavantes (1970), on the other hand, contended that fatalism is not a function of being a Mexican-American but of living in poverty, claiming that middle- and upper-class Mexican-Americans are not fatalistic. If fatalism is a cultural characteristic, it would be expected that Mexican-Americans would score more externally than less fatalistic cultures. On the other hand, if fatalism is not a cultural characteristic but a correlate of socioeconomic class, this contention would not be supported.

Another cultural characteristic of Mexican-Americans that could be related to locus of control is their tendency to express a traditional pride in their culture and a strong resistance to pressures applied to change them. Simmons (1966) pointed out that Mexican-Americans want to be full members of the larger society but not at the expense of giving up their cultural heritage. This resistance to external forces seemed to suggest a belief in internal locus of control, at least with respect to certain sets of values. In the area of familial relationships, Mexican-Americans value and maintain very close interpersonal ties among their immediate and extended family members (Gill & Spilka, 1962; Murillo, 1971). Cable and Minton (1971) suggested that family-centered environments could contribute to a greater perception of internal control. Thus, Mexican-American values associated with cultural pride and

133

close family ties suggested that they might score more internally on I-E than cultures without such predominant values.

To attempt to clarify the effects of the Mexican-American cultural background on locus of control, the responses of Chicano and Anglo college students to Rotter's (1966) I-E were compared in the present study. A criticism of research on the characteristics of Mexican-Americans has been that most generalizations are invalid because they are based on low income samples (Casavantes, 1970). In order to rule out such explanations, Anglo- and Mexican-Americans were matched on socioeconomic background. Cross-cultural researchers have suggested that examinations of the sub-categories of Rotter's scale can provide greater insight into differences among cultural groups (Reitz & Groff, 1972; Schneider & Parsons, 1970). Five sub-categories have been established: (1) luck, fate, (2) politics, (3) respect, (4) leadership, success, and (5) academic. Thus, in addition to hypothesizing cross cultural differences on the total I-E score, an exploratory investigation was made of cross-cultural differences on the five I-E sub-scales.

METHOD

Using Rotter's (1966) locus of control scale, data were gathered at Texas A & I University on a sample of 204 freshmen and sophomore students: 88 Anglo-Americans, 86 Mexican-Americans, 9 Blacks, and 21 from other ethnic groups. From this aggregate of respondents, it was possible to match 47 Anglo-Americans with 47 Mexican-Americans on socioeconomic background and sex. Socioeconomic background classification was determined on the basis of annual family income. Four categories were delineated: less than $5,000; 5,000 to 10,000; 10,000 to 15,000; and more than 15,000. The matched sample included 24 male pairs, 23 female pairs and 11 pairs, 21 pairs, 10 pairs and 5 pairs of Anglo- and Mexican-Americans in each ascending income bracket, respectively.

Subjects completed the I-E scale during class time. Instructions were read orally by the regular class instructor in each of the selected classes. Those students who did not wish to participate were not required to do so.

RESULTS AND DISCUSSION

Mean scores, standard deviations, and *t* values are presented in Table 1. Mexican-Americans were significantly ($p < .01$) less external than Anglo-Americans on the total scale score. Significant differences were also found on two of the five dimensional categories. Mexican-Americans were significantly less external on luck and fate ($p < .01$) and respect ($p < .02$). Differences on politics, leadership and success, and academics were not statistically significant.

The findings can be explained in terms of cultural values of the Mexican-American group. The family-centered orientation (Murillo, 1971) and the perennial resistance to give up their culture and heritage (Simmons, 1968) suggest belief in internal locus of control inasmuch as they indicate resistance to external influences. The interesting and significant finding that Mexican-Americans scored less external than Anglo-Americans on luck and fate contradicts the popular stereotype that Chicanos are fatalistic. Since socioeconomic status was controlled, Casavantes' (1970) contention that fatalism is not a Mexican-American cultural characteristic, but a function of socioeconomic status received support. Previous investigations which have suggested that Mexican-Americans lack feelings of personal control (e.g., Justin, 1970) usually did not take into account socioeconomic factors.

The finding that Mexican-Americans scored significantly less external on the re-

Table 1. Mean scores, standard deviations, and *t* values

I-E category	Anglo-Americans N = 47		Mexican-Americans N = 47		
	Mean	SD	Mean	SD	t
Total scale	10.98	4.30	8.79	3.34	2.76**
Luck, fate	3.28	1.90	2.21	1.39	3.10**
Politics	2.28	1.23	2.36	1.01	.37
Respect	2.45	1.18	1.89	.98	2.48*
Leadership, success	1.47	1.16	1.04	1.00	1.91
Academics	1.36	1.01	1.23	.94	.64

*$p < .02$
**$p < .01$

spect dimension is consistent with their cultural background. The fact that Mexican-Americans are usually polite and respectful toward others even when it is not an expression of true feelings (Murillo, 1971) suggests a great deal of internal control over this interpersonal dimension.

The findings reported here may seem unexpected because they are in direct opposition to the cultural stereotype that Mexican-Americans are fatalistic. Nevertheless, the explanations offered are based on their cultural characteristics and seem tenable. In sum, the finidngs not only contradict the stereotype that Mexican-Americans are fatalistic and controlled by external forces, but seem to suggest that their culture actually contributes to a greater perception of internal control.

REFERENCES

Cable, R. K. and Minton, H. L. Social class, race, and junior high students' belief in personal control. *Psychological Reports,* 1971, **29** (3, pt. 2), 1188-1190.

Cabrera, Y. A. A study of American and Mexican-American culture values and their significance in education. *Dissertation Abstracts,* 1964, **25,** 309.

Casavantes, E. Pride and prejudice: A Mexican-American dilemma. *Civil Rights Digest.* Winter, 1970, **3,** 22-27.

Gill, L. and Spilka, B. Some non-intellectual correlates of academic achievement among Mexican-American secondary school students. *Journal of Educational Psychology,* 1962, **53,** 144-149.

Justin, N. Culture, conflict, and Mexican-American achievement. *School and Society,* 1970, **98,** 27-28.

Murillo, N. The Mexican-American family. In N. N. Wagner and M. J. Haug (Eds.), Chicanos: *Social and Psychological Perspectives.* St. Louis: The C. V. Mosby Co., 1971, pp. 97-108.

Parsons, O. A., Schneider, J. M., & Hansen, A. S. Internal-external locus of control and national stereotypes in Denmark and the United States. *Journal of Consulting and Clinical Psychology,* 1970, **35,** 30-37.

Reitz, H. J. & Groff, G. K. Comparisons of locus of control categories among American, Mexican, and Thai workers. *Proceedings of the Annual Convention of the American Psychological Association,* 1972, **7** (pt. 1), 263-264.

Rogers, D. P. Personality traits and academic achievement among Mexican-American students. *Dissertation Abstracts International,* 1972, **33,** 2179-2180.

Rotter, J. B. Generalized expectations for internal vs. external control of reinforcement. *Psychological Monographs,* 1966, **80** (1, Whole No. 609).

Schneider, J. M., & Parsons, O. A. Categories on the locus of control scale and cross-cultural comparisons in Denmark and the United States. *Journal of Cross-Cultural Psychology,* 1970, **1,** 131-138.

Simmons, O. G. The mutual images and expectations of Anglo-Americans and Mexican-Americans. In Bernal Segal (Ed.), *Racial and ethnic relations.* New York: Thomas Crowell, 1966.

Tin-Yee Hsieh, T., Skyhut, J., and Lotsof, E. J. Internal vs. external control and ethnic group membership: A cross-cultural comparison. *Journal of Consulting and Clinical Psychology,* 1969, **33,** 122-124.

Stone, P. C., & Ruiz, R. A. Race and class as differential determinants of underachievement and underaspiration among Mexican-Americans. Paper presented at the annual convention of the American Psychological Association, 1971.

CHAPTER 12 NATIONAL ORIGIN AND GHETTO EXPERIENCE AS VARIABLES IN MEXICAN AMERICAN STEREOTYPY

ANTHONY GARY DWORKIN

The study of the stereotypes and self-images of native-born and foreign-born Mexican Americans (Dworkin, 1965) raised several questions not anticipated in the original research. One such question concerns the relative importance of national origin versus length of residence in the Mexican American ghetto to account for the divergence between NBMA and FBMA stereotypes of Anglos. This is especially relevant, since replications reported to this researcher have not always supported the 1965 findings. In cases in which replication has not corroborated the 1965 study, national origin alone, without consideration for length of ghetto exposure, constituted the FBMA definition. It should be recalled that the NBMAs were natural-born citizens of the United States, while FBMAs were still Mexican nationals who had lived in the United States six months or less—presumably not having had time to change their reference groups and stereotypes.

Dworkin (1970) compared NBMAs and FBMAs to determine whether the stereotypes held by each subgroup served as functional vocabularies of motives to articulate and rationalize different forms of civil rights protest. It was felt that the negative images of the Anglo held by NBMAs would justify protest activity of a more violent nature than could be rationalized by the positive images held by FBMAs. In fact, it was thought that FBMA imagery might rationalize attitudes and actions that would not challenge Anglo dominance. The data supported this hypothesis. However, at that time (1967) Mexican American willingness to engage in protest, violent or otherwise, was considerably less than that of other minorities such as black Americans. Only 3 per cent of the Mexican Americans and 37 per cent of the black Americans favored riots over other forms of protest, while 22 per cent of the Mexican Americans and 68 per cent of the black Americans gave riots qualified support. Furthermore, 41 percent of the Mexican Americans and 97 per cent of the black Americans supported nonviolent protest as preferable to no action.

Clear distinctions existed between FBMAs and NBMAs. None of the former and 27 percent of the latter felt that riots were effective. Furthermore 10 per cent of the FBMAs and 72 per cent of the NBMAs preferred nonviolent protest over no action at all. The 1970 article did imply that FBMAs might begin to adopt NBMA stereotypes and endorsement of violent and nonviolent protest as their residence in the ghetto lengthened and their experiences with Anglo discrimination increased.

It is the intention of the present paper to determine whether FBMAs living in the ghetto retain their favorable stereotypes of Anglos or eventually acquire the unfavorable images held by their NBMA counterparts. The data we collected to answer our question was cross-sectional and static, and as such we must infer process. Our sample consisted of 131 Mexican Americans living in the Los Angeles and Denver Standard Metropolitan Statistical Areas. The sample was divided into three categories: NBMAs, FBMA long terms, and FBMA recents. Of the Ss, 78 were NBMAs and 53 were FBMAs, of whom 21 were recent migrants to the United States (here less than six months) and 32 were long-term residents (greater than six months, but with a median of 9.6 years). All of the Ss were between the ages of 18 and 30; 60 had attended college; 72 had no formal education beyond high school; 54 were women and 77 were men.

Each S was administered a questionnaire by a Mexican American interviewer of the same age and sex. Stereotypes were collected using an open-ended format, used also in the 1965 study. Such a format allows the Ss to articulate their own descriptions instead of limiting them to predetermined checklist items. Duijker and Frijda (1960) and Ehrlich and Rinehart (1965) have recommended the open-ended technique. Several measures of stereotypy besides the actual images were obtained, including some of those identified by Edwards (1940) and Fishman (1956). Particularly relevant to our present discussion were three indices: Direction, Judged Quality, and Similarity to Self.[1] Factor analysis of the three indices generated a common dimension that we labeled Stereotype Ethnocentrism. This factor indicates that Ss stereotype unfavorably (Direction) and prejudicially (Judged Quality) those targets who are perceived by the Ss to be unlike themselves (Similarity to Self). Conversely, the favorable, nonprejudicial, and the similar cluster together. To embrace the similar and reject the different characterize in intergroup relations what we have classically thought of as ethnocentrism. When the medium of such ac-

ceptance and rejection involves stereotypy, we may call it Stereotype Ethnocentrism.

Factor scores for the Mexican American Ss were computed for Stereotype Ethnocentrism. The range of possible factor scores was from 1.0 to 3.0. Median factor scores were computed for each of the categories of Mexican Americans. The NBMA sample scored highest with a Stereotype Ethnocentrism median of 2.76; the long-term FBMAs were second with a median of 2.66; and the recent FBMAs had the lowest Stereotype Ethnocentrism with a median of 1.16. If we trichotomize Stereotype Ethnocentrism into high, medium, and low scores and crosstabulate these with the three categories of Mexican Americans, we arrive at a property space consisting of a 3×3 contingency table, as presented in Table 1.

In order to establish the importance of ghetto experience over national origin, it will be necessary to demonstrate that if NBMA stereotypes of Anglos are unfavorable, then the number of Ss with high Stereotype Ethnocentrism should be distributed in accordance with the following hypotheses:

H_1: There is no significant difference in the distribution of NBMA and FBMA long-term Ss on the Stereotype Ethnocentrism factor.

H_2: FBMA long-term Ss will have significantly higher Stereotype Ethnocentrism scores than FBMA recent Ss.

H_3: NBMA Ss will have significantly higher Stereotype Ethnocentrism scores than FBMA recent Ss.

Table 1 suggested that if H_1 and H_2 are tenable, then H_3 will also be tenable. Thus, we need only compute two 2×3 chi square tests of significance. Alpha was set at .01 in order to be cautious. Tables 2 and 3 present the results of those tests. With two degrees of freedom, the obtained chi square value for the test of H_1 is 0.747, which is not significant. As H_1 is actually a null hypothesis, we accept it and conclude that there is no significant difference between the distribution of NBMA and FBMA long-term Ss on the Stereotype Ethnocentrism factor.

The 2×3 chi square comparing the FBMA long-term Ss with the FBMA recent Ss yielded a value of 20.36, which for two degrees of freedom is significant at beyond

---

[1]Direction was defined as the valence of the stereotypes, and was coded in terms of whether the S felt his images were favorable, neutral, or unfavorable. Judged Quality was a generalized measure of the connotation of the stereotypes as determined by a panel of judges who coded the images as biased against the target, neutral, or biased in favor of the target. Similarity to Self was the degree to which the S felt that he himself possessed the same characteristic as he ascribed to the target.

Table 1. Stereotype Ethnocentrism scores for the three Mexican American subgroups

	NBMA	FBMA (long-term)	FBMA (recent)	Σ
Low	10	5	16	31
Medium	15	8	3	26
High	53	19	2	74
Σ	78	32	21	131

Table 2. Stereotype Ethnocentrism for NBMA and FBMA (long-term)

	NBMA	FBMA (long-term)	Σ
Low	10	5	15
Medium	15	8	23
High	53	19	72
Σ	78	32	110

$\chi^2 = 0.747$, d.f. = 2, $\alpha = .01$, N.S.

Table 3. Stereotype Ethnocentrism for FBMA (long-term) and FBMA (recent)

	FBMA (long-term)	FBMA (recent)	Σ
Low	5	16	21
Medium	8	3	11
High	19	2	21
Σ	32	21	53

$\chi^2 = 20.36$, d.f. = 2, $\alpha = .01$, $p < .001$.

the .001 level of confidence. We can thus accept H_2 as tenable. A significant difference exists in the distribution of recent and long-term FBMAs, with the FBMA long-term Ss displaying greater Stereotype Ethnocentrism toward the Anglo target group.

The tenability of H_1 and H_2 make it axiomatic that H_3 is also tenable. No difference exists in the Stereotype Ethnocentrism between NBMA and FBMA long-term Ss, while a significant difference exists between FBMA long-term and FBMA recent, and consequently a significant difference must exist between NBMA and FBMA recent (these two have the most extreme median Stereotype Ethnocentrism scores).

Table 4. Stereotypes mentioned by Mexican Americans to describe Anglos

	Group using the stereotype		
	NBMA	FBMA (long-term)	FBMA (recent)
Athletic	X	X	X
Well dressed	X	X	X
High economic level	X	X	X
Well educated	X	X	X
High social position	X	X	X
Materialistic	X	X	X
Bigoted	X	X	
Poor family life	X	X	
Greedy	X	X	
Prejudiced	X	X	
Snob	X	X	
Superiority complex	X	X	
Hypocritical	X	X	
Conformist	X	X	
Average intelligence		X	X
Good family life			X
Intelligent			X
Religious			X
Social			X
Average social position			X
Progressive			X
Clean			X
Hard-working			X
Friendly			X

In order to add further to the salience of the evidence of differences between FBMA recents on the one hand and FBMA long-term and NBMAs on the other, Table 4 presents a list of the most commonly mentioned stereotypes of the Anglo enumerated from the Mexican American subgroups. The images presented in the table represent only a partial listing, as we include only those stereotypes mentioned by 5 per cent or more of the Mexican Americans.[2] Examination of the table reveals

[2] Limiting the list to images held by 5 or more per cent of the sample achieved several things: (1) it made the list of free associations of stereotypes more manageable; (2) it permitted us to avoid presenting idiosyncratic or personal stereotypes as opposed to social stereotypes (see Secord and Backman, 1964); and (3) it brought the present research closer to the tradition established by those who rely upon adjective checklists and the Katz and Braly (1933) Index of Stereotypy format, thereby providing continuity to the literature.

that NBMA and FBMA long-term *S*s mentioned nearly identical stereotypes of the Anglo. The images contain many descriptions that are highly critical of the Anglo. The FBMA recent *S*s, however, mention many words not appearing on the lists by the other Mexican Americans, and nearly all of their images are favorable.

It now seems that national origin *per se* is not the variable which accounts for the FBMA-NBMA dichotomy found in Dworkin (1965). Rather, the relative amount of time each has been exposed to Anglo discrimination and prejudice (measured in terms of length of ghetto residence) is the essential component. Those who have communicated to this author that the NBMA-FBMA dichotomy is not a salient one, and who have taken national origin, without concern for the length of ghetto residence, to demarcate the NBMA and FBMA populations apparently have been in error.

REFERENCES

Duijker, H. C. J., and Frijda, N. H. National Character and National Stereotypes. Amsterdam: North Holland Publishing Co., 1960.

Dworkin, Anthony Gary. Stereotypes and Self Images Held by Native-Born and Foreign-Born Mexican Americans. Sociology and Social Research, 1965, **49**, 214-224.

Dworkin, Anthony Gary. Epilogue to Stereotypes and Self-Images of Mexican Americans. In John H. Burma (ed.) Mexican-Americans in the United States. Cambridge, Mass.: Schenkman, 1970.

Edwards, Allen L. Four Dimensions in Political Stereotypes, Journal of Abnormal and Social Psychology, 1940, **35**, 566-572.

Ehrlich, Howard J., and Rinehart, James. A Brief Report on the Methodology of Stereotype Research, Social Forces, 1965, **42**, 564-575.

Fishman, Joshua A. An Examination of the Process and Function of Social Stereotyping, Journal of Social Psychology, 1956, **43**, 27-64.

Katz, D., and Braly, K. Racial Stereotypes of 100 College Students, Journal of Abnormal and Social Psychology, 1933, **28**, 280-290.

Secord, Paul F., and Backman, Carl W. Social Psychology. New York: McGraw-Hill, 1964.

CHAPTER 13 SELF-CONCEPTIONS OF MIGRANT AND SETTLED MEXICAN AMERICANS[1]

VIKTOR GECAS

There are two major dimensions of the self-concept which have been the foci of empirical research: the evaluative and the substantive.[2] The evaluative component refers to the indivdual's *feelings* about himself, his self-esteem; while the substantive dimension refers to the content of a person's ideas about himself, typically expressed in the form of *identities.* Most of the research on the self-conceptions of Mexican Americans has stressed the evaluative dimension, with inconclusive results. For example, Coleman[3] and Hishiki[4] found the self-evaluations of Mexican American children to be significantly lower than those of Anglo children, while DeBlassie and Healy[5] and Carter[6] found no significant differences between these two groups. A number of other studies have explored the stereotypes and self-images of Mexican Americans.[7] Typically, these studies focus on various self-*attributes* expressed by these populations which have clearly identifiable positive or negative values, such as, "emotional," "familistic," "lazy," "religious," "authoritarian," etc. Much of this literature has concentrated on that cluster of values and traits associated with the concept of *machismo* as a pivotal aspect of the male's self-concept in Mexican culture.[8]

From Social Science Quarterly, 54 *(3)* (Dec., 1973), pp. 579-595.

[1]This is a revision of a paper presented at the annual meeting of the Pacific Sociological Association, May, 1973. This research was conducted as Project 1743, Department of Rural Sociology, Agriculture Research Center, College of Agriculture, Washington State University.

[2]For excellent reviews of research on the self-concept see Ruth Wylie, *The Self-Concept: A Critical Survey of Pertinent Research Literature* (Lincoln, Nebraska: University of Nebraska Press, 1961) and Ruth Wylie, "The Present Status of Self Theory," in E. F. Borgatta and W. W. Lambert, eds., *Handbook of Personality Theory and Research* (Chicago: Rand McNally and Co., 1968).

[3]J. S. Coleman, *Equality of Educational Opportunity* (Washington, D.C.: U.S. Government Printing Office, 1966).

[4]P. C. Hishiki, "Self-Concepts of Sixth Grade Girls of Mexican Descent," *California Journal of Educational Research,* 20 (March, 1969), pp. 56-62.

[5]R. R. DeBlassie and G. W. Healy, *Self-Concept: A Comparison of Spanish-American, Negro, and Anglo Adolescents Across Ethnic, Sex, and Socio-Economic Variables* (Las Cruces, New Mexico: ERIC-CRESS, 1970).

[6]T. Carter, "Negative Self-Concept of Mexican-American Students," *School and Society,* 95 (March, 1968), pp. 217-219.

[7]See Anthony G. Dworkin, "Stereotypes and Self-Images Held by Native-Born and Foreign-Born Mexican-Americans," *Sociology and Social Research,* 49 (Jan., 1965); G. Hewes, "The Mexican in Search of 'the Mexican'," *American Journal of Economics and Sociology,* 18 (Jan., 1954), pp. 109-223; and Ozzie G. Simmons, "The Mutual Images and Expectations of Anglo-Americans and Mexican-Americans," *Daedalus,* 90 (Spring, 1961), pp. 286-299.

[8]See Michael Maccoby, "On Mexican National Character," *Annals of the American Academy of Political and Social Science,* 70 (1967), pp. 63-73.

To be sure, these trait inventories do get at an aspect of self-concept, the attributive aspect, but they tend to neglect the categorical dimension of self-concept. Gordon's distinction between these two dimensions is worth noting:

The relevant categories denote the "kind of thing" the object is, whereas the attributes describe the object in terms of qualities that differentiate it from others of its kind. . . . Categories tend to have relatively clear boundaries and are inferred according to the logic of membership, exclusion, and inclusion. Attributes, on the contrary, are matters of degree and intensity.[9]

In most of our self-conscious experience, categories and attributes are closely related. For example, if we think of ourselves in gender terms, i.e., "man," we usually associate some qualities with it, such as, "a good man," "a tall man," etc. The point, however, is that research has focused on the qualitative, attributive aspects of self-concept to the neglect, largely, of the categorical dimensions.

The importance of the categorical dimension of self-concept is that it links the individual (psychologically) to social structures. It locates the individual in social space, a space consisting of the myriad of statuses and roles which a society provides to its members and which are integrated into various social structures. Social identity is the term frequently used to refer to the categorical aspect of self.[10] As Stone pointed out, identity establishes what and where the person is in social terms: "When one has identity, he is situated—that is,

cast in the shape of a social object by the acknowledgment of his participation or membership in social relations."[11] From this perspective, a person may have many identities depending on the diversity of social relations in which he engages. The structure of the self-concept, in fact, can be conceived as the hierarchical organization of a person's identities.[12]

The relative neglect of the identity component of self-concept in minority research is unfortunate because this dimension constitutes an important factor in the relations between minority and majority groups and between members of the minority group itself. For Mexican Americans, as well as for blacks and American Indians, political activism and ethnic self-assertion have been directly associated with the self-conscious development and projection of a new group identity. This is most clearly manifest in the process of renaming one's group, in giving it a new identity and a new value. For example, the more activist members of the Mexican American population have come to identify themselves as "Chicanos"; such American Indians prefer to be called "Native Americans"; and Negroes are now referred to as "blacks." The importance of the name used to refer to one's group is illustrated by Grebler, *et al.,* who noted considerable regional differences among Mexican Americans in the name used to denote their ethnic identity:

Californians stood firm for use of the word "Mexican-American." The Texans were resolutely in favor of "Spanish speaking." . . . The descendants of colonial New Mexicans, who often reject the term "Mexican" altogether, insist on some version of "Spanish." This might be "Spanish American," "Hispano" or "Spanish-surname."[13]

[9]Chad Gordon, "Self-Conceptions: Configurations of Content," in C. Gordon and K. J. Gergen, eds., *The Self in Social Interaction* (New York: John Wiley and Sons, 1968), p. 117.

[10]Viktor Gecas, D. L. Thomas and A. J. Weigert, "Social Identities in Anglo and Latin Adolescents," paper presented at the annual meetings of the Pacific Sociological Association, Portland, Oregon, 1972; Gordon, "Self-Conceptions," p. 117; George J. McCall and J. L. Simmons, *Identities and Interactions* (New York: The Free Press, 1966); and Theodore R. Sarbin, "The Culture of Poverty, Social Identities, and Cognitive Outcomes," in V. L. Allen, ed., *Psychological Factors in Poverty* (Chicago: Markham Publishing Co., 1970).

[11]Gregory P. Stone, "Appearance and the Self," in A. Rose, ed., *Human Behavior and Social Process* (Boston: Houghton-Mifflin Co., 1962).

[12]See Gordon, "Self-Conceptions," p. 117; Manfurd Kuhn and Thomas S. McPartland, "An Empirical Investigation of Self-Attitudes," *American Sociological Review,* 19 (Feb., 1954), pp. 68-77; and McCall and Simmons, *Identities and Interactions.*

[13]Leo Grebler, Joan W. Moore, and Ralph C. Guzman, *The Mexican-American People* (New York: The Free Press, 1970), p. 385.

Commitment to these identity labels was illustrated by Grebler when he pointed out that is was impossible for the Mexican American Political Association to merge with the Political Association of Spanish-Speaking Organizations largely because of the ideological commitment of each regionally based group to its own name.[14]

Along with ethnic group identity, other structural, interpersonal, personal, and group identities may be as consequential for Mexican Americans with respect to their actions and interactions with social systems. Farris and Brymer,[15] for example, argued that the Latin youth's integration in peer group and heterosexual relations and commitment to the identities located in these relationships have implications for success or failure in school. They found that it is the Mexican American youth who are alienated from their cultural peers who are most successful in school and those who are integrated tend to drop out.

What seems necessary at this point is a mapping operation to determine the identity patterns of Mexican Americans and to explore their variations for different categories within this population. It should be emphasized that Mexican Americans are a heterogeneous group of people, a point which has been stressed by many writers.[16] The elements or dimensions of diversity are numerous, perhaps as numerous as those in the society as a whole. But one dimension which has a special prominence for this ethnic group is the dimension of geographic mobility. Mexican Americans are disproportionately involved in migrant farm labor. There are about 460,000 migrant farm workers in the United States, most of these are concentrated in the western and southwestern States (California, Texas, New Mexico, Arizona, and Colorado). Over half of these workers are Americans of Mexican descent.[17] Although this represents only about 5 percent of the Mexican American population, many more are involved in this type of work at one time or another. Since the working conditions and life style of migrant labor make for a hard life, many leave the migrant stream as soon as economic circumstances permit.

How does migration as a *style of life* affect the self-conceptions of Mexican Americans? Controlling for the effects of income and occupation, what differences might we expect in the self-attitudes of migrant versus settled populations of Mexican Americans? There is a substantial body of writing in sociology on the psychological consequences of mobility or rootlessness for the individual—from the early products of the "Chicago School" which focused on the disorganizing effect of the city on various immigrant groups,[18] to more contemporary works by Lazarus, Murphy, and others.[19] The theme which frequently appears in these writings is the negative or detrimental effects of geographic mobility—effects such as alienation, anomie, personal disorganization, etc.[20] The extent

---

[14]*Ibid.,* p. 385.

[15]Buford Farris and Richard A. Brymer, "Differential Socialization of Latin and Anglo-American Youth: An Exploratory Study of the Self-Concept," in J. J. Burma, ed., *Mexican-Americans in the United States* (New York: Harper and Row, 1970).

[16]See Grebler, *et al., The Mexican-American People.*

[17]United States Senate Committee on Labor and Public Welfare, Subcommittee on Migratory Labor, "The Migrant Labor Problem in the United States," (1968 Report to the 90th Congress).

[18]Robert E. Park, E. W. Burgess, and R. D. McKenzie, *The City* (Chicago: University of Chicago Press, 1925); W. I. Thomas and F. Znaniecki, *The Polish Peasant in Europe and America* (Chicago: University of Chicago Press, 1918-20); Louis Wirth, "The Problem of Minority Groups," in A. J. Reiss, ed., *Louis Wirth on Cities and Social Life* (Chicago: University of Chicago Press, 1964).

[19]Judith Lazarus, B. Z. Locke, and D. S. Thomas, "Migration and Differentials in Mental Disease," *Milbank Memorial Fund Quarterly*, 41 (Jan., 1963), pp. 25-42; B. Malzberg, and E. S. Lee, *Migration and Mental Disease* (New York: Social Science Research Council, 1956); and H. B. M. Murphy, "Migration and the Major Mental Disorders: A Reappraisal," in M. Kantor, ed., *Mobility and Mental Health* (Springfield, Ill.: Thomas, 1965).

[20]For a more skeptical view of the relationship between migration and personal disorganization, see Charles Tilly, "Race and Migration to the American City," in J. Q. Wilson, ed., *The Metropolitan Enigma* (New York: Anchor Books, 1970).

to which these relationships can be applied to migrant Mexican Americans is questionable. In fact, there is reason to speculate that in a comparison of migrant and settled Mexican Americans, the migrants may have the more positive and integrated self-concepts. The rationale for this speculation is that migrant Mexican Americans, especially those migrating in family units, have undergone less acculturation and integration into Anglo society than have their settled counterparts. Both their mobility and (typically) their residence in isolated labor camps during the harvest season tends to inhibit involvement in local community organizations, institutions, and friendship relationships. As a result, the value systems derived from Mexican culture may be more prominent (less undermined) for this population, giving the migrant Mexican American's sense of self greater consistency and positive value.[21] From this view, acculturation may be more damaging psychologically than mobility. The findings of Farris and Brymer, cited above, give indirect empirical support to this interpretation.

The present study is an exploration of the self-conceptions of poor, rural migrant and settled Mexican Americans in terms of their identity patterns and their self-evaluations, with an emphasis on the former. What are the self-moorings of Mexican American men, women, and children of the rural poverty population? How do these self-conceptions differ for migrant and settled farm workers? What is the nature of the ethnic self-identifications of these groups?

METHOD
Sample and procedure

The findings which are reported here are part of a larger study of rural Mexican American families which focused on the educational and occupational aspirations of Mexican American youth. Data were gathered through extensive interviews with four family members of each family

selected: the father, mother, a grade school-age child and a high school-age child. A Spanish and an English version of the interview schedule was constructed. Our bilingual interviewers determined which version to use in any given case depending on the facility of the respondent. Eighty-five families were interviewed, by Mexican American interviewers, in the Yakima Valley of Washington State. The region is an agricultural area depending heavily on migrant farm labor.

The research design distinguished between two populations of Mexican Americans: migrants who follow the crops and are transient to the area, and those who have settled in various communities in the valley. We used two different sampling procedures to get at each of these populations. For the migrant population we relied on labor camps. After identifying all of the labor camps in the area which employed at least ten families or more, we attempted to draw a random sample. This proved rather fruitless, however, because of the difficulty we encountered from the owners and managers of these camps in getting access to many of the camps chosen.[22] We managed to gain access to 12 camps. Every family in a camp was contacted and those that qualified were interviewed. The qualifications were: (1) they had to be Mexican American, (2) have a family income under $5000, and (3) have a father, mother, 10-13 year old child, and a 14-18 year old child in the family available for interviewing. The last qualification was the most difficult and severely limited the number of families we were able to obtain.

The "settled" sample was drawn from three small towns in the area (populations about 5000) selected for their substantial and identifiable populations of Mexican Americans. An area was demarcated in each town, which was determined through reliable local sources to have the highest

---

[21]This, of course, does not mean that migrants find farm labor any more appealing than do settled farm workers. In fact, their work and living conditions are usually worse than those of settled workers.

[22]During the summer of 1971, when we were collecting our data, there was considerable tension between workers and owners due to the threat of unionization. The owners were suspicious of anyone entering the camps and talking to their workers, and they were very reluctant to give permission for this kind of activity.

Table 1. Sample characteristics of migrant and selected Mexican-Americans

	Migrant	Settled
Number of respondents	146	189
Fathers	35	48
Mothers	36	50
Sons	33	37
Daughters	42	54
Mean age		
Parents	43.6	41.7
Children	14.5	14.1
Family Size (mean)	8.8	7.4
Family Income (mean)	$2760	$3830
Place of Birth (parents)		
Mexico	49%	34%
Texas	44	59
Other	7	7
Parents' Education (in years)	4.0	4.8
Religion: Catholic	94%	90%
Type of Work (Father)		
Fieldwork	92%	63%
Other farm-related work	8	28
Non-agricultural work	0	9
Length of Time Lived in Washington State (Median Years for Parents)	0.6	14.0

concentration of Mexican Americans, and a house-to-house canvass was conducted to identify every qualifying family. A "settled" family was defined as one which had lived in the area for at least one year. The other qualifications for inclusion were the same as for the migrants. Almost all of the fathers in the settled sample were engaged in farm work in some way. Other characteristics of our samples are described in Table 1.

Measure of self-concept

Perhaps the simplest and most direct procedure for ascertaining who a person is, or rather, who he thinks he is, is to ask him to communicate what comes to his mind when he ponders the question, "Who am I?" This procedure was formalized by Kuhn and McPartland[23] in a measure which they called the Twenty Statements Test (TST) designed to get at the self-attitudes of individuals. The rules for this procedure are simple: "In the space provided below, please give twenty answers to the question, 'Who am I?' Answer as if you were giving the answers to yourself, not to somebody else." In our use of the TST, we modified the original technique in two ways: (1) we only asked for ten statements, because we've found that many people tend to run out of things to say after making ten statements, and (2) we had the interviewer write down the statements as given by the respondent.

The principal advantage of the TST as a measure of identities (IDs) is that it allows for an unlimited range of responses because of its minimal structure. The subject can express himself in ways which may be inaccessible to more structured self measures, such as adjective check lists, Q-sorts and semantic differentials. An even greater advantage of the TST over these other measures is that it allows for self-designations in terms of nouns as well as adjectives. It is through the noun form that we usually express our social identities, i.e., teacher, father, sportsman, etc.

The most important and difficult part of the TST is in the construction and application of coding categories.[24] Generally, we looked for a "mention" of a particular form category of self statement, and then compared the percents of persons in various groups mentioning this category. The basic coding system we used is a slightly modified and shortened version of the elaborate scheme developed by Gordon.[25] There are seven major groupings of categories in

---

[23]Kuhn and McPartland, "An Empirical Investigation of Self-Attitudes," pp. 68-77.

[24]For discussions and examinations of some of the more common coding systems used for the TST, and considerations of their validity and test equivalence, cf. B. J. Franklin and F. J. Kohout, "Subject Coded Versus Researcher Coded TST Protocols: Some Methodological Implications," *Sociological Quarterly,* 12 (Winter, 1971), pp. 82-89; Clark McPhail, "Respondents' Judgments of Self Statements," *Sociological Quarterly,* 9 (Spring, 1968), pp. 202-209; Stephen P. Spitzer, J. R. Stratton, J. D. Fitzgerald, and B. K. Mack, "The Self Concept: Test Equivalence and Perceived Validity," *Sociological Quarterly,* 7 (Summer, 1966), pp. 265-280; and Charles W. Tucker, "Some Methodological Problems of Kuhn's Self Theory," *Sociological Quarterly,* 7 (Summer, 1966), pp. 265-280.

[25]Gordon, "Self-Conceptions."

our coding system: (1) *Ascribed Charac-teristics:* identities conferred on the individual at birth which usually remain with him throughout his life and which serve to position the individual with regard to the major axes of differentiation in society; (2) *Roles and Memberships:* this set of social identities is to a greater degree under the control of the individual and structurally locates him in various social organizations; (3) *Abstract Identifications:* references to self as a member either of a universal category or a very particularistic category, such as, "a person," "a human being," "me," "unique"; (4) *Interests and Activities:* statements involving judgments, tastes, likes, intellectual and artistic concerns, and athletic activities; (5) *Material References:* references to the body as an object of self-conscious awareness as well as to other physical possessions and resources; (6) *Senses of Self:* assessment of self as a person of worth, of competence, as an actor in control of his life, and as a helpful or selfless person; (7) *Personal Characteristics:* the individual's typical manner of acting and his style of psychic functioning.[26] Along with these seven identity groupings, we also coded statements which clearly expressed posi-tive or negative evaluations of self, i.e., good, honorable, kind, strong, handsome and bad, ugly, mean, unhappy, etc.[27]

FINDINGS

An overall inspection of the identity patterns revealed in Table 2 indicates that poor Mexican Americans tend to locate themselves most frequently in the structural identities provided by society. Family, gender, and work constitute the most frequently mentioned identities for adults, with family being consistently the highest. It is interesting to note that of the various identities within family, "parent" occurs much more frequently than "spouse." This is comparable to the finding for children that "offspring" is a much more frequent identity than "sibling." It appears that vertical family relationships are more important sources of individual identity than are lateral bonds.

Differences between parents are relatively small and are in the expected direction: mothers mentioned family identities somewhat more frequently, while fathers were more likely to refer to their work or occupational roles. Similarly, social status, which was usually a comment concerning the respondent's poverty situation, and references to possessions and resources were more frequent concerns of the father, undoubtedly because the father is held more responsible for providing for the family. Much of the woman's activity, on the other hand, revolves around her family and home and this, then, constitutes a major arena for her self-definition.[28]

---

[26] A brief illustrative description of the content of the categories is as follows: *Gender:* I am a boy, woman, macho, sexy; *Age:* 17 years old, a kid; *Name:* Jose; *Ethnicity:* Mexican, Chicano; *Religion:* a Catholic, very religious, believe in God; *Family:* any reference to family, family members or family status; *Parent:* mother, father, parent; *Spouse:* husband, wife; *Offspring:* son, daughter; *Sibling:* brother, sister; *Work:* a worker, work hard, fieldworker; *Student:* a student, like school, get good grades; *Citizenship:* American, U.S. citizen, taxpayer; *Social Status:* I am poor; *Abstract Identification:* a person, human, unique, me; *Judgments and likes:* "I think" or "I like" statement; *Intellectual Concerns:* reads a lot, getting an education; *Sports:* play football, run fast; *Physical Self:* good looking, strong, tall, 5'10", healthy; *Possessions:* a car owner, have money; *Moral Worth:* good, honest, self-respecting; *Competence:* any talent or skill, i.e., a good swimmer; *Self-Determination:* try to get ahead, ambitious, confident; *Altruism:* helpful or help people; *Interpersonal Style:* friendly, shy, affectionate, aggressive; *Psychic Style:* happy, moody, proud, depressed.

[27] Inter-coder reliability was assessed for all of the coding categories. The average reliability coefficient for these categories is .88, and in almost all of the cases it is over .80. These coefficients were computed by dividing the number of identical codings, for two coders, by the total number of statements examined. The Spanish versions of the TST were first translated into English so that all of the coding was done in English.

[28] For descriptions of Mexican-American family life, see Leo Grebler, *et al., The Mexican-American People;* Fernando Peñalosa, "Mexican Family Roles," *Journal of Marriage and the Family,* 30 (Nov., 1968), pp. 680-689; Ross D. Staton, "A Comparison of Mexican and Mexican-American Families," *The Family Coordinator,* 21 (July, 1972), pp. 325-330.

Table 2. Percent of respondents mentioning identity category by family position

Identity	Father	Mother	Son	Daughter
Ascribed Characteristics				
Gender	55[a]	72	71	72
Age	1	1	16	20
Name	33	27	33	29
Ethnicity	35	29	41	32
Religion	21	29	21	14
Roles and Memberships				
Family or Kinship	85	91	44	50
Parent	64	84	0	0
Spouse	33	45	0	0
Offspring	4	6	31	27
Sibling	3	4	7	14
Occupation or Work	80	55	39	42
Student	6	1	21	44
Citizenship	5	0	3	2
Social Status	12	2	3	2
Peer	6	5	21	22
Abstract Identification	10	5	25	25
Interests and Activities				
Judgments, Tastes, Likes	13	17	23	19
Intellectual Concerns	8	8	14	22
Artistic Activities	4	0	14	9
Sports and Athletics	2	0	29	8
Material References				
Physical Self; Body Image	2	7	14	24
Possessions, Resources	20	8	7	3
Senses of Self				
Sense of Moral Worth	24	16	19	28
Sense of Competence	25	28	6	22
Sense of Self-Determination	22	8	7	8
Sense of Altruism	72	64	70	76
Personal Characteristics				
Interpersonal Style	37	22	24	35
Psychic Style	21	23	14	29
(N =)	(83)	(86)	(70)	(96)

[a] These percents represent the proportion of people within each family position designation who have mentioned a given identity category at least once.

The most frequent identity category for children is gender. Over 70 percent of boys and girls mentioned it. This is consistent with previous research on children and adolescents which has found gender to be a pivotal identity.[29] Family also constitutes a salient source of identities for children, appearing second in frequency of the structured identities. Girls are more likely to mention family and student IDs, indicating, perhaps, a greater commitment to these areas of social life, while boys are more likely to think of themselves in athletic terms. However, a concern with physical self and body image is more typical of girls (24 percent versus 14 percent). The body may be viewed by the girl as an instrument for the achievement of her major status, that of wife-mother, and so it becomes an important element in her self-concept.

Comparing the identity patterns of children and adults, we find that children more frequently mention peer references,

---

[29] See Gecas, *et al.*, "Social Identities in Anglo and Latin Adolescents," and Gordon, "Self-Conceptions."

abstract identifications, and interests and activities. Adolescents are likely to be more ambivalent about who they are in the categorical terms society provides and more prone to express personal, idiosyncratic identities. Abstract identifications do not integrate the individual very much into on-going social structures, and interests and activities have an exploratory quality about them. The child and adolescent is still in the process of establishing his consensual identities. An important arena for the establishment of *interpersonal* identities is the peer group. It is not surprising that this constitutes a more frequently mentioned identity for children than for adults.

There are some interesting commonalities across parents and children. "Sense of altruism," or the conception of self as a helpful, generous person, was very frequent for all four categories of respondents, with 70 percent of respondents mentioning it. It is clear that poor Mexican Americans think of themselves as helpful and unselfish people. A few identities received surprisingly low frequencies. Ethnicity and religion are the most conspicuous. Mention of cultural heritage or background is most frequent for boys (41 percent) and least frequent for mothers (20 percent), with an overall average of 34 percent mentioning it. This is surprising in view of the strong cultural ties attributed to Mexican Americans, especially those of the poverty sector. Farris and Brymer[30] also found a surprisingly low frequency of mention of ethnic identity by their Mexican American children and adolescents.

When we further explored the question of ethnic sef-identifications we found that the most frequent ethnic label used by both parents and children is "Mexican" and the second most frequent is "Mexican American." The other designations are inconsequential in terms of frequency, except for the finding that 10 percent of the boys identified themselves as "Chicano." If the designation "Chicano" indicates a greater sense of ethnic identification, and perhaps pride, then it is the adolescent male who appears to be most strongly committed to

[30]Farris and Brymer, "Differential Socialization of Latin and Anglo-American Youth."

Table 3. Ethnic self-identification by family position (in percents)

Ethnic designation	Fathers	Mothers	Boys	Girls
Mexican	67	69	51	51
Mexican American	25	27	34	35
Spanish American	0	0	4	7
Spanish	2	1	0	3
Chicano	1	0	10	3
No Response	4	3	0	1
(N =)	(83)	(86)	(70)	(96)

his ethnic identity. The previous finding that boys are most likely to express ethnic identities is consistent with this interpretation.

Now let us consider our two groups of Mexican Americans, migrants and settled, separately for any differences in identity patterns (Table 4). The most striking finding occurs at the evaluative or orientational level of self-conception. Migrants appear to have a more favorable image of themselves than do settled Mexican Americans. On three of the four categories of Senses of Self, migrants expressed more positive self-conceptions.[31] Migrant fathers, mothers, boys, and girls all expressed sense of moral worth and altruism more frequently than did their settled counterparts. Also, migrant parents had more statements indicating personal competence and, to a lesser degree, sense of self-determination than did settled parents. In summary, the migrant respondents have a more optimistic and generally higher conception of themselves than do the settled Mexican Americans. This impression is reinforced by the findings in Table 5 which clearly indicate that migrants also express positive statements about themselves more frequently than settled Mexican Americans. The percentage differences are substantial between the two groups and occur for members of each family position.

[31]The four categories comprising Senses of Self were scored for both positive and negative expressions, but only the positive statements are presented here because there were so few negative ones.

Table 4. Percent of respondents mentioning identity category by migrant status

Identity	Migrant				Settled			
	Father	Mother	Son	Daughter	Father	Mother	Son	Daughter
Ascribed Characteristics								
Gender	49	69	67	67	60	74	76	76
Age	0	3	3	17	2	0	27	22
Name	57	39	49	43	17	18	19	19
Ethnicity	43	36	36	33	29	24	46	31
Religion	26	42	27	17	19	20	16	11
Roles and Memberships								
Family or Kinship	86	97	49	67	85	86	41	37
Parent	63	86	0	0	65	82	0	0
Spouse	40	58	0	0	29	36	0	0
Offspring	6	8	27	31	3	4	35	24
Sibling	8	0	9	29	4	0	5	2
Occupation or Work	94	47	49	45	71	60	30	39
Student	3	3	24	50	8	0	19	39
Citizenship	0	0	3	3	8	0	3	2
Social Status	14	3	3	5	10	2	3	0
Peer	6	8	16	21	6	2	24	23
Abstract Identification	0	6	9	17	8	2	27	26
Interests and Activities								
Judgments, Tastes, Likes	11	11	24	17	15	22	22	20
Intellectual Concerns	6	8	12	24	10	8	16	20
Artistic Activities	3	0	12	2	4	0	16	15
Sports and Athletics	0	0	21	7	4	0	35	9
Material References								
Physical Self; Body Image	0	8	18	31	4	6	11	19
Possessions, Resources	26	8	12	5	17	8	3	2
Senses of Self								
Sense of Moral Worth	37	19	21	36	15	14	16	22
Sense of Competence	34	39	21	31	17	20	30	15
Sense of Self-Determination	31	11	6	12	17	6	8	6
Sense of Altruism	91	81	85	90	60	52	57	65
Personal Characteristics								
Interpersonal Style	40	31	27	36	35	16	12	35
Psychic Style	26	28	15	24	19	20	14	33
(N =)	(35)	(36)	(33)	(42)	(48)	(50)	(37)	(54)

Table 5. Percent of respondents indicating positive and negative self evaluations by migrant status

	Migrant families			
	Father	Mother	Son	Daughter
Positive Evaluations	71	69	58	76
Negative Evaluations	3	8	3	19
(N =)	(35)	(36)	(33)	(42)

	Settled families			
	Father	Mother	Son	Daughter
Positive Evaluations	46	40	38	48
Negative Evaluations	10	12	3	17
(N =)	(48)	(50)	(37)	(54)

This is consistent with our speculation that patterns of acculturation may be different for these two groups, which could have consequences for their self-evaluations. It also parallels the findings by Dworkin[32] on differences in self-conceptions of "foreign-born" and "native-born" Mexican Americans. Dworkin reasoned that this difference is due to the different *frames of reference* that the two populations were using to evaluate themselves. The foreign-born Mexican Americans had a more positive self-image and were more optimistic about their situation because they were comparing themselves with the people they had left behind in Mexico, and in that comparison they came off favorably. On the other hand, the Mexican Americans born in the United States were using the American society as their frame of reference. This explanation points again to the view that deprivation is relative and that one's level of self-evaluation is largely dependent on the reference group or frame of reference that one is using.

There are some other differences worth noting in the self-conceptions of migrant and settled Mexican Americans. The migrants appear to be more firmly rooted to structural sources of identity, i.e., our two groupings of Ascribed Characteristics and Roles and Memberships. With the curious exception of gender and age, migrant Mexican Americans more frequently mentioned name, ethnicity (except for boys), and religion, as well as family, work and student IDs, than did settled Mexican Americans. The latter, however, were somewhat more likely to define themselves in terms of interests and activities and abstract identifications.

This difference between the two groups in their patterns of self-definition could also be interpreted as being reflective of the process of acculturation and secularization. Migrant Mexican Americans, comprising a more recent population of immigrants, would be expected to have more of their traditional values and attitudes intact and to express these in their self-identifications. This interpretation gains credibility when we compare the frequency differences in ID categories between fa-

thers-mothers and boys-girls. The "traditional" pattern in Mexican culture is for a distinct sex-role segregation in the family and in society. The extent to which there are male-female differences in self-conception could be taken as an index of "traditionalism" or "non-traditionalism." Of the 28 identity comparisons between fathers and mothers, 18 are greater for migrant Mexican Americans while only 9 are greater for settled Mexican Americans. Furthermore, it is on the various structural identities that the differences are the most consistent, with migrant Mexican Americans having larger differences in 12 to 15 comparisons. The differences between boys and girls are less pronounced but are in the same direction. The decline in sex differences in self-concept for settled Mexican Americans can be viewed as their weakening commitment to traditional values which stress sex-role segregation.[33]

We also asked our respondents to indicate which of the statements they had made about themselves was most important to the way in which they think of themselves. The results of that question are presented in Table 6 and parallel, to a large extent, the patterns discussed in Tables 2 and 4. For both migrant and settled parents the parental identity emerges as the most important, and family in general (comprising family statements not specifically referring to family position) is rated high in importance. This is much more the case for mothers than fathers. Over half of the mothers in both samples of Mexican Americans rated their identity as parent as the most important. The identity of "spouse" does not receive nearly the prominence for either parent. Expectedly, work appears more important for men than women.

Differences between migrant and settled Mexican Americans seem to be greater for children than for their parents. The most important identity for settled children is gender. Thirty-two percent of boys and 37 percent of girls indicated their sex as the most important statement about themselves. For migrant children, religion is the most prominent identity for boys and

[32]Dworkin, "Stereotypes and Self-Images," p. 49.

[33]Cf. Grebler, *et al., The Mexican-American People.*

Table 6. Percent distributions of "most important self designation"

Identity[a]	Migrant				Settled			
	Father	Mother	Son	Daughter	Father	Mother	Son	Daughter
Ascribed Characteristics								
Gender	0	8	0	5	21	4	32	37
Name	3	0	15	10	0	0	5	4
Ethnicity	3	0	6	10	0	2	3	7
Religion	9	19	18	7	4	4	8	6
Roles and Memberships								
Family or Kinship	3	11	0	7	19	26	0	2
Parent	26	53	0	0	23	54	0	0
Spouse	0	8	0	0	2	0	0	0
Offspring	0	0	9	17	0	0	5	0
Sibling	0	0	0	5	2	0	0	0
Occupation or Work	26	0	9	7	8	0	3	7
Interests and Activities								
Sports and Athletics	0	0	6	0	0	0	14	0
Senses of Self								
Sense of Moral Worth	11	0	6	2	0	0	3	2
Sense of Competence	0	0	0	5	0	2	5	4
Personal Characteristics								
Interpersonal Style	0	0	3	7	4	0	3	7
Others	21	0	21	18	20	18	22	33

[a]Only those identity categories which had at least a 5 percent response rate by one of the groups of subjects were included in the table.

offspring is most important for girls. Name, ethnicity, religion, and work were more frequently mentioned as most important by migrant Mexican Americans, corresponding to the pattern in Table 4.

SUMMARY AND CONCLUSIONS

We mentioned earlier that structural identities "locate" an individual in social space by psychologically integrating him into various social structures. In this sense, migrants appear to be more firmly rooted in structural sources of identity (i.e., family, religion, work, ethnicity) stemming from their cultural heritage, than are the settled Mexican Americans. This difference was interpreted as reflecting the psychological consequences of acculturation which is probably greater for settled populations of Mexican Americans than it is for the relatively more isolated migrants.

But the biggest difference in the self-conceptions of migrant and settled Mexican-Americans was in their self-evaluations: migrants had a more positive and in general a more favorable view of themselves than did the settled Mexican Americans both with regard to general evaluations of self, and in terms of more specific evaluative self-statements referring to senses of moral worth, competence, self-determination, and altruism. Differential frames of reference or comparison levels were offered as an explanation for this difference. Here again the process of acculturation may be hard on the self-concept of the settled Mexican Americans experiencing it, as new expectations and frames of reference become adopted and at the same time one's economic and social conditions do not appreciably change.

Gender appeared as the most important identity for settled children, while religion, family, and name were more important to migrant children. This difference between settled and migrant children on gender identity is probably due to the greater opportunity for settled children to engage in dating, peer, and heterosexual relations, all of which are likely to accentuate sexual self-consciousness in the developing adolescent.

There were, however, a number of similarities between migrant and settled Mexican Americans in their identity patterns. For both groups the most important source of institutional and categorical self-moorings was the family. This is hardly surprising since the values placed on family as a source of emotional, psychological, and economic support to its members have been common themes in the literature on Mexican and Mexican American people. The woman especially tends to identify herself primarily as mother and only secondarily as spouse and in terms of such other categories as religion, gender, and personal qualities. Family identities are also quite important for men, but work and occupation compete with these for prominence in the order of self-designations.

For both adults and children, the most salient family bond is that of parent-child. Self-conceptions in terms of lateral relationships, e.g., spouse or sibling, were much less frequent and important. That this is not unique to Mexican American families is evident in the work of Lopata,[34] who found "mother" to be the most important family identity for the suburban Chicago women she studied. The crux of the idea of "family" may be, as Reiss[35] main-

tained, a group specializing in nurturant socialization. This lays stress on the parent-child relationship not only as the most important, but also as the *definitive* aspect of the family.

A surprising finding was the rather inconspicuous place of ethnic identity for both migrant and settled respondents. It was somewhat more important for children than parents, but in general it was below other identities, such as gender, religion, and family, in prominence. It may be that thinking of oneself in terms of cultural heritage is somewhat of a luxury which comes only after some of the more immediate concerns are alleviated. This could be one reason why the most outspoken Mexican Americans, and members of other minorities, tend to be relatively better educated and in better economic circumstances. The Chicano movement has been, essentially, a middle-class movement among Mexican Americans which is gradually filtering down to the lower-class ranks. As our findings indicate, this filtering process is affecting adolescent males the most, but even here the influence is not great. Social revolutions and even evolutions depend, to a large extent, on an increase in self-conscious group identification which can be translated into action.

[34]Helena Z. Lopata, *Occupation: Housewife* (New York: Oxford University Press, 1971).
[35]Ira Reiss, "The Universality of the Family: A Conceptual Analysis," *Journal of Marriage and the Family,* 27 (Nov., 1965), pp. 443-453.

CHAPTER 14 PSYCHOLOGICAL RESEARCH AND THE MEXICAN AMERICAN

AMADO M. PADILLA

Psychology is the science directly concerned with behavioral and social processes. As practitioners of this science, psychologists have been looked to for guidance in providing new and better ways of promoting human welfare. However, psychologists thus far have contributed little in bringing their knowledge and resources to bear on the pressing social problems that exist today.[1]

It is true that there has been a group of psychologists who have argued for involvement in the issues confronting society. It is not to this group of psychologists that this article is addressed, but to that community of psychologists who seek to maintain the status quo by continuing to support a psychology that de-emphasizes the promotion of human well-being.

For example, these psychologists have been unable to deal with the significant social problems that affect the Mexican Americans and other minority groups because they have confined themselves to a laboratory model of psychology.[2] A laboratory-oriented approach to psychology assumes that only when one can control and manipulate variables in a laboratory can one study behavior scientifically. Such an approach fails to recognize all of the cultural, environmental, and social influences that motivate the Mexican American.

On those rare occasions when these psychologists leave the laboratory and attempt to implement their hypotheses of behavior on people culturally different from themselves, they often resort to ethnocentric interpretations of their observations. Ethnocentrism is the tendency to evaluate people and experiences from the viewpoint of one's own group. Such an approach, when employed by a psychologist, serves to cloud his objectivity and often to retard his understanding of culturally different people, such as the Mexican American.

The purpose of this article is: (1) to show how some psychologists, because of their rigidity in adhering to a laboratory model and their own ethnocentrism, have created a situation which is intolerable to today's Mexican American, (2) to show how such approaches have resulted in inadequate and irrelevant psychological services, and (3) to offer recommendations for change. These objectives will be approached through an examination of the psychological literature that relates to certain issues centering on family-child relationships, bilingualism and intelligence tests, and mental illness and mental health practices among Mexican Americans.

FAMILY-CHILD RELATIONSHIPS

The psychological research community has not as yet dealt in depth with Chicano family-child relationships, but has relied on the writings of anthropologists and sociologists. Family-child relationships are described by these writers in overgeneralized statements. For example, the Chicano family is supposedly primarily authoritarian and patriarchal. The father maintains authority through tradition and force. He is aloof and inhibits his feelings of love and concern for his children. He is a poor model for his male children and consequently his children have difficulty in establishing adequate masculine identification.

The mother, in contrast, is submissive, quiet, obedient, and faithful to her husband. She is fatalistic in her philosophy of the world and dependent upon her husband and family. She is a good mother only because her children are an extension of her own dependency needs.[3]

Moreover, it is claimed that the Mexican American is not competitive, ambitious, or achievement oriented because these qualities have not been rewarded during his early childhood. What have been rewarded are dependence, obedience, compliance, and silence. He is not active, mobile, curious, or talkative. The Mexican-American child, because of his early childhood training, is forever expecting to have his dependency need fulfilled by the environment.

In summary, the stereotyped Mexican-American family has a high regard for authority, an adherence to tradition, a philosophy of acceptance and resignation, and a religious orientation. This view contrasts with the Anglo-American family, which values achievement and success, activity and work, efficiency and practicality, material comfort, equality of opportunity, freedom, science, democracy, and individual personality.[4]

For the sake of brevity, the important cultural differences in family-child relationships described by social scientists can be outlined as follows:

	Training	Activity	Time Orientation	Man-Nature Relationship
Mexican American	Dependence	Being	Present	Subjugation to Nature
Anglo American	Individualism	Doing	Future	Mastery over Nature

It should be pointed out again that these stereotypes have not originated from the writings of psychologists. However, they have been accepted by psychologists without concern for documentation. Inferences made about the Mexican American are made without concern for the cultural and ecological variability that exists among Chicanos. Chicanos occupy all positions on the social, economic, and educational ladder. Some persons are at the lowest step; others occupy positions at the top. Some Chicanos are rural, but most are urban dwellers. There are differences in cultural awareness; some Mexican Americans prefer total assimilation and acculturation, and others prefer a parallel system. Yet, to read the Anglo accounts of Chicanos, the numerous overgeneralizations that describe him are noticeable.

In addition, social scientists have studied the Mexican American from an assumption that total assimilation into the mainstream is desirable; therefore, because of the Chicano's resistance to assimilation, his family structure is at fault. This *modus operandi* has resulted in social scientists describing the Mexican-American family structure in negative terms with little or no concern given to the positive attributes of the Chicano family.

The achievement syndrome often found in the writings of Anglo social scientists offers a good example of the above discussion. Achievement motivation is a prized index often pointed to by Anglo researchers in drawing cross-cultural differences. Celia S. Heller states:

Parents, as a whole, neither impose standards of excellence for tasks performed by their children nor do they communicate to them that they expect evidence of high achievement. . . . The home also fails to provide the kind of independence training that . . . is highly functional for achievement. . . . It is not surprising, therefore, that these children seldom show initiative or freely express their own ideas.[5]

It is the contention here that Mexican-American parents are no different in what they want for their children from their Anglo counterparts. Chicanos want the same education and occupational opportunities for their children. However, they believe that these should be attainable without the loss of the Chicano value systems.

It is this kind of sensitivity to cultural values that social scientists and psychologists have failed to recognize in their study of the Mexican-American family. Only one study in the psychological literature has adequately recognized that the Mexican-American family orientation differs on many variables besides ethnicity. In this study, Ronald W. Henderson and C. B. Merritt showed that the potential for school success of Mexican-American children was dependent upon the number of intellectually stimulating experiences to be found in the home, rather than in a belief that the more "Americanized" the parents, the greater the potential for success. As Henderson and Merritt state, "The data seem to refute the common assumption that children from families that are 'most Mexican' in their behavior and outlook will have the most difficulty in school."[6]

The conclusion to be drawn from the above exposé on the family is that psychologists have allowed the misrepresentations and stereotypes of the Mexican-American family to persist because of their acceptance of these stereotypes. What is needed is a thorough examination of all the dynamic interactions that occur in the Chicano home situations. Only such an analysis will reveal how the Chicano family differs from the Anglo in child-rearing practices that result in different aspirational and achievement orientation. Such studies must include controls for socioeconomic status if the present state of knowledge about the Chicano family is to be clarified.

BILINGUALISM AND TESTS OF INTELLIGENCE

Psychometrics is an area of psychology that until recently enjoyed a major role in the study of racial and ethnic differences. The philosophical belief underlying intelligence testing is that men are not created equal in their intellectual capabilities and that such differences can be measured.[7] It is in this area that Mexican Americans have been intensively investigated.

A bibliographic search by the writer has indicated that no less than forty-eight of slightly over one hundred studies in the psychological literature pertaining to the Mexican American have in some way involved the issue of test performance and bilingualism. Many of these studies have shown that the intellectual functioning of Mexican-American children is below that of Anglo-American children. These studies have, more importantly, shown that the gap in intellectual functioning increases with age. It has been suggested that the major reason for this difference is due to the Spanish-speaking background of the Mexican-American child.[8]

It has also been suggested that bilingualism results in cognitive confusion that limits the child's ability to learn concepts as rapidly as a monolingual child. The usual conclusion drawn by educators from such suggestions is that the bilingual child, or child who is monolingual in Spanish, is a poor educational risk. Such conclusions have had clear racist implications, yet psychologists have failed to recognize the social significance of such messages. In short, such findings have been taken by some persons to mean that there are fundamental hereditary differences in intellectual capability between English-speaking and Spanish-speaking people.

Only recently, and under great pressure, have educators been forced to change their policies on the outcomes of intelligence tests. For instance, Chicano residents in California and certain communities in Texas have discontinued the educational tracking of their children based on mental tests.

Pressure has not yet been applied to psychometricians for a proper reevaluation of their tests. It is true that they have engaged for years in a continuous dialogue about the importance of cultural variables on intelligence measuring instruments; however, little progress has been made in developing culture-free tests or even culture-sensitive tests for various ethnic groups other than the Anglo American.[9] The standard psychological tests employed have not taken into account the cultural and environmental background of Mexican Americans. Nor have they included Chicanos in their standardization procedures. To illustrate the importance of these two factors, consider the implications that would be drawn if psychologists speaking only English were tested for intelligence in

Spanish, on instruments standardized with Mexican Americans!

Two avenues of research have shown that there is a need to reexamine the relationship of bilingualism to intellectual functioning. One of these directions focuses on neurological theorizing and the other on recent psychological findings that show how the learning of two languages at an early age facilitates cognitive development.

Wilder Penfield, a noted neurologist, has for many years advocated bilingualism as a way in which the cortex of the young child can be given additional stimulation. Of equal importance is the fact that at an early age the brain seems to possess a greater plasticity and capacity for acquiring languages. The secret lies in an action called the switch mechanism, a conditioned reflex that works automatically in the brain. This switch mechanism enables the child to switch from the vocabulary of one language to that of another language with ease, so that both languages are learned directly and without confusion.[10]

Further, it has been shown that in some situations bilingualism serves to facilitate intellectual performance and that in some cognitive areas knowledge of two languages might be advantageous.[11] Joshua A. Fishman believes that functions related to the labeling of objects at an early age are advanced by knowing two languages because the child is thus facilitated in his acquisition of a mature notion of the nature of labels. Labeling of objects is important because such an ability is the precursor to more elaborate cognitive skills involving the use of labels in sentences.[12]

A recent study using bilingual Mexican-American Head Start children showed these children to be superior to monolingual children in tasks involving the naming of objects and the use of names in sentences. These findings confirm Fishman's hypotheses about the importance of two-language learning. What has still to be determined is the import such research receives from the psychological community.[13]

What psychologists have failed to recognize is that the question of intellectual functioning is not one of bilingualism per se but is a matter of economic, cultural,

and situational factors. One factor that has received little consideration is malnutrition. Because it is unfortunately true that many Mexican Americans exist from day to day in a condition of poverty, it is not hypothetical to assume that many children are chronically malnourished. And it is a well-established fact that dietary deficiencies in young children are related to retardation in intellectual development and mental functioning.[14]

An interesting hypothesis has recently been advanced by Michael C. Latham and Francisco Cobos that may explain the depressed intelligence test scores of Mexican-American children and the observations made by anthropologists of these children. According to Latham and Cobos, a caloric-deficient diet results in a physiologic response to conserve energy for purposes of growth and for essential activities only. Thus, the child spends long periods of time passively and quietly. The time spent playing with his peers, verbalizing with his mother, manipulating objects, and stimulating his senses is limited. His subsequent poor performance on tests may then be due to his inactivity. Moreover, reports from anthropologists suggesting that Chicano children are inactive, compliant, and silent may be observations of the effects of malnutrition, rather than of Mexican-American child-rearing practices.[15]

The result of the misuse of psychological tests by psychometricians is that many Mexican Americans have come to have a negative self-concept. The negative self-concept has taken the form of the Chicano child's perception of himself as a failure in the educational setting; this image has consequently resulted in his withdrawal, only to find increased negative stereotypes of himself as an illiterate and uneducated burden on society. For many Chicanos these feelings have been repeatedly reinforced and have been transmitted from parents to offspring.

ADVANTAGES OF BILINGUAL TRAINING

To summarize, psychologists and educators have very adequately programmed the Mexican American into a "self-fulfilling prophecy" of failure through the use of inappropriate psychological measuring instruments. This situation can no longer be tolerated, but only with a concerted effort by the Mexican-American community in general, and the Chicano psychologist in particular, will such practices be corrected. Toward this goal, all people who share a bilingual-bicultural heritage should become advocates of early bilingual training for the following reasons:

(1) Bilingual training increases the early stimulation of the child that is so vital in the early phases of the educational process.

(2) There is sufficient evidence to show that such training increases the overall cognitive development of the child.

(3) Such training reduces the emotional shock that children undergo when forced to participate in a monolingual, in this case English, educational process.

(4) Such training reduces the social discomforts and stigma of having to operate at only the level of a single culture and language.

(5) Bilingual-bicultural training enhances the social mobility of the person as he grows into adulthood because he can communicate with the older members of his family at home and in the Anglo world on an equal basis.

(6) Finally, such training serves to enhance the mental health of the person because there is no interfering problem of marginality that sociologists have documented so well in persons who have lost their cultural and lingual heritage.

MENTAL ILLNESS AND MENTAL HEALTH PRACTICES

Chicanos have been perceived as child-like in their beliefs of what constitutes mental illness and in their mental health care practices. According to some psychotherapists, the Mexican American views illness as a suffering imposed by God that is not to be questioned because the imposed illness is part of God's plan for the universe. Because mental illness is part of a grand plan, it is a family affair as well as a community concern. It is seen in a religious and social context, rather than in the medical-scientific context of the Anglo society.[16]

It is this conception of illness that the psychologist and related mental health workers employ when attempting to understand psychopathology among the Chicanos. The psychological and mental health literature on this topic is filled with anecdotes of such folk beliefs as: *susto* (fright), *embrujada* (bewitchment), *mal ojo* (evil eye), *caido de la mollera*, and *empacho* (food-blocked intestine). Moreover, accounts of the practices of *curanderas* (folk healers) fill the pages of psychiatric journals.[17] These accounts make fascinating reading for the non-Chicano clinicians because they are replete with mysticism and because they stir the reader to the belief that the Chicano is at a primitive stage of development, desperately in need of assistance.

It is known that urban Mexican Americans do not differ overall from Anglo Americans in their perceptions of mental illness. However, there are some intra-group differences among Chicanos in their perceptions of mental illness that must be clarified. Among older and less acculturated Chicanos, there is greater reliance on such beliefs as the inheritance of mental illness, the effectiveness of prayer as a cure of mental illness, and a familistic orientation which maintains that the mentally ill person will recover sooner by remaining at home. It should be emphasized, however, that as Mexican Americans have become more urbanized, their perceptions do not differ substantially from other ethnic groups.[18]

Little is known about the prevalence of mental illness among the Mexican Americans. Little epidemiological work has been conducted on the incidence and manifestations of mental illness among the Mexican Americans. The limited existing data suggest that Mexican Americans, at least in the state of Texas, have a lower incidence of mental illness than do Anglo Americans. E. Gartly Jaco has suggested that these findings are attributable to the existence of a warm, supportive, extended family with strong values of mutual acceptance, care, and responsibility, which tend to protect Mexican Americans against the development of major mental illness.[19]

Two studies supporting Jaco's observation that the family structure is vitally important in an understanding of mental disorders among the Chicano have been reported. In the first study, Horacio Fabrega found that hospitalized Mexican Americans appeared to be more severely disturbed than their Anglo counterparts. More important is the fact that the families of these Mexican-American patients may have been tolerant and willing to assist, and consequently delayed seeking help or hospitalization for their mentally ill family member. It is this delaying procedure that appears to be the causal agent for the severity of the disorders found among the Mexican-American patients.[20]

A second study employing standard projective techniques found that the family occupies a much more influential role in the cognitive structure of Mexican Americans than is true of Anglos or blacks. Responses on the Thematic Apperception Test pointed out differences between the Mexican Americans and the other two groups in themes of family unity and in their characterization, particularly of father-son and mother-son relationships.[21]

Taken together, these studies are indicative of the positive attributes of the Mexican-American family structure, contrary to the description in an early section of this paper. Because of the supportive family structure, the family offers an excellent entry into the psychotherapeutic situation. It is unfortunate that psychologists and related mental health practitioners have not as yet capitalized on the Chicano family structure in providing mental health services for the Chicano. What actually has occurred is that Mexican Americans have been forced to seek mental health care in settings that have discriminated against them and have offered services which are culturally and emotionally irrelevant.[22]

It should be emphasized that Mexican Americans require the same quality of mental health care as other Americans; but it is true that clinical psychology and many of the traditional psychotherapeutic techniques are geared toward the middle class values and standards of the non-Chicano suburbanite. Many avenues of mental health care have excluded not only the Chicano, but all groups who differ from the model. Only when therapists become sensitive to the social, economic, and political dynamics of the Chicano and the barrio will the mental health care of the Chicano become relevant and adequate.

Mental health care, to be adequate for the Mexican American, must be preventive. It must focus on the mental well-being of the Chicano child and on the positive coping mechanisms that are characteristic of the adult who has been able to survive in an often hostile environment. It must also have bilingual-bicultural components that are responsive to the needs of the Mexican American.

RECOMMENDATIONS FOR A RESPONSIVE PSYCHOLOGY

Psychology can only become relevant for the Chicano when psychologists realize that the barrio is a living entity consisting of the interplay of intragroup and intergroup relationships, ecological factors, cultural differences, and developmental forces that motivate the behavior of the Chicano. The existing psychological knowledge of the Chicano has been obtained in poorly conceived and inadequately controlled cross-cultural investigations. Until well-planned experimental studies that bear directly on the needs of the barrio, rather than on the proclivities of the non-Chicano investigator, are conceived, Chicanos should perhaps call a moratorium on research in which they are involved as subjects.

Psychologists, as well as other behavioral and social scientists, must begin to realize that a science of behavior cannot be limited to one segment of a population. There must be a concern for individual differences, both within a group of people as well as between culturally different peoples. This new psychology that is to incorporate all people—be they from the suburbs, ghetto, or barrio—must seek to enhance the psychological well-being of all people. This aspect of the profession has for too long been neglected.

Toward this goal, psychologists must desist in their arrogance, that is, in the belief that because psychology is the study of behavior they know what will be best for people. Chicanos, as well as other minorities, have suffered from this arrogance when research and service programs have been planned. It is becoming clearer that the community must be involved in all phases of planning. Only when full community participation is accepted will psychology be a viable force which can plan, research, provide, and promote the well-being of all Americans.

An extension of this community participation includes the increased training of Chicanos in psychology. With proper training these new Chicano psychologists will be able to utilize their skills in serving the needs of the barrio.[23]

The Chicano stands at the crossroads of decision concerning the kind of psychological research and services he wants and needs most. If he uses his power to his advantage, he can dictate to psychologists the direction that their investigations should take. He can call a halt to the use of time-worn hypotheses and models. He can demand that studies by psychologists become interdisciplinary and sensitive to his culture. He can be sure that mental health service programs become relevant through the inclusion of bilingual-bicultural components. The Chicano can shape a psychology that will be meaningful to him and from which Anglos will prosper in their proper understanding of him. Only this two-way concern will bring an end to the Chicano's case history of neglect at the hands of psychologists.

NOTES

[1]George A. Miller, "Psychology as a Means of Promoting Human Welfare," *American Psychologist,* 24:1,063 (December 1969).
[2]In order to avoid confusion, Mexican American and Chicano will be used interchangeably in this article to encompass a group of people of Mexican descent who have been variously described by social scientists as Mexican, Mexican American, Spanish, Latin, Chicano, and so forth.
[3]Ari Kiev, *Curanderismo: Mexican-American Folk Psychiatry* (New York: The Free Press, 1968).
[4]Lyle Saunders, *Cultural Differences and Medical Care: The Case for the Spanish-Speaking People of the Southwest* (New York: Russell Sage Foundation, 1954).
[5]Celia S. Heller, *Mexican American Youth: Forgotten Youth at the Crossroads* (New York: Random House, 1967), pp. 37-39.
[6]Ronald W. Henderson and C. B. Merritt, "Environmental Backgrounds of Mexican American Children with Different Potentials for School Success," *Journal of Social Psychology,* 75:101 (June 1968).
[7]For a thorough examination of the reasoning of such a belief and the arguments that result, see Arthur R. Jensen, "How Much Can We Boost the I.Q. and Scholastic Achievement?" *Harvard Educational Review,* 39:1-123 (Winter 1969).
[8]Natalie T. Darcy, "Bilingualism and the Measurement of Intelligence: Review of a Decade of Research," *Journal of Genetic Psychology,* 103:259 (December 1963); and Hilding B. Carlson and Norman Henderson, "The Intelligence of American Children of Mexican Parentage," *Journal of Abnormal and Social Psychology,* 45:544 (July 1950).
[9]Anne Anastasi, *Differential Psychology* (New York: Macmillan, 1937).
[10]Wilder Penfield and Lamar Roberts, *Speech and Brain Mechanisms* (Princeton: Princeton University Press, 1959).
[11]Elizabeth Peal and Wallace E. Lambert, "The Relation of Bilingualism to Intelligence," *Psychological Monographs,* 76:1 (No. 27 1962).
[12]Joshua A. Fishman, "Bilingualism with and without Diglossia; Diglossia with and without Bilingualism," *Journal of Social Issues,* 23:29 (April 1967).
[13]Carol Feldman and Michael Shen, "Some Language-Related Cognitive Advantages of Bilingual Five-Year-Olds," *Journal of Genetic Psychology,* 118:235 (June 1971).
[14]Joaquin Cravioto, Elsa R. DeLicardie, and Herbert G. Birch, "Nutrition, Growth and Neuro-Integrative Development: An Experimental and Ecologic Study," *Pediatrics,* 38:319 (August 1966).
[15]Michael C. Latham and Francisco Cobos, "The Effects of Malnutrition on Intellectual Development and Learning," *American Journal of Public Health,* 61:1,307 (July 1971).
[16]Kiev, *Curanderismo*
[17]John Gillin, "Magical Fright," *Psychiatry,* 11:387 (November 1948); Margaret Clark, *Health in the Mexican-American Culture* (Berkeley: University of California Press, 1959); James Galvin and Arnold Ludwig, "A Case of Witchcraft," *Journal of Nervous and Mental Disease,* 133:161 (August 1961); and William Madsen, "Value Conflicts and Folk Psychotherapy in South Texas," in Ari Kiev (ed.), *Magic, Faith, and Healing* (New York: The Free Press, 1964).
[18]Marvin Karno and Robert B. Edgerton, "Perception of Mental Illness in a Mexican-American Community," *Archives of General Psychiatry,* 20:233 (February 1969); and Robert B. Edgerton and Marvin Karno, "Mexican-American Bilingualism and the Perception of Mental Illness," *Archives of General Psychiatry,* 24:286 (March 1971).

[19]E. Gartly Jaco, *The Social Epidemiology of Mental Disorders* (New York: Russell Sage Foundation, 1960).

[20]Horacio Fabrega, Jon D. Swartz, and Carole A. Wallace, "Ethnic Differences in Psychopathology-II: Specific Differences with Emphasis on a Mexican-American Group," *Journal of Psychiatric Research,* 6:221 (July 1968).

[21]Dale L. Johnson and Melvin P. Sikes, "Rorschach and TAT Responses of Negro, Mexican-American and Anglo Psychiatric Patients," *Journal of Projective Techniques,* 29:183 (June 1965).

[22]Marvin Karno, "The Enigma of Ethnicity in a Psychiatric Clinic," *Archives of General Psychiatry,* 14:516 (May 1966); Joe Yamamoto, Quinton C. James and Norman Palley, "Cultural Problems in Psychiatric Therapy," *Archives of General Psychiatry,* 19:45 (July 1968); Lawrence Y. Kline, "Some Factors in the Psychiatric Treatment of Spanish-Americans," *American Journal of Psychiatry,* 125:1,674 (June 1969); M. J. Philippus, "Successful and Unsuccessful Approaches to Mental Health Services for an Urban Hispano-American Population," *American Journal of Public Health,* 61:820 (April 1971); and E. Fuller Torrey, "The Irrelevancy of Traditional Mental Health Services for Urban Mexican-Americans," Paper presented at the Meetings of the American Orthopsychiatry Association, San Francisco (March 1970).

[23]Proof that such training programs are lacking can be seen when one compares the ratio of psychologists to the general population. Although there is one psychologist to approximately every 7,500 people, the ratio of psychologists to Chicanos is one to about every 160,000. These figures are based on a recent estimate of the number of Chicano psychologists by the Association of Psychologists for La Raza.

PART FOUR

EDUCATION AND INTELLECTUAL ASSESSMENT

Education has often been viewed as the key to success in American society. Accordingly, "equal educational opportunities" are guaranteed, to some extent, by law. It is becoming increasingly apparent, however, that requiring children's presence in school in no way assures that they will: (1) become educated or (2) be able to rise economically in accordance with their abilities and training. A number of excellent accounts have appeared in recent years dealing with the psychic crippling perpetrated on minority students by the schools (Herndon, 1965; Parsons, 1966; Kohl, 1967; Kozol, 1967).

Issues raised in attempts to explain the disturbingly poor educational performance of minority and lower socioeconomic status students have included "nature vs. nurture" speculations (Is environment or heredity most responsible? Does racial superiority in fact exist?); "personality" and "culture" explanations; teacher expectancy effects (the self-fulfilling prophecy phenomenon); and the effects of prejudice and oppression (Rieber & Womack, 1968; Ramirez, Taylor, & Petersen, 1971; Rosenthal & Jacobson, 1968; Anderson & Safar, 1967). By far the most hotly debated questions, though, revolve around bilingualism and IQ tests. Consequently, we have devoted the bulk of this section to these two topics. The articles that follow are of a somewhat more technical nature than those in other parts of this volume, but we hope that the nonprofessional reader will bear with us, for the issues developed by these writers are of major importance.

The 1934 article by Sanchez was one of the first in the academic debate that continues to this day over the intelligence, education, advantages, and disadvantages of bilin-

gual children and is still, more than four decades later, highly relevant. This in itself is an indictment of our educational system—that in over 40 years so little progress has been made in understanding and responding to the needs of bilingual students. While most studies continue to find that bilingual children in America do less well academically and score lower on intelligence tests, the method of instruction and attitudes toward bilingualism that these children encounter have more to do with their poor achievement and school adjustment than the fact of their bilingualism. As Padilla mentioned in the last section, bilingualism potentially has numerous advantages in promoting cognitive development and enhancing social mobility; but it is hardly an asset in a school system that, *contrary to all educational theory,* refuses to build on the language skills the entering pupil already possesses but instead insists on the sole use of the less preferred tongue. This policy is often carried to the extreme of punishing (and sometimes expelling) students for speaking any Spanish at all—even between friends in the halls. The net result of such practices is to turn out graduates (or dropouts) who are literate in neither tongue (Anastasi & Cordova, 1953).

The evidence is equivocal on whether children do better on IQ tests administered in their mother tongue; as San-

chez and others (Darcy, 1963; Sattler, 1974) have noted,
intelligence test scores are contingent upon both language
and acculturation factors. Translating a test is of no value
if the items have not been experienced by the child, and
it is especially futile if the dialect into which the test is
translated is not the child's own (for example, using the
Puerto Rican-dialect version of a test on Mexican Americans) or if the language of the home is a nonsystematic
combination of Spanish and English, as is often the case.

Far and away the biggest problem with standardized IQ
tests, though, is that the norms for their *interpretation*
simply do not apply to poor and minority children.

The relationship of the lay concept of "intelligence" to
IQ scores is a tenuous, often confused one. In the public
mind, "intelligence" is a unitary phenomenon, an attribute
that individuals possess in various degrees, and the IQ
score is an unchanging, precision measure of how much
intelligence one "has." (Unfortunately, quite a few professionals behave as if they also believed this.) Not so: intelligence, though there may be a "general" factor, is essentially an amalgam of numerous specific abilities, which
are defined in slightly different ways and given different
relative weightings in the theories of each of the different
test inventors. Furthermore, the IQ (intelligence quotient

—computed as a ratio of "mental age" to chronological age, times 100) is neither static (as Project Headstart demonstrated) nor a true measure of innate intelligence. Rather, IQ constitutes a quantified sample of *behavior* under a standardized (as much as possible) set of stimulus conditions. The instructions, tasks, test materials, and order of presentation are always the same, and insofar as it can be managed, the testing room environment and the tester's manner of interaction with the examinees are held constant. What cannot be controlled, however, are the variables the examinees bring into the situation. These include, not only their native intelligence (whatever that is), but also their momentary physiological and emotional state (Have they had breakfast? Are they coming down with the flu? Did they just have a fight with their best friend? Are they afraid of the tester? Are they motivated to do their best?) and their whole experiential history (see Sattler, 1974; R. L. Williams, 1970a).

The fundamental assumption behind intelligence tests, guiding both the selection and age-level placement of the items and the interpretation of a person's score, is that that person shares a common pool of experiences and values with all other members of his society, and in particular with the sample of the population on whom the test was originally perfected. Insofar as an individual's background differs from the societal norm, the test will be a less accurate indicator of true potential. Mercer's study indicates

the relative magnitudes of error due to sociocultural factors in the IQ scores of black and Chicano children at various socioeconomic levels. Tragically, many Chicanos have been stigmatized as mentally retarded on the basis of IQ test scores alone, and shunted off into classes for the mentally retarded or at best treated as mediocre intellects when in fact they are of average or superior ability. The necessity of taking additional criteria into account in making decisions about minority students is made painfully obvious by Mercer.

In reaction to abuses like the above, many minority citizens, including some psychologists, have called for a moratorium on IQ testing of minority group children (R. L. Williams, 1970b), at least until such time as new, more culture-fair tests can be devised. Unfortunately, to date no "culture-free" intelligence test has proved useful as a predictive measure. As Sattler (1974) observes, "In a sense, *no test can be culture-fair if the culture is not fair.*" The assumptions of white, middle-class, northern, urban, Protestant value orientations, attitudes, and childhood experiences that form the backbone of the most used IQ tests are also the assumptions around which our educational system is built, and this is precisely what gives them their predictive power.

What is seldom understood is that IQ tests are first, foremost, and perhaps only, *predictors of school performance;* this was their original, and still is, their main purpose. In-

nate, inherited "intelligence" is only one of many factors that correlate with success in school and is not necessarily even the most important; furthermore, it can only be measured indirectly—*inferred* from behavior. And behavior, of course, is a changeable thing, so *IQ tests are at best an indication of a person's level of functioning at one particular point in time.*

Such a behavior sample, though, can provide information of a far more useful type than simply an overall score, a single, numerical relative ranking. IQ tests are complex and tap many abilities and cognitive skills, and as the Meekers illustrate, the responses obtained can be broken down into categories according to the abilities they tap. The system the Meekers used is only one of a number of useful methods of analysis. By identifying a student's relative strengths and weaknesses in this manner (something that would be very difficult to do from just classroom records and teachers' observations), a much more intelligent plan can be made as to what teaching strategy to use with this child.

IQ tests, then, need not work against the minority child's welfare; however, the fact that they often do attests to the fact that *tests are only as "intelligent" as the people who use them.* Sattler (1974, p. 46) makes this point most effectively:

> Test scores should not be accepted as fixed levels of either performance or potential; instead, they may be used to determine the magnitude of the deprivation that is to be overcome by a planned program of remedial activities. Scores can also be used to compare disadvantaged children with one another. Still another way in which scores can be useful is to compare the child's current test performance with his previous test performance. In the last analysis, the examiner and other test users must accept the responsibilities involved in interpreting and in using educational and psychological tests.

> > "Many comparisons depend upon tests, but they also depend upon *our* intelligence, our good will, and our sense of responsibility to make the proper comparison at the proper time and to undertake proper remedial and compensatory action as a result. The misuse of tests with minority group children, or in any situation, is a serious breach of professional ethics. Their proper use is a sign of professional and personal maturity." (Deutsch et al., 1964, p. 144; in Sattler, 1974)

The "professional and personal maturity" requisite to intelligent use of IQ tests is that of, not just the psychologist who administers the test, but also the classroom teacher. As Ramirez indicates, making a determination of individual and/or group differences is an exercise in futility unless the teacher is willing and able to vary teaching methods to meet the diverse needs of the students. As he also points out, every cognitive "style" and teaching method has its uses and is the most "mature" or advantageous response in some situations, and teachers and students alike would find their personal effectiveness enhanced by the implementation of cultural democracy in education.

REFERENCES

Anastasi, A. & Cordova, F. A. Some effects of bilingualism upon the intelligence test performance of Puerto Rican children in New York City. *Journal of Educational Psychology,* 1953, *44,* 1-19.

Anderson, J. G., & Safar, D. The influence of differential community perceptions on the provision of equal educational opportunities. *Sociology of Education,* 1967, *40,* 219-230.

Darcy, N. T. Bilingualism and the measurement of intelligence: Review of a decade of research. *Journal of Genetic Psychology,* 1963, *103,* 259-282.

Deutsch, M., Fishman, J. A., Kogan, L., North, R., & Whiteman, M. Guidelines for testing minority group children. *Journal of Social Issues,* 1964, *20*(2), 129-145.

Herndon, James. *The way it spozed to be.* New York: Bantam Books, 1965.

Kohl, H. *36 children.* New York: Signet Books, 1967.

Kozol, J. *Death at an early age.* New York: Bantam Books, 1967.

Parsons, T. W., Jr. Ethnic cleavage in a California school. Unpublished Ph.D. thesis, 1966. Reviewed in "School bias toward Mexican-Americans," *School and Society,* 1966, *94,* 378-380.

Ramirez, M., III, Taylor, C., Jr., & Petersen, B. Mexican-American cultural membership and adjustment to school. *Developmental Psychology,* 1971, *4,* 141-148.

Rieber, M., & Womack, M. The intelligence of preschool children as related to ethnic and demographic variables. *Exceptional Children,* 1968, *34,* 609-614.

Rosenthal, R., & Jacobson, L. *Pygmalion in the classroom: Teacher expectation and pupils' intellectual development.* New York: Holt, Rinehart & Winston, 1968.

Sattler, J. M. *Assessment of children's intelligence.* Philadelphia: W. B. Saunders Co., 1974.

Williams, R. L. Black pride, academic relevance, and individual achievement. *Counseling Psychologist,* 1970, *2*(1), 18-22. (a)

Williams, R. L. Danger: Testing and dehumanizing black children. *Clinical Child Psychology Newsletter,* 1970, *9*(1), 5-6. (b)

CHAPTER 15 BILINGUALISM AND MENTAL MEASURES

A word of caution

GEORGE I. SÁNCHEZ

The great development shown in objectivity in education during the last two decades has led to the conception among those over-zealous to demonstrate the scientific accuracy attained in this field that we are at a point where mental capacities of children can be determined accurately by the mere *application* of the newly devised measuring instruments—standardized mental tests. While sound thinkers in the field of tests and measures have constantly cautioned against the superficial and unanalytical use of these instruments, the quest for a short-cut to critical and exhaustive study of the abilities of school children has led to numerous abuses and errors in the use of mental tests. This is especially true of those who, blindly accepting the doctrine of individual differences, fail to recognize the importance of the fundamental personal, social, and cultural differences of the pupils and of the extremely important question of differences in milieu.

While the misapplication of tests is a matter of general concern and evident in education generally, it is in the treatment of the problems presented by bilingual, or environmentally handicapped, children that the gravest mistakes have been made. The caution with which such prominent students as Terman, Garrett, Otis, Pintner,

From Journal of Applied Psychology **18:**765-772, 1934. Reprinted by permission.

Freeman and others have approached the use of tests in instances where language or environmental problems enter into the testing situation has been largely ignored or misinterpreted by those, who, equipped with the mechanical technique of application and scoring, have failed to place due weight on the analysis and evaluation of personal differences and of environmental problems.

The fact that tests have in a measure fulfilled their function of checking on the community of experience of children and on the extent to which children vary in profiting from common experiences has seemingly led many to assume that there is a universality in community of experiences. However, a test is valid only to the extent that the items of the test are as common to each child tested as they were to the children upon whom the norms were based. Only when community of experience actually exists can checks based on that assumption be valid, even if we grant that such checks do symbolize intellectual capacity—an "if" that has serious questions in itself.

The controversial nature of "intelligence" as such and of intelligence as a predetermined, hereditary faculty can easily be appreciated when one reads such works as Spearman's *Abilities of Man*[8] or Chapter X of Beard's (editor) *Whither Mankind*.[1] The latter reference is an illuminating and extremely readable treatment of the question of the relationship between "race" and intellectual achievement. Geo. A. Dorsey, in a humorously satirical manner, is unrelenting and even vicious in his attack upon those who have garbled the facts of genetics, eugenics, and heredity to champion the superiority of "Nordic" or "Aryan" "race." In unequivocal terms the glaring inconsistencies of the doctrine that "like begets like" and that civilization and intellectual accomplishment are linked irrevocably with Nordic heredity are set forth and ridiculed. In addition, outstanding anthropologists and geneticists are cited as authorities for the evidence against the deterministic assumption of a Nordic "corner" on brains. The chapter is a refreshing antidote to the widespread acceptance of the superiority of nature over nuture.

Yet, in spite of the uncertain basis upon which the fundamentals of mental tests rest, time and again students of the bilingual question insist on applying tests and accepting the results uncritically. To be sure tests are tools that should be used for what they are worth. The problem confronting the examiner is that of determining their worth in a particular situation. The worth of test-results lies in their proper interpretation and in the assistance which such interpretation lends to furthering the educational needs of the pupil. An IQ ratio, as such, *has no value.* It is only when that measure is used critically in promoting the best educational interests of the child that it has any worth-while significance to the educator. This means that an IQ of 70 is valuable only in relation to the hereditary, cultural, social, and educational background of the child and the way in which that past history can be utilized and improved in making the child the *best possible person he is capable of being.*

While on the surface an IQ of 70 means "moron," actually it means that only to the extent that the past history of the child has been assayed by the test in equal manner, with equal justice, and in equal terms as were the past histories of the children used as the criteria of the test. Even so, it is being granted for purposes of argument that such an assay is a valid one—that what is being sampled really represents evidence of "intelligence."

A few years ago Dr. T. R. Garth[2] of Colorado tested about 1,000 ("Mexican"?) Spanish-speaking children from different communities in Texas, Colorado, and New Mexico. He found that the median IQ of these children was 78, slightly above the point of demarcation for morons. In fact, 50 per cent of the fourth-grade children tested were of 71.8 IQ or below! Uncritical evaluation might lead to the conclusion that at least 50 per cent of the Spanish-speaking children represented by this large sample was unfitted to participate in any but the simplest tasks of life. Such a wholesale indictment of a people would be indefensible—yet such are the results of test *application.* Who would champion the thesis that half or more of the Spanish-speaking, *or any other such,* group is dull, borderline, and feeble-minded when it is generally accepted that only 7 per cent of "normal" groups may be so classified? However, such a champion would find test-results to support his cause!

The writer tested a second-grade group of bilingual children and found the median IQ to be 72.[5] Working on the assumption that the tests reflected a function of the school, remedial instruction in language and language arts was given over a two-year period with the result that the median IQ was "raised" to approximately 100, or normal. Thus the tests served a very useful purpose as tools though their value as yardsticks of "intelligence" was questionable throughout the entire procedure. The class proved to be a slightly superior group of students throughout later development. If initial test results had been accepted at face value, a large percentage of the children would have been classified as belonging in special classes for the dull and some even as belonging in institutions for the feeble-minded!

The Binet Tests, when evaluated for vocabulary difficulty,[6] have been found by the writer to contain many words that do not even appear in the best of recommended word lists for bilingual children—to say nothing of the possibilities that such lists do not represent actual word mastery on the part of the pupils. If many of the words of the tests are unknown, and many but casually familiar or just recently acquired, what can be said as to the experiences and operations, the background and rapport, presupposed by the very nature of the tests? While language handicap in all probability transcends mere speech or vocabulary difficulties, it seems evident that at the very least the removal of such difficulties is a prerequisite to the beginnings of proper measurement. Even so, it is dangerous to assume that by supplying word knowledge the language handicap has been removed.

One investigator[7] used a makeshift "translation" of a test and found that there was no language handicap because the IQ's were not raised by such procedure! What assurance did he have that the IQ's obtained from the "translated" test were comparable to the norms? Why should the IQ's be raised by his procedure? And, is the evidence conclusive that the IQ's were not raised? The whole question is that of whether or not the revised test was the same test as the original in terms of difficulty, suitability, validity, reliability, etc. Similar tactical errors are common in testing programs and in the thinking of many who deal with the bilingual problem.

Of particular interest is the use to which measures or estimates of abilities have been put in other phases of education. Too often professional and scientific use of measures of evaluation is circumvented by attitudes and emotions which have no place in the educational program. From the standpoint of educational theory there are considerations which transcend the practical questions of sentiment, desirability, opposition or acquiescence, etc. Miss Reynolds,[4] of the United States Office of Education, quotes a graduate student who argues for segregation because "the two nationalities do not associate much . . . Mexican children . . . do not want to play with American children," etc. She also quotes a Los Angeles school official: "Our educational theory does not make any racial distinction between the Mexican and the native white population. However, pressure from white residents of certain sections forced a modification of this principle to the extent that certain neighborhood schools have been placed to absorb the majority of the Mexican pupils in the district!" Dr. Paul Taylor[9] quotes a Texas school official: "We don't enforce the

attendance on the whites because then we would have to on the Mexicans." Many other such expressions are common and are clearly presented in the studies made by Dr. Taylor. How such attitudes can go hand-in-hand with scientific instruments is incomprehensible, if such instruments are to produce worth-while results. That this condition is one which contributes to the impairment of educational opportunity cannot be denied.

Though not necessarily attributable to questions of attitudes and prejudices, it is apparent to any one who takes the time to examine the records that the state educational system in New Mexico is not functioning efficiently with respect to the bilingual problem. For example, in 1932-33 there was a total of 24,810 Spanish-speaking children enrolled in the first and second grades of the public school system.[3] However, only 540 were enrolled in the twelfth grade—two per cent as compared with a percentage of fourteen for other children. In other words, and in spite of any and all excuses that might be offered, *the Spanish-speaking group is not receiving a comparable education.* Some might counter with the argument that the Spanish-speaking group does not have the capacities to continue in school, so they drop out or are eliminated. It could be granted, only for the sake of argument however, that the group has an average IQ of 85. This means that 50 per cent of the group is above that level and that certainly a number much greater than 540 is capable of doing twelfth-grade work. Then, who has failed—the child or the school? What of compulsory education? What of the duty and responsibility of the State? What of the democratic theory of education?

The flagrant violations of the fundamental aspects of the theory of education and of the social and economic goals of America that are observed in the practice of education among bilinguals point to the urgent need for greater real professionalization of the educational practitioners and of further public enlightenment. The frequent prostitution of democratic ideals to the cause of expediency, politics, vested interests, ignorance, class and "race" prejudice, and to indifference and inefficiency is a sad commentary on the intelligence and justice of a society that makes claims to those very progressive democratic ideals. The dual system of education presented in "Mexican" and "white" schools, the family system of contract labor, social and economic discrimination, educational negligence on the part of local and state authorities, "homogeneous grouping" to mask professional inefficiency—all point to the need for greater insight into a problem which is inherent in a "melting pot" society. The progress of our country is dependent upon the most efficient utilization of the heterogeneous masses which constitute its population—the degree to which the 2,000,000 or more Spanish-speaking people, and their increment, are permitted to develop is the extent to which the nation should expect returns from that section of its public.

It appears that to those whose interest lies in the field of technical evaluation of the question of the school and the bilingual child there has come the time when fundamentals must be determined. The relative responsibility of the school and of the child in the achievement of desirable goals must be examined. Is the fact that a child makes an inferior score on an intelligence test prima facie evidence that he is dull? Or is it a function of the test to reflect the inferior or different training and development with which the child was furnished by his home, his language, the culture of his people, and by his school? When the child fails in promotion is it *his* failure or has the school failed to use the proper whetstone in bringing out the true temper and quality of his steel?

The school has the responsibility of supplying those experiences to the child which will make the experiences sampled by standard measures as common to him as they were to those on whom the norms of the measures were based. When the school has met the language, cultural, disciplinary, and informational lacks of the child and the child has reached the saturation point of his capacity in the assimilation of fundamental experiences and activities—then failure on his part to respond to tests of such experiences and activities may be considered his failure. As long as the tests do not at least sample in equal

degree a state of saturation that is equal for the "norm children" and the particular bilingual child it cannot be assumed that the test is a valid one for that child. Under our theory of education *the Child cannot fail.* Nevertheless, for comparative purposes, a child or a group may be classed as inferior or superior by measures which do equal justice to the criterion and the child or group. The fundamental questions in mental tests of bilingual children, then, are primarily questions of validity, to wit:

I. Do the tests measure *in that particular child* what they purport to measure? The tests may be valid for the "average" child and still lack validity for an individual or for a particular group. Questions of culture, schooling, socioeconomic status, etc., loom big in this phase of the problem.

II. Are the assumptions on which the test was based for the original "norm" children applicable with equal justice to the particular case? If the use of a radio were assumed to sample intelligence, would a Navajo Indian living in a hogan be equally subject to such an assumption as average children, or would the tallying of sheep be a more desirable measure? Is "intelligence" abstract reasoning, memory, "g," "s," etc.? Whatever it is, are the assumptions of what it is justified universally?

While it would be shortsighted to propose the abandonment of mental tests in the bilingual problem, and nothing herein contained should be so interpreted, a note of caution in their use is in order. It should be borne in mind that a mental test is not a measure in the same sense that yardsticks or meters are measures. Mental tests are professional instruments which must be supplemented by intelligent and professional application and evaluation for the best interests of the child or group concerned.

CITATIONS

1. Beard, C. H. Whither Mankind. Longmans, Green, 1928.
2. Garth, T. R. The Intelligence of Mexican School Children. School and Society. XXVII, 1928; pp. 791-794.
3. N. Mex. Dept. Educ., Division of Information

and Statistics. Annual Financial and Statistical Report—1932-33.

4. Reynolds, Annie. The Education of Spanish-speaking Children. U.S. Office of Education Bulletin. No. 11, 1933.

5. Sánchez, Geo. I. Scores of Spanish-speaking Children on Repeated Tests. Ped. Sem. and Jr. Genetic Psych. March, 1932; pp. 223-231.

6. Sánchez, Geo. I. The Implications of a Basal Vocabulary to the Measurement of the Abili-ties of Bilingual Children. To appear: Jr. Social Psych.

7. Sheldon, W. H. The Intelligence of Mexican School Children. School and Society. XIX, 1924; pp. 139-142.

8. Spearman, Chas. The Abilities of Man. Macmillan, 1927.

9. Taylor, Paul S. Mexican Labor in the United States, U. of Calif. Publications in Economics. Vol. 6, No. 5.

CHAPTER 16 STRATEGIES FOR ASSESSING INTELLECTUAL PATTERNS IN BLACK, ANGLO, AND MEXICAN-AMERICAN BOYS—OR ANY OTHER CHILDREN—AND IMPLICATIONS FOR EDUCATION

MARY MEEKER
ROBERT MEEKER

Today it is common practice for those who speak on behalf of disadvantaged students to be against IQ testing in the schools. The basis of their opposition is a familiar scenario: A student is tested; the test may be, for a variety of reasons, inaccurate, and the test results often characterize the student as being below normal in intelligence. This characterization functions as a label which goes to the teacher and prompts attitudes and treatment that may be inappropriate and false and even worse, are subtly (or otherwise) transmitted to the student. The student, in turn, tends to reflect behavior that fulfills the teacher's expectation. In short, if the psychologist tells the teacher that Johnny is below average and if the teacher treats him as such, Johnny will respond accordingly, indicating that the practice of testing is little related to the reason for testing and the test results are not used appropriately, i.e., as diagnostic instruments for the purpose of curriculum development. This situation still is being repeated countless times in schools throughout the nation: the issue is what to do about it. To understand the issue better, one needs to follow the scenario one step further.

Once the problem is acknowledged, a

From Journal of School Psychology 11(4):341-350, 1973.

further dialogue ensues, in which there are four principals: those who represent the disadvantaged, those who are directly concerned with instruction, those who are involved in test construction, and, in the center of this dialogue, the school psychologist. Representatives of the disadvantaged are advocating the abolition of all IQ testing; psychometricians are analyzing the sources of test inaccuracies and are discussing means for making tests more valid, more reliable, and culture-free or criterion-referenced in nature; and, close at hand, the classroom teachers are requesting professional assistance for their daily encounters. The school psychologist must respond to all of them, and although it is the response to the classroom teacher that is critical, it is necessary to examine each response in turn.

To the representative of disadvantaged: The proposed abolition of IQ testing is well intended, but ill conceived. To deny teachers access to formal assessments is to force them to make informal assessments that are subject to the same sorts of deficiencies, which, not being exposed to scrutiny, are not open to easy identification and correction. This also denies the need for formal assessments that some students must have to meet legislated qualifications in many special programs.

To the psychometrician: Analyses of the sources of testing deficiencies are helpful, and the proposed programs for rectification are welcomed, but operations cannot be suspended while professionals wait for more reliable and valid instruments. The job of constructing better tests is an exacting task that takes time, but the educational need is always immediate and ongoing, so the best available instruments must be used.

The school psychologist is, then, in a position where he can neither forfeit nor defer responsibility. Many of the cited injustices of the present practices can be eradicated by making some changes in the professional services provided. To understand best the nature and importance of these changes, we need to reexamine the dynamics of the opening scenario. The inescapable conclusion drawn from that scenario is that deficient assessments are almost uniformly insufficient, if not detrimental, for the ensuing instruction. The problem is not the potentiality of error, so much as the fact that the assessment is so general in kind that, as a consequence, it bears little relation to treatment. If assessments are specific and prescriptively related to treatment, then there is considerably less chance that errors, when they do occur, will be perpetuated.

All of this serves as an extended prologue to considering the school psychologist's response to requests from classroom teachers for professional assistance. The response must not be as general, global, and unrelated to instructional treatment as an IQ score is. In this study the authors have analysed IQ test results using a specific and prescriptive technique in which (1) the IQ test responses on Binets are separated from the score and interpreted as indicators of individual or group profiles of abilities, and (2) these responses can serve diagnostically for an individualized program of training of intellectual abilities in children, and (3) this information can come from the psychologist to the teacher out of the traditional testing battery with little more effort on the part of the psychologist.

The rationale for the approach used in analysing Binet responses via Guilford's (1956) Structure of Intellect Model (SI) is covered in Meeker (1963, 1969). The application of Guilford's theoretical SI model has occasioned a need to change the initials to SOI, just as the S-R initials were changed to S-O-R to indicate application of S-R theory. The authors use SOI to indicate application of Guilford's SI to organismic responses. That is, since neither the Binet nor the WISC is rooted in a theory of human intelligence, yet purports to measure intelligence, Meeker (1963) devised a set of templates which would allow the examiner to place Binet and WISC responses into an SOI profile as a means of getting away from an IQ score and going to a profile or pattern of a child's intellectual responses. In this manner, rooting the IQ test in theory, it is possible to identify in the profile strengths and weaknesses which allow for prescriptive education.

Psychometricians have long questioned the (presumed) adequacy of a unidimensional index of intelligence. As early as the 1930's Alexander (1934), after Thurstone, found that general intelligence accounted for only 10% of success in shop achievement (spatial ability accounted for 13%, motivation for 48%, and 34% remained unaccounted). Research into specific intellectual abilities (as contrasted with general ability) has been developing ever since.

Most notable among these developments has been the work of Guilford and his associates (Guilford, 1956). Using factor-analytic techniques, they found sets of distinct intellectual abilities beyond those factored by Thurstone which could be conceptualized along three dimensions. They referred to these dimensions as the Structure of Intellect. Subsequent to this pioneering work other investigators (Meeker, 1963; Meyers, Dingman, & Orpet, 1964; Orpet & Meyers, 1966; Sitkei, 1966; Feldman, 1970; Ball, 1972) have found similar factors among normal, mentally retarded, physically handicapped, and gifted children.

The inadequacy of a general index of intelligence seems apparent and undoubtedly the trend toward differentiation will continue. Nonetheless, the instruments of general assessment will not be quickly or easily displaced in the school context for two reasons: First, the instruments are familiar to practitioners and they are, undeniably, statistically sound. Second, there is, at present, no practical substitute for the Binet and WISC; i.e., there are no differentiated abilities tests (group or individual) that can be used within the limits of time and personnel that are normally allocated to testing. In other words, general intelligence instruments, although inadequate, will find continued use as long as there are no practical specific-abilities tests available.

The Binet and the WISC have very limited diagnostic utility when reported as IQ scores and thus have offered little guidance for prescriptive treatment for minority, ethnic, or any other children. As a practical and interim remedy for this situation, Meeker (1963, 1969) has proposed a method for using Binet (or WISC) responses to derive differentiated assessments of samples of intellectual responses.

The Binet-SOI analysis (Meeker, 1963) was derived for several purposes and is based on several assumptions, chief among which are: that intellectual abilities underlie the learning of subject matter and that with practice, intellectual abilities can be developed just as academic skills can, if a diagnosis of those abilities can be made based upon the rooting of the Binet and WISC on a theory or model of intelligence. The responses from each standardized test would present the most reliable and valid material for the purpose of identifying individual responses. This method has been used extensively in studies by Meeker (1963, 1965, 1966, 1971), Feldman (1970), Brown (1971), Karadenes (1971), Has & Pereira (1972) and Manning (1973).

PURPOSE

A review of studies relating to intelligence indicates that in most cases a general IQ score is used as the basis for conclusions drawn from the findings. This study questions the correctness of such use, especially with minority children, and instead looks at item-responses from Stanford-Binet tests administered to 245 respondents. Using a technique described elsewhere (Meeker, 1963), the item responses were tallied according to the SOI scheme. All subjects were boys who resided in lower socioeconomic Los Angeles

urban communities. The authors were curious as to whether the typical 13-point disadvantaged differential score found when minority, ethnic, or LSES children are tested was indicative of the lack of specific intellectual abilities as defined by the SOI. We also were interested in identifying any specific group strengths and weaknesses and considered whether instruction would enhance their abilities of a formal academic nature. The comparable age 7-9 group was selected to see what, if any, changes occurred in its SOI abilities due to exposure to traditional school learning.

The group identity of the respondents was retained in the tally of each item-response; as a result, each datum is characterized by a five-way classification:

> GROUP—MAE (4-5), MAS (4-5), MAE (7-9), B (4-5), B (7-9), A (4-5), A (7-9).
> OPERATION—Cognition, Memory, Evaluation, Convergent and Divergent Productions
> CONTENT—Figural, Symbolic, Semantic
> PRODUCT—Units, Classes, Relations, Systems, Transformations, Implications
> SCORE—Correct, Incorrect

The five-way classification yields a potential data space of 1,260 cells; the sampling distribution in the data space was too irregular to support a full multiclassification analysis, so each of the major SOI dimensions was analyzed independently (with consequent loss of information pertaining to between-dimension interactive effects). Multiclassification analyses for each of the SOI dimensions showed highly significant differences.

GROUP × OPERATION × SCORE
$x^2 = 101.6457$ df = 24 $p < .0001$
GROUP × CONTENT × SCORE
$x^2 = 154.1713$ df = 12 $p < .0001$
GROUP × PRODUCT × SCORE
$x^2 = 170.044$ df = 30 $p < .0001$

Sample

Respondents were from one of seven groups:
(1) MAS (4-5) Mexican Americans, age 4 to 5, who took their tests in vernacular Spanish with a Mexican-American examiner.
(2) MAE (4-5) Mexican Americans, age 4 to 5, who took their tests in English; they spoke English as a primary lan-

Sample description

	Age range	IQ range	IQ mean	Sex	Number
MAS—4-5	4.9-5.9	79-113	90	M	37
MAE—4-5	4.9-5.9	77-123	95	M	33
MAE—7-9	7.0-9.11	76-144	101	M	35
BLACK—4-5	4.9-5.9	78-135	100	M	31
BLACK—7-9	7.0-9.11	77-153	103	M	24
ANGLO—4-5	4.11-5.9	80-132	101	M	33
ANGLO—7-9	7.0-9.11	79-145	104	M	64

guage; their parents spoke English and Spanish. An interpreter, when needed, was available during each examination.

(3) MAE (7-9) Mexican Americans, age 7 to 9, who took their tests in English; they spoke English as a primary language and their parents also spoke English and Spanish.[1]

(4) B (4-5) Blacks, age 4 to 5, tested in English by black examiners.

(5) B (7-9) Blacks, age 7 to 9, tested by black examiners.

(6) A (4-5) Anglos, age 4 to 5, tested by Anglo examiners.

(7) A (7-9) Anglos, age 7 to 9, tested by Anglo examiners.

One condition of the 4- to 5-year-old sample was that none had had any formal preschool education; that is, none had been in Head Start, nursery, or co-op preschool, thus obtaining SOI-Binet profiles on the 4- to 5-year-olds so as to have a sample of entering kindergarteners who were "uncontaminated" by formal education. The authors wanted to identify kinds of SOI abilities boys come to school with when they have had limited exposure to learning.

Each of the above relationships was further analyzed with regard to the within-group and between-group effects. These results are of greatest interest for this study since they afford two kinds of comparisons. The within-group analyses reveal general strengths and weaknesses profiles for each group, while the between-group analyses serve to anchor these evaluations in relationships to other groups,

[1]It was not possible to complete a sample of MAS (7-9) to contrast and compare with MAS (4-5).

and, by implications, to the general population. In other words, if a group shows particular strength in cognition (among the operations), that fact in itself would be helpful in planning instructional programs; if, in addition, the group also shows strength in cognition in comparison to other groups, this would serve to reinforce the evaluation. Thus, in interpreting the results the authors looked primarily to the within-group analyses, since they are most useful for instructional prescriptions, and secondarily to between-group analyses as a means of anchoring the group ability profiles. Summaries of the within- and between-group analyses for each of the major dimensions of the SOI are presented in Tables 1, 2, and 3.

Given such information, then, let us see how school psychologists might use this information. Suppose a given within-groups profile is an individual profile. For instance, the MA-S (4-5) profile indicates a general weakness in Memory. Since memory, visual, auditory, and kinesthetic skills are critical for reading, spelling, and arithmetic (Meeker, 1966; Feldman, 1970), then one must reason that the teaching of memory skills has to become an objective, and secondly that the teaching of memory must be sequenced and hierarchically articulated and should precede the teaching of reading, spelling, and arithmetic if there is a weakness in memory. Again, since the MA-S (4-5) profile is strong in Evaluation skills, Figural input, Units, Classifications and Systems thinking, then each of these, in turn, can be further enhanced and developed by means of using curriculum planned for that purpose (Meeker & Sexton, 1971).

Considering the Blacks (4-5) within-

Table 1. Aggregate group scores for operations categories (items passed/items failed)

Groups	Operations					Within group (between operation probabilities)
	Cognition	Memory	Evaluation	Convergent production	Divergent production	
Mexican Americans (CA 4-5) Tested in Spanish	522 / 392	96 / 103 Lʷ Hᵇ	235 / 163 Hʷ Hᵇ	137 / 107	38 / 75 Lʷ Lᵇ	p < .001
Mexican Americans (CA 4-5) Tested in English	336 / 242 Hʷ	55 / 127 Lʷ Lᵇ	146 / 105 Hʷ Hᵇ	124 / 137	45 / 48	p < .001
Mexican Americans (CA 7-9) Tested in English	148 / 164 Hʷ Lᵇ	91 / 134	59 / 109 Lʷ Lᵇ	89 / 85 Hʷ	34 / 69 Lʷ Lᵇ	p < .003
Blacks (CA 4-5)	380 / 293 Hʷ	81 / 148 Lʷ Lᵇ	140 / 169	134 / 157	46 / 66 Lʷ	p < .001
Blacks (CA 7-9)	278 / 270 Lᵇ	201 / Hᵇ	140 / 186 Lᵇ	172 / 182	95 / 94	p < .07
Anglos (CA 4-5)	391 / 274 Hʷ Hᵇ	86 / 181 Lʷ Lᵇ	155 / 166	166 / 164	55 / 75 Lʷ	p < .001
Anglos (CA 7-9)	754 / 566 Hʷ	353 / 514 Lʷ	362 / 435 Lʷ Lᵇ	389 / 361	224 / 206 Hᵇ	p < .001
Between groups (within operations) probabilities	p < .003	p < .001	p < .001	p < .28	p < .001	Hʷ–high within group Hᵇ–high between groups Lʷ–low within group Lᵇ–low between groups

groups profile as an individual profile, and comparing their entering strengths in Cognition, Figural, Units, and Classes thinking with the lack of significance in strengths or weaknesses for Blacks (7-9), one might hope that specific planning will retain those intellectual strengths and remediate the weaknesses shown in Memory, Divergent Production, and Symbolic and Transformational thinking. This can be done by using SOI curriculum. It does mean, therefore, that the focus in education will have to be placed on the teaching of intellectual abilities (as defined by Guilford and others) as preparation for learning subject matter. In the long run, the development of intelligence may prove more lasting than the learning of 9 and 144 as squares.

DISCUSSION

The authors offer these analyses as an illustration of the potential utility of specific ability assessment in the understanding of intelligence beyond the use of a general IQ score. To reiterate: Most studies have used the general IQ score as a basis for the reported findings. This study indicates that the score itself, alone, may be misleading in that the boys, (within groups, Table 3) except for the Blacks 7-9, show a dimensional strength in Figural Intelligence. Between groups the MA-S and MAE 4-5 are significantly strong in this ability. What is figural intelligence? It is the ability to comprehend, retain, and use any inputs into the child's environment which are gestalt or whole or concrete in form as opposed to the handling of

Table 2. Aggregate group scores for content categories (items passed/items failed)

Groups	Contents			Within group (between contents) probabilities
	Figural	Symbolic	Semantic	
Mexican Americans (CA 4-5) Tested in Spanish	566 / 220 H^w H^b	30 / 91 L^w L^b	432 / 529 L^w L^b	p < .001
Mexican Americans (CA 4-5) Tested in English	313 / 153 H^w H^b	23 / 84 L^w L^b	370 / 422 L^w	p < .001
Mexican Americans (CA 7-9) Tested in English	102 / 94 H^w L^b	66 / 111 L^w	253 / 356 L^b	p < .01
Blacks (CA 4-5)	313 / 236 H^w L^b	51 / 117 L^w L^b	417 / 480	p < .001
Blacks (CA 7-9)	190 / 154 L^b	145 / 150 H^b	551 / 601	p < .06
Anglos (CA 4-5)	318 / 211 H^w	49 / 123 L^w L^b	489 / 526	p < .001
Anglos (CA 7-9)	495 / 386 H^w L^b	255 / 387 L^w H^b	1332 / 1309 H^b	p < .001
Between groups (within contents) probabilities	p < .001	p < .001	p < .002	H^w–high within group H^b–high between groups L^w–low within group L^b–low between groups

numbers, codes, notes (Symbols), and words and ideas (Semantics). The psychologist then, must point out to teacher and curriculum specialists that these boys, if given opportunities and experiences to work with figural material before they are exposed to symbols and semantic ideas, will develop feelings of success, good self-concept, and confidence which go a long way in helping them through the rough spots they will have to face in the handling of Semantics, in which all of the disadvantaged except the 7-9 Anglos show a significant weakness.

The fact that the first-grade teacher begins her curriculum primarily with semantics, and certainly heaviest weighting is given to semantics in the traditional curriculum, is unfortunate for disadvantaged children. If the semantic and symbolic dimensions were parceled out of the IQ score through the accumulated totals profile, one could predict that these boys who score low on general IQ tests would score average or above average in figural intelligence.[2] There is parsimony in this approach to curriculum development in the conserving of esteem for disadvantaged boys. The psychologist, of course, can now make the test results relevant to the educational needs of the student. The teacher will feel she has had help because she is an applier and can organize her tasks from simple (units level) to complex (implica-

---

[2]See Meeker (1969) for developing an MA score on each of the separate dimensions by accumulated totals profiles.

Table 3. Aggregate group scores for products categories (items passed/items failed)

Groups	Units	Products Classes	Relations	Systems	Transformations	Implications	Within group (between products) probabilities
Mexican Americans (CA 4-5) Tested in Spanish	295 / 152 H^w H^b	137 / 59 H^w	168 / 187 L^w	179 / 114 H^w H^b	108 / 123 L^w	141 / 205 L^w L^b	$p < .001$
Mexican Americans (CA 4-5) Tested in English	168 / 120 H^w H^b	82 / 38 H^w	140 / 132	111 / 103 H^b	72 / 98 L^w L^b	133 / 168 L^w L^b	$p < .003$
Mexican Americans (CA 7-9) Tested in English	97 / 125 L^b	29 / 26 H^w	79 / 123	45 / 108 L^w L^b	56 / 63	115 / 116 H^w	$p < .001$
Blacks (CA 4-5)	181 / 158 H^w	83 / 47 H^w	159 / 149	117 / 145	77 / 138 L^w L^b	164 / 196	$p < .001$
Blacks (CA 7-9)	215 / 191	48 / 37	197 / 209	146 / 188	98 / 87 H^b	182 / 193	$p < .07$
Anglos (CA 4-5)	186 / 176	90 / 44 H^w	182 / 159	109 / 148 L^w	94 / 120 L^w	195 / 213	$p < .001$
Anglos (CA 7-9)	484 / 463 L^b	133 / 89 H^w	453 / 475	250 / 434 L^w L^b	251 / 189 H^w H^b	511 / 432 H^w H^b	$p < .001$
Between groups (within products) probabilities	$p < .001$	$p < .09$	$p < .06$	$p < .001$	$p < .001$	$p < .001$	H^w–high within group H^b–high between groups L^w–low within group L^b–low between groups

tions level) and thus can give the child school experience which makes him feel successful so that a very necessary condition for the learning of difficult material is fulfilled or accomplished. The structure of intellect model offers a sequence for the development of curriculum both horizontally (F-S-M) and vertically (U-C-R-S-T-I) (See Meeker & Sexton, 1971, SOI Abilities Workbooks). More than that, however, the horizontal order of presentation of materials allows the psychologist to provide optimum learning sequence; that is, if the child is strong in Figural Units, then he can be presented material which capitalizes on his strength; then a lesson in Semantic Units, in which he may be less capable, can be presented next. Thus, the SOI becomes much more than a neat task analysis system for presenting materials. It offers a personalized or individualized base for the presenting of subject matter. That is, the SOI materials develop intellectual strengths by using traditional subject matter as the vehicle. The teacher soon understands that intellectual abilities can be taught (such as Figural Units) through mathematics, language arts, science, etc.

Another area to which SOI patterns contribute for the purpose of planning is that of vocational and professional guidance. Certain intellectual abilities are more basic to particular vocations than others; these patterns are exhibited early. Although the SOI analysis was designed primarily to identify individual profiles of learning abilities, the group profiles are not dysfunctional for educational practice and individualized curriculum. Group results do have limitations for general instructional planning, for an individual student's profile of abilities on any or all of the SOI dimensions may be vastly different from his group's profile on any or all of the SOI dimensions. As obvious as this may be statistically, one nonetheless finds, in instructional practice, that group-type diagnoses are used as bases for prescribing individual treatment. The larger point at issue is that specific, treatment-related, individual assessment can be an immediate remedy for intelligence testing abuses.

If one keeps in mind that group profile data differ from an individual profile, and

if he must develop instruction, then he can make certain suggestions, and here are examples of making the test data relevant to teaching:

1. Disadvantaged boys are relatively strong in the ability to comprehend; therefore much more time should be devoted to the teaching of cognition.
2. Enough of the members of each group show memory weaknesses to warrant substantial time being devoted to development of specific auditory, visual, and kinesthetic memory abilities. Of all the five major operations, lack of memory skills is most predictive of failure to master academics (Meeker, 1966).
3. More experiences in creative, unstructured, open-ended fun-type tasks would help develop weak divergent production skills (Manning, 1972).
4. Symbolic and semantic thinking is generally weak; therefore introduction of either task into the curriculum should be preceded by, or associated contiguously with, figural tasks.
5. Evaluation skills, i.e., planning, judgmental reasoning tasks ought to be part of daily curriculum in a fail-safe, non-critical atmosphere using semantics.

REFERENCES

Alexander, W. P. Research in guidance. A theoretical basis. *Occupations,* 1934, *12,* 75-91.

Ball, R. S. Comparison of thinking abilities of 5-year-old white and black children in relation to certain environmental factors. Proj. 9-70-0067. Tempe, Ariz.: Arizona State University, 1972.

Brown, D. L. Variations in test response of preschool children by sex and socioeconomic level related to Guilford's structure of intellect. Unpublished doctoral dissertation, University of Pittsburgh, 1971.

Feldman, B. Prediction of first-grade reading achievement from selected structure-of-intellect factors. Unpublished doctoral dissertation, University of Southern California, 1970.

Guilford, J. P. The structure of intellect. *Psychological Bulletin,* 1956, *52,* 267-293.

Hays, B. M., & Pereira, E. R. Effect of visual memory training on reading ability of kindergarten and first grade children. *Journal of Experimental Education,*1972, *41* (1), 33-38.

Karadenes, M. A comparison of differences in achievement and learning abilities between Anglo and Mexican-American children when the two groups are equated by intelligence.

Unpublished doctoral dissertation, The University of Virginia, 1971.

Manning, E. *Teaching divergent thinking to gifted children.* Title III Project. Whittier, Calif.: East Whittier Schools, 1972.

Meeker, M. N. The NSWP behavior samplings of the Binet. Paper presented at the meeting of the American Psychological Association, Philadelphia, September, 1963.

Meeker, M. N. A procedure for relating Stanford-Binet behavior samplings to Guilford's structure of the intellect. *Journal of School Psychology,* 1965, *3,* 26-36.

Meeker, M. Differential syndromes of giftedness. *Journal of Special Education,* 1968, *2* (2), 185-194.

Meeker, M. N. *The structure of intellect: Its interpretation and uses.* Columbus, Ohio: Charles E. Merrill, 1969.

Meeker, M. An evaluation of a high school educationally handicapped class: A two-year follow-up of the measurables and unmeasurables. In *Educational therapy.* Seattle: Special Child Publications, 1971.

Meeker, M. N., & Sexton, K. M. *Structure-of-intellect abilities workbook,* 2nd edition. Los Angeles: Loyola University of Los Angeles, 1971.

Meyers, C. E., Dingman, H. F., & Orpet, R. E. Four ability-factor hypotheses at three preliterate levels in normal and retarded children. *Monograph of the Society for Research in Child Development,* 1964, *29,* 5.

Orpet, R. E., & Meyers, C. E. Six structure-of-intellect hypotheses in six-year-old children. *Journal of Educational Psychology,* 1966, *57,* 341-346.

Sitkei, G. Comparative structure of intellect in middle and lower class four-year-old children in two ethnic groups. Unpublished doctoral dissertation, University of Southern California, 1966.

CHAPTER 17 PLURALISTIC DIAGNOSIS IN THE EVALUATION OF BLACK AND CHICANO CHILDREN: A PROCEDURE FOR TAKING SOCIOCULTURAL VARIABLES INTO ACCOUNT IN CLINICAL ASSESSMENT

JANE R. MERCER

Pluralistic diagnosis is a set of procedures we are developing which attempts to take both adaptive behavior and sociocultural background into account in assessing the meaning of scores on standardized measures. This approach has developed as an outgrowth of findings from an epidemiology of mental retarda-

Portions of the materials presented in this paper were presented at the Meeting of the American Psychological Association, Washington, D.C., September 3-7, 1971; Kennedy International Symposium on Human Rights, Retardation, and Research, Washington, D.C., October 16, 1971 and the 10th Annual National Educators Association Conference on Civil and Human Rights of Educators and Students, Washington, D.C., February 18-20, 1972.

Data in this report have been collected under auspices of the following grants: Public Health Service Research Grant No. MH-08667, from the National Institute of Mental Health, Department of Health, Education and Welfare and Public Health Service General Research Support Grant No. 1-SO1-FR-0563202, from the Department of Health, Education and Welfare, Socio-Behavioral Study Center in Mental Retardation, Pacific State Hospital, Pomona, California; Public Health Service Grant No. PH43-67-756; McAteer Grant No. M8-14A and M9-14 from the California State Department of Education, Office of Compensatory Education.

tion which we have conducted in the City of Riverside, California over the past eight years. In order to explain clearly the rationale behind pluralistic diagnostic procedures, it is necessary to review, briefly, the conceptual model and design used in the Riverside epidemiology and to point out those findings from that study which are most relevant to our current topic.

SOCIAL SYSTEM PERSPECTIVE: THE LABELING PROCESS

Two contrasting conceptual perspectives were used in the Riverside epidemiology—a clinical perspective and a social system perspective. The social system perspective treated mental retardation as an achieved social status and a social role which some individuals play in some social systems. This aspect of the study focused on the labeling process and the characteristics of persons who achieve the status of mental retardate in various social systems in the community, especially the public school.

We contacted 241 organizations in the community and asked each organization to give us information on each mentally retarded person being served by that group. Because we were studying the labeling process, we did not impose a standard definition but asked each organization to use whatever definition was customarily used by its staff. After identifying those persons nominated by more than one organization, we found there were 812 unduplicated persons who had been nominated 1,493 times for the register. We grouped the 241 organizations into 8 categories to simplify our analysis: the public schools, law enforcement, private service organizations, private organizations for the mentally retarded, California Department of Mental Hygiene, medical facilities, public welfare and vocational rehabilitation, and religious organizations. We found that the public schools had contributed 429 persons to the case register, 340 of whom were not nominated by any other organization. The next largest contributors were medical facilities, 166 nominees, and the California Department of Mental Hygiene, 119 nominees. When we studied the number of persons jointly nominated by various types of organizations, the public schools clearly held the commanding position. They not only had labeled more persons as mentally retarded than any other organization but they shared their labels more widely throughout the community.

We compared the various kinds of information used by different agencies in labeling persons as mentally retarded. We found that the public schools rely primarily on IQ test scores. Ninety-nine percent of their cases had been given an IQ test but only 13% had received a medical diagnosis. Law enforcement agencies were similar to the schools. On the other hand, the Department of Mental Hygiene had both IQ test scores and medical diagnoses for over 90% of its nominees.

We then studied each type of formal organization to see what standards they were using in screening for mental retardation. We found that 46% of the persons nominated by the public schools had IQs above 70 and 62% had no reported physical disabilities. All other agencies, except law enforcement, were labeling persons with more deficiencies. For example, only 12% of those nominated by the Department of Mental Hygiene had IQs above 70 and only 11% were without physical disabilities.

We concluded that the public school system is the primary labeler in the community. The schools label the most persons as mentally retarded, share the most labels with other organizations, and label the most persons with IQs above 70 and with no physical disabilities. Any public policy directed at modifying labeling practices in the community must include modification of public school labeling practices. Any major change in the labeling policies of this single system would have a significant impact on labeling processes in the community as a whole.

Who gets labeled retarded?

We next studied the characteristics of the 812 who were holding the status of mental retardate in one or more organizations in Riverside at the time of our census. We found that 72% of the persons on the register were 5 through 20 years of age, only 7% were under 5 years of age, and only 21% were over 20. School-age children were "overlabeled" and preschool children and adults were "underlabeled" compared to their percentage in the general population of the community. Before children get to school, only those with the most physical disabilities and lowest IQs are identified. After graduation from school, only the most intellecutally and physically subnormal adults continue to be labeled.

We classified all persons on the case register into 10 groups according to the median value of the housing on the block on which they lived. We found that the persons in the lowest socioeconomic categories were greatly overrepresented on the register and those from higher statuses were underrepresented. When we studied ethnic groups, we found 300% more Mexican-Americans and 50% more Blacks than their proportion in the general population but only 60% as many English-speaking Caucasians (Anglos) as would be expected. Because most Mexican-Americans and Blacks in Riverside come from lower socioeconomic backgrounds, ethnic group and socioeconomic status are correlated. When we held socioeconomic status constant, we found that Anglos were still underrepresented and Mexican-Americans were still overrepresented in the case register but Blacks appeared in their proper proportion.

Ethnic disproportions were especially marked among public school nominees. There were four-and-a-half times more Mexican-American children and twice as many Black children labeled retarded as would be expected from their proportion in the population and only half as many Anglo children. When we compared Riverside school data with data from other school districts in the State of California, we found that this overrepresentation of Mexican-American and Black children in classes for the educable mentally retarded was statewide and not just a local pattern.

FINDINGS FROM THE CLINICAL PERSPECTIVE

A second phase of our study was the clinical epidemiology conducted from a clinical perspective. This perspective is commonly adopted by persons in the fields of medicine, psychology, social work, and education. Within the clinical perspective there are two definitions of "normal" which tend to be used simultaneously and interchangeably: the pathological model and the statistical model. The pathological model, developed in medicine, defines diseases or handicaps by the biological symptoms which characterize them. A person is categorized as "abnormal" when pathological symptoms are present and "normal" when there is an absence of pathological signs. On the other hand, the statistical model defines abnormality according to the extent to which an individual varies from the average of the population on a particular trait. Ordinarily, if an individual is more than two standard deviations above or below the mean for the population on which a measure was standardized, he is regarded as "abnormal." The clinical perspective regards mental retardation as an attribute of the individual. His symptomatology may exist as an entity regardless of whether it has been identified and labeled by significant others in his social milieu. The trained diagnostician with his clinical measures may detect abnormalities not apparent to lay persons.

Definitions

The definition of mental retardation operationalized in the clinical phase of our study was that of the American Association of Mental Deficiency.

Mental retardation refers to subaverage general intellectual functioning which originates during the developmental period and is associated with impairment in adaptive behavior. (Heber, 1961)

This is a two-dimensional definition. Before a person may be diagnosed as mentally retarded, he must be subnormal in both intellectual performance and adaptive behavior. Evidence of organic dysfunction or biological anomalies is not required.

In the same document, "subnormal" is defined as performance on a standard measure of intellectual functioning which is greater than one standard deviation below the population mean, approximately the lowest 16% of the population (Heber, 1961). Educational practice generally places the dividing line somewhat lower. The highest IQ test score for placement in a class for the educable mentally retarded ranges between 75 and 79, depending upon local usage. This cutoff includes approximately the lowest 9% of the population. The test designers suggest a cutoff that more closely conforms with traditional definitions, an IQ below 70, approximately 3% of the population (Wechsler, 1958; Terman & Merrill, 1960). In the clinical epidemiology, all three cutoffs were used and the results compared.

Operations

Intellectual adequacy was measured in the clinical epidemiology by using standardized measures of intelligence, primarily the Stanford-Binet LM and the Kuhlman-Binet. We conceptualized adaptive behavior as an individual's ability to play ever more complex roles in a progressively widening circle of social systems. Because there are no generally accepted measures of adaptive behavior, we developed a series of 28 age-graded scales for this purpose drawing heavily on the work of Doll and Gesell, especially for the younger years (Doll, 1965; Gesell, 1948, 1956). Questions were answered by a respondent related to the person being evaluated.

Sample

The research design called for a first-stage screening of a large sample of the population of the community using the adaptive behavior scales and then a second-stage testing of a subsample using standardized IQ tests. We called these samples the screened sample and the tested subsample, respectively.

The screened sample was a stratified area probability sample of 3,198 housing units in the city of Riverside, California, selected so that all geographic areas and socioeconomic levels in the city were represented in their proper proportion. The 46 interviewers were college educated, 36 were teachers. Spanish-speaking interviewers were assigned to all households with Spanish surnames. Black interviewers were assigned to interview in housing located in predominately non-White neighborhoods. Anglo interviewers were randomly assigned the remainder of the households. In each household, one adult member, usually the mother, served as respondent and provided information about all other members of the household to whom she was related. Interviews were completed in 2,661 of the 2,923 occupied housing units, an overall response rate of 90.7%. In all, 6,907 persons under 50 years of age were screened.

There were 483 persons selected for individual intelligence testing on the basis of a disproportionate random sampling frame. Tests were completed on 423 persons for an overall response rate of 87.6%. Intelligence test scores were also secured from other sources for an additional 241 persons, making a total of 664 scores available. Each person in the tested subsample was assigned a weight according to the number of persons he represented in the larger, screened sample.

Typology of mental retardation

A simplified version of our working typology of mental retardation is shown in Table 1. The American Association of Mental Deficiency definition contains two primary symptoms—subnormality in intellectual performance and subnormality in adaptive behavior. Combinations of these two dimensions produce four major types of persons: the clinically retarded, the

Table 1. Typology of mental retardation

	Intellectual performance	Adaptive behavior
Clinically retarded	Subnormal	Subnormal
Quasi-retarded	Subnormal	Normal
Behaviorally maladjusted	Normal	Subnormal
Normals	Normal	Normal

quasi-retarded, the behaviorally maladjusted, and the normals. The clinically retarded are those who are subnormal in both IQ and adaptive behavior. The quasi-retarded are those who are subnormal in IQ but normal in adaptive behavior. The behaviorally maladjusted are those who have normal IQs but are subnormal in adaptive behavior. The normals are those who pass both dimensions. In this paper we are concerned primarily with two categories in this typology, the clinically retarded and the quasi-retarded.

FINDINGS AND CONCLUSIONS
Conclusion I: cutoff level for subnormality should be lowest 3% (IQ below 70)

As noted earlier, three cutoff levels are currently used for defining subnormality—the American Association of Mental Deficiency proposes the lowest 16% of the population; educational usage defines the lowest 9% as subnormal; and traditional practice has been to define the lowest 3% as subnormal. We examined the impact of using each of these cutoffs.

The behavioral characteristics of the adults in our sample who failed the traditional criterion, the lowest 3%, was compared with adults who failed only the educational of the AAMD criteria. We found that the majority of the adults who were failing at a 9% or the 16% criterion were, in fact, filling the usual complement of social roles for persons of their age and sex: 83.6% had completed 8 grades or more in school, 82.6% had held a job, 64.9% had a semiskilled or higher occupation, 80.2% were financially independent or a housewife, almost 100% were able to do their own shopping and to travel alone, and so forth. Differences between their performance and that of persons failing the traditional criterion differed at the .001 level of significance on 21 out of 26 of the comparisons made. It is clear that most adults who appear in the borderline category were managing their own affairs and did not appear to require supervision, control, and care for their own welfare. Their role performance appeared neither subnormal nor particularly unusual.

We found that rates for subnormality using only an IQ test score, ranged from

21.4 to 36.8 to 72.8 per 1,000 for the total population of the community at each successive criterion. When a two-dimensional definition was used, that is, persons had to fail both IQ and adaptive behavior before being defined as clinically retarded, rates shrank to 9.7, 18.9, and 34.7 per 1,000 for the total population at each criterion level. There were significant differences by ethnic group and socioeconomic status. We found that rates for clinical retardation, using the two-dimensional definition, increased from 4.4 to 6.1 to 9.6 per 1,000 for the Anglo population but increased from 4.1 to 22.4 to 53.1 per 1,000 for the Black population and from 60.0 to 127.4 to 238.4 per 1,000 for the Chicano population. Similar disparities appeared for low status as compared to high status persons, regardless of ethnic group. Proportionately more low status persons and persons from minority ethnic groups are defined as clinically retarded, as the cutoff level for subnormality is raised.

We compared the findings from our field survey with the actual labeling practices of clinicans in the community and found much higher rates from the field survey than from actual labeling practices when the 16% or the 9% cutoff was used. The greatest correspondence between field survey rates and rates of labeling occurred when the traditional 3% cutoff was used.

We concluded that the 3% cutoff, that is, IQ below 70 and adaptive behavior in the lowest 3% of the population, was the criterion most likely to identify those in need of special assistance and supervision and least likely to stigmatize as mentally retarded, persons who would be filling a normal complement of social roles as adults. Persons scoring in the so-called "borderline" category should be regarded as low normals rather than as clinically retarded.

Conclusion II: both IQ and adaptive behavior should be evaluated in making diagnoses

Although the American Association of Mental Deficiency proposes the two-dimensional definition of mental retardation which we used in our study, in actual clinical practice most clinicians measure only intelligence in a systematic fashion when making assessments. We examined the probable consequence of clinicians using only an IQ test score rather than measuring both IQ and adaptive behavior in reaching a diagnosis of retardation.

First, we compared the social role performance of the quasi-retarded, that is, those who failed only the IQ test, with the clinically retarded, school-aged child, that is, those who failed both the IQ test and the adaptive behavior scales. The clinical retardate is reported to have had more trouble learning, is more frequently behind the school grade expected for his age, has repeated more grades, and is more likely to be enrolled in special education classes. The quasi-retardate, in spite of a low IQ test score, has avoided falling behind his age mates or being placed in special programs. We found that 80% of the quasi-retarded adults had graduated from high school; they all read books, magazines, and newspapers; all had held jobs; 65% had white-collar positions; 19% had skilled or semi-skilled positions, and 15.7% were unskilled laborers. All of them were able to work without supervision; participated in sports; traveled alone; went to the store by themselves; and participated in informal visiting with coworkers, friends, and neighbors. In other words, their social role performance tended to be indistinguishable from that of other adults in the community.

There was 54.7% shrinkage in the rate of mental retardation for the total population of the community, at the 3% criterion, when adaptive behavior was measured as well as IQ. However, the shrinkage varied by ethnic group and socioeconomic status. There was no shrinkage for Anglos. Every Anglo who had an IQ below 70 was also in the lowest 3% in adaptive behavior. On the other hand, 60% of the Chicanos and 90.9% of the Blacks who had IQ test scores below 70 passed the adaptive behavior measures. Comparable results were found at the other two criterion levels. A similar pattern appears for socioeconomic status but is less pronounced than in the case of ethnic group.

The most important aspect of these figures is the finding that, at the 3% cutoff, the evaluation of adaptive behavior contributed little additional information to that provided by the IQ test for Anglos.

However evaluation of adaptive behavior was important in evaluating persons from ethnic minorities and lower socioeconomic levels—persons from backgrounds that do not conform to the modal social and cultural pattern of the community. Many of them may fail intelligence tests mainly because they have not had the opportunity to learn the cognitive skills and to acquire the knowledge needed to pass such tests. They demonstrate by their ability to cope with problems in other areas of life that they are not comprehensively incompetent.

We concluded that clinicians should develop a systematic method for assessing adaptive behavior as well as intelligence in making clinical assessments of ability and should operationalize the two-dimensional screening procedure advocated by the AAMD ten years ago.

Conclusion III: sociocultural factors should be systematically taken into account in interpreting clinical scores

Our third major conclusion was that the IQ tests now being used by psychologists are, to a large extent, Anglocentric. They tend to measure the extent to which an individual's background is similar to that of the modal cultural configuration of American society. Because a significant amount of the variance in IQ test scores is related to sociocultural characteristics, we concluded that sociocultural factors must be taken into account in interpreting the meaning of any individual score.

Specifically, we studied two different samples of persons to determine the amount of variance in IQ test scores which could be accounted for by sociocultural factors. The first group were the 100 Chicanos, 47 Blacks, and 556 Anglos from 7 months through 50 years of age for whom IQs were secured in the field survey or in the agency survey and for whom we also had information on the sociocultural characteristics of their families. Eighteen sociocultural characteristics were dichotomized so that one category corresponded to the modal sociocultural configuration of the community and the other category was nonmodal. IQ was used as the dependent variable in a stepwise multiple regression

in which the 18 sociocultural characteristics were used as independent variables. The multiple correlation coefficient for this large heterogeneous sample was .50 (p < .001), indicating that 25% of the variance in the IQs of the 703 culturally and ethnically heterogeneous individuals in this group could be accounted for by sociocultural differences.

In a similar analysis, 1,513 elementary school children in the public schools of Riverside were studied, using 13 sociocultural characteristics of their families as independent variables and Full Scale WISC IQ as the dependent variable. The 598 Chicanos and 339 Black children in the sample included the total school population of the three segregated minority elementary schools which then existed in the district. The 576 Anglo children were randomly selected from 11 predominantly Anglo elementary schools in the district. The multiple correlation coefficient was .57, indicating that 32% of the variance in the IQs of this socioculturally heterogeneous group of elementary school children could be accounted for by differences in family background factors. Sixty-eight percent of the variance was residual, that is, unaccounted for.

Not only did sociocultural characteristics account for a large amount of the variance in IQ test scores in the large samples which combined all three ethnic groups, but they also accounted for a large amount of the variance in IQ within each ethnic group. A series of stepwise multiple regressions were run for Chicanos and Blacks, separately, using IQ as the dependent variable and sociocultural variables as the independent variables.

In Table 2, the first set of correlations present the findings for the 100 Chicanos in the field survey. Eighteen sociocultural variables were correlated .61 with IQ and accounted for 37.2% of the variance in the measured intelligence of this group. The five sociocultural characteristics most significant in the stepwise regression were: living in a household in which the head of household has a white-collar job; living in a family with five or fewer members; having a head of household with a skilled or higher occupation; living in a family in which the head of household was reared

Table 2. Sociocultural component of IQ for Chicanos and Blacks

| | Field survey | | | | | Full scale WISC: Children 6-14 years | | | | | |
| | Chicanos (N = 100) | | | Blacks (N = 47) | | | Chicanos (N = 598) | | | Blacks (N = 339) | |
Sociocultural variable[a]	R	% Variance	Sociocultural variable[a]	R	% Variance	Sociocultural variable[a]	R	% Variance	Sociocultural variable[a]	R	% Variance
Head white-collar	.37[c]	13.7	Mother reared in north	.27[b]	7.3	Less than 1.4 per room	.24[c]	5.8	1-5 in family	.21[c]	4.4
1-5 in family	.43[c]	18.5	Head white-collar	.33[b]	10.9	Mother expect some college	.32[c]	10.2	Mother expect some college	.30[c]	9.0
SES index head 30+	.47[c]	22.1	Head male	.35	12.3	Head 9+ years education	.34[c]	11.6	Head married	.35[c]	12.2
Head reared urban area	.49[c]	24.0	Nuclear family	.38	14.4	English all or most of the time	.36[c]	13.0	SES index head 30+	.39[c]	15.2
Head reared in U.S.	.54[c]	29.2	Own home	.41	16.8	Own home	.37[c]	13.7	Own home	.41[c]	16.8
Total—18 variables	.61[c]	37.2	Total—17 variables	.52	27.0	All 17 variables	.39[c]	15.2	All 16 variables	.44[c]	19.4

[a]All sociocultural variables are stated in the direction of sociocultural modality.
[b]Significant at the .05 level of significance.
[c]Significant at the .01 level of significance.

in an urban environment and was reared in the United States.

There were 47 Blacks in the field survey for whom we had information on all variables in the analysis. Findings on such a small number are less reliable, but the multiple correlations coeffeint between IQ and sociocultural characteristics was .52, accounting for 27% of the variance in IQ test scores. The five best indicators were: having a mother reared in the North; having a head of household with a white-collar job; having a male head of household; living in an intact family, and living in a family which is buying its own home.

For the elementary school children, all 17 variables were correlated .39 with Full Scale IQ for Chicano children and .44 with Full Scale IQ for the Black children. This means, that sociocultural characteristics could account for 15.2% of the variance in the IQ test scores of Chicano children and 19.4% of the variance in the IQ test scores of Black children.

In brief, Chicano elementary school children with higher IQ test scores tend to come from less crowded homes and have mothers who expect them to have some education beyond high school. They have fathers who were reared in an urban environment (over 10,000 population) and who have a ninth grade education or more. They live in a family which speaks English all or most of the time and is buying its home. Black children with the highest IQ also come from families that have characteristics similar to those of the modal configuration of the community. They come from families with less than six members; have a mother who expects them to get some college education; have parents who are married and living together in a home which they either own or are buying; and have a father who has an occupation rated 30 or higher on the Duncan Socioeconomic Index (Reiss, 1961). Thus, the more the family is like the modal sociocultural configuration of the community, the higher the IQs of Black and Chicano children on the WISC. Clearly, sociocultural factors cannot be ignored in interpreting the meaning of standardized intelligence tests when evaluating the child from a non-Anglo background. The tests are measur-

ing, to a significant extent, the child's exposure to the Anglo core culture.

DEVELOPING A SOCIOCULTURAL INDEX FOR CLASSIFYING CHILDREN BY FAMILY BACKGROUND

The findings from the multiple regression were used to group each Black and Chicano elementary school child who was given the WISC into one of five groups according to the extent to which his family background conformed to the modal configuration for the total community of Riverside. Each child was given one point for each family background characteristic which was like the dominant society on the five primary sociocultural variables related to Full Scale IQ for his ethnic group. If his family was similar to the modal configuration on all five characteristics, he received a score of five. If his background was similar to the dominant configuration on four characteristics, he received a score of four, and so forth.

The drawings in Figure 1 depict the scores of Chicano children in the various sociocultural groupings and compare them with the distribution of scores for children on whom the test was standardized. The average IQ for the entire group of Chicano children was 90.4, approximately two-thirds of a standard deviation below the mean for the standardization group. The 127 children from backgrounds least like the modal sociocultural configuration of the community, having no or only one modal characteristic, had an average IQ of 84.5, borderline mentally retarded by the American Association of Mental Deficiency criterion. The 146 children with 2 modal characteristics had a mean IQ of 89.0, those with 4 modal characteristics had a mean IQ of 95.5, and those with all 5 modal characteristics had a mean IQ of 104.4. When social background was held constant there was no difference between the measured intelligence of Chicano and Anglo children.

In Figure 2, the situation is just as dramatic for Black children. The total group of 339 Black children had an average IQ of 90.5 when there was no control for sociocultural factors. The 47 children who came from backgrounds least like the modal configuration of the community had

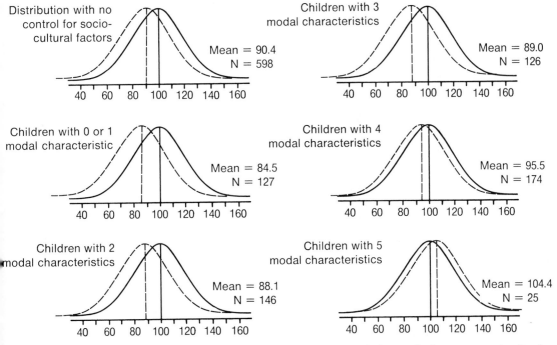

Fig. 1. Convergence of the average IQ test scores of Chicano children with the standard norms as sociocultural factors are increasingly controlled.

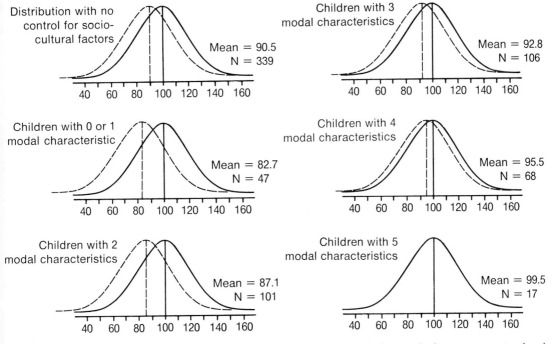

Fig. 2. Convergence of the average IQ test scores of black children with the standard norms as sociocultural factors are increasingly controlled.

an average IQ of 82.7. Those with 2 modal characteristics had an average IQ of 87.1. Those with 3 modal characteristics had an IQ of 92.8, those with 4 characteristics an average IQ of 95.5, and those with 5 characteristics an average IQ of 99.5, exactly at the national norm for the test. Thus, Black children who came from family backgrounds comparable to the model pattern for the community, did just as well on the Wechsler Intelligence Scale for Children as the children on whom the norms were based. When sociocultural differences were held constant, there were no differences in measured intelligence.

PLURALISTIC DIAGNOSIS IN THE EVALUATION OF BLACK AND CHICANO CHILDREN

During the past twenty years, one of the great achievements of public education in America has been the development of special education programs designed to meet the special needs of handicapped children. It would be a tragedy if these valuable programs were to be jeopardized because of inadequacies in assessment procedures which have labeled many children as "retarded" who are from non-Anglo backgrounds. There are viable alternatives to present practices. Assessment procedures can be modified to take sociocultural factors into account and programming can be altered to reduce stigmatization and to keep many children who are now in self contained special education classrooms in the educational mainstream.

Present procedures in labeling mental retardates are essentially Anglocentric. They systematically militate against persons from lower socioeconomic statuses and from non-Anglo backgrounds because they categorize behavior resulting from cultural differences as "subnormal" and do not take adaptive behavior in non-academic settings into account.

Pluralistic assessment would seek to remedy those deficiencies in current clinical practice by expanding the amount of information used in making educational and clinical decisions and by increasing the number of normative frameworks within which a particular set of scores is interpreted. Plualistic assessment would be based on four types of information: (1) a

sociocultural modality index score based on information about the social milieu into which the person has been socialized to be used as the basis for determining which normative framework is most appropriate for interpreting his performance, (2) a measure of adaptive behavior interpreted within the socioculturally relevant normative framework, (3) the measure of general academic readiness (IQ test) interpreted within the socioculturally relevant normative framework to determine the extent to which the individual's score reflects sociocultural factors, and (4) the same measure of general academic readiness (IQ test) interpreted within the standard norms to determine whether the person is likely to succeed in a regular public school academic program without supplementary help.

First, school psychologists should be required to secure systematic information about the child's adaptive behavior in nonschool situations—at home, in the neighborhood, and in the community. If a child is performing adequately in these settings, then it is clear that his problems are school specific and that he is not comprehensively retarded. His program should be planned with the expectation that he will probably be able to fill his adult roles acceptably and that his primary needs are for special help with academic tasks. For him, special tutoring, programmed learning, cross-age teaching, remedial reading, or similar programs are to be preferred to the self contained classroom and a curriculum for the mentally retarded.

Second, school psychologists should be required to secure systematic information about a child's sociocultural background which can be used in interpreting the meaning of his IQ test score.

A pluralistic, sociocultural perspective would evaluate the general academic readiness of each child as measured by the typical Anglocentric IQ test in terms of two frameworks simultaneously—the standardized norms for the test and the norms for the sociocultural group to which the child belongs. His position on the standardized norms indicates his probability of succeeding in a regular class in the American public school system as it is now constituted. His position in the distribution of scores of other children from similar sociocultural backgrounds, children who have had approximately the same opportunity to acquire the knowledge and skills needed to answer questions on an intelligence test designed by an Anglo American society, will provide a more accurate indication of his potential for learning if enrolled in appropriate educational programs. If a child scores more than one standard deviation above the mean of his sociocultural group, then he probably has high normal ability, even if his actual IQ is 100—average by the standard norms of the test. Conversely, a child who achieves a score of 75 on an IQ test when he comes from the least modal sociocultural background is within the normal range for persons, like himself, who have had little exposure to the cultural materials needed to pass the typical intelligence test. His educational program should be planned on the assumption that he is a person with normal learning ability who may need special help in learning the ways of the dominant society.

Third, only persons in the lowest 3% of the population on both adaptive behavior and "intelligence" (IQ below 70) should be regarded as mentally retarded.

Our problem in the past has been that a large number of children with widely different characteristics and very different needs have been grouped under one label, the mentally retarded, and have been given one undifferentiated program. What is needed is a more sensitive system for identifying children in need of specific education programs and a whole continuum of special education programs carefully targeted for children with specific needs. Special education programs should be planned on the premise that every child be kept in the educational mainstream if at all possible. The self contained classroom should be a treatment reserved only for the comprehensively retarded.

Figure 3 presents, schematically, how such a continuum of special education programming might look. At the far right are those children in the regular classroom who need no special help beyond the regular classroom program. The group to their left consists of those children who can be maintained full time in the regular classroom if they are given some additional individual help by tutors, mothers helpers, cross-age tutors, or other persons working under the direction of the regular classroom teacher.

The next group consists of those children who need more intensive assistance from a trained special education teacher for a few hours a week outside the regular classroom. Children in this group would be those who need remedial reading, English as a second language, or other types of programs requiring special teaching skills. Closely related to this group are those children who may have regular, daily periods in a resource room, a crisis room, or other special program but are still, primarily,

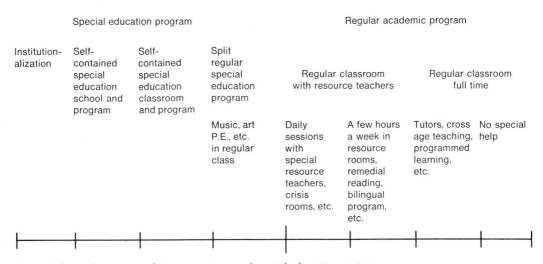

Fig. 3. Schema for conceptualizing a continuum of special education services.

enrolled in the regular academic class-room.

The four categories to the extreme left are heavily weighted toward special education. However, even within the special education program, there can be differentiated treatments. Some children may have a program split between regular and special classes, sharing music, art, physical education, and other nonacademic classes with regular students. The comprehensively retarded would spend their entire day in a self contained special education classroom and program while still remaining in the same school building with their brothers, sisters, neighbors, and friends. Only the comprehensively retarded with physical handicaps or other special needs which require a specially designed physical plant would be isolated in self contained special schools or institutions.

One of the most distressing current developments in special education in some regions of the United States has been the precipitious reassignment of many children to the regular classroom program from self contained special education classrooms with no provision for a continuum of special education services to meet their needs. It would be a serious step backwards if, as a result of modifying assessment procedures, we eliminate programs needed to serve children. Relabeling is not some magic panacea which suddenly enables children from socioculturally nonmodal environments to achieve in the mainstream of public education. It is essential that the children who received and were eligible for special education in the past continue to receive special services to supplement their educations in the regular classroom. It is essential that money be provided to continue support for special education services for them. Changes in the types of assessment and the types of programming must not be used as excuses for saving money by eliminating needed services to children. Instead, the financial support and the efforts of special education teachers should be redirected into providing a wider variety of special services geared to keeping as many children as possible in the educational mainstream and educating each child to his own maximum potential.

ACKNOWLEDGMENT

We wish to thank key persons from the Riverside Unified School District for their support and advice in our research efforts: Past Superintendent of Schools, Bruce Miller; Superintendent of Schools, Raymond E. Berry, Albert Marley, Director of Pupil Personnel Services; Former Director of Pupil Personnel, Richard Robbins; Mabel C. Purl, Director of Research and Testing. From the Alvord School District we acknowledge with gratitude the help of Robert W. Hocker, Director of Pupil Personnel; and J. Martin Kaeppel, Psychometrist.

AUTHOR'S NOTE

A more comprehensive and detailed analysis and report of the referral process, the clinical testing process, the assumptions and inferences of the clinicans, and the pluralistic evaluation process discussed herein appear in a forthcoming volume entitled *Labeling the Mentally Retarded,* University of California Press.

REFERENCES

Doll, E. A. *Vineland Social Maturity Scale, condensed.* (Rev. ed.) Manual of Direction. Minneapolis: American Guidance Service, Inc., 1965.

Gesell, A. L. *Studies in Child Development.* New York: Harper & Row, Publishers, 1948.

Gesell, A. L. *Youth: The Years From Ten to Sixteen.* New York: Harper & Row, Publishers, 1956.

Heber, R. F. A manual on terminology and classification in mental retardation. *American Journal of Mental Deficiency,* 1961, 64. Monograph Supplement. (2nd ed).

Reiss, A J., Jr. *Occupation and Social Status.* Glencoe, N.Y.: The Free Press, 1961.

Terman, L. M., & Merrill, M. A. *Stanford-Binet Intelligence Scale.* Boston: Houghton Mifflin Co., 1960.

Wechsler, D. *The Measurements and Appraisal of Adult Intelligence.* (4th ed.) Baltimore: The Williams & Wilkins Co., 1958.

PUBLICATIONS BY THE AUTHOR RELATED TO THIS STUDY

Labeling The Mentally Retarded, University of California Press, (in press).

Who is normal? Two perspectives on mild mental retardation. In E. G. Jaco (Ed.), *Patients, Physicians and Illness.* (Rev. ed.) Glencoe, N.Y.: The Free Press, 1972.

Institutionalized Anglocentrism: Labeling mental retardates in the public schools. In Peter Orleans and William Russell, Jr. (Eds.), *Race, Change, and Urban Society.* Urban Affairs Annual Review, Vol. V., Los Angeles: Sage Publications, Inc., 1971.

Sociocultural factors in labeling mental retardates. *The Peabody Journal of Education,* April, 1971, 48(3), 188.

The meaning of mental retardation. In Richard Koch, & James Dobson (Eds.), *The mentally retarded child and his family: A multidisciplinary handbook.* New York: Brunner-Mazel, Inc., 1971.

Sociological perspectives on mild mental retardation. In H. Carl Haywood (Ed.) *Social-cultural aspects of mental retardation: proceedings of the Peabody NIMH Conference.* New York: Appleton-Century-Crofts, 1970.

The ecology of mental retardation. *The challenge of mental retardation in the community.* The proceedings of the 1st Annual Spring Conference of the Institute for the Study of Mental Retardation. University of Michigan, Ann Arbor, Michigan, May, 1970, 55.

The School as a selecting-labeling system. *Journal of School Psychology,* 1967, 5(4), 270-279, (with Robins and Meyers).

Social system perspective and clinical perspective: Frames of reference for understanding career patterns of persons labeled as mentally retarded. *Social Problems,* 1965, 13(1), 18-34. Reprinted in Martin S. Weinberg (ed.), *Deviance: The Interactionist Perspective.* New York: MacMillan, Inc., 1967.

Key conceptualizations in the sociology of mental retardation. *Human growth and diversity.* California Association of School Psychologists and Psychometrists, 1965, 68-82.

CHAPTER 18 COGNITIVE STYLES AND CULTURAL DEMOCRACY IN EDUCATION[1]

MANUEL RAMIREZ III

The emphasis on acculturation in the melting pot ideology,[2] which has been adopted by most educational institutions, has contributed to the continuance of the assumption that values and life styles which differ from those of the middle class United States are inferior and must be abandoned. Cubberly, a renowned American educator, supported this belief. Referring to people of minority groups who had settled in urban centers of the East Coast, he stated,

. . . everywhere these people settle in groups or settlements, and . . . set up their national manners, customs, and observances. Our task is to break up these groups or settlements, to assimilate and amalgamate these people as a part of our American race, and to implant in their chil-

dren, as far as can be done, the Anglo-Saxon conception of righteousness, law and order, and our popular government, and to awaken in them a reverence for our democratic institutions and for those things in our national life which we as a people hold to be of abiding worth.[3]

This attitude has led to the use of the family-is-damaging model[4] in the development of educational programs for people of minority groups in this country. In fact, in the case of some ethnic groups, it would be more accurate to say that a *culture*-is-damaging model has been applied. That is, the cultures of some ethnic groups (particularly blacks, Indians, and peoples of La Raza) have been viewed by educational institutions as interfering with the intellectual and emotional development of children and hindering the development of life styles and values typical of mainstream U.S. culture.

Chicano culture has long been viewed as inferior by educational institutions. The belief that Spanish interferes with the Chicano child's ability to learn English and that loyalty to his family and ethnic group competes with his loyalty to the "American way of life" is reflected in programs being

From Social Science Quarterly, 1973; **53**(4):895-904.

[1]This is a revision of a paper presented at the annual meeting of the American Psychological Association, Washington, D.C., September, 1971. The author is indebted to Barbara Goffigon for her help in preparing this paper. For a more extensive discussion of this topic see Manuel Ramirez and Alfredo Castaneda, *Cultural Democracy in Education and Mexican American Children,* to be published by Seminar Press.

[2]Alfredo Castaneda, "Melting Potters vs. Cultural Pluralists: Implications for Education" in Alfredo Castañeda, *et al., Mexican-Americans and Educational Change* (Riverside, Calif.: Mexican-American Studies, U.C.R., 1971).

[3]Elwood P. Cubberly, *Changing Conceptions of Education* (Boston: Houghton Mifflin Co., 1909), pp. 15-16.

[4]Robert D. Hess, "Parental Behavior and Children's School Achievement: Implications for Head Start," *Critical Issues in Research Related to Disadvantaged Children* (Princeton, N.J.: Educational Testing Service, 1969).

implemented across the country, many of which are labeled "compensatory." Many Mexican American children have been assigned to classes for the mentally retarded merely because they do not speak or understand English and/or because they are unfamiliar with information familiar to children of middle class U.S. culture.[5]

REJECTION OF LEARNING STYLES

Institutional practices based on the assimilationist melting pot philosophy disregard the individual's experiences in his home and in his barrio. The person concerned must either conform to the demands of these institutions or leave them. Rejection of an individual's culture is accompanied by rejection of his established learning, incentive-motivational, human relational and communication styles. Thus, he is being asked to abandon these styles and to adopt new ones. Instead of reinforcing and utilizing the culturally unique learning and communication styles of members of minority groups, educational institutions have chosen to ignore them and have attempted to impose styles of their own choosing.

CULTURALLY DETERMINED LEARNING STYLES

Culturally unique learning styles represent a critical variable in the education of the culturally different. Lesser and his colleagues have shown that members of different ethnic groups exhibit different patterns of intellectual ability, each group performing better in some areas than in others.[6] The results showed that the intellectual patterns varied for each of four ethnic groups and that the patterns were similar for different socioeconomic groups within the same culture. These findings imply that intellectual patterns observed in these cultural groups, *are manifestations of culturally unique learning styles.* That is, each culture emphasizes the importance of achievement in certain areas. Parents and other agents of socialization employ culturally sanctioned teaching styles to develop certain interests and aptitudes in children.

Kagan and Madsen have compared the performance of Anglo, Mexican, and Mexican American children in cooperative and competitive situations.[7] When rewards could only be earned if the children participating in a task cooperated with each other, Mexican children were the most cooperative, Mexican American children next most cooperative, and Anglo children the least cooperative. When, in turn, the children were given a competitive set on the same task, Anglo children were more competitive than either Mexican or Mexican American children. The School Situations Picture Stories Technique (a variation of the TAT) was administered by Ramirez, Price-Williams, and Beman[8] to Mexican American and Anglo American fourth grade children of the same socioeconomic status. When the stories were analyzed for need achievement as defined by McClelland and his colleagues[9] Anglo children scored slightly higher than Mexican Americans. When stories were analyzed for need achievement for the family (e.g., the child achieves so that members of his family benefit from his achievement and/or are proud of him) Mexican American children scored significantly higher than Anglo children. These findings again document cultural differences in children's performance.

---

[5]J. T. Chandler and J. Plakos, "Spanish-Speaking Pupils Classified as Educable Mentally Retarded," (California State Department of Education, 1969).

[6]G. S. Lesser, G. Fifer, and D. H. Clark, "Mental Abilities of Children from Different Social-Class and Cultural Groups," *Monographs of the Society for Research in Child Development,* 102 (1965).

[7]Spencer Kagan and M. C. Madsen, "Cooperation and Competition of Mexican, Mexican-American, and Anglo-American Children of Two Ages Under Four Instructional Sets," *Developmental Psychology,* 5 (July, 1971), pp. 32-39.

[8]Manuel Ramirez, Douglass Price-Williams and Alma Beman, "The Relationship of Culture to Educational Attainment," (Houston: Center for Research in Social Change and Economic Development, Rice University, research in progress).

[9]D. C. McClelland, J. W. Atkinson, R. A. Clark, and E. L. Lowell, *The Achievement Motive* (New York: Appleton, 1953).

CULTURAL DEMOCRACY

Differences in learning styles between members of different ethnic groups are the result of socialization practices reflecting the values of these groups. Institutions which have followed the melting pot philosophy have favored that set of styles characteristic of the United States middle class. Hence, many people in this country have been denied academic, economic, and social success. Educational programs which are not based on the unique learning styles of the people they serve do not provide culturally relevant learning environments and are culturally undemocratic. They reject the cultural background of their students and create conflicts by forcing these students to question the values and learning experiences which they have acquired in their homes and neighborhoods. The results of these practices are reflected in school drop-out rates and in the low levels of educational attainment of members of minority groups. Schools are too often institutions of acculturation rather than of education. If we are to eliminate these undemocratic practices and ensure that educational institutions respect cultural differences evident in our society, we must encourage the adoption of a new philosophy, that of cultural democracy. The right of each individual to be educated in his own learning style must be explicitly acknowledged.

This implies that the individual has a right to maintain a bicultural identity, that is, to retain his identification with his ethnic group while he simultaneously adopts mainstream United States values and life styles. This philosophy encourages institutions to develop learning milieus, curriculum materials, and teaching strategies which are sensitive to the uniqueness each individual brings to the classroom. Because cultural democracy focuses on the importance of the teacher-learner relationship, it implies increased humanism in the educational processes.

COGNITIVE STYLES AND CULTURAL DEMOCRACY

Since cognitive styles subsume variables related to learning styles, they can be used to assess both the individual and the institution, permitting determination of the ex-

tent to which the institution reflects the styles of the students it serves.

Witkin and his colleagues have identified two cognitive styles—field-dependence and field-independence:

In a field-dependent mode of perception, the organization of the field as a whole dominates perception of its parts: an item within a field is experienced as fused with organized ground. In a field-independent mode of perception, the person is able to perceive items as discreet from the organized field of which they are a part.[10]

We have selected field dependence/independence as the conceptual framework for our analysis of the relationship of Mexican Americans to educational institutions because it has been studied widely in a cross-cultural context, and because it clearly relates cognitive styles to unique cultural socialization practices.

Although Witkin's conceptual scheme is very useful in implementing cultural democracy in the school, there are some problems connected with it. Too much emphasis has been placed on the presumed advantages of field independence and the disadvantages of field dependence. Field independent socialization styles have been generally described in more favorable value-laden terms than field dependent child rearing practices.[11] It is only a short step from such descriptions to the conclusion that some cultures are pathological because they interfere with the development of field independent characteristics in children. In fact, Witkin's theory of differentiation could easily lead to the aforementioned conclusion. The theory states that all people are field dependent or undifferentiated at birth. As they develop they become more field independent or differentiated. Relationships between parents and children which lead to field dependence in children are classified as interactions which interfere with the development of differentiation. The concept of differentiation, then, assumes that field dependence

[10]H. Witkin, "A Cognitive Approach to Cross-Cultural Research," *International Journal of Psychology,* 2 (No. 4, 1967), p. 236.
[11]Herman A. Witkin, R. B. Dyke, H. F. Faterson, D. R. Goodenough, and S. A. Karp, *Psychological Differentiation* (New York: John Wiley & Sons, 1962).

is a more "rudimentary" stage of development. Such a presumption excludes the possibility that a field dependent cognitive style may develop independently of a field independent style. In fact, cross-cultural research has shown that members of some cultures tend to be field dependent while people in other cultures tend to be field independent.[12] This would seem to indicate that cultures, through socialization practices, tend to encourage the development of either relatively more field dependent or field independent cognitive styles in children. The fact that most research shows that children in most cultures tend to do better on the Rod and Frame and Embedded Figures Tests as they grow older does not exclude the fact that they may also be becoming more field dependent. There simply is no way to measure development of field dependence at present. That is, the Rod and Frame and Embedded Figures Tests may be adequate measures of field independence but not of field dependence.

The hypothesis that field independence and field dependence are two separate cognitive styles is supported by Cohen, who identifies two conceptual styles—analytic and relational—which are similar to field dependence and field independence:

. . . the analytic cognitive style is characterized by a formal or analytic mode of abstracting salient information from a stimulus or situation and by a stimulus-centered orientation to reality, and it is parts-specific (i.e. parts of attributes of a given stimulus have meaning in themselves). The relational cognitive style, on the other hand, requires a descriptive mode of abstraction and is self centered in its orientation to reality; only the global characteristics of a stimulus have meaning to its users, and these only in reference to some total context.[13]

The fact that field dependent and independent cognitive styles may be two separate cognitive styles should not be taken to indicate that a person cannot be both field dependent and field independent. In fact, our observations have led us to conclude that many adults and some children are indeed bicognitive and are able to function in the situationally appropriate style.

There is another caution which should be mentioned with respect to Witkin's conceptual framework, the use of the word dependence. It is far too easy to make the assumption that what is meant by field dependence is dependent personality. In addition, the word dependent is value-laden. For these reasons we have decided to substitute the word "sensitive" for dependent. (From this point on field sensitive will be used instead of field dependent.) As can be seen from the research reviewed below the word sensitivity better describes the behavior of people with this cognitive style. It is their greater sensitivity to the social and physical environment which distinguishes them from field independent individuals on many tasks.

PREFERRED MODES OF THINKING, PERCEIVING, REMEMBERING, AND PROBLEM SOLVING

Early work by Goodenough and Karp,[14] and Witkin,[15] uncovered an interesting pattern of correlations between measures of cognitive style and different subtests of the Wechsler intelligence scales. The subtests of the Wechsler scales cluster into three major factors: a *verbal* dimension, an *attention-concentration* dimension, and an *analytic* dimension. The only cluster of subtests found to correlate to a significant degree with measures of field sensitivity-independence was that of the analytic dimension. Thus, individuals scoring toward the field independence end of the dimension tended to score higher on such subtests as Block Design, Object Assembly, and Picture Completion. No difference was found between field sensitive and field independent individuals on the other two sub-sets of test items. The frequent finding that field independent individuals tend to score higher on measures of intelligence than field sensitive individuals may be in-

---

[12]Witkin, "A Cognitive Approach," pp. 233-250.

[13]Rosalie Cohen, "Conceptual Styles, Culture Conflict, and Non-Verbal Tests of Intelligence," *American Anthropologist,* 71 (Oct., 1969), pp. 828-856.

[14]D. R. Goodenough and S. A. Karp, "Field Dependence and Intellectual Functioning," *Journal of Abnormal and Social Psychology,* 63 (March, 1961), pp. 241-246.

[15]Witkin, *et al., Psychological Differentiation.*

terpreted to indicate an advantage held by field independent subjects in responding to items of the analytic dimension.

Research has also shown that when the test materials are characterized by an abstract or impersonal nature, field independent individuals appear to have an advantage. However, a markedly different pattern becomes evident when the test materials focus on social or human factors. Field sensitive individuals have been found to give longer and more complex stories to picture cards designed to assess verbal expressiveness.[16] Field sensitive individuals appear to remember faces and social words more often than field independent individuals, though their incidental memory for non-social stimuli is not generally superior.[17]

It appears, then, that in some form or another, field sensitive individuals are more influenced by, or more sensitive to the human element in the environment. Field independent individuals have an advantage in testing situations which de-emphasize the human element, situations in which the testing material is relatively more impersonal. They are more able to isolate parts from a whole, and are less constrained by conventional uses of objects and materials.

Characteristics which differentiate field sensitive from field independent individuals then, are those which reflect preferred modes of relating to, classifying, assimilating, and organizing the environment. These descriptions do not represent "cultural disadvantage" or "deficiency."

FIELD SENSITIVITY-INDEPENDENCE AND INCENTIVE MOTIVATIONAL STYLES

The term, incentive-motivational style, may be defined as a preference for a set of goals and rewards (incentives). These incentives are represented by changes in the environment which indicate, symbol-

ize, or have become associated with support, acceptance, and positive recognition of behavior. Preferred incentives refer to those sets of environmental events which effectively influence behavior. Of concern here is how effectively different environmental events influence, modify, or reinforce behavior.

Examination of the research into differences in incentive-motivational styles again reveals that field sensitive persons are more influenced by the human element in the environment than are field independent persons.

Disapproval and approval (praise) exhibited by an authority figure appears to be more effective with field sensitive children than with field independent children. For example, it has been found that the performance of field sensitive children is depressed when an authority figure indicates disapproval by remarking, for example, "This doesn't seem like the kind of group that can do well; you're not as fast as the other groups." Conversely, field sensitive children are motivated more effectively under conditions in which the authority figure indicates approval through praise: "This is a very bright group; you certainly have caught on faster than most children."[18] The tendency for field sensitive children to seek approval from the authority figure is consistent with the observation that when stress was introduced into a testing situation, field sensitive children tended to orient, or look up to the face of the adult examiner about twice as often as field independent children.

One of the differences between the incentive-motivational styles of field sensitive and field independent individuals is related to the *interpersonal* dimension. For example, field sensitive individuals are more likely to be motivated by those forms of reward which offer personalized support and recognition or acceptance.

FIELD SENSITIVITY-INDEPENDENCE AND INTERPERSONAL PERCEPTIONS

The concept of field sensitivity/independence provides some interesting and sug-

[16]*Ibid.*
[17]Samuel Messick and F. Damarin, "Cognitive Styles and Memory for Faces," *Journal of Abnormal Psychology,* 69 (March, 1964), pp. 313-318; and D. Fitzgibbons, L. Goldberger and M. Eagle, "Field Dependence and Memory for Incidental Material," *Perceptual and Motor Skills,* 21 (Dec., 1965), pp. 743-749.

[18]Norma Konstadt and Elaine Forman, "Field Dependence and External Directedness," *Journal of Personality and Social Psychology,* 1 (1965), pp. 490-493.

gestive insights into the dynamics of interpersonal perceptions between student and teacher. In a recent study by Di Stefano,[19] five extremely field independent teachers and five extremely field sensitive teachers were asked to describe 11 students by means of 21 bi-polar semantic differential scales[20] and 25 single adjective scales selected from the Peabody. The students who were described were also classfied as field sensitive or field independent, and were asked to describe the teachers in the same manner. Di Stefano's main conclusion was that "people with similar perceptual styles tend to describe each other in highly positive terms, while people whose perceptual styles are different have a strong tendency to describe each other in negative terms."[21] Three other findings are of special interest: (1) teachers tended to rate students of their own perceptual style as more successful than those of the opposite style; (2) field sensitive teachers tended to be slightly more lenient in their grading than field independent teachers, and field independent teachers were more critical in grading field sensitive students; and (3) field independent teachers tended to concentrate on the areas of science and mathematics.[22]

These results demonstrate the possible existence of a somewhat unusual form of professional discrimination. If teachers view students with perceptual styles similar to their own as being more successful, or potentially more successful, they are likely to offer these students more encouragement and possibly higher grades.

ASSESSING THE COGNITIVE STYLE OF MEXICAN AMERICANS

The initial discussion of field sensitivity-independence mentioned its relationship to socialization practices of cultures. Witkin and his colleagues[23] have identified socialization practices related to the development of field sensitivity in children. They have labelled these the field sensitive socialization cluster.

When the socialization practices of Chicanos from traditional[24] communities are compared with those of the field sensitive socialization cluster, many similarities are found. This is especially true in the area of indicators concerning separation of the child from the mother and family. The Chicano child is encouraged to be responsible and independent, aggressive and assertive, as long as he is achieving for the family and/or protecting it. While the middle class Anglo is typically encouraged to establish an identity independent of the family, the Chicano from a traditional community is encouraged to always view himself as an integral part of the family. He is reared in an atmosphere which emphasizes the importance of interpersonal relationships. Consequently, he develops great sensitivity to social cues, and to the human environment in general. This would lead us to predict that Chicanos reared in traditional communities are likely to be field sensitive.

The results of two studies (one in Houston, Texas, and another in Riverside, California) confirm this prediction. In the Houston study, 120 fourth graders, 60 Mexican Americans, and 60 Anglo children of the same social economic class and religion (Catholic) were tested with the Portable Rod and Frame Test. The results shown in Table 1 indicate that, as predicted Mexican American children scored in a more field sensitive direction. In the Riverside desegregation study[25] 596 Mexican American and 571 Anglo children from grades kindergarten through six were tested with the Man in the Box, an instrument similar

[19]Joseph J. Di Stefano, "Interpersonal Perceptions of Field Independent and Dependent Teachers and Students," Working Paper Series No. 43 (London, Ontario: University of Western Ontario, Nov., 1970).

[20]C. E. Osgood, G. J. Suci and D. H. Tannenbaum, *The Measurement of Meaning* (Urbana: University of Illinois Press, 1957).

[21]Di Stefano, "Interpersonal Perceptions of Field Independent and Dependent Teachers and Students."

[22]*Ibid.*

[23]Witkin, *et al., Psychological Differentiation.*

[24]For example, Mexican American culture has been described as traditional, dualistic, and atraditional, the first of these being that which most closely identifies with Mexican culture and values, the last, that which has most adopted middle class American values.

[25]D. Canavan, "Field Dependence in Children as a Function of Grade, Sex, and Ethnic Group Membership," paper presented at the American Psychological Association meeting, 1969, Washington, D.C.

Table 1. Mean portable rod and frame test scores of Mexican American and Anglo American fourth grade students

| | Mexican Americans (N = 60) | | Anglos (N = 60) | | | |
	$\overline{X}$	SD	$\overline{X}$	SD	t	p
Males	14.56	7.80	6.97	7.07	4.06	< .001
Females	17.26	6.80	9.51	8.71	3.84	< .001

Table 2. Mean portable rod and frame test scores of teachers and Mexican American students

| | | Mexican American students | | | | | |
| Teachers | | Grade 1 | | Grade 4 | | Grade 6 | |
M	F	M	F	M	F	M	F
1.83	2.71	18.26	20.21	14.70	16.89	9.43	14.52

to the Portable Rod and Frame. The results, again, supported the hypothesis that Chicano children are more field sensitive than Anglo children.

THE FIELD SENSITIVE MEXICAN AMERICAN AND THE FIELD INDEPENDENT INSTITUTION

I am hypothesizing that the primary reason for failure of educational institutions to fulfill the needs of the majority of Mexican Americans, and others in this country, is that they are not sensitive to the cognitive styles of these people. That is, these institutions are oriented toward serving the person who is relatively more field independent.

Fifty-three teachers and 711 students of several elementary schools in the Los Angeles metropolitan area which have high concentrations of Mexican American students were tested with the Portable Rod and Frame Test. The results presented in Table 2 show that teachers and Mexican American students differ greatly in cognitive style. The teachers are far more field independent.

Cohen has also found that the curriculum, assessment instruments and learning environments in most schools are biased in the direction of the analytic style, similar

to field independence.[26] When one considers the results of the Di Stefano study, it can be concluded that most schools represent culturally undemocratic learning environments for Mexican American children. That is, it could be predicted that Mexican American students are being viewed as less capable by their teachers and are being given lower grades.

COGNITIVE STYLES AS VEHICLES FOR DEVELOPING CULTURALLY DEMOCRATIC LEARNING ENVIRONMENTS

Cognitive styles may make it possible to implement the philosophy of cultural democracy in education. Preliminary observations we have made on the teaching strategies of a small sample of field sensitive and field independent elementary school teachers indicate that there is considerable difference in their approaches to teaching. Field sensitive teachers, for example, express more warmth in their relationships with students and appear to be more sensitive to personal feelings and interests of students. Field sensitive teachers also use social rewards, tend to humanize

---

[26]Cohen, "Conceptual Styles, Culture Conflict, and Non-Verbal Tests of Intelligence."

and personalize curriculum materials and are more likely to employ structured guidance and the deductive approach in presenting curriculum to students. Field independent teachers, on the other hand, appear to be more formal and aloof in their relationships with students. Field independents also tend to use more formulas and graphs (mathematical and scientific abstractions) in their class presentations, are more likely to encourage students to work independently and to use the inductive approach in presenting curriculum.

We hope that this research will lead us to techniques which we can employ to train teachers to teach in both styles and also to write curricula and develop assessment instruments which reflect both the field sensitive and field independent styles. The development of such educational environments would allow children of any cultural background to acquire the ability to function in either cognitive style and consequently increase their level of achievement.

PART FIVE
MENTAL HEALTH

The area of mental health cannot be separated from all of the topics previously discussed in this volume: the problems of poverty and racial discrimination, family relations and cultural conflicts, educational and employment experiences, and contact with the law. The unavailability of mental health care of adequate quality and quantity to members of the lower socioeconomic strata is one of our nation's gravest failings. Since the publication of Hollingshead and Redlich's (1958) monumental study, on the relationship of social class to mental illness, it has been reaffirmed time and again that the prevalence of serious mental illness is highest among the poor. And it is among the poor that availability and utilization of professional treatment are lowest. If they receive treatment at all, the poor and ethnic minority members are likely to receive predominantly physical forms of therapy—drugs or electroconvulsive (shock) treatment. The values of such treatments are increasingly being questioned, as is the medical model that underlies their use (Cowen and coworkers, 1967), and the urgency of the need for quality mental health care becomes ever more apparent.

Armando Morales' Santa Barbara paper is an excellent starting point for the consideration of mental health issues as they apply to Chicanos. He has brilliantly integrated the historical trends that have shaped modern attitudes toward the Mexican and the poor, and the expression and results of racism in the social sciences, law enforcement, and mental health care. Although our emphasis in this section is on the quality and availability of treatment, it is important to understand the societal pressures and common experiences that contribute to the mental health and the mental illness of Chicanos. We have explored these factors in preceding sections, and Morales' article serves to synthesize the foregoing material with the issues considered here.

Yamamoto and his associates have studied the patient-therapist relationship with regard to the effect of ethnocentrism on the quality of mental health care offered to the

"visible minorities." They found that psychiatrists tend to
dislike and avoid prolonged and close therapeutic contacts
with minority group members. A later study (Yamamoto,
et al., 1967) found that therapists low in ethnocentricity
treated minority patients more often and longer. The belief
is widespread that the poor are incapable of benefiting
from the insight therapy favored by the middle class (see
Padilla). One cannot help suspecting that this belief is a
result of the insecurity such patients evoke in their middle-
class therapists. Add to class differences a linguistic barrier, and the difficulty of the situation for the therapist and
the patient becomes almost insurmountable. Some of these
difficulties of Anglo therapist–Chicano patient interaction
are illustrated in Morales' (1971) article, *Distinguishing
psychodynamic factors from cultural factors in the
treatment of the Spanish-speaking patient.* Even a therapist being aware of cultural differences is no guarantee
that the patient will be able to make himself understood,
for the therapist may fall into the trap of overlooking pathology that fits the ethnic group's stereotype.

Marcos, et al. discuss the effect of interview language
itself on the diagnostic impression the hospitalized Spanish-speaking patient leaves with the doctors. Interestingly, even patients with a larger English than Spanish
vocabulary presented more pathology in English-language

interviews than they did in Spanish, casting doubt on the common practice of conducting sessions in English if at all possible. A cluster of six characteristics out of a total of 18 rated were found to be consistently distorted by interviewing in the patient's second language. Based on this finding, the authors hope to develop a "yardstick to minimize some of the constant errors resulting from the interview language" for use by monolingual English speakers. While this might prove helpful in the diagnosis of bilingual patients, it would be of little value in subsequent treatment sessions. As Edgerton and Karno point out, "Spanish is the language of the family and thus of intimacy. The switch from this language to the more formal and impersonal idiom of English—even should the patient and his relatives be linguistically capable of such a switch—may well defeat any effort by the psychiatrist to enter the affective world of his patient." In view of the importance attached to communication problems in theories about schizophrenia and family disorders and the necessity of establishing and mantaining rapport, it seems strange that so little thought is given to this problem in most clinical settings. The employment of a translator seems to be considered the ultimate concession, yet this too has a distancing, filtering effect on communication.

Karno and Morales and their associates at the East Los

Angeles Mental Health Service have graphically demonstrated what can be done for, and with, Mexican American
patients when professionals care enough to try—to learn
Spanish and to overcome the kinds of organizational problems discussed by Miranda and Kitano that so alienate Chicanos and other "outsiders" to the dominant culture. Many
supposedly untreatable patients were found to be quite responsive to intensive psychotherapy presented in "a context of cultural and linguistic familiarity and acceptance."

This conducive context, as several contributors to this
section indicate, is not so very different *in principle* from
the Anglo beliefs and ideals. As Edgerton and Karno found,
Mexican perceptions of what Anglos define as mental
illness are in near total agreement with the Anglo assessment of these behaviors; and Gonzales stresses that,
although folk beliefs persist, they *coexist* rather than compete with the conventional, modern understanding of mental illness. Even the folk illnesses and treatments are not
that foreign to "modern medicine": they show a good deal
of sophistication in terms of psychosomatic relationships.

Fabrega and Wallace's study perhaps speaks most directly to the issue of cultural acceptance. Their findings
support the anomie theorists' contention that alienation
from society—lack of adherence to any group's norms—is
closely related to mental illness. This factor clearly differentiated the study's outpatient population from the nonpatient comparison group. It is interesting to note that neither set of norms—the Anglo nor the Mexican—was more
highly correlated with mental health *or* illness than the
other. It was the fact of identification with some one group,
rather than any aspect of the values identified with, that
was salient. This lack of commitment would seem to be
a more useful definition of failure to acculturate than is
noncommitment to the dominant (Anglo) values, which is
the criterion most often used in acculturation studies of
Chicanos.

The parallels between this plurality of paths to mental
health and the "cultural democracy" in education advocated by Ramirez are obvious. We should be able to develop
a mental health care delivery system compatible with and
supportive of Mexican American values and identities. Eligio Padilla outlines some of the stumbling blocks to the
communication and implementation of Chicano desires in
regard to mental health services at the present time. In
addition to their small representation within the professions and the insensitivity of the government and the professions to their special needs, Chicanos face along with
everyone else the problem of insufficient workers and
money to meet the mental health needs of the nation.

Under current legislation, Federal funding of community mental health centers is phased out over a period of
a few years under the assumption that they will become
self-sustaining. In poor communities, this is an unrealistic
expectation and perpetuates the existing discrimination
against the poor in the availability of mental health care.

Furthermore, the "medical model" of mental disorders, around which community mental health services are organized, is very "expensive" in terms of worker requirements, so much so that some highly respected observers have suggested that we can never *hope* to fulfill all the nation's needs using it.

The solution Padilla espouses—abandonment of the medical model of psychological disorders and development of treatment techniques that are based on social learning theory and can be applied by workers with less extensive training—has been gaining in popularity. But others, like Cervando Martinez, have cautioned against throwing out the medical model prematurely. There are so many questions about the therapeutic efficacy of the different treatment modalities as applied to Mexican Americans that need empirical answers; the Chicano movement is only now serving to bring these into focus. It is clear that there is need for a variety of approaches including medical and social learning models. Time and a committment to truth will help us to understand those ways that are the most effective.

But even without further research, it is obvious that the inequality of services along racial and economic lines must be faced squarely and immediately, both by professionals and by government; that what manpower now exists should be deployed more equitably; and that active recruitment of indigenous talent at all levels of service must begin in earnest. The shame of discriminatory neglect and distortion must not be allowed to continue.

REFERENCES

Cowen, E. L., Gardner, E. A., & Zax, M. *Emergent approaches to mental health problems.* New York: Appleton-Century-Crofts, 1967.

Hollingshead, A. B., & Redlich, F. C. *Social class and mental illness.* New York: John Wiley & Sons, Inc., 1958.

Morales, A. Distinguishing psychodynamic factors from cultural factors in the treatment of the Spanish-speaking patient. In Wagner, N. N., & Haug, M. J. (Eds.), *Chicanos: Social and psychological perspectives* (1st edition). St. Louis: The C. V. Mosby Co., 1971, pp. 279-280.

Yamamoto, J., James, Q. C., Bloombaum, M., & Hattem, J. Racial factors in patient selection. *American Journal of Psychiatry,* 1967, *124,* 630-636.

CHAPTER 19 THE IMPACT OF CLASS DISCRIMINATION AND WHITE RACISM ON THE MENTAL HEALTH OF MEXICAN-AMERICANS

ARMANDO MORALES

My assignment for this conference was to write a paper focusing on white racism and its impact on the mental health of Mexican-Americans in Southern California. I'm sure that any analysis of these problems will be representative of those situations that Mexican-Americans find themselves in in other areas throughout the Southwest. Some of the social problems found in Mexican-American communities are the following:

1. Deficient educational achievement due to the lack of educational opportunities
2. Excessive unemployment
3. Broken homes
4. Excessive numbers of police in Chicano communities
5. Police-community friction
6. The overrepresentation of Mexican-Americans in jails and prisons for offenses related to drinking and drugs
7. The gross lack of mental health treatment facilities in Chicano communities
8. The general unavailability of psychiatric manpower—particularly bilingual mental health professionals, and
9. Societal resistance toward the funding of community mental health centers directed *by* and *under Mexican-American* community control and sanction.

This paper was presented at the Western Interstate Commission for Higher Education conference on "Mexican-American Mental Health Issues," June 10, 11 and 12, 1970, in Goleta, California.

Why are these conditions found in Mexican-American, Black, Puerto Rican and other poor, ethnic communities? I suggest the answer lies in (1) the brutal discrimination that Americans practice toward the poor; (2) racism; and (3) an institutionalized delivery system of mental health care that emphasizes quality, individualized psychiatric treatment for the affluent, and an almost complete denial of quality mental health care for those that need the services the most—the poor![1] In order to better understand how class discrimination, racism and the paucity of mental health programs currently affect Mexican-Americans, an exploration of the origins of these inhumane attitudes has to be considered.

These attitudes originated in 18th century England largely as the result of the political economy writings of Adam Smith and Thomas Malthus. England was in the midst of the great industrial revolution which found the government catering to the interests of the commercial class. The poor were ruthlessly economically exploited which contributed to increased poverty but these problems were of little concern to the middle class, for they developed a rationale—"laissez-faire"—the doctrine of free enterprise with no government intervention. The implication was that out of unrestricted competition the strong would survive and society would benefit.

Adam Smith in *Wealth of Nations* believed that one of the roles of the state was the defense of the rich against the poor. He regarded public assistance for the poor as an artificial and evil arrangement which consumed money which could have been used for wages. To furnish "unearned subsistence" (welfare) Smith concluded, was to further human misery.[2]

Thomas Malthus in his *Essay on Population* believed that populations would always outrun the food supply. War, pestilence and famine were seen by Malthus as "positive" checks on the growth of populations. He strongly argued that any government welfare assistance to the poor would only help increase their misery.[3] The "don't prolong the misery of the poor—let them die" attitudes advocated by Smith and Malthus easily fed into the philosophy of Social Darwinism championed by Herbert Spencer (1820-1903), an Englishman. Spencer, borrowing Darwin's biological theories regarding lower forms of life, extended them to man and originated the term "survival of the fittest." Spencer opposed all state aid to the poor because they were unfit and should be eliminated! In his words, "The whole effort of nature is to get rid of such, to clear the world of them, and make room for the better. If they are sufficiently complete to live, they do live, and it is well they should live. If they are not sufficiently complete to live, they die, and it is best they should die."[4] Spencer's doctrines had great impact on American thought and were thoroughly absorbed.[5]

In the Social Darwinistic militant phase, society is organized chiefly for survival. It bristles with military weapons, trains its people for warfare, relies upon an autocratic state, submerges the individual, and imposes a vast amount of compulsory cooperation.[6] This is why today we find that over 66% of our annual national budget of 200 billion goes for *military* purposes. Only 34% of the national budget is available for all other government expenditures. This includes health, education, welfare, agriculture, national resources, pollution, post offices, roads and foreign relations.[7] To be more precise, America spends $480.00 per person for war and only $14.00 per person for health!

This is why the richest country history has ever produced maintains thirty-two million people living in poverty. Michael Harrington claims that there are forty to fifty million people living in poverty in the United States.[8] The majority of the poor in America are white although the blacks, American Indians, Mexican-Americans and Puerto Ricans suffer from the most intense and concentrated impoverishment of any single group.[9]

Having the greatest medical, physical and professional resources in the world, America has to painfully accept the fact that twelve countries (including France, communist East Germany, Switzerland and Japan) have lower infant mortality rates than the United States.[10] This is also why sixteen Mexican-Americans starved to death in the barrios of San Antonio in 1965.[11] These are also the inhumane values that account for the lack of mental health services in Chicano communities.

In addition to class discrimination, the various manifestations of white racism[12] may be seen affecting the mental health of Mexican-Americans. From 15th and 16th century chronicles, we learn that the Aztecs, then numbering twenty million, developed a wealthy and powerful empire in central Mexico. Their culture was highly developed and in that atmosphere flourished highly advanced forms of psychiatry and psychotherapy. Dr. Diaz Infante, a Mexican psychoanalyst who worked with the late father Angel Garibay of the National University of Mexico in translating Indian writings, reports that Aztec therapy was given by competent personnel and in institutions of high repute. The Aztecs had an amazing grasp of psychology and translations of their documents show that they developed concepts about ego formation and psychic structure similar to those advanced by Sigmund Freud almost *five hundred years later!* These concepts appear in an Aztec document about dream interpretation.[13]

The Aztec physicians knew how to recognize persons who were manic, schizoid, hysterical, depressive or psychopathic. Such persons were treated by a variety of methods including an early form of brain surgery, hypnosis, and specific herbal potions for specific disorders. With the colonization by Spain in the early 16th century,

Spanish medicine based on European concepts was introduced. Spanish colonial physicians still held primitive ideas about the causes of disease. They believed that it was a punishment for sins caused by devils who had taken possession of the patient's body and spirit.[14] Because military might became associated with racial superiority, it was also concluded that Spanish medical practices were superior to that of the Aztecs. One can only speculate what great impact Aztec psychiatry might have had on the Western world and the United States had it not been for the racism practiced by the Spaniards. In spite of this, however, the first hospital for the mentally ill was founded in Mexico City in 1567. The first hospital for the mentally ill was not founded in the United States until 1732 in Philadelphia—one hundred and sixty-five years later!

Racism was the underlying dynamic of the "Manifest Destiny" called upon by American expansionsists to support the conquest of Mexico in the mid 1800's. It was written that Mexicans "must amalgamate or be lost in the superior vigor of the Anglo-Saxon race, or they must utterly perish."[15] This Anglo-Saxon dogma became the chief element in American racism in the imperial era that politically and economically has exploited the Mexican in the United States right up to the present time.

Stereotypes are created by the dominant group as a means of negatively identifying and keeping the minority group in a subordinate, inferior position.[16] Many criminal stereotypes of Mexican-Americans were developed by Anglo-American society which provided the basis for current institutional racism. William Wilson McEuen, reporting on a survey of Mexicans in Los Angeles in 1914 under the supervision of Emory S. Bogardus, one of the country's outstanding sociologists, stated:

The excessive use of liquor is the Mexican's greatest moral problem. With few exceptions both men and women use liquor to excess. Their general moral conditions are bad when judged by the prevailing standards. It seems just, however, to say that Mexicans are unmoral rather than immoral since they lack a conception of morals as understood in this country. Their housing conditions are bad, crime is prevalent, and their morals are a menace to our civilization. They are illiterate, ignorant and inefficient and have few firm religious beliefs.[17]

They were described as a "child race" without the "generations of civilization and culture back of them which support the people of the United States."[18] Another commonly held stereotype of Mexicans in Los Angeles was that they were carriers of knives. With the dominant groups clinging to these attitudes and stereotypes toward a minority group, the informal policy is in subtle ways communicated to law enforcement as to what they might expect or "look for" in their contacts with that minority group. This leads to what Robert K. Merton called a "self fulfilling prophesy." It is not surprising to find, therefore, that although Mexicans comprised 5% of the population, Los Angeles Police Department records in 1913 revealed that 24.3% of all drunk arrests were Mexicans and that 75.5% of all "carrying concealed weapons" arrests were also Mexicans.[19] Nearly 30% of all arrests and convictions for "suspicion" resulting in ninety to one hundred and fifty days in jail sentences were Mexicans—by far more than any other ethnic group per ratio of population.[20] Since Mexicans were viewed at that time as a "child race" by the dominant group and police, it is clear to see why they were more frequently under *suspicion* like children, hence arrested.

Today we find that drunk and drunk driving arrests account for a little over 50% of all offenses in the Mexican-American East Los Angeles community—a significantly higher ratio than in other communities. For example, the East Los Angeles area with 259,275 population accounts for 9,676 drunk and drunk driving arrests per year compared to the 95% white, non-Spanish surname West Valley area with a population of 260,832, where there are only 1,552 drunk and drunk driving arrests per year. One might conclude that the larger number of arrests in the Mexican-American community might be due to a greater incidence of alcoholism in the community. This is not the answer as the Division of Alcoholic Rehabilitation of the California Department of Public Health reports identical ratios of alcoholism to population—8,143 alcoholics per 100,000 population.[21] The answer lies in the large numbers of police that are assigned to the Mexican-American community—375 officers averaging 13.5 officers per square mile as compared to 151 officers averaging 3.5 officers per square mile in the white, non-Spanish surname community. The major crime ratios are practically identical, 1.4%.

With the exception of three or four Alcoholics Anonymous groups in East Los Angeles, and a modest public health satellite service, there are no detoxification or professional services available for Mexican-Americans with drinking problems. Apparently the only treatment facility continues to be the Los Angeles County Jail where people of Spanish surname comprise 25% of the jail population for offenses mostly related to drinking. Not only is the father's mental health affected by being punished in jail for his medical symptom, but there is now evidence to show that committing a father to jail is soon accompanied by a depression in the school performance of his *children.*[22]

Another Mexican-American criminal stereotype that has existed for well over fifty years is related to narcotics. In 1930, when the population of California was 5,677,251, persons of Spanish surname numbered 262,801 or 4.6% of the population. However, persons of Spanish surname were greatly *overrepresented* in prison population, 9.3% to 14.5%, from 1918 to 1930—the average percentage being 12.4% during this period.[23] A comparison of the Spanish surname population with the total as to the nature of their crimes revealed that they were more frequently arrested for violations of the "State Poison Act," which related to narcotics (mostly marijuana).

The California State Narcotic Committee in 1931 concluded that marijuana had a *widespread use* throughout Southern California among the Mexican population.[24] The committee arrived at this inaccurate conclusion based upon a very small number of cases and generalized to the larger Mexican population. Statistical evidence reveals that during the five month period from January 1, 1930, to May 31, 1930, there were 152 arrests for narcotics

offenses (56% marijuana, 26% morphine, 14% opium and 2% heroin) in Los Angeles —site of the largest Mexican population in the United States. Of those arrested, *63* were Mexican—certainly not representing "widespread use among the Mexican population." This is how racial stereotypes are generated that eventually become institutionalized.

Celia Heller's book *Mexican-American Youth,* published in 1966 and in 1969 in its fifth printing, contributes to the perpetuation of this historical stereotype. On the basis of an insignificant number of cases, 221 out of a Los Angeles 24 years and under youth Spanish-surname population of 424,000, she believes that narcotics play a *significant part* in the lives of Mexican-Americans.[25] While Mexican-Americans are underrepresented in California state hospitals (3.3%), they are *vastly overrepresented* in prison. Of 40,000 adult parolees and prisoners in California, 20% or 8,000 are Mexican-American, primarily for offenses related to narcotics. At the California Rehabilitation Center, a state prison facility for narcotic users which has 2,700 prisoners, *44%* or 1,188 of the inmates are Mexican-Americans.[26] Does this suggest that Mexican-Americans utilize narcotics more than other groups? Facts lead one to a different conclusion. It has been known for several years that physicians and nurses comprise the *largest single group* of narcotic addicts in the country but the record shows this group to be grossly underrepresented in the arrest and conviction columns.[27] This is just another dramatic example of class discrimination and institutional racism.

I do not want to leave the impression that one *only* finds problems related to drinking and narcotics in the Mexican-American community, but these issues were highlighted to demonstrate how California had developed institutionalized approaches for "handling" Mexican-Americans based on historical, racial stereotypes.

Schizophrenia, for example, is a world mental health problem which reportedly affects one out of ten persons. This figure is generally accepted in the United States. The Los Angeles County Mental Health Department reveals that 13% to 17% of its out-patients in ten regional services carry the diagnostic label of psychosis—mostly schizophrenia. The County East Los Angeles Mental Health Service located in a Mexican-American community, easily reports a percentage figure *twice* this number.

Undoubtedly there are many treatment approaches to schizophrenia although Finland and Belgium report very progressive approaches. Finland emphasizes a skilled family psychotherapy approach with light emphasis on medication[28] while Belgium is famous for its Geel community approach where there exists sensitive community understanding and therapeutic support of psychotic and retarded patients.[29] European countries deploy their psychiatrists in treating the more difficult, chronic psychotic cases and leave the treatment of neurotics to para-professionals and mental health aides. In the United States we do the opposite—we assign the difficult, chronic psychotic patients to paraprofessionals and aides, and the neurotic patients are by and large seen by psychiatrists and psychologists in private practice.

A strong reliance on medication for the management of psychotic patients in poor communities eventually becomes an *antitherapeutic measure* as the patient is never able to realize his fullest psychotherapeutic and social potential. Paraprofessionals and community aides will eventually become discouraged with these patients. Intensive, comprehensive therapeutic approaches based on *skilled, quality service* must be instituted in Mexican-American communities. Quality health care should not be an economic privilege— it is a basic human right! The mental health problems that Mexican-Americans are currently experiencing in society are very much related to impoverished, socioeconomic conditions found in Chicano communities. They are the casualties of what Dr. Ernesto Galarza has called "institutional deviancy."[30] The role of mental health workers should not be only to provide treatment to people in need—not merely to help them "adjust" to society's deviant systems. Rather, the task is to change those conditions that are the underlying causes of the problems. This, therefore, calls for *social action* by mental

health workers, the recipients of the services, and the Chicano community. This approach, however, poses a dilemma and a very serious question to consider. Will the establishment, public and private resources, fund a comprehensive mental health agency that provides treatment *and* attacks the underlying causes of the problems?

REFERENCES

1. August B. Hollingshead and Fredrick C. Redlich. Social Class and Mental Illness (New York: John Wiley & Sons, Inc., 1958), pp. 216-217. Hollingshead and Redlich concluded in their study that (1) a definite association existed between class position and being a psychiatric patient, and (2) the lower the class, the greater the proportion of patients in the population.
2. Blanch D. Coll. Perspectives in Public Welfare (Washington, D.C.: U.S. Department of Health, Education, and Welfare, 1969), p. 9.
3. T. Walter Wallbank and Alastair M. Taylor. Civilization: Past and Present (New York: Scott, Foresman & Co., 1955), p. 168.
4. Richard Hofstadter. Social Darwinism in American Thought (Boston: Beacon Press, 1944), p. 41.
5. Ibid., p. 50.
6. Ibid., p. 42.
7. "The Crisis is Mounting," National Association of Social Workers Special Report, Los Angeles Area Chapter, 1970.
8. Michael Harrington. The Other America (New York: The Macmillan Co., 1963), p. 185.
9. Ibid.
10. Frank Falkner. "Infant Mortality: an Urgent National Problem." Children **17**:83, May-June, 1970.
11. Stan Steiner. La Raza: The Mexican-Americans (New York: Harper & Row, Publishers, 1969), p. 152.
12. There is no one basic definition of racism but for the purposes of this paper, Webster's definition of racism will be adopted. Webster defines racism as the assumption that psychocultural traits and capacities are determined by biological race and that races differ decisively from one another which is usually coupled with a belief in the inherent superiority of a particular race and its right to domination over others.
13. Guido Belsasso. The History of Psychiatry in Mexico, Hospital and Community Psychiatry **20**:342, Nov., 1969.
14. Ibid.

15. Richard Hofstadter. op. cit., pp. 171-172.
16. Arnold Rose. The Roots of Prejudice (Paris: UNESCO, 1951), p. 11.
17. William Wilson McEuen. "A Survey of the Mexican in Los Angeles," unpublished Master's Thesis, University of Southern California, 1914, p. 100.
18. Ibid., p. 102.
19. Ibid., p. 80.
20. Ibid.
21. "California State Plan for Community Mental Health Centers," State of California, Department of Public Health, Bureau of Health Facilities Planning and Construction, June, 1968, p. 301.
22. Sidney Friedman and T. Conway Esselstyn. "The Adjustment of Children of Jail Inmates." Federal Probation **XXIX**:59, Dec., 1965.
23. National Commission on Law Observance and Enforcement. Report on Crime and the Foreign Born, United States Government, 1931, p. 202.
24. Ibid., p. 205.
25. Celia S. Heller. Mexican-American Youth: Forgotten Youth at the Crossroads. (New York: Random House, 1966), p. 74.
26. As reported to the writer by CRC Board Member Martin Ortiz at a "Correctional Reforms" conference held in East Los Angeles on June 28, 1969.
27. M. Nyswander. Narcotic Addiction, American Handbook of Psychiatry (New York: Basic Books, Inc., 1959), p. 616.
28. Yrjo O. Alanen, Aira Laine, Viljo Rakkolainen and Simo Salonen, "Evolving the Psychotherapeutic Community: Research Combined with Hospital Treatment of Schizophrenia," paper presented at the conference "Schizophrenia—the Implications of Research Findings for Treatment and Teaching," sponsored by the National Institute of Mental Health, Washington, D.C., May 30 to June 2, 1970.
29. Jan Frans Schrijvers. "The Significance of the Geel Family Care Plan for The Study and Treatment of Schizophrenia." Paper presented at the conference on "Schizophrenia" in Washington, D.C., on May 30 to June 2, 1970.
30. Ernesto Galarza. "Institutional Deviancy: The Mexican-American experience," public address delivered at the Western Interstate Commission for Higher Education conference on "Mexican-American Mental Health Issues," June 10, 11 & 12, 1970, Goleta, California.

CHAPTER 20 CULTURAL PROBLEMS IN PSYCHIATRIC THERAPY

JOE YAMAMOTO
QUINTON C. JAMES
NORMAN PALLEY

What happens to a patient of a "visible minority group" when he seeks psychiatric treatment? At the Los Angeles County General Hospital Psychiatric Outpatient Clinic we found out what happened to such a minority group patient after he applied for treatment and was seen initially by a therapist.

We were especially interested whether these minority group patients were offered therapy and if so, what type. By "visible minority group" we mean Negroes, Mexican-Americans, and Orientals and not one of the ethnic Caucasian groups, i.e., minority groups, who are easily distinguishable from the majority Caucasian group. In our clinic, a patient can get individual therapy, group therapy, or drug therapy. Some patients are seen once and are discharged as being unsuitable for therapy or not needing psychiatric treatment. Our interest in this problem stems

From Arch. Gen. Psychiat. **19**:45-49, 1968. Reprinted by permission.

This is a revised version of a paper read before the Seventh Western Divisional Meeting of the American Psychiatric Association, Hawaii, August 1965.

This research was supported in part by project grant MH-00954 from the National Institute of Mental Health, Public Health Service.

George Moed and Neil Fond provided technical assistance.

The use of the computer was provided by the Health Sciences Computing Facility, University of California at Los Angeles.

from the fact that our Outpatient Clinic population includes a large number of Negroes, Mexican-Americans, and a few Orientals and we knew of no studies which dealt with this particular problem.

In our review of the literature we found a study by Rosenthal and Frank[1] which reported that in their clinic, Negro patients were less often selected for individual therapy and those who were seen were seen fewer times than their Caucasian counterparts. There is also a substantial body of literature on the general problems of lower-class patients and the problems of meeting their expectations when they apply for treatment.[2-10] However, none of these discussed the racial groups among the lower-class patients. These contributions which discuss the treatment of minority groups do so within the context of patients who have been engaged in the treatment process.[11]

In contrast, our paper discusses the experience of a large group of Negro and Mexican-American patients as they were seen initially in the clinic, selected for treatment or discharged, and with a follow-up for up to one year after the initial interview. In the summer of 1964, 594 patients were seen.

Of these consecutive new patients, 387 (65%) were Caucasian, 149 (25%) were Negro, 53 (9%) were Mexican-American, and 5 (1%) were Oriental. These categories were selected by the patients from an in-

Table 1. Race and sex

	Women		Men		Total	
	Percent	*No.*	*Percent*	*No.*	*Percent*	*No.*
Caucasian	40.4	230	24.7	157	65.1	387
Negro	17.5	104	7.6	45	25.1	149
Mexican-American	5.7	34	3.2	19	8.9	53
Oriental	0.5	3	0.4	2	0.9	5

formation form and we have reason to believe from smaller samples (almost 15% of the samples had Spanish surnames) that some of the Mexican-American groups listed themselves as Caucasians. Thus the above percentage of Mexican-American is probably less than actual.

Table 1 shows the sex distribution of the patients in our study. There were more women than men in each of the ethnic groups with a proportion of almost 2:1. The specific ratio of women and men varied with race, with 59% women in the Caucasian group, 60% in the Oriental, 64% in the Mexican-American, and 70% in the Negro.

In order to understand the results we asked that each patient and therapist fill out a questionnaire about the interview or treatment. We hoped this could give us clues as to the reasons why a patient was not taken into therapy. It would also give us some information about the therapist and his feelings toward the patient and vice versa. The data from the questionnaire was tabulated along with demographic data such as sex, income, education, and the therapeutic course of the patient.

We asked the therapist to fill out the following questionnaire after the patient was discharged from the clinic.

Post treatment rating scale
1. I think these visits by the patient have made him feel
   much worse   somewhat worse   no change
   somewhat better   very much better
2. How did you feel toward the patient?
   disliked him very much   disliked him
   average   liked him   liked him very much
3. What is your opinion concerning the patient's prognosis to improve in treatment if he would be seen as often as twice a week for a year?
   very poor   poor   average   good
   excellent

4. Do you think the patient could benefit from additional visits?
   _____ yes   _____ no
   If yes, underline how many
   1 or 2   3-10
   11-25   over 25
5. Do you think the patient got what he wanted from treatment?
   _____ yes   _____ no

When we received notification of the discharge we contacted the patient either personally, by phone, or by mail and asked that they fill out the following patient's questionnaire.

Survey of patients' attitudes
1. I think these visits to the clinic have made me feel
   much worse   somewhat worse   no change
   somewhat better   much better
2. How did you feel toward the therapist?
   liked him very much   liked   average
   disliked   disliked him very much
3. What did you think of the therapist's ability?
   very poor   poor   average   good
   excellent
4. Do you think you could benefit from additional visits?
   _____ yes   _____ no
   If yes, underline how many
   1 or 2   3-10
   11-25   over 25
5. Did you get what you wanted from treatment?
   _____ yes   _____ no
   Comments _____
   _____
6. Did your family or friends influence you as to whether you should continue or leave treatment?
   _____ yes   _____ no
   Continue _____ yes Leave _____ yes
                _____ no   _____ no
   Comments _____
   _____
7. Did you feel the therapist was prejudiced?
   _____ yes   _____ no

Table 2. Type of treatment and race

	Caucasian		Negro		Mexican-American		Oriental	
	Women	Men	Women	Men	Women	Men	Women	Men
Evaluation	76	64	42	15	13	4	—	—
Follow-up clinic	38	19	26	14	8	7	—	2
Group < 10	11	8	2	3	—	1	—	—
> 10	16	13	1	—	—	—	—	—
Individual < 10	61	36	30	12	11	3	1	—
> 10	27	17	3	1	2	4	2	—
Total	230	157	104	45	34	19	3	2

Most of the patient's questionnaires we completed via the phone, i.e., one of the authors called the patient and asked him to answer the questions.

The therapists were all Caucasian and consisted of psychiatrists, psychiatric residents, psychologists and psychiatric social workers, and a group of fourth year medical students.

The types of treatment offered are individual therapy where the patient sees the therapist for 50 minutes once or twice a week; group therapy where the patient is seen in group once or twice a week and the Follow-up Clinic where the patient is seen briefly and given tranquilizers. Patients in the Follow-up Clinic are seen at intervals up to two months for medication.

There are a large number of patients who are seen once and are discharged. There is also a group of patients who were offered further appointments, but did not keep them after the intitial interview.

RESULTS

At the end of the study period, 79 patients were still in treatment. Of the 515 patients who were discharged, we were able to get 301 matched patient-therapist questionnaires.

In order to compare the therapeutic experiences of the diverse ethnic groups we tabulated the number of visits and the sex and race. Table 2 includes all patients.

The figures are largely self-explanatory and show that there is a much larger proportion of Caucasians who stay for more than ten visits. Our minority group patients were much more often seen in the Follow-up Clinic (where they saw the doctor briefly and had drugs prescribed) or discharged after the initial interview. Relatively few were offered or seen in group therapy or individual therapy. This table shows that one half of the Caucasians, less than two fifths of the Mexican-Americans, and less than one-third of the Negroes received individual or group sessions.

Even more dramatic is the difference in the numbers of patients who have been seen for more than ten individual psychotherapy hours. We feel that this group of patients are most "popular" with the therapists and have demonstrated a congruency of values and attitudes with those of the therapists. The therapists must more often feel able to emphasize, to temporarily identify themselves with these "popular" patients. Of the Caucasian patients, 11.4% were in this category, of the Mexican-Americans 11.3%, and of the Negroes only 2.7%. We shall discuss the significance of these data subsequently.

The last group in our study are those 79 patients who have persevered and remained in treatment beyond the nine-month period of our study. Two thirds of these patients were women, a slightly higher proportion than at the beginning. When categorized by race, there were 62 Caucasians, 11 Negroes, 4 Mexican-Americans, and 2 Orientals. If we were to dichotomize this patient population by sex and look at the distribution in individual or group therapy versus "Follow-up Clinic" (our minimal contact clinic where drugs are often prescribed), there is a startling contrast. There are 17 Caucasian men in individual therapy or group therapy, and there are no non-Caucasian men in indi-

Table 3. Type of treatment at end of study by race

	Caucasian		Negro		Mexican-American		Oriental	
	Women	Men	Women	Men	Women	Men	Women	Men
Individual therapy	15	7	3	—	1	—	2	—
Group therapy	11	10	1	—	—	—	—	—
Follow-up Clinic	13	6	4	3	3	—	—	—

Table 4. Feelings of therapists and patients*

	Much disliked	Disliked	Average	Liked	Liked much
Therapists	2.4	8.3	44.6	40.5	4.2
Patients	3.0	7.5	45.0	40.0	4.5

*Expressed in percentages.

vidual or group therapy! Only three non-Caucasian men, all Negro, survived the nine-month period in the Folow-up Clinic where the doctor-patient contact is minimal. Table 3 illustrates the treatment of the total surviving group.

The relative paucity of non-Caucasian men in the group tested for this length of time suggests the possibility that with this group there are factors either in the patient, the therapist, or the patient-therapist situation that lead to the self-termination, discharge, or mutual ending of treatment at a far greater rate. Not only do they less often apply for treatment, but they receive less lengthy and intensive therapy. The therapist's ethnocentricity may cause him to be less accepting, or the minority group patient may feel that the therapist does not understand and that no help is forthcoming. We do plan to evaluate these variables in future studies.

Since the data were punched on cards we were not able to match each therapist's response to a particular patient's response. We plan to do this later by hand. When we compared the responses of the patient's with those of the therapist's, the similarities are striking. For example, the therapists said that 51.4% of the patients had improved—and 62% of the patients

agreed. The therapists felt that 44.6% of the patients had gotten what they wanted —and 47.1% of the patients concurred. Again, the opinion about additional visits being of benefit were 66.1% and 73.2% respectively. These data certainly suggest that our therapists were sensitive to our patients' realities. We are aware that this contrasts with the results of previous studies. One possible conclusion here would be that our therapists are more alert to social class factors.

Along with the congruency of the above mentioned findings, there was similarly 44.5% of the patients who said they like the therapist in comparison to 44.7% of the therapists who said that they like the patients. The results are shown on Table 4.

We found that the family or friends had little influence as to whether a patient continued or quit therapy. A patient's continuing or leaving therapy was a factor of the patient-therapist relationship. We wanted to know if the patients felt the therapist was prejudiced. We were mainly interested in the minority group responses and we were surprised that a number of Caucasian patients felt the therapist was prejudiced towards them. The results were somewhat surprising in that 6.1% of the Negro patients, 4.3% of the Mexican-

American patients, and 4.3% of the Caucasian thought the therapist was prejudiced.

We did not expect such a large number of Negroes would say the therapist was prejudiced but this also did not appear to be an overt factor in the acceptance or rejection of a patient for treatment.

A pattern of response was revealed by our Caucasian patients when compared by education. Those who were most well educated said that they had not gotten what they wanted, and they also felt that additional visits would be beneficial. Those with the least education largely felt that they had gotten what they wanted from treatment and also were almost unanimous in feeling that additional visits would help.

In the future, we plan to cross-tabulate our data to see if where the therapist said that he like the patient, therapy was more intensive or longer in duration. And similarly with the patient who likes the therapist; does he stay longer, is he more intensively treated?

The constructive result of this study is that we know that our patients from different cultural backgrounds are less often offered or receive intensive therapy. In order to ascertain the reasons for this difference, we are now evaluating the ethnocentricity of the therapists and we will correlate this with the destiny of these same patients. Since our ethnic men pose problems in not surviving as continuing patients, we also plan to study them more in depth to see if their life histories may suggest "poor ego strength" to the culturally unsophisticated therapist. Perhaps the experience of being disadvantaged has left our patients with attitudes of distrust, disenchantment, and hopelessness which cause them to leave treatment earlier.

SUMMARY

We followed the destiny in treatment of 594 consecutive patients in the Psychiatric Outpatient Clinic at the Los Angeles County General Hospital. Our specific interest was to compare the treatment experience and the responses of the patients and their therapists to similar questions concerning improvement, feelings of liking or disliking, whether additional visits would be of benefit, and whether or not the patient had gotten what he wanted. In addition, the patients were asked if they felt the therapist was capable, and the therapists were asked the patient's prognosis. These data were tabulated and cross-tabulated on a computer, and we compared the results among the patients, 65% of whom were Caucasian, 25% Negro, 9% Mexican-American, and 1% Oriental. We were able to obtain all the data for 301 patients and when these data were analyzed we found that our non-Caucasians seldom criticized their therapists. Of the Negro patients, 6.1% felt that the therapist was prejudiced, 4.3% of the Caucasian, and 4.3% of the Mexican-American patients felt that the therapist was prejudiced towards them. When we compared the treatment experiences of our patients, 50% of the Caucasians, 40% of the Mexican-Americans, and only 33% of the Negroes were seen in either individual or group psychotherapy. This means that our ethnic patients were more often discharged or seen for minimal supportive psychotherapy. After nine months, there were only 79 patients in active treatment, with 78% Caucasian, 14% Negro, 5% Mexican-American, and 3% Oriental. Three Negro men were the only non-Caucasian men left after nine months and all of them were in the Follow-up Clinic, where they were seen for minimal support. Our therapists felt that they disliked 10.7% of their patients, while 10.5% of the patients disliked the therapists. This study has certainly shown us that a problem exists. The minority group patient receives the least intensive therapy. We are currently studying the ethnocentricity of the therapists and the life-experiences of Negro men in order to find some answers which may improve our techniques of treatment.

REFERENCES

1. Rosenthal, D., and Frank, J. D.: The Fate of Psychiatric Clinic Outpatients Assigned to Psychotherapy, J Nerv Ment Dis **127**:330-343 (Oct) 1958.
2. Adler, L. M.; Goin, M.; and Yamamoto, J.: Failed Psychiatric Clinic Appointments, Relationship to Social Class, Calif Med **99**:388-392 (Dec) 1963.
3. Albronda, H. F.; Dean, R. L.; and Starkweather, J. A.: Social Class and Psycho-

therapy, Arch Gen Psychiat **10**:276-283 (March) 1964.

4. Brill, N. Q., and Storrow, H. A.: Social Class and Psychiatric Treatment, Arch Gen Psychiat **3**:340-344 (Oct) 1960.

5. Haas, K.: The Middle-Class Professional and the Lower-Class Patient, Ment Hyg **47**:408-410 (July) 1963.

6. Goin, M. K.; Yamamoto, J.; and Silverman, J.: Therapy Congruent With Class-Linked Expectations, Arch Gen Psychiat **13**:133-137 (Aug) 1965.

7. Lief, H. I., et al: Low Dropout Rate in a Psychiatric Clinic, Arch Gen Psychiat **5**:200-211 (Aug) 1961.

8. Heine, R. W., and Trosman, H.: Initial Expectations of the Doctor-Patient Interaction as a Factor in Continuance in Psychotherapy, Psychiatry **23**:275-278 (Aug) 1960.

9. Redlich, F. C.; Hollingshead, A. B.; and Bellis, E.: Social Class Differences in Attitudes Toward Psychiatry, Amer J Orthopsychiat **25**:60-70 (Jan) 1955.

10. Yamamoto, J., and Goin, M. K.: On the Treatment of the Poor, Amer J Psychiat **122**:267-271 (Sept) 1965.

11. Seward, G. Psychotherapy and Culture Conflict, New York: The Ronald Press, 1956.

CHAPTER 21 THE EFFECT OF INTERVIEW LANGUAGE ON THE EVALUATION OF PSYCHOPATHOLOGY IN SPANISH-AMERICAN SCHIZOPHRENIC PATIENTS

LUIS R. MARCOS
MURRAY ALPERT
LEONEL URCUYO
MARTIN KESSELMAN

Psychiatric ratings of ten schizophrenic patients whose native language was Spanish disclosed more psychopathology when the patients were interviewed in the English language than when they were interviewed in Spanish. Some evidence suggested that there were clinically important changes in the patient attributable to his problems in speaking in a second language. The clinician's frame of reference must also be taken into account: what is applicable to native English-speaking patients cannot be directly applied to the evaluation of persons from other cultures.

At Bellevue Psychiatric Hospital, as in many other urban centers, Spanish-speaking patients comprise a significant proportion of the patient population (1, 2) while Spanish-speaking psychiatrists are un-

From Am. J. Psychiatry **130**(5):549-553, May 1973. Copyright 1973, the American Psychiatric Association.

Dr. Marcos is Clinical Instructor and Postdoctoral Fellow, Department of Psychiatry, Downstate Medical Center, State University of New York, 450 Clarkson Ave., Box 88, Brooklyn, N.Y. 11203. Drs. Alpert, Urcuyo, and Kesselman are all associated with the New York University Medical School Department of Psychiatry, where Dr. Alpert is Associate Professor of Psychiatry, Dr. Urcuyo is Staff Psychiatrist, and Dr. Keeselman is Assistant Professor of Psychiatry.

This study was supported in part by Public Health Service grant MH-08618 from the National Institue of Mental Health.

The authors wish to express their appreciation to Paul Beatty, Florence Diamond, Victor Martin, Sanghae Park, and Nelly Pastoriza.

common. As in many psychiatric facilities, it is a frequent practice to have patients whose mother tongue is not English evaluated by psychiatrists who speak only English. If the patient is able to communicate at all in English the examination is done in this language. Only if the patient is entirely non-English-speaking might an interpreter be used. Our purpose in the research reported here is to assess the influence of interview language on the psychiatric evaluation of schizophrenic patients whose native tongue is Spanish.

A number of authors (3-7) have pointed out the need for mental health professionals who possess both fluency in Spanish and a sensitive understanding of the Spanish-American culture. It is difficult to measure the sensitivity of a clinician to an unfamiliar culture, and it is not surprising that there has been little direct experimental work studying this issue. However, the sheer ability to speak a language is less elusive to measurement and, considering the emphasis on communication dysfunction in some theories of psychopathology, it is surprising that the role of interview language in the assessment of pathology in bilingual patients has received very little experimental attention.

We could find only one report on this topic. In this report, Del Castillo (8) described several clinical experiences in which Spanish-speaking patients appeared obviously psychotic during native-tongue interviews but seemed much less so, and even without any overt psychotic symptoms, when the interview was conducted in English. In this latter report, the interviews were part of pretrial examinations. The interviewer was free to conduct the interview in any manner he chose in order to accomplish this goal. Under these circumstances it is difficult to evaluate the extent to which the interview procedure, apart from the interview language, contributed to the difference in detected pathology. Morever, the issue of legal competence is a somewhat circumscribed one and may reflect only certain components of the psychiatric evaluation.

We have recently developed a method for obtaining standardized psychiatric mental status evaluations utilizing a combination of prerecorded interview questions and closed-circuit television. This procedure has been described in detail elsewhere (9, 10). In effect, it provides a reliable method for minimizing interview variability and for attaining a permanent record that may be rated under well-controlled conditions. The method has been shown to be at least as sensitive as the standard face-to-face procedure in the assessment of level of psychopathology and in the estimation of response to treatment. Utilizing this method, we undertook a study of the effect of interview language on the rating of psychopathology. It was our expectation that by separating the rater from the interview situation we would be able to derive a clearer understanding of this effect.

METHOD

Ten recent admissions to the adult services of Bellevue Psychiatric Hospital were selected for this study. The criteria for admission to the study were as follows: 1) diagnosis of schizophrenia, made independently by two psychiatrists; 2) no evidence of organic brain disorder; 3)

Table 1. Description of the patient sample

Subject	Sex	Age	Years of education	Years in United States	Wechsler vocabulary score English	Spanish	Diagnosis	Drug treatment
1	M	21	9	3	10	20	Chronic undifferentiated schizophrenia	300 mg. chlorpromazine
2	F	34	9	24	27	38	Chronic undifferentiated schizophrenia	400 mg. chlorpromazine
3	M	32	10	20	36	38	Paranoid schizophrenia	200 mg. chlorpromazine
4	F	31	12	25	35	49	Paranoid schizophrenia	400 mg. chlorpromazine
5	M	34	11	17	23	42	Chronic undifferentiated schizophrenia	30 mg. trifluoperazine
6	M	31	9	10	56	68	Paranoid schizophrenia	20 mg. trifluoperazine
7	F	34	5	18	9	28	Chronic undifferentiated schizophrenia	300 mg. chlorpromazine
8	F	29	6	6	12	40	Chronic undifferentiated schizophrenia	400 mg. chlorpromazine
9	M	21	9	20	60	34	Paranoid schizophrenia	350 mg. chlorpromazine
10	M	42	7	39	50	18	Chronic undifferentiated schizophrenia	30 mg. trifluoperazine

Spanish as the native language; 4) fluency in English sufficient to participate in English psychiatric interviews; and 5) willingness to volunteer for the study. Patients were not informed as to the aim of the study. In table 1 the background and clinical characteristics of the patients are listed.

Four psychiatrists contributed independent ratings of the videotapes. Two had Spanish as their mother tongue and two were English-speaking. The four psychiatrists were experienced in the use of the Brief Psychiatric Rating Scale (BPRS) (11) and had previously participated in training sessions designed to establish acceptable levels of interrater reliability. Raters were blind as to the purpose of the study and to the admission criteria as well.

In order to study the interrater reliability between English- and Spanish-speaking raters, one of the English and one of the Spanish raters viewed ten additional videotape interviews of English-speaking schizophrenic patients. Interrater reliability for these ratings, based on the total pathology scores, was r = .85 (t = 4.56, p < .01). The means of the total pathology scores were 50 for the English-speaking rater and 49 for the Spanish-speaking rater. These mean scores were not statistically different (t = 1.04, df = 9, p < .3).

Closed-circuit television recordings were made of standard psychiatric interviews in English and Spanish. Half of the patients participated in the English interview first and vice versa. The two interviews were spaced no more than 24 hours and no less than 20 hours apart. During this period no change was made in the patient's medication. An English-speaking or Spanish-speaking clinician was present during the interview; however, his participation was minimal since the interview questions had been put on audiotape. The English and Spanish questions which were identical, were presented in the same order. The videotape recordings of the English-language interviews were independently rated by the two English-speaking psychiatrists; the interviews in Spanish were also rated independently by the two Spanish-speaking psychiatrists. Finally, both the English and the Spanish versions of the vocabulary subtest of the Wechsler Adult Intelligence Scale (12) were administered to the patients after the psychiatric interviews had been completed.

RESULTS

To determine whether the language of the interview would have an effect on the amount of pathology detected by the raters, we computed the total pathology score for each patient. This score, which is the sum of the ratings on the 18 BPRS scales for the two raters per language, is presented for each patient in figure 1. In this figure it can be seen that more pathology was detected during the English interview for each patient. The mean score for the English-language interviews was 93

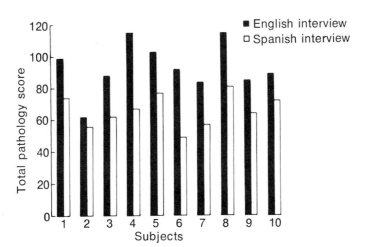

Fig. 1. Total BPRS pathology scores for each subject in English and Spanish interviews.

and for the Spanish-language interviews 65; the difference was highly significant statistically (t = 7.11, p < .001). Interrater reliability for the Spanish-speaking raters was .91 (t = 6.31, p < .001). The difference between the mean levels of pathology detected by the two Spanish raters was not statistically significant. Interrater reliability for the English-speaking raters was also .91. The means of the total pathology scores were 48 for English-speaking rater 1 and 45 for English-speaking rater 2. The difference between these means, although small from a clinical point of view, was statistically significant (t = 2.61, p < .05). However, this difference between the English-speaking raters would not contribute to the difference between the English and Spanish ratings. It was English-speaking rater 1 who, together with Spanish-speaking rater 1, participated in the preliminary reliability study in which it was found that English-speaking rater 1 and Spanish-speaking rater 1 detected equivalent levels of pathology. Since English-speaking rater

2 tended to rate lower than English-speaking rater 1, this would if anything tend to decrease the levels of pathology detected on the combined English ratings.

From this analysis it is clear that our bilingual patients have been judged to demonstrate more pathology when they have been interviewed in English. To determine whether this increment in pathology in the English-language interviews reflected a simple constant added to the amount of pathology detected in the Spanish-language interviews, the product-moment correlation between the total pathology scores in English and Spanish was computed, and was found to equal .64. This correlation was significantly different from zero but was lower than the correlation we usually obtain when two of our experienced raters evaluate the identical behavioral sample. (The five-percent confidence limits for a correlation of .64 with an N of 10 are .36 and .81.) The lowering of interrater correlation across languages might be interpreted as suggesting that patients are dif-

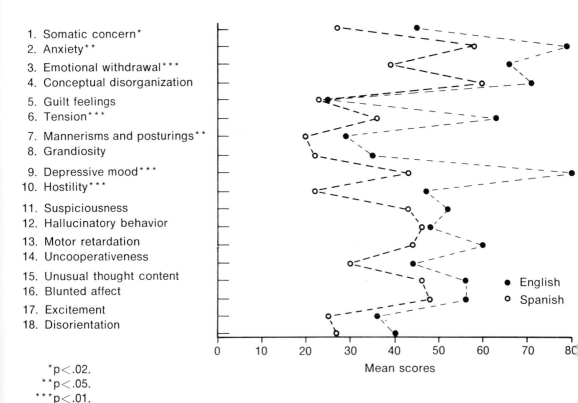

1. Somatic concern*
2. Anxiety**
3. Emotional withdrawal***
4. Conceptual disorganization
5. Guilt feelings
6. Tension***
7. Mannerisms and posturings**
8. Grandiosity
9. Depressive mood***
10. Hostility***
11. Suspiciousness
12. Hallucinatory behavior
13. Motor retardation
14. Uncooperativeness
15. Unusual thought content
16. Blunted affect
17. Excitement
18. Disorientation

● English
○ Spanish

*p<.02.
**p<.05.
***p<.01.

Fig. 2. Pathology score for each BPRS scale in English and Spanish interviews.

ferentially affected by the language of the interview.

We will now report the effect of the language of interview on the individual BPRS scales. In figure 2 the mean score for each scale is presented for both the English and Spanish interview. The mean scores are significantly elevated for seven of the 18 scales (t test between correlated means). The scales most affected by the language of the interview were "tension," "depressed mood," "hostility," "anxiety," "emotional withdrawal," and "somatic concern."

The differences between the English and Spanish interviews for the rest of the scales were not statistically significant.

DISCUSSION

Our results indicate that Spanish-American patients are consistently rated as showing more pathology when they are interviewed in English. Even the two patients who obtained higher vocabulary scores in English than in Spanish were evaluated as presenting more pathology in their English-language interview. The vocabulary score is not a direct measure of language fluency, but this finding would suggest that caution should be taken in the psychiatric evaluation of patients whose first language is not English, including those who appear competent in it.

Our results disagree with those of Del Castillo (8), who conducted interviews in both Spanish and English and felt that he uncovered more pathology in Spanish interviews with Spanish-American patients. A factor that might have contributed to the discrepancy could be related to the different effects of pathology in the two studies. In Del Castillo's setting it was to the advantage of the patients to demonstrate enough pathology to avoid trial. Our patients frequently want to minimize their symptoms in order to elude long-term hospitalization. Patients who are more competent in Spanish may be better able to communicate the level of pathology that will produce the most desirable disposition for them. However, it is unlikely that the amount of pathology detected in a psychiatric examination is simply a function of the impression the patient wishes to make.

There are three general factors that should be considered here—one related to the raters, one related to the patients, and one residing in the interaction between the raters and the patients. First, we might hypothesize that patients are actually the same in the English and the Spanish interviews. The average patient recieved a total pathology score of 46.5 for his English interview and 32.5 for his Spanish interview. The higher pathology scores given by the English-speaking raters or the lower scores given by the Spanish-speaking raters could reflect rater prejudice. Brody (13) has mentioned the possibility of positive as well as negative prejudice; he has attributed the roots of prejudice to intrapsychic factors within the prejudiced individual.

Whether the ratings of the English or the Spanish interview are taken as reflecting the "true" pathology, the 14-point difference between the ratings can be seen as representing the mean of a distribution of prejudice points and could be viewed as separable from the distribution of pathology points. If this were so it would be difficult to explain the high interrater correlation between the two English-speaking and the two Spanish-speaking raters (for both, $r = .91$), since if prejudice points were attributes they might be expected to be distributed more randomly across the patients and would thus dilute the correlation. Of course, pairs of raters might share identical stereotypes; we cannot eliminate such a possibility with these data.

To further check on the prejudice hypothesis, a multiple correlation was computed between the English Pathology Score, the Spanish Pathology Score, and the Spanish Vocabulary Score. The reason for looking at these independent predictors was that they were patient variables unavailable to the English-language rater. The multiple correlation was .83, and each of the predictors independently added significantly to the correlation analysis of variance (ANOVA). It is hard to imagine any simple prejudice mechanism through which these orderly relations could operate from predictors not accessible to the rater.

Although we can account for a significant part of the difference between the English and Spanish ratings in terms of patient variables, we cannot exclude the possibility that both positive and negative rater prejudices contributed to the different levels of pathology found.

The second factor that might operate to produce the increment in English interview pathology is related to the hypothesis that the patient changes when he is required to speak English. Under the best of circumstances, schizophrenics find it difficult to describe their experiences. They may be tense when speaking in English (scale 6). They may just "give up" in their attempt to communicate and appear more emotionally withdrawn (scale 3) and uncooperative (scale 14). We have some evidence that this factor was operative; we will report differences between the patient's responses to identical questions in Spanish and English in a separate report (14).

The third factor derives from the fact that the raters frame of reference is not applicable to the special problems of the Spanish-American patient. For example, in a previous study we showed that when an English-speaking patient becomes depressed, a number of things change in the way he speaks; these include an increased duration of articulations and markedly increased pause times (15). Some of these changes may also be found when an individual speaks in a language in which he is less competent, so that the rater might confuse the effects of translation with the effects of depression (scale 9). Similarly, Mahl (16) has demonstrated that speech disturbances are verbal indicators of anxiety. We have found more of the speech disturbances that Mahl has described in our patients while they speak English and thus would expect elevation in the anxiety ratings (scale 2).

In addition, under this factor the problems of norms for cross-cultural ratings might be subsumed. For example, Fernandez-Marina (17) has described the "Puerto Rican syndrome," emphasizing the conversion reaction component. Fabrega and associates (18) and Wolf (19) have noted an increased frequency of somatic complaints in Mexican-American and Puerto Rican patients. Thus one might expect an elevation on scale 1 ("somatic concern"). Spanish-speaking raters appear to have a more culturally relative attitude and seem better able to evaluate these patients' statements within the context of their Spanish-American cultural background.

CONCLUSIONS

In a study of ten schizophrenic patients whose mother tongue was Spanish we found that psychiatric ratings reflected greater psychopathology when the patients were interviewed in English than when they were interviewed in Spanish. Although a contribution from rater prejudice (both positive and negative) could not be excluded, there was evidence suggesting clinically relevant changes in the patient attributable to the problems of speaking in a second language. There were also indications that the clinician's frame of reference, which is applicable to native English-speaking patients, cannot be directly applied to the evaluation of patient behaviors that are influenced not only by psychopathology but by cross-cultural, cross-language factors as well.

Because of the limited number of trained professionals who are competent in Spanish, we expect the practice of interviewing patients in their less competent language to continue. We are currently in the process of analyzing the verbal and nonverbal communication differences from our closed-circuit television recordings to ascertain the nature of the differences. We are also trying to determine whether we can provide the English rater with a yardstick to minimize some of the constant errors resulting from the interview language.

REFERENCES

1. 1968 Statistics. Albany, NY, New York State Department of Mental Hygiene Statistical Department, 1973
2. Department of Commerce, Bureau of Census: Statistical Abstract of the United States. Washington, DC, US Government Printing Office, 1971
3. Edgerton RB, Karno M: Mexican-American bilingualism and the perception of mental illness. Arch Gen Psychiatry 24:286-290, 1971
4. Fitzpatrick JP, Gould RE: Mental illness among Puerto Ricans in New York: cultural condition or intercultural misunderstanding? Am J Orthopsychiatry 40:238-239, 1970
5. Karno M: The enigma of ethnicity in a psy-

chiatric clinic. Arch Gen Psychiatry **14:**516-520, 1966

6. Karno M, Edgerton RB: Perception of mental illness in a Mexican-American community. Arch Gen Psychiatry **20:**233-238; 1969

7. Kline LY: Some factors in the psychiatric treatment of Spanish-Americans. Am J Psychiatry **125:**1674-1681, 1969

8. Del Castillo JC: The influence of language upon symptomatology in foreign-born patients. Am J Psychiatry **127:**242-244, 1970

9. Alpert M: Television tape for evaluation of treatment response. Psychosomatics **11:**467-469, 1970

10. Alpert M, Marcos LR, Kesselman M: Evaluation of closed-circuit television as the clinical sample for the assessment of psychopathology and the estimation of treatment response (in preparation)

11. Overall JE, Gorham DR: The brief psychiatric rating scale. Psychol Rep **10:**799-812, 1962

12. Wechsler D: The Measurement of Adult Intelligence, 4th ed. Baltimore, Williams & Wilkins, 1958

13. Brody EB: Psychiatry and prejudice, in American Handbook of Psychiatry, vol 3. Edited by Arieti S. New York, Basic Books, 1966, pp 629-642

14. Marcos LR, Urcuyo L, Kesselman M, et al: The effect of the language barrier on the evaluations of Spanish-American patients (submitted for publication)

15. Alpert M, Frosch WA, Fisher SH: Teaching the perception of expressive aspects of vocal communication. Am J Psychiatry **124:**202-211, 1967

16. Mahl GF: Measuring the patient's anxiety during interviews from "expressive" aspects of his speech. Trans NY Acad Sci **21:**249-257, 1959

17. Fernandez-Marina R: The Puerto Rican syndrome: its dynamics and cultural determinants. Psychiatry **24:**79-82, 1961

18. Fabrega H, Rubel AJ, Wallace CA: Working-class Mexican psychiatric outpatients. Arch Gen Psychiatry **16:**704-712, 1967

19. Wolf KL: Growing up and its price in three Puerto Rican subcultures. Psychiatry **15:**401-433, 1952

CHAPTER 22 MEXICAN-AMERICAN BILINGUALISM AND THE PERCEPTION OF MENTAL ILLNESS

ROBERT B. EDGERTON
MARVIN KARNO

Attitudes towards mental illness and the usage of language are related; both reflect cultural distinctions with lasting psychological involvements. Mental health professionals are needed who possess both fluency in Spanish and sensitive understanding of the culture of the Mexican-American poor.

It was in 1928 that Edward Sapir noted that persons who speak different languages live in different worlds, not the same world with different labels attached. More than 50 years of research in bilingualism on the relation of language to culture has produced a set of complex and contradictory findings which have led to lively disagreement regarding the effects of bilingualism on cognitive and perceptual processes as well as on attitudes and

From Arch. Gen. Psychiat. 24:286-290, March 1971.

Accepted for publication April 13, 1970.

From the Neuropsychiatric Institute, Los Angeles.

Reprint requests to the Neuropsychiatric Institute, 760 Westwood Plaza, Los Angeles 90024 (Dr. Edgerton).

This research was supported by the California Department of Mental Hygiene, Research grant No. 64-2-37. Computing assistance was obtained from the Health Sciences Computing Facility, UCLA, sponsored by National Institute of Health grant FR-3. Data processing and statistical analysis was carried out by Lois Crawford. Eunice Mason Hill served as field interviewing supervisor. We wish also to acknowledge the assistance of the Social Science Research Institute, University of Hawaii (National Institute of Mental Health grant MH 09243).

values.[1-2] Therefore, while it is generally accepted that the language one speaks affects the way in which the environment is perceived, valued, and spoken about, the extent and direction of these influences are by no means demonstrated.

Most of the nearly 750,000 Mexican-Americans in Los Angeles County today are largely bilingual. However, for the most part, Spanish remains the language of childhood of the family and therefore of emotion, while English, on the other hand, is the language of the school, the job, and the alien, "Anglo" world. This communication will explore some of the relationships between this bilingualism and attitudes toward mental illness. The research reported here was conducted in two subcommunities of the larger East Los Angeles area—Belvedere and Lincoln Heights. The major research effort was devoted to a systematic household interview which was administered to Anglo and Mexican-American residents of these two East Los Angeles communities. This survey was designed to gather quantitative data concerning perceptions and definitions of, and attitudes toward mental illness which could be compared across the two communities. (Simultaneously, ethnographic field studies were carried out in the same two communities in an effort to obtain additional qualitative information and to lend a sense of social and historical context to the interview responses.) The survey was developed and pretested over a year's time. The final version was 18 pages in length, including approximately 200 questions involving biographic, demographic, and attitudinal information, in addition to a variety of items that dealt explicitly with mental illness. The core of these mental illness items was formed by eight short vignettes that, in everyday language, described persons who were depicted as suffering from what psychiatrists generally consider to be psychiatric disorders. Five of these vignettes were most important: (1) paranoid behavior in an adult male, (2) severe depression in a middle-aged woman, (3) interpersonal conflict in a married couple, (4) an acute schizophrenic reaction in a teen-aged girl, and (5) aggressive delinquent behavior in a teen-aged boy.

The interviews were carried out in either English or Spanish depending upon the preference of the respondent. All interviewers were fluently bilingual. Of the 444 Mexican-Americans interviewed, 260 (approximately 60%) took the interview in Spanish. A block sampling design within each community was employed for the random selection of households, and within households, adult members were selected as respondents by a random probability technique. The interview was not identified to the respondent as dealing with either health or mental health; instead, it was identified as a university-based study which was concerned with the kinds of problems that can arise in all people's lives. (The first question to deal with mental illness, or apparent mental illness, did not occur until halfway through the interview.) Interviews lasted between one and two hours, the rapport was typically good, and the refusal rate was well within acceptable limits.[3]

BACKGROUND OF THE PROBLEM

Our original interest in this research was an effort to determine whether the widespread under representation of Mexican-Americans in both private and public psychiatric treatment facilities throughout the southwestern states could be related to differences in their perceptions of, or attitude toward, mental illness. Consequently, we compared the responses of 444 Mexican-Americans with 224 Anglo-Americans who were also residents of East Los Angeles. As indicated in an earlier report, this comparison between the attitudes of Anglo-Americans and Mexican-Americans indicated that there were remarkably few differences between the two populations.[3] The two populations perceived the same behaviors as being evidence of mental illness, and their attitudes toward such behaviors were remarkably consistent. However, while Mexican-Americans as a group only rarely differed significantly from Anglo-Americans as a group, it was apparent that there were some marked differences among the 444 Mexican-Americans whom we interviewed.

Consequently, we searched for variables which would permit us to discriminate among these Mexican-American respondents with regard of, or attitude toward, mental illness. For example, we examined such variables as age, sex, religion, education, occupation, number of years spent in the United States, as well as certain attitudes toward language, education, and occupation, not to mention certain beliefs regarding the etiology of mental illness (eg, that mental illness is caused by sin), and the treatment of mental illness (eg, that the most effective treatment for mental illness is prayer). When we attempted to relate each of these variables to responses concerning mental illness, we found that these relationships were characteristically few and small, seldom approaching statistical significance. What is more, when these variables were intercorrelated, it was discovered that the relationships between them were typically weak.

We also combined a number of these variables in an effort to increase the number of mental illness related response differences, as well as the magnitude of these differences. When this was attempted, that combination of variables which produced the largest number of statistically significant relationships to mental illness responses was this: all of those persons who were born in the United States, educated nine or more years, and took the interview in English, versus those persons who were born in Mexico, educated eight or fewer years, and took the interview in Spanish. This combination of variables clearly represents a contrast in acculturation (as reflected in education and place of birth) as well as a difference in language usage, and as such it was a potent predictor of response to mental illness questions. To our surprise, however, there was a still more discriminating comparison. In fact, by far the best predictor among all possible variables was simply the language in which the respondent took the interview. And since our goal was to discover that variable or combination of variables which would best discriminate among these 444 Mexican-Americans with regard to their answers to our questions about mental illness, we shall report here the response differences that were noted when Mexican-American respondents were divided into those who took the interview in Spanish and those who took the interview in English.

LANGUAGE OF THE INTERVIEW AND ITS RELATIONSHIPS

Although there were not statistically significant differences between men and women in their choice of Spanish or English, there were differences in the ages of the two groups, with those who were younger being more likely to answer in English, and those who were older (particularly those over 57) more likely to take the interview in Spanish. There was also a clear difference in the place of birth, with 81% of those taking the interview in English being born in Los Angeles, and 77% of those who took the interview in Spanish being born in Mexico. This difference also extended to education, with 70% of those who chose Spanish having eight or fewer years of schooling, and 65% of those who chose English having more than eight years of education. There was another difference with regard to expressed fluency in either language; those who took the interview in English, with very few exceptions, characterized their normal language usage as bilingual. Of those who took the interview in Spanish, more than 66% characterized themselves as speaking Spanish "only or mainly"; fewer than 33% characterized themselves as "bilingual."

For persons in each language category, Spanish and English, there was substantial unemployment. For example, 22% of those respondents who took the interview in English said that the head of household in their family was unemployed. Among those who took the interview in Spanish this figure was 41%, the larger percentage being largely a product of the fact that 17% of these heads of household were retired. There were also differences with regard to church attendance and the importance of religion. Those who took the interview in Spanish said that religion was more important in their lives than did those who took the interview in English; in addition, their church attendance was more frequent, with 63% of the Spanish language respondents attending church once a week or more, opposed to 37% among the English respondents.

Despite these sizable differences between English and Spanish speaking respondents, there was remarkable agreement among them when attitudes toward Spanish and English as languages were examined. For example, when asked whether a Mexican-American child should learn to speak Spanish well, 90% of those who took the interview in Spanish said emphatically "yes," but 95% of those who took the interview in English gave the same answer. Similarly, virtually all respondents rejected the idea that their children should learn to read and write only English, insisting instead that they also become literate in Spanish. When asked whether children should speak English in the home before going to school, 83% of those persons who chose Spanish answered affirmatively and so did 90% of those who chose English. These findings suggest that while these two populations differ with regard to their knowledge of English, or their comfort in its use, they share the belief that their children should learn to live as bilinguals.[4-5]

When we examined the expressed language behavior of our respondents, however, it was abundantly clear that these adults did not participate equally in a bilingual world. Those who took the interview in English tended to live in a world in which English was far more important, whereas those who took the interview in Spanish lived in what was very largely a Spanish language environment. For example, the

English speakers listened to the radio in English and watched English language television programs, but those who took the interview in Spanish typically listened to Spanish radio programs (these are available not only from Mexican stations but from a number of local Los Angeles stations) and they regularly watched Spanish language television programs. For example, 51% of those who took the interview in Spanish said that they watched channel 34 (an all Spanish language television channel presenting a variety of programming) "everyday or almost everyday." Only 15% of the English speakers watched channel 34 this often. Although there were no differences between the two populations with regard to the motion picture entertainment that they sought out (very few attended motion pictures and when they did, these films were primarily in English), there were substantial differences with regard to what they read. For example, 75% of those who took the interview in English read an English language newspaper, "daily or almost daily"; only 36% of the Spanish speakers did the same. On the other hand, whereas 5% of the English speakers read a Spanish newspaper, 34% of the Spanish speakers read such a paper "daily or almost daily." What is more, although neither population read magazines with great frequency (37% of the English speakers and 50% of the Spanish speakers said that they "never or almost never" read a magazine), there was a considerable difference with regard to the reading of religious magazines. Such magazines were never read by the English speakers, but 17% of those who took the interview in Spanish read such magazines "frequently."

It would appear then, that these respondents lived a far greater percentage of their lives in one language than the other—they listened to, spoke, and were more comfortable in either Spanish or English, not both. The question at issue is whether persons who live in different worlds of language also live in different worlds with regard to mental illness.[5] It is again apparent, as it was when we compared Mexican-American responses with Anglo American responses, that there was a considerable degree of similarity between the mental illness responses of those who took the interview in English and those who took it in Spanish. For example, there were no differences with regard to their attitudes toward severe paranoia nor with regard to their attitudes toward marital conflict. What is perhaps more surprising, there were no differences between them regarding the nature or severity of problem behavior involving narcotics. What is more, the English and Spanish speakers agreed entirely in their attitudes toward the effectiveness of psychiatric treatment and the curability of mental illness in general.

Despite the fact that in over 75% of the responses concerning mental illness there were no statistically significant differences between those persons who chose to take the interview in English and those who chose to take it in Spanish, there were some differences that merit our attention. We shall discuss these differences under six general headings.

Depression

On the basis of our reading of the literature on Mexican-American and Mexican family structure, we had anticipated that the role of the elderly, particularly the role of the aging mother, was such that Mexican-Americans would regard involutional depression as a more serious matter than would Anglo-Americans, and indeed, that appeared to be the case. For those who took the interview in English (here, we make the assumption that these people were less involved with the culture of Mexico than those who took the interview in Spanish) involutional depression was seen as being less serious than it was by those who took the interview in Spanish.

The vignette to which these responses were made is reproduced below:

Mrs. (Brown) (Gonzalez) is nearly 50, has a nice home and her husband has a good job. She used to be full of life, an active, busy woman with a large family. Her children are now grown and in recent months she has changed. She sits and broods for hours, blames herself for all kinds of bad things she thinks she has done, and talks about what a terrible person she is. She has lost interest in all the things she used to enjoy, cannot sleep, has no appetite, and paces up and down the house for hours.

Although both populations agreed that the woman whom we described as a depressive mother was "sick," the English speakers far more often saw the source of her sickness as "loneliness," whereas the Spanish speakers described her as suffering from a "nervous" condition.

Delinquency

We had anticipated that those persons who most closely identified with Mexican-American culture would be more tolerant of Mexican-American gang activity than those who more closely identified themselves with Anglo-American culture.

The vignette we presented is given below:

Ken (Marcos) is only 15 but has been in an awful lot of trouble. He looks for fights, has a terrible temper, and stays away from school. His older brothers are married and settled down and never got in trouble like Ken. He's been arrested for car theft and there have been knifings in his gang and he's been in juvenile hall and at probation camp. His parents are worried but don't know what to do because he never wants to talk to them and is almost never home.

The responses to this vignette did not conform to our expectations. Instead, those who took the interview in English were more tolerant of this delinquent gang activity than were those who took the interview in Spanish. What is more, when asked what should be done about young men who engaged in such activities, we found that the English speakers said that these delinquent boys needed either love from their parents or help from a psychiatrist: on the other hand, those who took the interview in Spanish said that what was called for was the intervention of the police, or harsher discipline on the part of the parents. And when respondents were asked if an emotional problem were involved in the behavior of these delinquent boys *(un problema emocional)* the English speakers generally said "yes" and the Spanish speakers generally said "no." What is more, these differences were maintained even when the greater age of the Spanish speaking respondents was controlled for, so that we cannot conclude that this is merely an age-related difference. The difference was this: English speakers saw the cause of delinquency in the parent-child interaction; the Spanish speakers held that the child was primarily at fault.

Schizophrenia

We had anticipated that the more Mexican the orientation of the respondent, the greater would be his fear of and aversion toward the behavior that characterizes schizophrenia. The findings in this regard are equivocal, but there is at least one distinction that bears notice. When presented with the following vignette describing the behavior of a 17-year-old girl in her last year of high school, Mexican-Americans—whether they took the interview in English or in Spanish—agreed that this girl had a problem and that it was serious.

Jane (Walker) (Mendez) is 17 and in her last year of high school. She has always been a moody girl and has never gotten along well with people. A few months ago she began to cry all the time and to act very afraid of everyday things. She has stopped going to school and stays at home. She screams at her parents and a lot of the time doesn't make any sense at all. She has talked about hearing voices talking to her and thinks that she is really somebody else than herself.

Further, they agreed that something should be done about this problem and that it was a kind of "sickness." However, they disagreed with respect to the way in which they spoke of this sickness. As we noted in an earlier paper,[3] Anglo Americans confronted by this same vignette referred to the girl as suffering from a "mental" illness, whereas Mexican-Americans in general referred to her condition as a "nervous" problem. When the two language categories among the Mexican-American respondents were compared, this difference continued; those who took the interview in English referred to her illness as "mental" and those who took the interview in Spanish referred to "nerves" $(P < 0.001)$.

Inheritance of mental illness

When asked whether or not they believed that mental illness is often inherited, Mexican-American respondents differed most dramatically when compared by language choice. Of those who took the interview in English, 58% said "no," and only 27% said "yes"; of those who took the interview in Spanish, 64% said "yes, mental illness is often inherited," and only 23% said "no." Without here judging the relative correctness of these answers in light of recent psychiatric research, we would note that the belief in the inheritance of mental illness is probably more characteristic of Mexican "folk culture" than it is of modern Anglo-American culture.[5-15]

Treatment of mental illness

As mentioned before, the two language groups were in agreement with regard to the effectiveness of various psychiatric and nonpsychiatric forms of treatment for mental illness. In one area however, they disagreed dramatically. That area concerned the effectiveness of prayer. Having already noted that those respondents who took the interview in Spanish were seemingly more involved with religious activities than those who took the interview in English, it comes as no surprise that those who took the interview in Spanish believed prayer to be far more efficacious than did the English speakers (of the Spanish respondents, 84% said that prayer could "cure" mental illness; only 15% of the English respondents agreed). We would again note that belief in prayer as an effective treatment for mental illness is far more characteristic of Mexican "folk culture" than it is of modern Anglo-American culture.

Role of the family

There is agreement in the literature on rural Mexico and on Mexican-Americans in the United States that a major focus in these cultures is familism—a basic value orientation toward intimacy, integration, and enduring relationships within the family. Thus, in the Mexican-American family there has been reported to be a strong pressure for a family (or extended family) to solve its own problems, especially its emotional problems, within a family context.[5-15] Family solidarity with regard to the treatment of emotional disorders was strongly confirmed by our findings. Thus, those who took the interview in English agreed with the Anglo-Americans that a mentally ill person would *not* best recover from his illness by staying with his family. On the contrary, those who took the interview in Spanish disagreed, saying that recovery would best be effected if such a person could remain *with* his family. Should this finding prove to be generalized,

it could have considerable significance for an understanding of the reluctance of some Mexican-Americans to expose a family member to psychiatric treatment, should it be thought that such treatment would require hospitalization or some other form of separation from his family.

If the psychiatrist is to understand this familistic orientation, he must be aware that family solidarity is not merely a cultural commitment, but a psychological one as well. But he must also understand that Spanish is the language of the family and thus of intimacy. The switch from this language to the more formal and impersonal idiom of English—even should the patient and his relatives be linguistically capable of such a switch—may well defeat any effort by the psychiatrist to enter the affective world of his patient.

CONCLUSIONS

Responses given by 444 Mexican-Americans in East Los Angeles to a household survey interview of beliefs and perceptions of mental illness were, in general, not very different from those given by 224 Anglo-Americans, but within the Mexican-American group there were some significant differences. The most potent variable in predicting such variation in responses was the language in which the respondent took the interview.

The 260 Mexican-Americans who took the interview in Spanish, differed from the 184 Mexican-Americans who took the interview in English in six response categories: (1) depression, (2) juvenile delinquency, (3) schizophrenia, (4) the inheritance of mental illness, (5) the effectiveness of prayer, and (6) familistic orientation.

These differences suggest that, at least in East Los Angeles, the more commonly described cultural traits of Mexican-Americans—eg, fatalism, familism, strong attachment to formal religions values, patriarchal authoritarianism, and conservative morality regarding deviant behavior—are applicable (and even then with many exceptions and qualifications) only to those persons who speak mainly or only Spanish, and secondarily, to those who were also born in Mexico, and educated eight or fewer years.

In East Los Angeles, Mexican-Americans who speak mainly or only Spanish reflect the above-mentioned characteristics in their perceptions of mental illness, and in so doing, differ meaningfully from those who are bilingual or mainly monolingual in English. The latter tend to have been born in the United States and to have had nine or more years of formal education. Their language usage expresses their acculturation, and they are essentially indistinguishable from Anglo-Americans in their perception of mental illness.

Our data make any clear separation of language and culture quite meaningless. However, we can conclude that language usage and attitudes toward mental illness are related and that both reflect cultural distinctions with lasting psychological involvements. Our findings point to the need for mental health professionals who possess both fluency in Spanish and sensitive understanding of the culture of the Mexican-American poor.

REFERENCES

1. Diebold AR: The Consequences of Early Bilingualism in Cognitive Development and Personality Formation, in Norbeck E, et al (eds): *The Study of Personality: An Interdisciplinary Appraisal.* New York, Holt Rinehart & Winston Inc, 1968.
2. Haugen E: *Bilingualism in the Americas: A Bibliography and Research Guide,* Publication of the American Dialect Society, No. 26, University, Alabama, University of Alabama Press, 1956.
3. Karno M, Edgerton RG: Perception of mental illness in a Mexican-American community. *Arch Gen Psychiat* **20**:233-238, 1969.
4. Trejo AT: *Mexican American Survey Project: Summer Youth Program, Venice, California, Summer—1967.* Los Angeles, Welfare Planning Council, special report No. 75, 1968.
5. Madsen W: Mexican-Americans and Anglo-Americans: A comparative study of mental health in Texas, in Plog S, Edgerton R (eds): *Changing Perspectives in Mental Illness.* New York, Holt Rinehart & Winston Inc, 1969.
6. Madsen W: *The Mexican-Americans of south Texas.* New York, Holt Rinehart & Winston Inc, 1964.
7. Jaco EG: Mental health of the Spanish-Americans in Texas, in Opler MK (ed): *Culture and Mental Health.* New York, Macmillan Co, 1959.
8. Jaco EG: *The Social Epidemiology of Mental Disorders.* New York, Russell Sage Foundation, 1960.
9. Kiev A: *Curanderismo: Mexican-American Folk Psychiatry.* New York, Free Press of Glencoe Inc, 1968.
10. Saunders L: *Cultural Differences and Medical Care: The Case of the Spanish-Speaking People of the Southwest.* New York, Russell Sage Foundation, 1954.
11. Saunders L: Healing ways in the Spanish southwest, in Jaco EG (ed): *Patients, Physicians and Illness.* New York, Free Press of Glencoe Inc, 1958.
12. Rubel AJ: Concepts of disease in Mexican-American culture. *Amer Anthropol* **62**:795-814, 1960.
13. Rubel AJ: *Across the Tracks.* Austin, Tex, University of Texas Press, 1967.
14. Schulman S: Rural healthways in New Mexico. *Ann NY Acad Sci* **84**:950-958, 1960.
15. Clark M: *Health in the Mexican-American Culture.* Berkeley, Calif, University of California Press, 1959.

CHAPTER 23 A COMMUNITY MENTAL HEALTH SERVICE FOR MEXICAN-AMERICANS IN A METROPOLIS

MARVIN KARNO
ARMANDO MORALES

The second largest ethnic minority population in the United States and the largest ethnic minority population in the Southwestern United States comprises persons of Mexican birth or descent, most often designated as Mexican-Americans. In 1966 it was estimated that there were about two thirds of a million Mexican-Americans residing in colonies outside the Southwest, as compared to the estimated four and one third million in the five Southwestern states of California, Arizona, Colorado, New Mexico and Texas.[1] About one out of ten of California's twenty million residents and Los Angeles County's seven million residents are of Mexican birth or descent.[2]

In the summer of 1967, the Los Angeles County Department of Mental Health established a regional mental health service in the residential heart of the nation's largest, urban, Mexican-American community, East Los Angeles. A year and a half had been devoted prior to that time to the complex problems of planning, staffing and housing what was designed to be a unique professional program for a unique community.

The "community" to be served by the program included the East and Northeast

From Comprehensive psychiatry, Grune & Stratton, Inc., in press. Reprinted by permission.

Mental Health Districts of Los Angeles County, composed of the communities of Belvedere, Boyle Heights, City Terrace, East Los Angeles (a much smaller community of unincorporated Los Angeles County subsumed within the larger, generic "East Los Angeles" community), El Sereno, Highland Park, Lincoln Heights and Montebello, all lying immediately east of the Los Angeles City downtown area but still generally considered to be part of the central Metropolitan core. These communities consisted of 341,000 persons according to the 1960 U.S. Census. That figure should have been scaled upward by 10% to 30% according to many observers, to include the larger number of persons, particularly Mexican Nationals, believed not counted in the Census. The 1960 Census indicated that 61% of the East Los Angeles population was Spanish surnamed, but by 1965, a special census sub-sampling of a large part of this community indicated that this figure had climbed to 76% and at the present time may be well over 80%.[3]

The Mexican-Americans in East Los Angeles are not "poor" by world standards; however in terms of high unemployment rates, limited competitive job skills, a low level of educational achievement, crowded living space, deteriorated housing and high indices of communicable disease, they suffer a poverty similar to that of the

Negro population in Los Angeles.[4] Educationally and politically, the Mexican-American is in even a less fortunate position than the Negro in Los Angeles.[4,5]

The East Los Angeles community had been long recognized as a "desert" area in regard to professional mental health services. Lukens, in 1963, had documented the marked difficulties that confronted Mexican-American clients of social service agencies in East Los Angeles in obtaining mental health services.[6]

As a means of assessing the community's views concerning mental health and illness, a formal, university-based, social-psychiatric research project was initiated in 1964, concerning mental health attitudes and practices in the East Los Angeles Mexican-American community. From the study, it was learned that Mexican-Americans did not perceive and define mental illness in markedly different ways from Anglos, although they were strikingly underrepresented as patients in psychiatric facilities throughout California.[7] It was also known that "folk psychotherapy" or curanderismo was probably not a significantly used alternative to formal mental health services,[8] but that family physicians did serve as an active although inadequate (in amount as well as in professional depth and breadth) receiving and sustaining mental health resource in the East Los Angeles community.[9] It had been discovered that about 40% of the Mexican-American residents of East Los Angeles spoke only or mainly Spanish and hence professional persons would have to be able to work professionally in Spanish to reach those most in need of care.[7] It was also known from previous investigation that mental health personnel in a traditional, Anglo, middle-class psychiatric clinic in Los Angeles tended to be less sensitive to and less effective with Mexican-American (and Negro) patients than Anglo patients of comparable socioeconomic status.[10] Finally, discussions with the only psychiatrist in the border city of Tijuana, Mexico, had revealed that Mexicans and Mexican-Americans in California would travel from Los Angeles, Bakersfield, and even Fresno, hundreds of miles each way, to obtain culturally familiar and linguistically relevant personal psychiatric service.

These above mentioned factors as well as many others were particularly considered in the staffing and locating of the mental health service.

STAFFING

The staffing pattern for which personnel were recruited was that of the basic "module" designed by the Mental Health Department for each of its regional mental health services and included twenty one full-time positions. These were four psychiatrists, one the Regional Chief of the service; one Ph.D. clinical psychologist; four psychiatric social workers, one a supervisor; three senior public health nurses; a medical case worker; a rehabilitation counselor; a community services coordinator, for liaison work with a wide variety of community groups and agencies; and six secretarial-clerical personnel. Later another position, that of community worker, was added. The latter position was intended to be (and was) filled by a person from the community to be served. The position did not require any formal mental health or other professional training, but there was provision for the opportunity to learn a variety of helping roles, eventually leading to a career in mental health care.

A key decision was to recruit, to the greatest possible extent, Spanish-speaking personnel for all positions. Another decision was to recruit persons who had lived in, worked in, or otherwise "knew," identified with, and had strong commitment to the community to be served. These recruitment criteria were, of course, secondary to qualities of personal and professional competence and integrity.

The entire initial full-time staff of twenty-one was recruited over two and one half years time. Two of the first and most important positions to be filled were those of Community Mental Health Psychologist and Supervising Psychiatric Social Worker. Both positions were filled by persons of Mexican descent who had grown up in, been educated in and were well known in the East Los Angeles community. They provided much of the critical leadership and design of the program and embodied a rare combination of sociocultural awareness and concern and clinical competence. Fifteen of the staff were completely fluent in Spanish, four were conversant (with varying degrees of limitation) in Spanish, and three persons had a rudimentary knowledge of Spanish but enthusiastically and rapidly learned more. Ten of the twenty-two had been born in and had grown up in East Los Angeles. Twelve of the staff were Mexican-American, and two were of other Latin-American (Cuban and Peruvian) descent. There was a remarkably high degree of social, personal and professional involvement on the part of staff in the community itself, and with but a few exceptions, a very cohesive esprit de corps, somewhat in the nature of a shared, secular, missionary role. The characteristics of the professional staff obviated the use of translators in the diagnostic and therapeutic process, an awkward device which has been utilized experimentally in a New York City Mental Health program serving Puerto Ricans, ". . . as a functional solution to the language barriers."[11]

SERVICE QUARTERS

Six to twelve months of delay in making the program operational were incurred by the insistence on finding permanent quarters which would be in the heart of the residential East Los Angeles community, would be convenient for public and private transportation, and would be comfortable and inviting for staff as well as patients and their families. All of these criteria were met by the building selected, a former seminary of Spanish Colonial architectural design; tile roofed, with a long, arched front patio, and front and rear enclosed garden courtyards. All offices have windows, and the atmosphere is distinctly non-clinical and relatively non-institutional, thanks to the use of color and the aesthetics of the property itself. A much less convenient and far less comfortable and attractive building could have been occupied sooner, but the wait for the desired quarters, though frustrating at the time, was more than worthwhile in hindsight.

THE PROGRAM

The programs of the Los Angeles County Department of Mental Health are based firmly in a public health oriented philosophy of preventive services, which has stemmed from an acute awareness of the immensity of unmet mental health needs and the scarcity of resources to meet those needs in the Los Angeles metropolis.[12]

The translation of this philosophy into action in East Los Angeles, as elsewhere in the County, placed emphasis on professional mental health consultation, largely as defined by Caplan,[13] to a wide variety of community service agencies, including private and public welfare agencies, public and private (viz., parochial) schools, health agencies and professionals, law enforcement and probation officers, the clergy, and antipoverty programs. As backup to such consultation, short-term, crisis-oriented treatment is provided, utilizing individual, family, group and chemical therapy. Such treatment is reserved primarily for patients derived out of consultations: viz., those clients of consultees for whom specific, professional mental health services are indicated. In addition, referrals of patients are accepted directly from other agencies, as are walk-ins, but the effort is consistently made to utilize consultation in place of automatic acceptance into treatment of referrals.

Ad hoc consultation involves the discussion by phone or in person between one staff member (or more) of a care-taking or help-giving agency on the one hand, and a mental health professional on the other, concerning the mental health problems of one or more clients or patients. The emphasis in the East Los Angeles program was strongly on what Caplan defines as client centered consultation, although many agencies requested or would have preferred consultee or agency centered consultation.[13] Ongoing consultation, utilizing regular meetings at a given time and place with agency personnel, also usually client centered, was early established with a number of community agencies by staff of the East Los Angeles Mental Health Service.

Inservice training regarding mental health consultation consisted mainly of apprenticeship—the accompaniment of one professional staff member or more, having little or no experience in mental health consultation, with an experienced "senior consultant" in the consultation experience itself. The trainee or "alternate," as the trainee was called, would at first take an observer role, later a participant role, and then would eventually be ready to undertake independent consultation. This provided an intimate and comfortable teaching experience. Weekly meetings devoted to in-service training in mental health consultation were provided for all staff. Additionally, "alternates" requested and received weekly mental health consultation supervision by the designated director of mental health consultation services.

THE FIRST 200 PATIENTS

As already mentioned, short-term direct treatment of patients was planned as an integral part of the program. Fees were charged, based on a sliding scale related to the patient's economic status. The minimum fee was fifty cents and the maximum fifteen dollars per treatment session. Patients receiving welfare assistance did not pay. In order to gain a perspective on the population we were in fact serving, we surveyed characteristics of the first 200 consecutive patients accepted into direct treatment during the initial months of operation of the mental health service.

About four out of five of the patients were referred by care-taking agencies or personnel. The remainder were self-referred, having seen our sign in front of the building (printed in Spanish and English), or were referred by family or friends.

The sex ratio of the patients was 40% male, 60% female, compared to the community's overall distribution of 49% male, 51% female. The median age of the patients was 31 years, compared to the approximately 28 years for the community. The ethnic distribution of the 200 patients was as follows: Mexican-born, 32%; U.S.-born of Mexican descent, 54%; of other Latin-Americn descent, 4%; Anglo, Oriental and Negro combined, 10%. These figures were reassuringly indicative of representativeness from the community in regard to the patients we were serving. The overrepresentation of female to male patients is common to many psychiatric outpatient settings. Approximately 25% of the patients were diagnosed as psychotic (almost wholly schizophrenia), the remaining 75% representing a broad range of the conventional diagnostic categories.

Communication is a critical dimension of psychiatric treatment, and the language usage characteristics of the patients are important to note. A five-point scale was used to assess language usage of each patient. The everyday language usage of the patients of Mexican or other Latin American descent was noted by the therapist of each patient. The distribution was approximately 28% Spanish-speaking only, 11% Spanish-speaking mainly, 21% bilingual (about equal usage of Spanish and English), 27% English-speaking mainly, and 13% English-speaking only. This finding that about two out of five Spanish-surnamed patients spoke only or mainly Spanish corresponds with the figure obtained on a nonpatient Mexican-American population surveyed in East Los Angeles in a prior and independent study.[7] This fact also tended to confirm the representativeness of our patient population from the community served.

Our work as clinicans in the East Los Angeles Mental Health Service had been preceded by experience in psychotherapeutic work with Anglo middle-class and low-income patients in both public and private settings. We believe strongly from such experience that Mexican-American patients respond at least as well as their Anglo counterparts when they are offered professionally expert treatment in a context of cultural and linguistic familiarity and acceptance. Indeed, as noted by Morales previously (1967), alleged "cultural factors" may often be overinterpreted in a stereotypic manner, to the detriment of an adequate clinical understanding of the Spanish-speaking patient by the Anglo therapist.[14] It is expected that future controlled investigations will more definitively test this clinical impression.

We cannot at this point assess the influence of the overall program, including the consultation and education services, on the East Los Angeles community. We do feel safe in asserting that the program has been as effective as those of the Los Angeles County Mental Health Department established in nine other ethnic and non-ethnic communities of low to middle socio-economic status in Los Angeles County.

We presume that this was made possible by the careful planning involved, and the special characteristics and dedication of the staff.

REFERENCES

1. Samora, J., and Lamanna, R. A.: Mexican-Americans in a Midwest Metropolis: A Study of East Chicago, Advance Report 8, Mexican-American Study Project, sponsored by the Ford Foundation and the UCLA Graduate School of Business Administration, 1967.
2. U.S. Bureau of the Census. U.S. Censuses of Population and Housing: 1960. Census Tracts. Final Report PHC(1)-82. U.S. Government Printing Office, Washington, D.C., 1962.
3. U.S. Bureau of the Census. Current Population Reports, Series P-23, No. 18, Characteristics of the South and East Los Angeles Areas: November, 1965, U.S. Government Printing Office, Washington, D.C., 1966.
4. Social and Educational Problems of Rural and Urban Mexican-American Youth. Proceedings of the 12th Annual Southwest Conference. Sponsored by Occidental College in the City of Los Angeles (April 6, 1963), and the Rosenberg Foundation.
5. Fogel, W.: Education and Income of Mexican-Americans in the Southwest, Advance Report 1, Mexican-American Study Project, sponsored by the Ford Foundation and the UCLA Graduate School of Business Administration.
6. Lukens, E.: Factors Affecting Utilization of Mental Health Services by Mexican-Americans, an Exploratory Study. Sponsored by the Mental Health Development Commission of the Los Angeles Welfare Planning Council and the School of Social Welfare, University of California, Berkeley. June, 1963.
7. Karno, M., and Edgerton, R. B.: Perception of Mental Illness in a Mexican-American Community, Archives of General Psychiatry **20**:233-238 (Feb.), 1969.
8. Edgerton, R. B., Karno, M., and Fernandez, I.: Curanderismo in the Metropolis: The Diminished Role of Folk Psychiatry among Los Angeles Mexican-Americans, Amer. J. Psychother. **XXIV**(1):124-134 (Jan.), 1970.
9. Karno, M., Ross, R. N., and Caper, R.A.: Mental Health Roles of Physicians in a Mexican-American Community, Community Mental Health Journal **5**(1), 1969.
10. Karno, M.: The Enigma of Ethnicity in a Psychiatric Clinic, Archives of General Psychiatry **14**:516-520, (May), 1966.
11. Bluestone, H., Bisi, R., and Katz, A. J.: The Establishment of a Mental Health Service in a Predominantly Spanish-Speaking Neighborhood of New York City, Behavioral Neuropsychiatry **1**:12-16 (Aug.), 1969.
12. Brickman, H. R.: Community Mental Health—The Metropolitan View, Amer. J. Pub. Health **57**:641-650 (April), 1967.
13. Caplan, G.: Principles of Preventive Psychiatry, New York: Basic Books, 1964.
14. Morales, A.: Distinguishing Psychodynamic Factors From Cultural Factors in the Treatment of the Spanish Speaking Patient, The Psychiatric Bulletin of the Gilfillan Clinic, Rosemead, Calif., Spring, 1967.

CHAPTER 24 BARRIERS TO MENTAL HEALTH SERVICES: A JAPANESE-AMERICAN AND MEXICAN-AMERICAN DILEMMA

MANUEL MIRANDA
HARRY H. L. KITANO

INTRODUCTION

When ethnic minority communities encounter the majority community in urban settings, the conflict in values and cultures presents monumental problems for those attempting to provide social services as well as those in need of assistance. No small part of this difficulty has been experienced in the mental health area, where traditionally trained mental health workers are continually confronted by clients possessing markedly different life experiences and cultural values. Questions as to where the ultimate responsibility lies in overcoming the barriers to effective delivery of mental health services to the ethnic minority communites perplex even the most knowledgeable of professionals.

The problem is exacerbated if ethnic groups refrain from accepting the use of mental health services currently available. In line with this, one may ask whether they are not using the services because of greater mental health within the culture, or whether the lack of utilization is based on other reasons. Part of the problem is to then define mental health.

While disagreement exists as to the "best" definition of mental health, it is generally accepted that mental health includes people's feelings of worth in the context of the total cultural and societal system as well as within the identifiable groups to which they belong. Therefore, the absence of opportunities to meet basic and culturally determined needs in a society in which ethnicity may be viewed as a barrier toward mobility constitutes a gap between individual aspiration and the feeling of effectiveness. This gap thus becomes the source of a great deal of mental anguish and frequently leads to serious emotional disturbance.

Viewing psychological functioning from this broader definition as opposed to the myopic "illness model" (Albee, 1969; Szasz, 1960), it becomes apparent that the ethnic minorities are generally more hampered in fulfilling their psychological and social potential relative to their nonethnic counterparts (Cobb, 1972; Coles, 1966). This problem continues to exist because of the tendency of mental health professionals to concentrate their efforts in areas that ignore the ethnic position.

This chapter attempts to discuss the problems encountered by two ethnic minority populations in their efforts to bridge the cultural gap through use of mental health facilities. The underutilization of mental health facilities by the Mexican-American and Japanese-American populations has been well documented (Padilla & Ruiz, 1974; Kitano, 1969). The fact that these two populations exhibit the lowest rates of utilization of mental health services relative to other ethnic minority groups (Sue & McKinney, 1975; Karno & Edgerton, 1969) provided the impetus to write an article discussing the significant commonality of avoidance within these two populations.

But even though the two groups are similar in terms of their underrepresentation, they are vastly different in such variables as size, history, and culture. Glib explanations attributing their infrequent use of mental health services to *their culture* may have to be reexamined.

For example, according to the 1970 U.S. Census there were 591,290 Japanese Americans in the United States, with the heaviest concentrations in Hawaii (217, 307) and California (213,280). In contrast, the same census period reported more than five million residents as being Americans of Mexican descent, with almost 80% of them residents of the five southwestern states of Arizona, California, Colorado, New Mexico, and Texas.

The median total family income of the Japanese Americans in 1970 was $13,511, as compared with $7,334 for those with a Spanish surname. In terms of income below the poverty level, 7.5% of the Japanese Americans and 25.0% of those with a Spanish surname were in this category. Median years of education showed that for those Japanese Americans, 16 years of age or older, the years of school completed was 12.6, while only 48% of those with a Spanish surname have completed high school.

THE JAPANESE AMERICAN

The most common reaction among friends and fellow professionals concerning Japanese-American mental illness is to ask, "Is there any?" For it has become a matter of popular opinion that this minority is currently viewed as a "problem-free" group, including the opinion that they have low records of deviant behavior including very little mental illness.

However, the actual evidence of mental illness (or its counterpart, mental health) remains "data to be gathered," and perhaps a true incidence of the phenomena is probably impossible to attain. We refer to the "funneling effect" (Kitano, 1969) whereby rates of mental illness (as well as

other "problem behavior") are related to the level of observation and measurement so that different judgments are made by looking at various sides of the funnel. For example, the "true incidence" of mental illness (assuming that there are reliable and valid measures of the behavior) may be at the top or wide end of the funnel whereas the "official rates," generally recorded by hospitals, clinics, and health agencies, may be measuring the problem from the narrow or bottom end.

In an effort to obtain estimates of the incidence of mental health problems among the Japanese Americans in the United States, Kitano (1969) designed a study to obtain measurements from various observational levels. He asked Japanese-American social workers, psychologists, and psychiatrists to delve into their own background of growing up in an ethnic community and to use this *participant observational* technique to ascertain their diagnosis of mental health needs in the ethnic community. The respondents were unanimous in their observation that many Japanese Americans with whom they had been associated could have used professional services, but (as far as they knew) none had ever gone for such treatment. One of the most common problem areas revolved around parent-child and husband-wife difficulties. As one psychiatrist commented:

Every time I give a public lecture (usually sponsored by a church or service club) on family problems, sexual information, or child rearing, the place is packed and they ask all kinds of questions. Some of the questions are remarkably naive and others appear to indicate quite a bit of conflict but I'm sure the questioners will never go [directly] for professional services. (Kitano, 1969, p. 260)

The generalization was that there would be high interest and many signs of "needs" within the Japanese-American community (including good attendance at lectures and programs) but virtually no follow-up. Therefore, from one position on the funnel, the evidence is that Japanese Americans are a "need group," but that they do not use the professional services.

Support for the generalization that the Japanese Americans do not often use mental health resources comes from another level of the funnel. Family service agencies and child guidance clinics provide another view of "problems." We attempted to study Japanese Americans using family services and child guidance clinics in Los Angeles several years ago and found less than five active cases. Current information indicates almost no change, so that the generalization that Japanese Americans seldom use larger community resources is a valid one.

Data from California and Hawaii indicates Japanese Americans are disproportionately represented in the state mental hospitals. For example, data from the California State Department of Mental Hygiene for 1950, 1960, and 1964 shows that the Japanese American (and also the Mexican American) were among the lowest groups hospitalized (Kitano, 1969). More recent data from Hawaii also supports the notion that rates of hospitalization for mental illness remain low. For example, although Japanese Americans comprised 28.3% of the Islands' population, they represented only 10.9% of the inpatients and 11.8% of the outpatients with the Hawaii State Department of Mental Health (1974).

A study by Sue and McKinney (1975) in the state of Washington confirms the findings that Asian Americans underutilized community mental health facilities; further, of those using professional services, 50% dropped out after the first session. For example, the Japanese, Chinese, and Filipinos combined represented only 0.6% of the patients while comprising 2.38% of the population of the state of Washington. Therefore, the data is consistent with the notion that Japanese Americans are not seen by the community mental health agencies in any significant numbers.

THE MEXICAN AMERICAN

There appears to be little quesiton that Mexican Americans, for the most part, reject traditionally-oriented mental health services. In a study performed in California, where the Mexican-American population was estimated to be between 9% and 10%, Karno and Edgerton (1969) found that Mexican Americans accounted for only 2.2% of State Hospital admissions, 3.4% of State Mental Hygiene Clinic ad-

missions, 0.9% of the admissions to State University psychiatric facilities, and 2.3% of inpatient admissions to facilities jointly supported by state and local agencies. In addition, Mexican Americans made up only 3.3% of the inpatient population of California's state hospitals for the mentally ill.

In an earlier study, Jaco (1960) analyzed the incidence of psychosis recorded by public and private mental health facilities in the state of Texas during the years 1951 and 1952. Jaco discovered that relative to expected frequencies (as determined by representative populations), Anglos registered three times as many cases of psychosis relative to Mexican Americans. Jaco's conclusion that it was the "warm, supportive and reasonably secure" aspects of the Mexican-American subculture that accounted for the low identification of psychosis appears untenable when contrasted with studies describing the numerous "high stress indicators" existing within Mexican-American communities (Torrey, 1968 and 1969). The fact that limited education, lower income, inadequate housing, and limited communication ability with the dominant culture exist within the Mexican-American barrios strongly supports the contention that the true (though undetected) incidence of mental disturbance will be higher in these communities relative to those of the Anglo.

Bloom (1966) analyzed the first admission data for all public and private psychiatric facilities within a selected Colorado county. Mexican Americans were shown to be significantly underrepresented in both facilities, with major differences (as to be expected) attributable to the private settings. Bloom concluded that the lower rates of Mexican-American admissions into private institutions could be attributed not only to the economic barrier presented by these facilities but also the greater tolerance of deviant behavior in the Mexican-American communities.

The belief that Mexican Americans tend not to use mental health facilities because of their greater tolerance of the occurrence of deviant behavior, or that they define mental illness in significantly different ways relative to Anglos, finds little support from attitudinal studies conducted in this area. Karno and Edgerton (1969) gathered quantitative data on the perceptions, definitions, and responses to mental illness held by Anglo and Mexican-American residents of the two East Los Angeles communities. Their major approach was to conduct systematic household interviews. Analysis of their data led to the following conclusions:

> We do not believe that the underrepresentation of Mexican Americans in psychiatric treatment facilities reflects a lesser incidence of mental illness than that found in other ethnic populations in this county. For example, our data indicate that large numbers of Mexican Americans in East Los Angeles seek treatment for obviously psychiatric disorders from family physicians. In responses to our interviews, it might be added, Mexican Americans in our study expressed the conviction that they often suffer from psychiatric disorder.

An additional contention frequently offered to explain the low utilization of mental health services by Mexican Americans is the existence of *naturalistic* systems within the Mexican-American communities. This subtle reference to the *culture of poverty* has motivated many mental health administrators to allow the *Mexicans* to do their thing, as a substitute for using what power they have at their disposal for the development of improved intervention techniques. People with little money and little or no ability to influence change in social service delivery systems by necessity turn to other people, since they may be the only resource. The point, however, is whether this turning to *one's own* is the preferred solution, as opposed to the only available alternative.

Support for the position that naturalistic mental health systems do not explain low utilization rates among Mexican Americans is found in a study conducted by Edgerton, Karno, and Fernandez (1970). These researchers studied the existence of faith healing within a Mexican-American community to determine the extent that folk psychiatry was being practiced. While acknowledging its existence, these investigators felt that the use of the system was minimal and that it could not be used to explain the underutilization of health services. A similar conclusion was reached by Nall and Spielberger (1967) in their study

of tubercular Mexican Americans in Texas.

The underrepresentation of Mexican Americans in mental health facilities must be considered from the perspective of an interacting complex of social and cultural factors. Certainly to be considered within this complex is the tremendous obstacle that *bureaucratic-like* mental health agencies present to the Mexican American. The series of embarrassing questions and forced exposure that Mexican-American clients must confront in seeking assistance precipitate feelings of vulnerability that can immobilize their initial motivation to seek therapy. This self-esteem reducing process, which is frequently felt by the Anglo patient as well, is greatly heightened within the Mexican American. The compounding of other obstacles (for example, language, unfamiliarity with agencies, fear, and hostility toward Anglos) precipitates a crisis within the individual that often requires Herculean efforts to overcome. The answer thus stems more from the necessity to understand those components of the system maintaining the barriers, as opposed to conducting inquiries into the personality deficits of the Mexican American.

It therefore appears that although we have two widely disparate ethnic groups, they are similar in their nonuse of social service facilities. The question as to why leads to an analysis of the service delivery system and the inherent barriers within its processes.

PROBLEMS OF SERVICE DELIVERY

The problems of service delivery can be analyzed in a number of ways. Gilbert (1972) suggests that the problem can be organized around the following: fragmentation, inaccessibility, discontinuity, and unaccountability. In addition to these four general system problems, several specific factors exist that may help to explain the nonuse of facilities by the Mexican-American and Japanese-American population. Two of the more likely factors to cause problems are the *lack of information* and *different ethnic styles.* The interaction among all six of these factors is hypothesized to explain ethnic nonparticipation. These six categories are not mutually exclusive and have some degree of overlap, but it is our belief that they provide the general framework for the following analysis.

Lack of information

Lack of information (including misinformation) about mental health services is a major issue for ethnic communities. Misperceptions and ignorance about the *psychiatric culture* pervade most levels of Mexican-American and Japanese-American life so that they can be termed *unknowledgeable* when dealing with social and emotional problems and professional services. In contrast, other groups can be termed "knowledgeable"; for example, their social gatherings and family get-togethers may be heavily laced with psychological talk; they may discuss who is in therapy; there may be much "parlor diagnosing" of emotional problems, and there is usually a relative, friend, or family member who is in psychology, psychiatry, social work, or some other related counseling profession. Such a background provides information and a *mental health culture* so that there is familiarity with the social services and what they entail.

The Mexican American and the Japanese American are not an integral part of this network. There remains an uneasiness about discussing psychological and mental health problems, and if such a topic comes up, it is often dealt with through uneasy laughter or by referring to a wise old uncle who has all the answers. As a consequence, unrealistic expectations often arise about counseling, therapy, and such practical matters as cost, who to go to, how to get there, the kinds of treatment, different techniques, and therapeutic effectiveness. Therefore, many who might want to seek help simply don't know how to go about it, and if they did find a way, they might not remain, since the surrounding support systems may be lacking.

Although there is a current rise in the number of Mexican Americans and Japanese Americans entering the mental health professions, it is in the beginning phase. Some attempt to educate the groups about mental health is mandatory if services are to be effective; or, to take the opposite tack, some attempt to educate the professionals about these groups and where they are may be even more important.

The lack of familiarity compounds the problem of options. Ignorance and misperceptions may create anxieties that preclude the realistic use of mental health services. Rather than viewing suggestions about treatment as a number of options, ethnics may feel forced to attend, which then creates other kinds of problems.

Ethnic styles

Ethnic styles refers to those aspects of ethnic behavior concerning mental health and mental illness (including diagnosis and treatment) that limit the use of professional help. Ethnic styles and the lack of information are closely related.

The recognition and subsequent definition of mental health problems is one of the critical steps toward the use or nonuse of professional services. In a study of mental illness among Japanese Americans in the United States, Hawaii, and Japan, Kitano (1970) found that there was little initial recognition of mental illness in modern-day clinical terms; rather there was the belief on the part of family and friends that an individual was malingering or just not behaving correctly. Therefore, the usual mode of treatment was to lecture, to moralize, and to punish; when these techniques failed, friends, relatives, and neighbors were called in for their advice. More often than not they would offer the same prescriptions, so that one plausible explanation for the lack of ethnic clients in agencies deals with a differing ethnic style. But it would be an error to attribute the major reason for the avoidance to ethnic styles since this remains but one of a number of factors.

Another ethnic style relates to the concept of trouble. Visible minorities such as the Japanese American and the Mexican American have attempted to adapt to racism and discrimination through a *low posture* and being as little trouble as possible to the majority community. The existence of mental illness is associated with trouble, which therefore is something to hide or to be explained away in some other fashion. One obvious consequence of this would be the broad denial of problems if this were directly asked of the patient.

Fragmentation

Operationally, fragmentation implies an ineffective organization of available mental health services. Providing the appropriate services or techniques in handling an emotional problem is certainly a step in the right direction, but if these services are organized in such a fashion as to tax the client's understanding and/or patience, the effectiveness of service delivery is seriously reduced. Because most community mental health centers are organized along the lines of the medical model, questions are raised about their appropriateness. Consistency from a nonethnic perspective may be viewed as fragmentation from the ethnic position.

For example, in many mental health centers it is standard operating procedure to screen the potential client through an intake worker, who then refers the client to a therapist, who often will schedule several hours of diagnostic testing before initiating the therapeutic relationship. This rather laborious and time-consuming procedure often leaves ethnic minority patients feeling alienated and unable to comprehend why no one seems interested in responding to their immediate concerns. This, from the ethnic minority perspective, is fragmentation.

More often than not, the Mexican-American mental health client complains of impersonalization and detachment when describing experiences with mental health centers (Kline, 1969). Many Spanish-speaking mental health workers point to the failure of traditional mental health services to *personalize* their relationships with Mexican-American clients. As a result of this, it becomes less than surprising that most Mexican-American clients reject the therapeutic process as confusing and inappropriate (Karno & Edgerton, 1969).

More often than not, the Mexican-Ameri- that detract from the immediate implementation of a personal relationship must be given serious attention. The failure to develop a centralized relationship (that is, a specific and continuous therapeutic relationship) increases the risk of reinforcing

negative expectations of an aloof and distant process in the solution of their (the Mexican-American clients') problems. The importance of this issue is underlined by the fact that in some settings half of the Mexican-American clients do not return for a second or third appointment following their initial contact (Miranda, 1974). The need to develop a culturally relevant intake process that would minimize confusion and maximize the feeling of personal involvement appears vital.

Similar statements can be made about Japanese Americans. The shifting from one professional to another is not a part of the Japanese-American orientation; in fact the Japanese-American social structure encourages staying with one person (Nakane, 1970; Kitano, 1974), so that fragmentation can easily be interpreted as rejection or to mean that the therapist does not care. Further, the Japanese-American system encourages personalism through proper introductions, which are often with the *heads* of institutions, so that if the client is seen by professionals other than the *head* there may be feelings of rejection. It comes as no surprise that so many Japanese Americans do not return for their second appointment (Sue & McKinney, 1975).

As for the language barrier, much has been written about its importance in establishing the therapeutic relationship (Cohen, 1970). This variable undoubtedly has an immeasurable effect in facilitating the task at hand. In addition to language, the availability of mental health personnel whose own cultural heritage is similar to the client's holds much significance (Bloombaum, Yamamoto, & James, 1968). With increased awareness of these important variables, many mental health facilities have actively sought to employ bilingual-bicultural mental health workers. But more often than not, ethnics are restricted to community liaison work or to function as interpreters during the initial screening. The failure to utilize bilingual-bicultural staff in a centralized relationship results in a disruptive process that seriously contributes to the ethnic client's inability to form a positive and continuous attachment to the therapeutic relationship.

Discontinuity

Those few Chicanos and Japanese Americans electing to seek mental health services frequently report a sense of unreality about the process. If the ethnic client is fortunate enough to obtain a professional who is sympathetic to the presenting problem, a very large gap continues to exist between the activities occurring during the therapy hour and the activities the client must face upon returning to the community. This problem is obviously not limited to therapy with ethnics but its seriousness is greatly magnified for the ethnic minority client. To discuss how one *feels* about a situation in order to bring suppressed feelings into consciousness is fine. But the expression of feelings is not enough. The therapist must provide a linkage between feelings and some eventual course of action, which also takes into account the lack of realistic alternatives faced by visible, powerless minorities. We are not advocating the *concrete versus abstract myth,* which is held to account for much therapeutic failure among ethnics. We emphasize that most ethnic minorities are severely limited in acquiring those resources necessary to overcome sheer survival problems, so that a focus on emotional issues may almost seem a luxury. To suggest to individuals with adequate financial and other supports that they should accept responsibility for their lives and act in accordance with their personal desires and wishes is one thing. It is an entirely different matter to make this recommendation to an individual overwhelmed by *realistic* perceptions of powerlessness.

The reality problems faced by most ethnic minorities in this country are staggering. To assume that the expression of feelings will eventually result in a rewarding experience (as is often assumed when dealing with middle-class neurotics) is myopic. The search for effective behaviors, a realistic look at alternatives, the development of an identity in which the *rewards* are to identify with and to become what one can never be (for example, a blonde, blue-eyed Anglo), an understanding of racism, and the development of a behavioral repertoire that will enable an individual to advance and still not antagonize the majority group are of higher priority than the sheer expression of feelings. It is incumbent upon the therapist to assist in the development of feasible behavioral alternatives in addition to serving as a catalyst for the surfacing of suppressed feelings. Failure to work toward this continuity of affect and action generally results in client frustration and eventual termination of therapy.

In terms of a continuous treatment plan, an open-door scheduling procedure has the most productive results. Since the life-stress problems with which most ethnics must deal frequently precipitate emotional setbacks, mental health centers should be prepared to maintain a continuous interaction with the ethnic client. Most ethnic clients do not have the luxury of postponing significant decisions until they have had time to engage in a consultative relationship. The ability to remain flexible as an accommodation to the life-style of the ethnic client provides a positive perception of the mental health clinic's relevance. Unlike their middle-class white counterparts, most ethnic clients have more to deal with than attitudinal issues (for example, self-concept). The development of workable solutions requires a constant reevaluation and reaffirmation of behavioral objectives. Consultation often cannot *wait until the next appointment.* Many ethnic clients refuse to deal with barriers indigenous to traditional mental health clinics unless their problems have reached crisis proportions (Philippus, 1971), so that the relevant orientation must be consistent with this crisis state.

The problems facing ethnic clients are generally multiple and complex, so that they require the services of a number of agencies. But a *single agency–specialized treatment* model necessitates referrals for the treatment of multiple problems, which may be viewed as rejection and discontinuity by the Mexican-American and Japanese-American client. The issue may be resolved through the development of a multi-service agency that provides the continuity lacking in the separate agency–separate problem approach.

Inaccessibility

For years the only mental health facilities used by ethnic minorities (and as a last resort) were the state mental hospitals. They were typically large and isolated and, in spite of their large size, constantly overcrowded. Instead of treatment, they offered custodial care. Many patients lived out their lives in them. A major departure from this situation came with the passage of the Mental Retardation Facilities and Community Mental Health Center Construction Act of 1963. This act, with subsequent amendments, made it possible for communities throughout the nation to develop comprehensive mental health programs. The goal was to make these services accessible to *every* resident!

Money is a severe problem in the development of mental health centers in areas heavily populated by ethnic minorities. Federal grants for the construction and staffing of these centers falls far short of meeting all the costs. Construction projects have averaged, for all centers, $1,500,000; and Federal aid has covered only about 30% of this (Segal, 1973). The cost of operating a center, as estimated by applicants for Federal assistance, runs to about $750,000 a year; no more than 40% of this is covered by Federal funds for salaries. Matching funds, thus, must be provided both for building the center and for paying staff salaries.

The low tax base in most areas containing ethnic populations leads to some serious problems in meeting the matching funds obligation. In some cases, communities heavily populted by ethnic minorities have had to hold a series of special elections in order to implement a special tax to support a center. The specter of increased taxation on family budgets already strained to the breaking point has prevented the development of centers in the most needy areas.

The inability to build centers in areas with low tax bases has led to the incorporation of these areas by large centralized agencies located in middle-class, urban areas. The inadequacy of this alternative has been discussed by numerous writers (for example, Torrey, 1969). The geographic isolation of these centers frequently necessitates a lengthy bus ride for residents in the poorer sections of the involved area. Not only does the distance impede the frequency of self-referrals, but

the cost of transportation and the lack of adequate child care further serves to decrease the utilization of the centralized facilities.

A second major problem in ethnic minority mental health is the lack of an effective professional working staff. A disproportionate share of psychiatrists, psychologists, social workers, and other mental health personnel are white, monolingual, and located in middle-class to upper-middle-class urban areas. Those administrators electing to work in areas populated by ethnic minorities find it extremely difficult to put together a competent basic staff. The alternative has been that of hiring expensive part-time consultants who attempt to monitor the work of indigenous nonprofessionals. Two centers known to the present writers that are attempting to meet the needs of the Mexican-American and Japanese-American communities are entirely dependent (because of limited resources) on the services of university students!

In other centers, individuals without professional education or training are being asked to fill jobs usually restricted to trained professionals. We do not wish to downgrade the effectiveness of indigenous paraprofessionals, since much has been written about their effectiveness in providing communication links with the ethnic minority communities, but it is disconcerting to witness the ease with which mental health administrators assign complex mental health tasks to people poorly prepared to handle them. The romanticizing of the indigenous paraprofessional has led many mental health professionals to withdraw from ethnic communities.

It is our opinion that the ethnic communities are *not* asking that the nonethnic professional abandon the problem. What is being asked is that well-trained and experienced mental health professionals provide assistance as well as an opportunity for the development of competent ethnic minority mental health workers. This training cannot occur in a vacuum. The need for highly specialized services in education, speech pathology, neurological disabilities, and vocational training cannot be provided solely by indigenous paraprofessionals. The withdrawal of these specialists from the ethnic minority communities simply contributes to the multitude of problems that every ethnic minority must confront.

A more subtle issue involving inaccessibility deals with the relationship between the majority-group professional and the minority-group client. Chin (1974) refers to the *filters* that lead to selective perceptions when the American views mainland China, and the reciprocal image that the Chinese wish the American to see. Similarly, the training, experiences, and techniques of the professionals filter their perceptions of Mexican Americans and Japanese Americans, and these groups also respond by allowing only selective portions of themselves to be seen by the professional. This interaction may be central to understanding the inaccessibility issue.

For example, past research, limited experiences, and mass media have generally influenced and filtered majority-group perceptions of the Mexican American and Japanese American. The general impressions are often stated in stereotypes—closely knit families, nonverbal people, unlikely candidates for psychological treatment. The Mexican-American and Japanese-American filter may reinforce the stereotypes since the following may be the image they desire to show to the majority—invisible minorities who can take care of their own emotional and psychological problems, and groups who tend to mind their own business when it comes to personal problems. From our point of view *all groups* have similar problems and needs, but the filters (from both sides) allow only selected parts to be seen, so that services that can be beneficial for both parties are neglected and unused.

Unaccountability

The issue of unaccountability refers to insensitive decision-making processes in existing systems of mental health services. The fact that virtually all ethnic minority communities have experienced difficulty in influencing these processes calls for a serious reevaluation of the existing leadership structure in community mental health.

In an excellent analysis of the antecedents leading to unaccountability in the mental health field, Lerner (1972) focuses on the insidious process of problem distortion created by the bureaucratization of service delivery systems. The complexity and enormity of providing mental health services in a large urban area is cited as the justification for bureaucratic models as the most efficient way to organize large staffs with diverse talents. Central to bureaucracy is the premise that functions should be specialized and standardized by assigning duties consistent with a *master plan.* Top-level administration assumes the task of defining program ends and the means to obtain them, while conjointly allocating responsibility to frontline personnel for focusing on program means. But few frontline personnel participate in defining the goals.

More realistically, as pointed out by Lerner, "powerful administrators name the collective end without defining it and then construct overall plans cafeteria style by choosing the techniques that they currently prefer and rationalizing these as requisite means to the undefined end" (Lerner, 1972, p. 167). The obvious implication here is that both the means and ends (that is, therapeutic outcome) for handling client problems is defined and determined by the exisitng values set by program administrators. A more irrational and undemocratic process would be difficult to conceive.

The result of this type of bureaucracy is to develop subcomponents that function to handle discrete, specific, and highly-defined problems (that is, family therapy or crisis intervention). The difficulty in handling a client who fails to neatly fall into these therapeutic subsets generally results in frustration, or even rejection by the bureaucratized system. The individuals most likely to experience these shortcomings in the system are the clients and those staff members who must deal directly with them. Unfortunately, these are the very people within the bureaucracy with the least amount of power to correct the deficiencies. The investment of power in an administrative structure that has minimal or no contact with the *frontline* realities of therapeutic encounter leads to serious distortions of existing reality. The fact that Mexican-American and Japanese-American clients have felt this distortion of reality with virtually no recourse to the system perpetuating it constitutes unaccountability in its most malignant form.

More recently, efforts have been made to include consumers in the composition of mental health boards. While applauding this effort in principle, experience has taught us that in actuality these token representations have distorted beyond recognition the definition of consumer. To illustrate the point, one of the authors was asked to join a board as a *consumer* representative in spite of the fact that he held a doctorate in clinical psychology and was functioning as a therapist in a university setting! When he attempted to point this out to the Chairperson of the Board, he was quickly assured that *consumer* simply meant someone who was not providing mental health services in a community mental health agency. The Chairperson enthusiastically pointed to a long list of health service personnel serving as consumer representatives on other mental health boards throughout the country. Efforts to convince the Chairperson of the necessity of selecting individuals receiving, or who had recieved, services as truly representative consumers were met with accusations of subversive efforts to undermine the system, or soft-headed liberalism.

It appears to the present writers that the restoration of accountability in mental health requires a redistribution of the input sources that lead to program development. The decision as to how services should be provided, as well as what they should consist of, requires an equal *say so* among administrators, service providers, and consumers. Substituting an authoritarian hierarchy with one emphasizing a collegial relationship would greatly assist in the establishment of meaningful external responsiveness and open internal communication.

SUMMARY

We have analyzed two groups widely dissimilar in ethnic backgrounds, and presented a number of hypotheses concerning their nonuse of mental health facilities. The hypotheses included lack of information, ethnic styles, fragmentation, inaccessibility, discontinuity, and unaccountability. Although there is some empirical data to support the hypotheses, no systematic study testing the variables and their interaction has been conducted, so that the generalizations remain in the *to be studied* stage.

Nevertheless, the choice of two different groups, the Mexican Americans and the Japanese Americans, helps to focus on the problem of service delivery. If we had only taken one group for analysis, the temptation to place the blame on the culture would be high, as has generally occurred in other studies in this area. Those studies focusing on the Mexican American have pointed to the problem of poverty, to the *culture,* or to their general *inabilities* that create the barriers toward a more effective use of services. But many Japanese Americans are not poor; they are well educated, and their culture is also different. And yet they, like the Mexican Americans, do not use the available services. It is our hypothesis that the major responsibility lies with the purveyors of the delivery system. It is their rigidities, their models, their concepts, and their attitudes that create the barriers for the two groups. It may also be a commentary on our bureaucratic ineptness when newer proposals or models for service delivery, attempting to break the old modes, require approval from those very individuals responsible for the design of the present structures. More specifically, advancement of frontline workers to high-level administrative positions requires a certain adherence to the *party line.* Those individuals stressing the inequities within the system are rarely given the reins of power required for meaningful change. The situation thus becomes one in which those individuals least able to understand the need for change are in the best position to institute it!

It is difficult to remain neutral and objective social scientists, waiting for all of the facts before recommending any programs, since such a stance supports a tragic status quo. We assume that ethnic groups have as much, if not even more, mental health problems as the majority, yet our evidence clearly indicates that they do not avail themselves of the resources that are rightfully theirs. Therefore, ethnics are not able to meaningfully join in the argument about the effectiveness of mental health services or whether individual or group therapy is more efficient. All of these *in-house* issues appear as luxuries from the Mexican-American and Japanese-American perspective, since we are given little opportunity to participate and to truly understand their implications or how one changes their direction.

REFERENCES

Albee, G. W. The relation of conceptual models of disturbed behavior to institutions and manpower requirements. In F. N. Armhoff, E. A. Rubinstein, & J.C. Speisman (Eds.), *Manpower for mental health*. Chicago: Aldine, 1969.

Bloom, B. L. A census tract analysis of socially deviant behaviors. *Multivariate Behavioral Research*, 1966, *1*, 307-320.

Bloombaum, M., Yamamoto, J., & James, Q. Cultural stereotyping among psychotherapists. *Journal of Counseling and Clinical Psychology*, 1968, *32* (1), 99.

Chin, R. Theory and practice of pedagogy in the People's Republic of China. Seminar paper given at the University of California at Los Angeles, November 4, 1974.

Cobb, C. W. Community mental health services and the lower socioeconomic classes: A summary of research literature on outpatient treatment. *American Journal of Orthopsychiatry*, 1972, *42*(3), 404-413.

Cohen, R. E. Preventive mental health program for ethnic minority populations: A case in point. Paper presented at the meetings of the XXXIX Congreso Internacional de Americanistas, 1970, Lima, Peru.

Coles, R. Racial problems in psychotherapy. *Current Psychiatric Therapies,* 1966, *6,* 110-113.

Edgerton, R. B., Karno, M., & Fernandez, I. Curanderismo in the metropolis: The diminishing role of folk-psychiatry among Los Angeles Mexican Americans. *American Journal of Psychotherapy*, 1970, *24*(1), 124-134.

Gilbert, N. Assessing service delivery methods: Some unsettled questions. *Welfare in Review*, 1972, *10*(3), 1-9.

Jaco, E. G. *The social epidemiology of mental disorders: A psychiatric survey of Texas.* New York: Russell Sage Foundation, 1960.

Karno, M., & Edgerton, R. B. Perception of mental illness in a Mexican-American community. *Archives of General Psychiatry*, 1969, *20*(2), 233-238.

Kitano, H. H. L. Japanese-American mental illness. In S. Plog & R. Edgerton (Eds.), *Changing perspectives on mental illness*. New York: Holt, Rinehart and Winston, 1969, pp. 248-256.

Kitano, H. H. L. Mental illness in four cultures. *The Journal of Social Psychology*, 1970, *80,* 121-134.

Kline, L. Y. Some factors in the psychiatric treatment of Spanish Americans. *American Journal of Psychiatry*, 1969, *125*(12), 1674-1681.

Miranda, M. R. Acculturation and drop-out rates among Mexican-American psychiatric clients, Unpublished research study, 1974.

Nakane, C. *Japanese society.* Berkeley: University of California Press, 1970.

Nall, F. C., & Spielberg, J. Social and cultural factors in the responses of Mexican Americans to medical treatment. *Journal of Health and Social Behavior,* 1967, *8*(4), 299-308.

Padilla, A. M., & Ruiz, R. A. *Latino mental health: A review of literature.* Washington, D.C.: National Institute of Mental Health, 1973.

Philippus, M. J. Successful and unsuccessful approaches to mental health services for an urban Hispano-American population. *Journal of Public Health,* 1971, *61*(4), 820-830.

Sue, S., & McKinney, H. Asian-American clients in the community mental health services. *American Journal of Orthopsychiatry*, 1975, *45*(1), 111-118.

Szasz, T. S. The myth of mental illness. *American Psychologist*, 1960, *15*, 113-118.

Torrey, E. F. The case for the indigenous therapist. *Archives of General Psychiatry*, 1969, *20*, 365-373.

Torrey, E. F. Psychiatric services for Mexican Americans. Unpublished manuscript, 1968.

CHAPTER 25 VALUE IDENTIFICATION AND PSYCHIATRIC DISABILITY: AN ANALYSIS INVOLVING AMERICANS OF MEXICAN DESCENT

HORACIO FABREGA, Jr.
CAROLE ANN WALLACE

The demographic features and value identifications of a sample of psychiatric outpatients and a probability sample of nonpatients are compared. Both groups were Americans of Mexican descent and lived in border regions of South Texas, an area characterized by competing cultural systems and known to be undergoing social change. The nonpatient group had a significantly higher level of economic self-sufficiency and also showed higher measures on the variables of education, occupation, and marital stability. Scalogram analysis was used to better define group differences in value identification. Answers to the items of the value questionnaire reflected either traditional (Mexican) or nontraditional (Anglo) value preferences. Analysis showed that the two groups did not differ significantly in the way they conformed to scale requirements, and that there were no significant differences between the groups in degree of traditionalistic emphasis. Comparing how the individuals of each group were distributed across the value continuum between traditionalism and nontraditionalism, however, showed that the nonpatient group had a significantly larger proportion of individuals who preferred either extreme of the continuum as compared to the patients. It is suggested that the results involving the demographic variables imply group differences in social productivity and assimilation. These differences, in turn, may relate to the implications of the distributional patterns of the groups on the value scale rather than to differences in the overall extent of identification with traditional values.

A current assumption in psychiatry is that individuals who live in areas that are undergoing cultural change experience psychological distress as a reslt of having to cope with the deprivation and social disorganization that often accompany this change (Graves, 1967; Leighton, 1960;

Reprinted from Behavioral Science 13:362-371, 1968, by permission of James G. Miller, M.D., Ph.D., Editor.

This study was supported by the Texas Department of Mental Health and Mental Retardation, and by Commissioner John Kinross-Wright.

Murphy, 1959).[1] The model assumes, first of all, that for an individual to develop high psychological organization and adaptive skills, attitudes, roles and behavior

[1] The definitions of value given in Parson and Shils (1954, pp. 59 and 411) are used in this study. References to general existential premises (as used in Kluckhohn and Strodtbeck, 1961) are excluded. Since, as will be elaborated on subsequently, operational criteria and measurement procedures are brought to bear on individuals with regard to a limited number of circumscribed behavioral situations, psychological notions of value and attitude also appear relevant. (For a discussion of these interrelated issues see Parson ard Shils, 1954, pp. 383-433.)

patterns learned in the home should be internally consistent and similarly valued by the parents. Ideally, there should also be a high degree of correspondence between the sentiments and strategies learned in the home and those generally followed and socially sanctioned in the community. This correspondence is always short of perfect; in conditions of social disruption and cultural modification it is diminished, and as a result, an individual is not as well prepared to cope with the different demands and alternatives he encounters outside the home. Male family members usually experience the psychological effects of social system modifications more directly, since the social and economic responsibilities of females tend to keep them in the home, and they are thus less likely to have contact with mediating circumstances. In conditions of disruptive social change this differential effect of the social system on family members is augmented, contributing to family instability. In many other ways, the social and economic deprivations that often characterize environments undergoing change can directly undermine the security and stability of the family as a functioning system, producing interpersonal conflicts and altering socialization patterns. Individuals of minority ethnic groups can have these results of social change (parental disharmony, attitude conflicts, and discrepancy between sociocultural premises validated in the immediate social group as opposed to those sanctioned in the larger social system) accentuated if they live in an environment where their traditional values are in conflict with and undermined by the competing values of the dominant group. The result of these and related considerations is that individuals living in these circumstances experience psychological distress and/or symptoms when the disruptions in their customary patterns are felt. The continued need to modify those patterns and values related to the achievement of economic success in the larger community creates further interpersonal conflicts and anxieties because these modifications can entail changes in commitments and loyalties that also affect situations involving family and peer group activity where the modified values may be socially censured or deemed reprehensible. Others have im-

plied that the undermining of a group's ethos can in itself produce purposelessness, emptiness and an impaired sense of identity which can lead to specific symptoms (Erikson, 1950; Hallowell, 1950).

In general, for individuals of ethnic minority groups, conditions of acculturation have psychological implications that resemble those accompanying sociocultural change. This is because these conditions also involve change and hence require adjustment and adaptation to an environment substantially different from the one to which the individual is accustomed. There is, in fact a great deal of work in psychology and anthropology which has demonstrated in variety of settings the existence of "maladjustment" or personality problems in individuals who are in different stages of acculturation. (For reviews see Lindzey, 1961; Spindler and Spindler, 1963; and Wallace, 1962.) A conclusion of many of these studies is that acculturation results in, or is the cause of the psychological dysfunction, and many studies in psychiatry implicitly follow this rationale. There are few rigorous and well controlled studies that have established this, however, primarily because of the failure to deal with the methodological problem of health-illness definition (Blum, 1962; Milbank Memorial Fund, 1953); the work conducted in Canada (Leighton, Harding, Macklin, Macmillan, and Leighton, 1963) and Yoruba (Leighton, Lambo, Hughes, Leighton, Murphy, and Macklin, 1963) does indicate a high association between social disorganization and psychiatric symptomatology. Efforts have recently been made to conceptually analyze the varied psychiatric implications of social and cultural change (Fried, 1964; Leighton, 1959). This report will present the results of investigating social and cultural features of psychiatric patients and nonpatients who reside in a setting characterized by these changes.

THE STUDY

The study was conducted in border areas of South Texas where previous social scientific work has already demonstrated the existence of competing values and attitude systems that involve Americans of Mexican descent (Madsen, 1964; Rubel, 1966; Simmons, 1961). The differing value orientations and the social changes taking place have, in fact, been directly implicated in the adjustment problems that many Mexican Americans manifest (Heller, 1966; Madsen, 1966). In addition, in this ethnic group, well documented demographic characteristics (that is, level of employment, education, income, occupational differentiation, and fertility estimates) (Browning and McLemore, 1964; Mittlebach and Marshall, 1966) exist which point to circumstances of social deprivation that in many independent studies have been shown to be relevant to psychiatric "illness" or symptomatology (Dunham, 1961; Mishler and Scotch, 1965). Social background variables of this type may well be associated with psychiatric problems in this particular setting and this study attempts to investigate this possibility.

The rationale employed here can be said to be epidemiologic (MacMahon, Pugh, and Ipsen, 1960) as demographic features and the psychocultural emphases (values, attitudes, and related belief systems) of a group of psychiatric outpatients are compared to those of nonpatients of similar socioethnic background. This is done to clarify the relationship of these social and cultural factors to psychiatric disability. The sociological indices examined are those which reflect an individual's social functioning (such as education, occupation, and employment status). The attitudes and values compared are those which have been described as being typical and quite traditional for this group (Diaz-Guerrero, 1955 and 1964; Kluckhohn and Strodtbeck, 1961; Madsen, 1964; Rubel, 1966). For instance, there is heavy emphasis on allegiance and closeness to relatives who make up the extended family. General acknowledgment is made of the male's superiority, and authority; and respect and protection are shown females because of their purity, sanctity and vulnerability. Jobs are positively valued only if the individual employee is treated in a way which makes him feel he is personally respected by the employer; considerations of salary, promotions, and impersonal "work conditions" are secondary. Judging from interviews and observed medical practices, western scientific premises about the nature of disease, both causation

and cure, are not accepted; a rich and elaborate folk system prevails instead. These emphases and many others typically characterize Mexican and Mexican American individuals living in nonurban, folk-rural settings. It is known that these Mexican "traditions" have persisted and currently compete with Anglo-American ways in the Southwestern part of the United States. The psychological modifications that often take place in Mexican American individuals as a result of participation and involvement in the essentially Anglo society (Social Science Research Council, 1954) are important determinants of an individual's success in achieving socioeconomic security. Since these kinds of psychological changes are said to be personally stressful and are also believed to be related to psychiatric symptomatology, it is pertinent to investigate the value identification of samples of patients and nonpatients exposed to acculturative pressures, and to analyze the relationship of these pressures to social functioning.

If a difference in the extent of traditional value emphasis (strict adherence to Mexican folk values) is found between a group of patients and a group of nonpatients under conditions that allow comparison, then this attitude dimension might relate in a direct or indirect way to the existence of the behavior problem that prompted treatment. However, cognitive issues such as values and related belief systems are known to ultimately contribute to the type of medical aid an individual seeks (Freidson, 1960; Rubel, 1960; Saunders, 1954), and so a difference in degree of "traditionalism" in the two groups may simply reflect the type of treatment selected and may not allow clarification of the relationship between value identification and psychiatric disability. In other words, nonpatients could be more traditional and experience no less psychiatric symptomatology than patients; the difference in degree of traditionalism between the two groups could simply be a result of the fact that "patients" asked for help in the (Anglo) psychiatric setting, whereas "nonpatients," who may have similar psychological problems, used native curanderos or other folk procedures. In the event of a clear difference in degree of tradicionalism, the nature of the values held by each of the two groups would specify if value identification reflects mode of treatment selection or is possibly related to the psychiatric symptomatology. Independent of degree of value identification, individuals of each group may pattern the attitude items in a different manner. Also, if the attitudes of the two groups are partitioned along a particular dimension or continuum, the distribution of individuals in one group might differ from that of the other. Either of these latter two possibilities might exist regardless of whether the two groups differ in overall traditionalistic emphasis. Examination of this pattern of distribution may then suggest if value identification is related to the psychiatric disturbance. This study attempts to investigate these related problems.

METHOD
Patients

Seventy-six Mexican Americans accepted for outpatient psychiatric care during a six-month period at an adult mental health clinic in South Texas were used as the patient sample.[2] The interviews were conducted in Spanish by an American of Mexican descent who was intimately familiar with the background culture and with the communicational style. This person functioned as a lay interviewer and was unaware of the design, aim and implication of the study. Information pertaining to age, sex, occupation, income, education, and marital status was collected. Other background features included place of birth, nationality of parents, number of years residing in Texas, number of adults residing in the household, the frequency of household moves during the preceding three years.

Nonpatients

Using a probability sampling plan, forty-eight persons were selected from a representative small town served by the clinic. Census tract maps which divided the town into blocks and roughly described the quality of the homes in different areas were made available by the Department of Health. The blocks were numbered and

then, using a table of random numbers, different homes in each block were selected. The same individual who had interviewed the patients in the clinic setting also visited the selected homes. In neighborhoods predominantly inhabited by Mexican Americans, approximately 60 separate homes were selected, of which five were subsequently found to be unoccupied. Only adult members of households were interviewed. Because an initial sex ratio of 2:1 female was obtained in the clinic population, this same ratio was followed in the community.[3] Since the sampling process may have biased the social characterization of the two groups by leading to the selection of a greater number of employed and financially self-supporting adult nonpatients, final categorization of the variables likely to be affected (income, occupation, and employment status) was made by considering the family as the analytical unit.[4] Any resulting differences were thus likely to be more meaningful.

Value questionnaire

Each individual was also administered a questionnaire (in Spanish) dealing with social themes that importantly characterize this ethnic group.[5] Because their rate of literacy is low for both the English

[2] This study was made possible through the cooperation of Gary Miller, M.D., Director, and the staff at the Harlingen Adult Mental Health Clinic in Harlingen, Texas.

[3] Few females (1 or 2) refused. Men, because of employment status, were more difficult to contact; often several appointments had to be made; in several cases (illness, work out of town) realistic reasons intervened. In only about 5% of the cases was there refusal to cooperate.

[4] The occupation of the principal breadwinner was used to classify the occupational status of the family. If no member of the household was employed then the family was classified as unemployed. The income of all household members was considered the family income and included earnings (wages, salaries, self-employment income), social security benefits, and pensions. Those households receiving public assistance (in the form of money or commodities) or contributions from persons outside the household were classified as "non-self-supporting families" when the amount received from these sources exceeded 50% of the total family income.

[5] The questionnaire resulted from collaborative work with Dr. Arthur J. Rubel during the summer of 1966. This was made possible by a grant from the Hogg Foundation for Mental Health.

and Spanish languages, the questionnaire was verbally administered on an individual basis. The characteristics of this questionnaire and the rationale for coding the responses have already been reported (Fabrega, Rubel, and Wallace, 1967). Each item (N = 18) consisted of a brief story involving individuals in a social situation. As previously suggested, themes such as family solidarity, behavior toward parents and relatives, attitude and orientation toward work, interpersonal relations, and folk medical emphases were presented. A conflict was posed in the story and a choice between two alternatives was required of the respondent. His choice resolved the conflict and at the same time reflected his underlying value orientation. Responses coded traditional were those emphasizing 1) lack of individual autonomy vis-a-vis family and elders, 2) particularistic as opposed to universalistic value choices (in work settings or in personal relations with institutions), 3) acknowledgement of folk as opposed to scientific medical constructs, 4) disavowal of the English language at home, and 5) stereotyped conceptions regarding gender differences in role prescriptions and behavior. "Traditionalistic" options reflected commitment to and agreement with the values of the native Mexican culture. If the respondent chose the alternate option, this was taken to mean that he did not follow the traditional emphases of the Mexican group in those behavioral situations depicted by that item.

The content of the items which made up the questionnaire was drawn from personal experience gained from field work in Mexican and Mexican American settings as well as from a review of pertinent literature. Conflict situations were selected which focused sharply on issues, social relations, and strategies involving means-ends choices that are known to saliently distinguish the Anglo from the Mexican American sociocultural premises. Options resolving the conflicts were structured to exemplify Mexican as opposed to Anglo values. A priori decisions and judgments, in other words, were the basis for dichotomizing responses into traditional and nontraditional (Anglo) categories. As a result of this coding rationale, the manner in which an individual answered or resolved the social situations presented in the ques-

tionnaire was used to measure his value identification.[6] Educational attainment in the groups studied was low and this, plus the fact that anxiety often precluded prolonged concentration, led to a simplified presentation which contributed to the dichotomous coding system.

Utilizing the traditional and nontraditional response coding, the items were subjected to the Cornell technique of scalogram analysis (Edwards, 1957; Torgerson, 1955; Green, 1954). The responses of both patients and nonpatients were combined when subjected to this analysis, with their identities excluded.[7] With an individual's total score a measure of his "tradition-

---

[6] The questionnaire was pretested on a group of Americans of Mexican descent with differing value identifications who were sensitive to the conflicts that result from competing Latin-Anglo traditions. Their responses and comments to the questionnaire indicated that the items were both clear and pertinent. The vernacular (Spanish) of the questionnaire was developed in intimate collaboration with an American of Mexican descent who had grown up in the area where the study was conducted. The intrasubject stability of the questionnaire (test-retest reliability, using a one-week interval) was evaluated on a small sample of hospitalized Latin psychiatric patients (N = 15). This sample primarily consisted of individuals who were diagnosed as psychotic and in treatment on an acute ward of a state hospital. The product-moment correlation for the total traditional score was 0.91.

[7] It is here conceptualized that the items of the questionnaire, each of which refers to a behavior situation which reflects the respondent's preferred value orientation in the domain by demanding choice, can be hierarchically ordered. This order is equivalent to or approximates an underlying unidimensional scale that indicates the respondent's strength of commitment to traditional values. Individuals can be allocated to different positions in this scale. For this study, an eight-item scale reflecting degree of traditionalistic orientation resulted; this met the criteria for a Guttman scale. The coefficient of reproducibility was 0.91. Item marginals were used to compute the minimal marginal reproducibility and this value was 0.71. Only one of the eight items had a modal value that substantially exceeded a value of 0.80 (0.85), and no response category had more errors than nonerrors. Each item of the scale averaged a test-retest stability of 0.89. Only one item was below 0.85 (0.81).

alism" (that is, degree of reliance on values and attitudes consistent with the "native" culture), parametric and nonparametric statistical tests were used in comparing relationships between variables in the two groups. Only two-tailed significance regions were employed.

RESULTS

Background characteristics

Table 1 summarizes these results for both the patient and nonpatient groups. As can be noted, the samples were similar in many respects.[8] Although the marital status comparison was compounded by a sampling bias which decreased the likelihood that single individuals would be included in the nonpatient group, it was felt that a higher proportion of marital instability existed in the patient sample. Quantification on this variable was not attempted, however. Significant differences were found when the two groups were compared on variables related to unemployment and "outside" support. In the patient group, more families were unemployed ($\chi^2 = 13.72$, $p < .001$) and more instances of support from sources outside the household were reported ($\chi^2 = 13.52$, $p < .001$). In addition, a median test was used to compare the family income of the groups. Again the patient group was found to fall significantly below the median ($\chi^2 = 26.23$, $p < .001$).

When a two-factor index of social position, as outlined by Hollingshead (1957), was used to rank the families according to social class, the nonpatient group was placed in a higher position. The majority of both groups were in the lowest class, however, and to further clarify their comparability, an index of social position was analyzed through its separate components, education and occupation, as scaled by Hollingshead's code. A chi-square test found no difference in the educational

---

[8]The nonpatient control group had a higher proportion of females. This gender difference resulted because the sampling plan followed was based on an early estimate of the clinic data which later proved to inaccurately characterize the patient group. The variables were routinely tested for sex differences and no significant results were obtained.

Table 1. Background characteristics of the patient and nonpatient samples

Characteristics of individuals	Patients $N = 76$	Nonpatients $N = 48$
Age:		
Mean	38.1	36.7
Standard Deviation	14.3	12.1
Median	34.5	32.8
Range	18-76	18-66
%Males	43.4	29.2
%Married	46.1	85.4
%Separated or divorced	13.1	6.3
%Widowed	7.9	8.3
Mean number of children*	4.4	4.1
Standard Deviation	3.2	2.5
Median number of years education	5.4	7.0
%Catholic	81.6	91.7
%Protestant	15.8	8.3
%Non-citizens	19.7	20.8
%Born in Texas	65.8	77.1
%Born in Mexico	27.6	22.9
%of Native born parents	31.6	25.0
%of Foreign born parents	39.5	50.0
Mean number household moves in preceding 3 years	.8	.8
Standard Deviation	1.2	1.1
%Non-English speaking	36.8	22.9
Mean number years residing in Texas	30.0	32.1
Standard Deviation	16.9	11.3

Characteristics of families		
Median family income†	$1850	$3050
%Families unemployed†	52.6	18.8
%Families non-self-supporting†	34.2	2.1
Mean number adults living with person	1.8	1.7
Standard Deviation	1.3	1.2

*Single individuals were excluded for this computation.
†Using the χ^2 test, differences between the two groups were found to be significant beyond the .001 probability level.

level of the two samples. (A median test used with the number of years of education failed to show a difference but the median of 7.0 for the nonpatient group was higher than the median of 5.4 for the patient group.) The occupational level did show a significant difference ($\chi^2 = 4.70$, $p < .05$). However, since the classficiation scheme placed the unemployed families in the lowest occupational division, these individuals were then excluded and a separate analysis was done. The resulting chi-square computations failed to produce a significant figure, though the nonpatient group did have more people in the higher occupational levels. The most prominent differences, therefore, were felt to be in employment status, income, assistance from sources outside the household, and perhaps to some extent marital stability, with a trend toward nonpatients having higher levels of education and occupation.

Value orientation

The median test was used to analyze the relationship of education, age, and nationality of parents to magnitude of individuals' value scores. None of these tests reached significance though all showed directional trends, with those who were older, less educated, and of foreign parentage tending to display higher traditionalism scores. When the two end regions of the value scale were used (scores of 0 and 1 vs. 7 and 8), this trend was enhanced and approached significance levels, with parents' nationality showing statistical significance ($\chi^2 = 4.78$, $p < .05$). There were no male-female differences with regard to value score or distribution on the scale continuum.

The frequency of nonscale response patterns in the two groups was compared and no difference was obtained using the chi-square test for significance. The mean number of response errors of each group was computed, and using the t-test, no significant differences were found. No trend that would suggest underlying differences with regard to adherence to scale requirements was noted. These latter sets of findings would suggest that with regard to the restricted value domain measured by the scale, the two groups do not differ in the way their members hierarchically organize attitude items when consistency is invoked. Assuming scalability, in other words, most individuals give perfect response patterns at different scale positions, and those who do not are randomly distributed between the two groups.

Using the midpoint of the continuum, the two groups were compared to detect a possible association between group status and degree of traditionalism. The two groups did not show chi-square differences which would indicate that either group had a significantly higher proportion of traditionalistic *or* nontraditionalistic individuals. (The mean traditional scores of both groups were compared and no significant differences resulted when the t-test was applied.) However, when the three scale regions (nontraditionalistic, mixed or intermediate, and very traditionalistic) were compared, it was found that non-patients

Table 2. Value scale positions and distribution of subjects on scale continuum*

A. *Scale positions*

Non-traditionalistic	Mixed or intermediate	Very traditionalistic
0-1	2-6	7-8

B. *Number of subjects by scale position*

	0-1	2-6	7-8		Intermediate	Extremes
Patients	7	59	10	Patients	59	17
Nonpatients	11	24	13	Nonpatients	24	24

*The first part of the table indicates the scale positions (or value scores) included in the different scale regions used in the analysis. The second part shows the number of individuals of each group in the different scale regions.

were overrepresented in both extreme positions and underrepresented in the mid-region (see Table 2). The converse was the case with the patient group. This difference in the way individuals were distributed along the scale in the two groups is significant ($\chi^2 = 10.34$, $p < .01$). This means that in comparison to the patient sample, the nonpatient group shows a greater proportion of both nontraditionalistic and very traditionalistic individuals (see Table 2).

DISCUSSION

Though the findings dealing with the social background variables may be interpreted from a developmental level to reflect a greater degree of social competence (see Zigler and Phillips, 1960) on the part of nonpatients, they also imply greater assimilation (Shannon and Morgan, 1966). Results indicate then that social functioning and economic assimilation are higher in the nonpatient group. Since neither parametric nor nonparametric statistical tests indicated a significant difference in degree of traditionalism between the two groups, the salient features of each group (high social performance and psychiatric "illness") cannot be ascribed to overall differences in the extent of traditionalistic emphases. This means, for instance, that patients cannot properly be said to be more or less acculturated if the latter is defined using attitudinal dimension. In general, this aspect of the findings suggests that there is some independence between the cognitive-attitudinal and the socio-economic dimension of acculturation. In addition, because individuals of each group hierarchically ordered the scale items in a similar way, the seeking of psychiatric care does not appear to be associated with a deviant or different manner of cognitively structuring the particular sociointerpersonal themes used in the value analysis. In other words both groups are equally consistent and employ similarly ordered criteria and schemes when they are forced to resolve behavioral conflicts that involve competing value systems.

The finding that each group was distributed differently along the scale can be viewed from two perspectives. First, it was found that each of the four extreme scale positions (0, 1, 7 and 8) had proportionately more nonpatients than patients. Secondly, although nonpatients were equally divided between extreme and intermediate regions, more than three-quarters (78 percent) of the patients were found in the central part of the scale. Nonpatients thus take either a very traditional posture or one that is its converse, namely very nontraditional. Patients, on the other hand, seem to follow both traditional and nontraditional patterns to a moderate extent, having proportionately fewer individuals with identifications manifesting commitment to either pole of the value continuum. In the absence of knowledge about the life history and the actual behavior of the nonpatients, it is of course difficult to infer that an association exists between value commitment and psychiatric adjustment. It appears *as if* patients are balanced between or avoid very traditionalistic and nontraditionalistic emphases, whereas proportionately more nonpatients (one-half of this group to be exact) have chosen these "total or exclusive" orientations (end points of the value continuum). From the data obtained, it cannot be determined if this preference for exclusive positions is in fact psychologically stabilizing or constrictive.

As mentioned at the offset, culture contact situations can be assumed to be stressful to individuals of a minority group undergoing acculturative changes. This is a conclusion that has frequently been reached by many different observers. The stress may be due in part to the fact that decisions, strategies, identifications, and goals must be chosen from among alternatives that often entail contradictory or conflicting premises (Chance, 1965; Miller, Galanter, and Pribram, 1960; Rioch, 1958). In the setting reported in this study, the nonpatient group was noted to be more successful (in terms of social functioning), and was also found to manifest values and attitudes that indicated "exclusive or total" orientations. In other words, non-patients showed a preference for exclusively Mexican or Anglo American resolutions to the social situations that made up the questionnaire. If they reflected traditional (Mexican) values in relations with family, for instance, they were also more likely to espouse folk conceptions, acknowledge Mexican masculinity-femininity notions, and prefer particularistic social relationships in work situations. Likewise if nontraditional (Anglo American) options were chosen in one type of situation, they were also more likely to be followed in others. There was, thus, greater similarity between the types of underlying value orientation which influenced choices in differing social circumstances. It may be that orientations of this type enable greater psychological organization and improved social performance by allowing individuals to function with fewer (more general) premises. Thus, by exclusively relying on either Mexican or Anglo choices in many differing behavioral contexts psychological consistency is maintained and productivity increased. Love and special respect for one's parents and elders (a Mexican trait), for example, may conflict or prove inconsistent with the pursuit of a career requiring social autonomy (an Anglo trait), if parents overtly or covertly censure this latter strategy. The anxiety resulting from this cognitive inconsistency or conflict of values may interfere with adequate work performance, which, if severe, may lead to interpersonal difficulties with a spouse. In other words, if exclusive orientations are followed, the goals and strategies of many different contexts may be ordered and followed more efficiently since they share underlying premises and are consistent, and this may lead to higher social performance. If this reasoning is correct, the results of this study indicate that proportionately fewer patients manifest this kind of psychological organization and that this may contribute to their poorer social performance.

REFERENCES

Blum, R. H. Case identification in psychiatric epidemiology: Methods and problems. Milbank Mem. Fund Quart., 1962, **40**, 253-288.

Browning, H. L., & McLemore, S. D. A statistical profile of the Spanish-surname population of Texas. Austin, Texas: Bureau of Business Research, The University of Texas, 1964.

Chance, N. A. Acculturation, self-identification, and personality adjustment. Amer. Anthrop., 1965, **67**, 372-393.

Diaz-Guerrero, R. Neurosis and the Mexican family structures. Amer. J. Psychiat., 1955, **112**, 411-417.

Diaz-Guerrero, R. La dicotomia activo-pasivo en la investigacion transcultural. In Proceedings of the ninth congress of the Interamerican Society of Psychology. Miami, Dec. 17-22, 1964.

Dunham, H. W. Social structures and mental disorders: Competing hypotheses of explanation. In Causes of mental disorders: A review of epidemiological knowledge, 1959. New York: Milbank Memorial Fund, 1961, Pp. 227-265.

Edwards, A. L. Techniques of attitude scale construction. New York: Appleton-Century-Crofts, 1957.

Erikson, E. H. Childhood and society. New York: W. W. Norton & Co., 1950.

Fabrega, H., Jr., Rubel, A. J., & Wallace, Carole Ann. Working Class Mexican psychiatric outpatients: Some social and cultural features. Arch. Gen. Psychiat., 1967, **16**, 704-712.

Freidson, E. Client control and medical practice. Amer. J. Soc., 1960, **65**, 374-382.

Fried, M. Effects of social change on mental health. Amer. J. Orthopsychiat., 1964, **34**, 3-27.

Graves, T. D. Acculturation, access, and alcohol in a tri-ethnic community. Amer. Anthrop., 1967, **69**, 306-321.

Green, B. F. Attitude measurement. In G. Lindzey (Ed.) Handbook of social psychology, Vol. I. Massachusetts: Addison Wesley, 1954, Chapter 9.

Hallowell, A. I. Values, acculturation and mental health. Amer. J. Orthopsychiatry, 1950, **20**, 732-743.

Heller, C. S. Mexican-American youth: Forgotten youth at the crossroads. New York: Random House, 1966.

Hollingshead, A. B. Two factor index of social position. New Haven, Conn.: 1957. (Monograph supplied by author.)

Kluckhohn, F. R., & Strodtbeck, F. L. Variations in value orientations. New York: Row, Peterson & Company, 1961.

Leighton, A. H. Mental illness and acculturation. In I. Galdston (Ed.) Medicine and anthropology. New York: International University Press, 1959, Pp. 108-128.

Leighton, A. An introduction to social psychiatry. Illinois: Charles C Thomas, 1960.

Leighton, D. C., Harding, J. S., Macklin, D. B., Macmillan, A. M., & Leighton, A. H. The character of danger. New York: Basic Books, 1963.

Leighton, A. H., Lambo, T. A. Hughes, C. C., Leighton, D. C., Murphy, J. M., & Macklin, D. B. Psychiatric disorder among the Yoruba. Cornell University Press, Ithaca, New York, 1963.

Lindzey, G. Projective techniques and cross-cultural research. New York: Appleton-Century-Crofts, 1961.

MacMahon, B., Pugh, T. F., & Ipsen, J. Epidemiologic methods. Boston: Little, Brown & Company, 1960.

Madsen, W. The Mexican-Americans of South Texas. New York: Holt, Rinehart & Winston, 1964.

Madsen, W. Anxiety and witchcraft in Mexican American acculturation. Anthrop. Quart., 1966, 39, 110-127.

Milbank Memorial Fund. Definition of a case for purposes of research in social psychiatry. In Interrelations between the social environment and psychiatric disorders. New York: Milbank Memorial Fund, 1953, Pp. 117-157.

Miller, G. A., Galanter, E., & Pribram, K. H. Plans and the structure of behavior. New York: Henry Holt & Company, 1960.

Mishler, E. G., & Scotch, N. A. Sociocultural factors in the epidemiology of schizophrenia. Int. J. Psychiat., 1965, 1, 258-295.

Mittlebach, F. G., & Marshall, G. The burden of poverty. Los Angeles: Mexican-American Study Project Advance Report 5. Division of Research, Graduate School of Business Administration, University of California, 1966.

Murphy, H. B. M. Social change and mental health. In Causes of mental disorders: A review of epidemiological knowledge. New York: Milbank Memorial Fund, 1959, Pp. 280-329.

Parson, T., & Shils, E. A. (Eds.) Toward a general theory of action. Massachusetts: Harvard University Press, 1954.

Rioch, D. M. The biological roots of psychoanalysis. In J. J. Masserman (Ed.), Science and psychoanalysis. Vol. I. Integrative studies. New York: Grune & Stratton, 1958, Pp. 1-28.

Rubel, A. J. Concepts of disease in Mexican-American culture. Amer. Anthrop., 1960, 62, 795-814.

Rubel, A. J. Across the tracks: Mexican-Americans in a Texas city. Austin, Texas: The University of Texas Press for the Hogg Foundation for Mental Health, 1966.

Saunders, L. Cultural difference and medical care. The case of the Spanish-speaking people of the Southwest. New York: Russell Sage Foundation, 1954.

Shannon, L., & Morgan, P. The prediction of economic absorption and cultural integration among Mexican-Americans, Negroes, and Anglos in a northern industrial community. Hum. Org., 1966, 25, 154-162.

Simmons, O. The mutual images and expectations of Anglo-Americans and Mexican-Americans. Daedalus, 1961, 286-299.

Social Science Research Council (summer seminar on acculturation). Acculturation: An exploratory formulation. Amer. Anthrop., 1954, 56, 973-1002.

Spindler, G., & Spindler, L. Psychology in anthropology: Applications to culture change. In S. Koch (Ed.) Psychology: A study of a science. Study II. Empirical substructure and relations with other sciences. Vol. 6. Investigations of man as socius: Their place in psychology and the social sciences. New York: McGraw-Hill, 1963, Pp. 510-551.

Torgerson, W. S. Theory and methods of scaling. New York: John Wiley & Sons, 1965.

Wallace, A. F. C. Culture and personality. New York: Random House, 1962.

Zigler, E., & Phillips, L. Social effectiveness and symptomatic behaviors. J. Abnorm. Soc. Psychol., 1960, 61, 231-238.

CHAPTER 26 THE ROLE OF CHICANO FOLK BELIEFS AND PRACTICES IN MENTAL HEALTH

ELENA GONZALES

This chapter focuses attention on the issue of mental health in formulating services for Chicanos. The irrelevancy of mental health services for Chicanos has been documented in a number of studies (Karno, 1966; Karno and Edgerton, 1969; Torrey, 1970). The ineffectiveness of mental health services has often been attributed to the continued use of the traditional mental health model that interprets behavior in *intrapsychic terms* (Padilla, 1971). Nevertheless, the concepts of mental health and mental illness prevalent in mental health facilities for Chicanos continue to be implemented in the traditional framework within the dominant cultural context (Sanchez, 1971). Those studies that have examined the issue of underutilization of mental health facilities by Chicanos have bypassed the mental health issue and instead focus on the *mental health problem* and advocate modifications of the traditional mental health model in terms of specific procedures. For instance, Karno (1966) points to the intake procedure as a possible barrier to utilization of mental health facilities. In this regard, he states:

In addition to avoidance of ethnicity (by clinic personnel) there is another factor operative in the clinic which may significantly contribute to therapeutic failure with ethnic patients. This is the pervasive use of and reliance upon a model for the psychiatric historical interview which derives directly from the classical medical history. This is an information-retrieving process which, to a remarkable extent, systematically ignores the socio-cultural context of the patient's life.

Along this same vein, Philippus (1971) criticizes the formal, bureaucratic delivering system in most mental health facilities as a major factor in the underutilization of such facilities by Chicanos. He advocates the use of an informal, personal approach with much reliance on neighborhood personnel who are bilingual.

Karno and Morales (1971), in their description of a community mental health service for Chicanos in East Los Angeles, agree with Philippus in emphasizing the need for Spanish-speaking personnel. They also advocate the need for personnel who are committed to social, personal, and professional involvement in the community. They do not directly address themselves to the use of the traditional mental health model. Emphasis is placed on the need for treatment to occur in a context of cultural and linguistic familiarity and acceptance. The assumption seems to be that there is no need to alter the traditional psychotherapy models, but only deliver them in Spanish and in an atmosphere that outwardly is more *culturally* attuned to Chicanos. The inclusion of bilingual personnel often overlooks the real need for bicultural personnel. Sanchez (1970), in his article stated this position: "The posture to integrate Spanish-speaking personnel with no change in philosophy is assimilative in nature and avoids the central issue of what is mental health."

Padilla (1971), who questioned more directly the value of the traditional mental health philosophy and treatment, proposed that social learning theory offered a more appropriate model for treatment with minorities and the poor. While this is a step in the right direction, the issue of who will define the kinds of interpersonal skills and social systems most useful in maximizing human potential is not discussed.

Padilla and Ruiz (1973), examining the reasons behind the underutilization of mental health facilities by Chicanos, indicate that the more likely explanation is institutional policies that discourage self-referrals from Chicanos or that discourage continuation in treatment once referred. Variables that are considered influential in this regard are culture-bound values of the therapists and cultural differences.

Studies on acculturation indicate that those individuals who have rejected their traditional values are more susceptible to mental stress and disturbance (Ramirez, 1971). If mental health facilities and personnel are maintaining an assimilative stance, they are a factor in contributing to the stress they propose to treat. Evidence thus far indicates that cultural democracy, not policy of assimilation, enhances mental health (Ramirez, 1971). It appears that it has been the ethnocentric orientation of modern medicine, psychiatry, and psychology that has been a barrier to Chicano acceptance and use of modern medical facilities and physicians. Anglo professionals have had the political and social power to maintain overrepresentation of their own world view and to disparage those who differ from their own values and perceptions. Where mental health facilities are sensitive to language and cultural needs of Chicanos, patronage has increased (Karno and Morales, 1971; Philippus, 1970). Caution must be exercised to ensure that increased sensitivity to chicanismo is not simply the same old package in brighter and different wrappings.

The question of what is culturally relevant for Chicanos needs to be confronted if we are to maintain cultural representation for the Chicano in the mental health field. This chapter presents the culturally relevant aspects of folk beliefs and practices as they relate to Chicanos. It is suggested that mental health is better served when the traditional perspectives of distinct cultures are recognized, appreciated, and represented in mental health facilities.

In order to place Mexican-American folk beliefs and psychiatry in clear relationship to Chicanos, it is important to understand that the term Chicano does not define a static unitary entity of people who are of Mexican-American descent. Rather, it encompasses a large diverse group of people who share a common heritage, and experience the common enemies of discrimination and poverty. There are differences among Chicano people in terms of their geographical location and history, generational affiliations and socioeconomic status. The cultures in which Chicanos participate create for them a world view distinct from Anglo reality but not totally separated from that dominant view. Culture for Chicanos, as for any group of people, is a dynamic process and is in a state of constant change. Caution must be taken not to create a cultural stereotype to which all Chicanos are expected to conform.

The inclusion of this chapter on curanderismo affirms that the issue of who defines mental health and how it is defined must be examined from a Chicano's perspective. The dominant Anglo culture has maintained the position of defining what constitutes mental health and mental illness, and present facilities reflect this in their use of the traditional mental health models and techniques for treatment. This chapter offers some alternative direction and perspective toward resolving the mental health needs of Chicanos. The traditions and historical development of Chicanos should be examined and understood before alternative mental health models and techniques are considered. Mexican-American folk beliefs and practices encompass the traditional ways that many Chicanos have cared, and continue to care, for their physical and psychological ills. They represent a particular world view that has its own unique configuration of human values. An understanding of this aspect of Chicano tradition and life may enhance the process of developing responsive and meaningful mental health models and facilities for this ethnic minority.

WHAT IS CURANDERISMO?

The term curanderismo is used in transcultural psychiatry to refer specifically to Mexican-American folk psychiatry. The term will be used here in a broader aspect to encompass the general domain of traditional medical concepts and practices. Confusion arises when an aritficial separation is attempted between physical health and illness and mental health and illness. This is an unnatural separation within the traditional cultural context of Chicanos. Three separate aspects within the traditional medical concepts and practices will be distinguished. These are: (1) a set of traditional folk medical beliefs and practices, (2) the set of ritualistic acts traditionally considered to have favorable effects on health, and (3) the use of folk medical curers, curanderos.

Mexican and Mexican-American traditional culture is rich in folk medical lore and practices. Current folk medicine has historical foundations in: (1) European medicine of the 15th and 16th centuries, (2) Spanish-Catholic tradition, and (3) Indian heritage of the Aztecs, Mayans, and others (Kiev, 1968). Many of the concepts and practices are not at variance with modern medicine. Certain concepts that have been differentiated sharply from modern medical notions are: (1) *mal ojo,* (2) *mal de susto,* (3) *empacho,* (4) *mal puesto* (sorcery), and (5) *caída de la mollera.* These concepts are defined and the traditional treatment for each is described below.

Mal ojo, literally translated "bad eye," is believed to be a result of excessive admiration or desire on the part of another person. Symptoms indicative of this illness are sleepiness, a general malaise, and, frequently, a severe headache. The recommended treatment is to find the person who has cast the mal ojo (usually unintentionally) and have him manually caress the victim. Mal ojo is not generally interpreted as a consequence of evil intention (Nall and Speilberg, 1967). Rubel (1966) relates a tale of mal ojo by Telésforo, who had doubts about the realities of such a thing, but was convinced by a personal incident in his own life.

You know, the other day before I came to work I shaved, took my whiskers and all off. When I was outside I met a woman who looked at me and said, "You just shaved, didn't you? Took your whiskers off?" Well, I went on to work, and pretty soon I was feeling sick, and then I felt real hot. Well, I went up to Mrs. Brown, my boss, and said, "You know, I don't think I'm going to make it today!" So she put her hand up to my head and said, "Wow!" Boy, my head was really burning! I went on home and got into bed and around nine my brother came home and said, "Come on, let's go see the doc." So I went to see the doc and he gave me a shot, and gave me some pills and I went on back to bed. I wasn't feeling any better, so I told my wife to go on over to that woman's house and bring her over here. She came over with my wife, and she ran her hands over my face and said, "Well, you looked so young and cute that I guess that's why I noticed you." Well, she went away then, and pretty soon I began to feel better. I went back to work the next day and Mrs. Brown said, "Well, you sure were sick yesterday!" (Rubel, 1966, p. 158)

Reports of *mal ojo* are more commonly told about young children and women who are believed to be more susceptible to mal ojo because of their weaker physical status.

Last week my cousin's cute little baby had *ojo.* In the hours of the late afternoon my cousin was holding her child out in their front yard. One of the neighborhood men returning from work stopped to talk with the couple, remarking on the child's cuteness. Then he went on his way. That night when they put the child to bed, it began to cry and remained inconsolable through most of the night. Even though I slept in the other part of the house I could hear them moving about with the child. Very early the next morning I could hear my cousin leave the house as she went next door to speak to our neighbor who is a relative of the man with whom they had chatted the evening before. She asked the neighbor to do her the favor of requesting the man to stop at our house on his way to work. The neighbor went and roused the man with strong eyes. On his way to work the man stopped at our place and went into the other room where he ran a hand over the child's face and forehead, cooing to her and talking to her. He didn't remain any longer than about five minutes. When he left, the baby had stopped crying. (Rubel, 1966, p. 159)

Mal de susto, literally translated "illness from fright," is a syndrome believed to be the result of an emotional traumatic experience. Basic symptoms include restlessness during sleep, feelings of listlessness, loss of energy, and, occasionally, night sweats. Susto is part of a complex set of beliefs in which the individual is thought to be composed of a corporal being and one or more immaterial souls or spirits that may become detached from the body and wander freely (Rubel, 1964). In mal de susto, the individual is believed to have experienced a soul loss. If the treatment is administered at home it includes doses of herb tea (hierba buena preferably) and ritually *sweeping* the victim with a branch while prayers are recited. It is common practice to consult with a curer (curandero), in which case the treatment consists of an initial diagnostic session between healer and patient to determine the episode that caused the illness. In the process of coaxing the soul back to the corporal being, the patient is massaged and often sweated. He is also *swept* or rubbed with some object to remove the illness from the body (Rubel, 1964). The following is an example of mal de susto.

On a Sunday outing, Ricardo, the older boy (five years old) suffered an attack of susto. The rest of the family romped in and about the water of a local pond, but Ricardo demurred. Despite coaxing and taunts, especially from his seven-year old sister, Ricardo would have nothing to do with the water, but climbed into the automobile and went to sleep. He slept throughout the afternoon and did not even awake when he was taken home after dark and put to bed. That night he slept fitfully and several times talked aloud in his sleep. On the following morning, the parents decided that Ricardo had suffered a susto. It was caused, they reasoned, not by fear of the water but by the family's insistence that he enter the pond—a demand to which he was unable to accede. They brought him to a local curer to have his soul coaxed back to his body, thus be healed of soul loss. (Rubel, 1964, p. 273)

Empacho is believed to result from food clinging to the wall of the stomach in the form of a ball, which is believed to prevent the food from breaking up. The quality of food consumed is believed to be a common cause of empacho. It is also believed to result from malicious contamination of one's food by a personal enemy. Treatment includes administration of small doses of a mercury derivative (greta), and rubbing and gently pinching the spine. Prayers are recited continuously during the massaging therapy.

Rubel (1966) stresses that empacho is caused by a complex interaction of social and physiological forces. It is most likely to result in a situation in which another individual is allowed to override one's personal autonomy. Using an informant in the town of Mexiquito, Texas, Rubel's description follows:

Empacho is caused by eating something that you don't really want, as if I went outside and called one of the children and told him, "Come in and eat!" Well, if he didn't really want to, then empacho might result. Empacho is like having a ball form in the seat of your stomach; it burns like a fire (lumbre). Empacho has to be taken care of as soon as possible for it is dangerous. After three months it is beyond cure, and one would die from it. If you allow too much time to pass, then you lose all the flesh, all of your weight, and you become thinner and thinner. Your body is drying out. (1966, p. 166)

Caída de la mollera (fallen fontanel) is the one illness believed to affect children only. Infants in particular are believed by some Chicanos to have a fragile skull formation. The mollera (fontanel) is that part of the skull situated at the very top of the head. The counter-poise pressure of the upper palate is believed to be responsible for maintaining this position. If a blow upon the youngster's head occurs, the fontanel may be dislodged, causing it to sink. Once this happens, the upper palate is forced to depress and blocks the oral passage. After a fall, a child is carefully examined to determine if there is any unusual declivity in the skull. If such a depression is found, a treatment is begun to correct caída de la mollera. Caída de la mollera is also thought to result from pulling the nipple out of the infant's mouth too vigorously. In this case, the fontanel is believed to be sucked down into the palate. Treatment for caída de la mollera can be any combination of three procedures performed either separately or together. First, a finger is inserted into the child's mouth to supposedly push the palate back into place. Secondly, the child can be held over a pan of water so that the tips of the hair barely touch the water. Thirdly, a poultice, usually made from fresh soap shavings, is applied to the depression. It is believed that the most effective treatment includes all three procedures (Martinez and Martin, 1966).

Mal puesto, or sorcery, is considered a consequence of one of three kinds of social relationships: a lover's quarrel, an unrequited affair, or a reflection of invidiousness between individuals or nuclear families. Dramatic mania is a characteristic symptom of mal puesto. When mania is present, the individual is aware that he is possessed by another individual. Mal puesto is characterized by its chronicity and unresponsiveness to cure of any kind. Rubel (1966) relates a story told by an informant in Mexiquito to illustrate how mal peusto is thought to work.

A young woman describes a case in which the victim, who was one of her acquaintances, failed to return the affection of a suitor. He, aware of her lack of interest, offered her an orange soda. After drinking the soda she became demented (se volvia loca), surely he had placed something in her soda (echo algo). Her face turned color, her eyebrows drew tightly together, and her eyes became huge; she was, in fact, a very ugly sight. She had an appetite only for orange soda; all other food was rejected because of her suspicion that it contained hairs and insects (cabellos and animalitos). Her nights became sleepless nightmares because of the dogs and turkeys which she thought crawled upon, leaped, kicked and bruised her body. Inasmuch as only she was aware of those creatures, her family proved powerless to protect her despite their concern. On the mornings following such attacks she arose covered by bruises and other marks of her anguished travails. She was taken from one healer to another; from curandero to physician, physician to curandero, without respite and to no avail. (Rubel, 1966, p. 169)

Although *brujeria* (witchcraft) is another term used alternately with mal puesto, no studies reviewed by Rubel gave any evidence that there are specialists or *brujas* (witches) practicing mal puesto exclusively either to cause or to cure this condition. Many illnesses are attributed to witchcraft but the causal agent is usually unspecified others; *los vecinos* (the neighbors) or *la gente* (other people) are the agents of mal puesto especially when invidious elements are involved. In the case of a lovers quarrel, an individual can easily be specified.

The folk beliefs described above are clearly divided into two groups, natural and unnatural (*mal naturales* and *mal artificiales* or *mal puesto*). Mal naturales are thought to be in the realm of God, and mal artificiales in the realm of the devil. All the folk illnesses are closely linked with social relationships and most of them are connected with faulty interpersonal relations. These folk illnesses are only a few of the many folk beliefs held by many Chicanos in the Southwest. These have been dealt with more completely because they are the folk beliefs most commonly verified in the literature.

The second aspect of folk beliefs and practices are the magico-religious or propitiatory ritual practices. Although a common trait of Chicano folk culture, beyond documentation of their existence, they are the least studied of the three areas of folk beliefs and practices. Nall and Speilberg (1967) list four types of such practices as having particular importance. These are: (1) promise-making, (2) visiting shrines, (3) offering medals and candles, and (4) offering prayers. An example of these practices is evident in the continuous visits to the Don Pedrito Shrine on the Los Olmos Ranch. Early recording of such visits was made by Ruth Dodson, who in 1930, visited the grave of Don Pedrito on All Soul's Day and wrote that ". . . the wire fence that surrounded the small cemetery was falling down but the grave was covered with flowers. . . ." (1951, p. 68). In 1950, she visited the site again.

On last All Soul's Day, in 1950, seventy years after he first came to Los Olmos Ranch—now a ghost ranch itself—people came for miles to visit his grave. They entered a cemetery of twenty-five graves through a gate over which is a placard written in Spanish. It reads, "A Memorial to Don Pedrito Jaramillo from Señor Cortez and His Cooperators." Visitors kneel at his grave and pray; they say the rosary. They bring candles in glass containers with the figure of the Virgin of Guadalupe printed in colors on the glass to light and place at his grave; they bring wreaths of artificial flowers and statues; they bring other votive articles of many kinds. All is performed in fulfillment of vows made to the spirit of Don Pedrito or in supplication.

Written petitions taken from a visitors' book placed at Don Pedrito's grave site give further examples of these propitiatory practices.

Don Pedrito:

I ask you to help me in my work and in all sickness that I may have. Please grant me this request which I make of you this 20th of January of 1957. I promise always to come and bring you flowers and a candle. May I get well of my sickness in the name of God and the spirit of Don Pedrito J.

Signed/female

Mr. and Mrs. _____ of King Ranch:

Don Pedrito, I ask of you that you do me the favor of curing my son and daughter, that they get well and help me in my work and I promise I'll come and watch over you and bring flowers. My son is _____ and my daughter is _____ in the name of God and Don Pedrito.

Initials

I came to visit and bring you flowers and candles, and to beseech you to help me in my trip to see the doctor. I pray that he be a competent doctor.

Your faithful slave
and devotee,

Signed/female

(Romano-V, Octavio 1965, p. 1163).

One study conducted by Nall and Speilberg (1967) shows that the adherence to propitiatory religious rituals by Chicanos is not related to the acceptance of a modern medical regime. It can be assumed then that Chicanos do not rely solely on such practices for cure, but consider them an aid in expediting a remedy for various illnesses.

The third aspect of folk belief and practice relates to the use of *curanderos* or *curanderas* (folk healers). To understand the function of healers in Chicano culture, it is important to be aware of the differences among healers. Romano-V (1965) gives a clear description of the healing hierarchy.

It is possible that a given healer may have influence over a very small circle of followers, while another's influence transcends communal boundaries and touches the lives of many hundreds of people. Similarly, a given healer's influence might also cross the boundaries of social class. The sphere of influence which a healer may have, then, will constitute the core variable upon which the following societal model will be constructed. Beginning with the sphere of influence at its most minimal expression, and proceeding to the maximal in terms of number of followers and geographical area involved, the following hierarchical spectrum emerges: 1) daughter; 2) mother; 3) grandmother; 4) experienced neighbor, incipient full-time healer, male or female; 5) village or neighborhood (urban barrio) healer, male or female; 6) town or city (enclave) healer, male or female; 7) regional healer (more than one village or city), urban and rural, male or female; 8) international healer, urban and rural, Mexican or American, male or female; 9) international, religious, folk-saint, male or female. The hierarchical positions outlined in this model beginning in the nuclear household and culminating in the international setting are relatively fixed. The specific membership; however, is fluid in that individual healers may move up or down in the hierarchy, remain in a given position, or even drop out of the healing vocation altogether. (Romano-V, 1965, p. 1154)

It is important to keep in mind this hierarchy while evaluating the studies that have been done on curanderos. Many of them focus on the use of a regional healer or international healer and do not relate to the frequency with which the daughter, mother, grandmother, or neighbor is used in the nuclear or extended family. Rubel's (1966) study is an exception. He gives clear indication that in the Mexican-American community he studied, neighbors or regional healers are consulted only after family healers and their remedies, which include administering various herbs made up in various teas coupled with prayers or treating for one of the folk illnesses, have been used.

Many charismatic healers have been recognized as having special healing powers. One such curandero is the famous Don Pedrito Jaramillo, mentioned earlier in this chapter.

Don Pedrito Jaramillo was born in Guadalajara, Jalisco, in August, 1829. He had already declared himself a healer prior to his arrival in Texas in 1881 when he was 52 years of age. He initially established himself as a neighborhood healer at Los Olmos Creek. Don Pedrito claimed "that God had bestowed on him the power to heal the sick, to say which prescription, given in the name of God and executed with faith and in the name of God, had the power to heal. He claimed no healing power of himself. His mission was to help the sick through their faith in God's power to heal them" (Dodson, 1951, p. 12). He lived a life of self-imposed poverty and never solicited payment for his services. He traveled extensively throughout the Southwest and by 1893 his reputation as a healer was widespread. Don Pedrito would prescribe his cures wherever the patient would ask his help. This flexibility was described by an elderly survivor of the time, Don Miguel. "Don Pedrito would help everybody and he would prescribe inside, outside, anywhere even on the road. It was so strange how he would prescribe so rapidly" (Romano-V, 1965, p. 1161).

Don Pedrito never married and never was known to have a family of his own although he adopted a son. He died in 1907 after 25 years of healing in the Southwest.

Another charismatic healer not often written about is Teresa Urrea, who also acquired international reputation. Born in 1872 or 1873 in Ocoroni, Sinaloa, Mexico, Teresa began her healing at the age of sixteen. Because of political pressures, she was exiled to the United States in 1892. At the time of her expulsion from Mexico, Teresa had been acclaimed as Santa Teresa de Cabora for her many healing feats. While she was in Arizona and Texas, many Mexicans crossed the border to seek her cure. She gave her services free of charge to all who asked. She traveled throughout the United States for a number of years as part of a "curing crusade" in what she believed to be a philanthropic venture. She married in 1900 and gave birth to two daughters before her death in January of 1906 in Clifton, Arizona (Rodriguez and Rodriguez, 1972).

There are no special initiations, dream experiences, or ordeals required to become a curandero. Most healers learn through apprenticeship. One of the main underlying assumptions is that healing comes from God and, therefore, abnormal mental states are not prerequisites for the healer. But it does happen that charismatic curanderos have given certification by their experience with repeated dreams or usual mental states that they are the recipient of a special gift *(don)* from God. For instance, Teresa Urrea's healing power is attributed to her having experienced an unusual mental state.

Teresa's healing power was a result of a cataleptic state she experienced during her first few months at Cabora. It lasted three months and eighteen days. During the first fourteen days in the trance, Teresa's heartbeat became fainter and fainter until it seemed to cease altogether. Believing her dead, her family began preparations for her burial. An all night wake was held and late that night as the women knelt around her saying their prayers and fingering their rosaries, Teresa revived, raised herself up, and inquired as to what was going on. For the three months following that occurrence, Teresa was in a state of abstraction. It is reported that Teresa said, "For three months and eighteen days, I was in a trance. I know nothing of what I did during that time. They told me, those who saw, that I could move about but they had to feed me; that I talked strange things about God and religion, that people came to me from all over the country, and if they were sick or crippled, I put my hands on them and they got well. Of this I remember nothing, but when I came to myself, I saw they were well." (Rodriguez and Rodriguez, 1972, pp. 51-52)

Don Pedrito Jaramillo is said to have obtained his gift for healing in a dream. The story is described by Dodson (1951).

Don Pedrito related that when he was a poor laborer in Mexico (some say he was a shepherd), working for half a bushel of corn and the equivalent of five dollars a month, he suffered an affliction of the nose (his picture shows a prominent scar just below the bridge). One night he said he was suffering so much that he went out into the woods to a pool of water. He lay down and buried his face in the mud at the edge. This relieved him. He stayed there treating himself with the mud. At the end of three days he was well, but his nose remained disfigured. . . . He returned to his house and lay down and slept. After a while a voice awakened him and told him that he had received from God the gift of healing. At the same time, the voice told him that his master was sick and that he had the power to cure him. He got up and went to his master. He prescribed the first thing that came into his mind. After this manner he prescribed always. . . . Thus began the work of this curandero. (Dodson, 1951, pp. 12-13)

The curanderos power to heal is not looked on with awe. Healing is derived from God and the curandero is merely God's agent. The curandero relies sometimes on religious paraphernalia such as crosses and pictures of the saints. He does most of his healing at home in front of an altar. Because the curandero is usually a very religious person in the eyes of the community, his motives are unchallenged and he is trusted. Although the curanderos' reputation is made according to his successes, he is not blamed for his failures since the group accepts the role of God's will in all matters of health.

The curandero cares for both the minor and severe disorders of the community. The less severe disorders are those resulting from a variety of social, familial, and cultural experiences. The severe disorders are of two kinds: certain physical ailments that are also recognized by modern medicine and folk illnesses described previously (Kiev, 1968).

There are a number of studies of a descriptive nature (Kiev, 1968; Rubel, 1966; Romano, 1965; Foster, 1953) giving valuable information on the functions of curanderos. There is no study that gives complete information on how many curanderos there are throughout the United States. It can be assumed that there are local curanderos in every rural and urban area in which Chicanos are living, but it is difficult to obtain census-like information because the practice of medicine by nonlicensed individuals is considered illegal. Usually a curandero's whereabouts

and reputation are carried by word of mouth, but very often curanderos advertise their services. In larger urban areas this is especially true. In a very large urban area like New York, it is not uncommon to be handed a leaflet like the one at the bottom of the page.

How to distinguish between the charlatans and the sincere curanderos is important. Traditionally, it is considered unacceptable for a curandero to profit from rendering services to the sick. An unsolicited contribution is given for such services but those unable to offer a contribution are not denied care.

Studies that attempt to compare the use of curanderos with modern clinics often attempt to measure the use of one to the exclusion of others to obtain the comparative value of the two. The assumption that the adherence to folk beliefs and practices precludes the use of modern medical facilities and personnel is seriously questioned (Nall and Speilberg, 1967; Rubel, 1966; Lubchansky et al., 1970). Folk healers are often used for certain illnesses, but a modern physician may also be consulted.

Rubel feels that wandering among healers who might hold promises about health and illness in startling contrast to each other is not incongruous behavior on the part of Chicanos. He states that "treatment of a patient by his mother on one night, a physician on the next, and a spiritualistic curandero on the third does not seem inconsistent to Chicanos. The cure

---

Sra. Doris Consejera y Adivinadora Se hecha la baraja Mensajera de Dios	Señora Doris Counselor and Fortuneteller Messenger of God
Se resolveran sus problemas de amor, negocio, enfermedades y de sus problemas familiares. Se reuen los separados. Le ayuda en sus trabajos. Le resuelve su problema del alcoholismo. Le ayuda en sus dolores y enfermedades. Le librara de todos los sufrimientos que Ud. tenga. No hay problema tan grande que ella no le pueda resolver. Con una sola visita a esta mujer milagrosa usted se convencera. Ella tiene el poder que Dios le ha dado. Por sus oraciones Ud. ha de ser muy feliz. Venga a verla hoy mismo. **Se hecha la baraja.**	She can dissolve your problems of love, business, illness, and domestic difficulties. She can unite those who are separated. Give help in your work. Give resolution to your alcoholic problems. She gives help in your pain and sickness. She liberates you from all your sufferings. There are no problems so large that she is unable to resolve them. You will be convinced with one visit only to this miraculous woman. She has sanction from God. For your oration [prayer] you will be made very happy. Come and see her immediately.

is the thing; by what means or by whom is purely academic" (Rubel, 1966, p. 200). This pragmatic nature of Chicanos is often overlooked in the discussion of the use of curanderos.

HOW DOES CURANDERISMO RELATE TO CURRENT MENTAL HEALTH NEEDS OF CHICANOS?

Interaction of culture and mental health and illness

First, the existence of folk beliefs and practices reaffirms the relevance and role of culture in mental health and illness. It is important to realize that culture plays a strong role in determining the specific ways in which individuals deal with and perceive their environment. Anglo-Western culture, because of its dominance in economical and political spheres, has been able to overrepresent its own cultural ethno-centric view of the world, especially in the development of psychiatry. Culture influences the form of conflict, behavior, and psychopathology that occurs in members of the culture (Opler, 1959). The boundaries between cultural and biological phenomena can be differentiated by studying the particular world view of a specific people and its social system. When we speak of adjustment we are talking about the individual in relation to the social environment. It is then very important to consider the individual within his own social context. Specific socio-cultural systems significantly affect the definition and process of adjustment, deviance, and maladjustment. This is not to say that culture is a cause of maladjustment as is often implied in the literature related to Chicano cultural values. Each culture has its own stress points and strengths. Each has its own social network for regulating interpersonal interactions. Data on the cultural context in which the individual is functioning is important in planning services and determining cultural stress points and potential resources.

A number of studies attempt to document the existence of folk beliefs as an indication of distinct concepts of disease and mental illness in Chicanos. Many of them are descriptive in nature (Rubel, 1966; Kiev, 1968) and provide valuable information on the nature of disease in Chicano communities and culture and its relation to social systems. Rubel describes the strong persistence of four illnesses: (1) *caída de la mollera* (fallen fontanel), (2) *empacho* (intestinal disorders), (3) *mal ojo* (evil eye), and (4) *susto* (shock) in New Lots, a small town of 1500 inhabitants located in the lower Rio Grande Valley of southern Texas. Persons of Mexican descent comprised three-fifths of the total population at the time of this study. Regarding the function of folk illnesses and cures, Rubel indicates that health and illness are intimately linked with social relationships. In particular, Rubel states that:

> It is of considerable interest to note that when a patient or his family considers an illness to have been precipitated by faulty interpersonal relations, the presumed agent of that condition is never portrayed as an Anglo. Furthermore, in spite of the saliency of the intergroup antagonisms between Chicanos and Anglos in New Lots, there is no evidence to indicate that such hostilities are symbolized by illness. In Mexiquito, illness is appropriate to communicate intragroup, but not intergroup social stresses. (Rubel, 1966, pp. 171-172)

Most studies agree that disease among Chicanos must be viewed as social phenomena with social explanations. Kiev (1968) studied Chicanos in the San Antonio area and believes that this social aspect of curanderismo is the strongest force behind folk beliefs and practices.

> Thus, disease among the Mexican-Americans must be viewed not only as a unique personal experience but also as a social phenomenon with social explanations. All persistent, acute, severe, and bizarre sickness is believed to be caused either by the punitive action of God or by the malevolence of others. God punishes man for neglecting religious obligations, for breaches of ritual prohibition, or because he cannot live well with others. When social conflicts are not apparent, they are searched for or supernatural forces are invoked. Therapy is often a matter of reconciling disturbed social relationships, thereby simultaneously ridding the patient of his pathological symptoms. Thus, the folk medical systems in traditional or modified form provide channels for anxiety reduction and treatment for individuals in need. (Kiev, 1968, pp. 19-20)

Implicit in the descriptive data is the assumption that Chicano perception of mental illness and health is distinct from Anglo-Americans. Empirical data to support this assumption is not available. The few studies that have attempted a comparative analysis of how Anglo-Americans and Chicanos perceive, define, and respond to mental illness indicate that differences may not be as sharply differentiated as the descriptive data supposes (Karno and Edgerton, 1969; Rosenthal et al., 1969). Generalization of the comparative data is limited because of the small, geographically restricted populations on which they were conducted and the methodology employed. With this in mind, two studies that attempted a comparative analysis are summarized below.

Karno and Edgerton (1969) attempted to evaluate these differences in a study directed at accounting for the discrepancy between reported low incidence of mental illness (based on utilization of mental health facilities) and what was suspected to be a much higher incidence of mental illness in the Chicano population. The study was conducted in an East Los Angeles area in which Chicanos represented 10% of the 7 million residents. A comparative analysis was made of the responses given by 444 Chicanos and 224 Anglo-Americans of similar socio-economic status during a systematic household interview. The content of the interview was contained in an 18-page booklet with 200 questions that solicited biographical, demographical, and attitudinal information. To compare attitudes toward mental illness and health, the Star technique was employed whereby behavioral characteristics of fictional characters with various mental disturbances were given. Male respondents representing the household head were asked to respond to the following type of description:

Mrs. Brown is nearly 50, has a nice home, and her husband has a good job. She used to be full of life; an active, busy woman with a large family. Her children are now grown and in recent months she has changed. She sits and broods for hours, blames herself for all kinds of bad things she thinks she has done, and talks about what a terrible person she is. She has lost interest in all the things she used to enjoy, cannot sleep, has no appetite, and paces up and down the house for hours.

After hearing this vignette, the general question asked was, "What do you think about this woman?" Karno and Edgerton made three tentative conclusions regarding the underutilization of psychiatric facilities by Chicanos based on this preliminary study: (1) Chicano cultural tradition does not cause Chicanos to define mental illness in significantly different ways than do Anglos, (2) underutilization does not reflect a lesser incidence of mental illness in Chicano communities, and (3) underrepresentation is accounted for by complex social and cultural factors. Of those factors at play within the social and cultural context, folk medicine, folk psychotherapy, and "Mexican culture" in general are considered to be of minor importance in relation to the other social and cultural factors, such as language barriers, the active role of the family physician in mental health, and the self-esteem reducing nature of agency–client contacts.

Although no significant difference between the two groups in the perception and definition of mental illness is postulated, this does not dispute the possibilities that qualitative differences do exist. Indication is that Chicanos, like Anglos, use the same behavioral cues as indices of mental disturbance, but that there still might be qualitative differences in assumed etiology and significance of such mental states that are culturally distinct (Martinez and Martin, 1966).

In another study, Rosenthal et al. (1969), using a structured interview format, obtained comparative data on the extent and intensity of acceptance of certain medical child care practices among non-Anglo, lower income Anglo, and upper income Anglo women in Tucson, Arizona. An attempt was made to determine to what degree the social perception of agreement with these beliefs is a function of respondents' ethnic and income group. In total, 139 subjects were interviewed: 37 non-Anglo, 52 lower income, and 50 upper income Anglo females. The results of the survey-like study are summarized as follows:

Belief in magical childcare procedures was studied in non-Anglo and lower and upper-class Anglo-American women. The non-A group accepted the main cures investigated significantly more than did the low-A group which in turn displayed significantly less rejection of each belief and their aggregate than did the upper-A group; thus, not only cultural milieu but also socio-economic level within Anglo-American society affected acceptance of the healing practices. The sizable group difference derived more from the intense disagreement of Anglo women than from strong agreement with the belief complex by the non-A group. In regard to the cures, the upper-A group differentiated themselves from their community and from Negros, and differentiated their community from Mexican-Americans more than either of the other groups. Unlike both other groups who perceived belief congruence between Negro and Mexican-American people, the lower-A women distinguished sharply between these outgroup minorities. Although the non-A group felt magical practices were more common in the older generation than did the other women, all groups judged that such cures would be used less often, if at all, by the next generation of mothers. (Rosenthal et al., 1969, p. 12)

This is one of the few studies to attempt qualification of folk belief practices in relation to other social-psychological variables. Also, it is one of the few studies to employ statistical analysis of the data to determine significant differences in attitudes. The child care beliefs that are emphasized could be categorized as in the general area of old wives' tales and not specific folk beliefs unique to Chicano culture. For instance, respondents were asked to express agreement or disagreement on such items as "infant's eyes roll in funny ways because the soft spot lets the content (filling) inside the head press down" and "babies fed on the bottle may get big navels because air from the bottle presses into the tummy." Beyond making an assertion that these specific magical child care procedures are accepted by the non-Anglo group in relation to the lower and upper socio-economic Anglo group, no overall differences in perception of childhood ills and cures can be made.

The Karno and Edgerton and Rosenthal et al. studies illustrate the difficulty of making a determination of culturally relevant beliefs and practices unique to a subculture comparative to the dominant group. Obtaining adequate cross-sectional representation of all members of the subculture is one problem. In the Karno and Edgerton study, males were used as subjects because of their position in the family

and their accessibility. Yet, it has been shown that very often females practice and administer folk remedies. In making any comparisons, differences in generational, regional, and socio-economic position need to be considered. More importantly, there is need to verify that the area of inquiry is representative of one or the other culture whether it is the dominant one or not. The weight of the descriptive material indicates that Chicanos may maintain two systems of beliefs and practices regarding illness and health (Rubel, 1966; Madsen, 1964; Torrey, 1969). One system is shared with the dominant culture and the other is from traditional Chicano culture. In this case, Karno and Edgerton's findings are not surprising since they show that Chicanos share concepts of illness and health commonly held by Anglos. A more relevant test would be to rewrite the vignettes to describe typical folk beliefs and practices and to then analyze the comparative responses of Anglos and Chicanos.

General view of illness and health

Given the scarcity of empirical data to document distinct differences in perception of mental illness and health based on cultural affiliation, this section summarizes the generalizations made concerning Chicanos' views of mental illness based on descriptive data. Kiev (1968) categorizes Chicanos' views of illness and health into four areas. The first is the religious view of illness, whose foundation is the belief that life is ordained by divine will. If God's commandments are kept, good health and happiness will be bestowed. Sin is considered one of the causes of illness. Sickness is rationalized by the belief that God allows people to suffer in order to learn. One cannot question God's plan and so the individual who suffers patiently is seen as helping God to achieve his purpose. The individual's suffering is seen in a social context as it becomes a family affair or even a community concern because suffering is meaningful for other "children of God." To a Chicano whatever the illness or the class of the healer, whether curandero or physician, the final outcome of the curing venture is dependent on the will of God. Rubel (1966) attests to this by indicating that

Primero Dios (God first!) is an axiom that consistently and fervently accompanies discussion of illness or injury. Another such phrase *(Santos no puede si Dios no quiere)* indicates that even the saints may not cure if God proves unwilling (p. 198). Yet this fatalistic verbalization does not interfere with Chicanos' pragmatic action-oriented behavior toward illness. A cure for an illness is sought by the family when one of its members is ill and every means possible is used to obtain relief.

Secondly, illness is viewed sociologically when it is not considered a chance event, but is inextricably bound to the religious history of the individual and the group. Changes in traditional patterns of life are felt to violate God's will and as such are a source of potential difficulty. Kiev states: "The roots of illness are thus attributed in part to the pattern of life and the values emphasized in Anglo society, which violate the religious values of a family-centered, static agrarian society" (p. 36). All the folk illnesses are related to social interactions among family members and the community. Thus, it does appear that interpersonal relationships are a part of Chicanos' views of illness and health. Generally, the strongest distinction between Chicanos' and Anglo-Westerns' views of illness is that, for the latter, illness is an impersonal event, whereas, for Chicanos, it is a social as well as a biological fact (Kiev, 1968).

Thirdly, Chicanos have a supernaturalistic view of illness. This encompasses the acceptance of both good and evil influences. The basic assumptions are that the mind can influence matter, that words and wishes have creative power, that communication with the dead is possible, and that the dead can influence life on earth. This aspect of illness is seen especially in mal de susto when an individul experiences soul loss. Also, the ritualistic acts, *promise-making* and lighting candles, are a part of this supernaturalistic view of illness. Prayer is believed to be a way of communicating with saints and members of the family who are dead in order to solicit their aid in the curing process.

Fourthly, there is the *naturalistic* view. Health is the result of caring for the body properly—of maintaining a balance between the extremes.

Prevalence studies

Most reports on folk illness and practices of folk cures among Chicanos directly or indirectly assert a widespread prevalence of such beliefs. Few reports provide data that would allow for accurate estimation of how many people within a given population have knowledge of, or subscribe to, belief and practice or participation in such phenomena. A great number of reports deal with more rural Chicano populations especially in Texas communities. Other areas in the Southwest are not as completely reported on or investigated and the urban areas in which a higher degree of acculturation is assumed to dilute such beliefs and practices have received the least amount of attention. An exception to this general trend is a study by Martinez and Martin (1966) in which 75 Mexican-American housewives, living in a public housing project near the business district of Dallas, were interviewed to determine the extent of knowledge about folk illnesses and treatment. Knowledge of five folk illnesses: (1) *mal ojo,* (2) *empacho,* (3) *caída de la mollera,* (4) *susto,* and (5) *mal puesto* were investigated by means of an open-ended interview. Findings indicate that 97% of the women knew about each of the five diseases. Eighty-five percent had some specific knowledge about symptoms, treatment, and etiology of the diseases except mal puesto.

Regarding the prevalence and use of folk healers or curanderos studied, Martinez and Martin showed that a majority of the women were aware that senoras were in the immediate locale and more than one-half of them had been treated by a senora at some time during their life. In the study, a distinction between senoras and curanderos is made, indicating that the majority of the women had knowledge of senoras (nine such individuals were identified) while only one-fifth reported knowledge of a curandera (one curandera was identified). It is assumed here that senoras are neighborhood curers who have not declared themselves formal curanderas and maintain or confine their treatment to the immediate neighborhood locale.

The study also showed that visits to physicians or the local health clinic were reported by three-fifths of the subjects interviewed. Services rendered by these Anglo sources were for medical reasons other than relief from folk ailments. More importantly, the study showed that adherence to folk beliefs and curative practices does not preclude reliance upon physicians and other medical facilities. The authors theorize that:

Many Mexican-Americans participate in two insular systems of health beliefs and health care. A woman identified by many of the respondents as a curandera demonstrated this compartmentalized participation. At the close of the interview, she said, "I have to go take a nap now. My doctor says I need plenty of rest, and I don't want to disobey his orders."

Another study by Nall and Speilberg (1967) confirms the findings that folk medical beliefs and practices do not act as inhibiting factors for the acceptance of modern medical regimes. A sample of 53 tuberculosis subjects drawn from the "closed" tuberculosis case files of the McAllen Branch of the Hidalgo County, Texas Health Unit were used as subjects. This study investigated whether folk medical beliefs, the practice of propitiatory religious acts, and the use of folk curers, influenced or inhibited the acceptance or rejection of treatment for tuberculosis. Findings indicated that none of these traditional practices and beliefs inhibited the acceptance of modern medicine. On the other hand, a number of social integration indices were found to relate to the subjects' acceptance or rejection of the treatment regime. In particular, findings showed that integration into the ethnic subcommunity favored nonacceptance of the treatment regime and vice versa. The authors speculate that Chicano socio-cultural forces build strong ties to the family and to the ethnic community into the model Chicano personality so that a high degree of psychological dependency is manifested. The treatment regime for tuberculosis demands lengthy periods of confinement away from the family and the ethnic subcommunity and thus presents demands on the integrated Chicano that are stressful and thus difficult to meet.

Creson and McKinley (1969) indicate that in an interview with 25 Chicano patients of low socio-economic status, the concept of folk illness was deeply entrenched. Thus, the patients were resistant to the influences of Anglo-American culture and its scientific medicine.

Only one study (Holland, 1963) attempted to qualify the intensity of adherence to folk beliefs and practices among Chicanos themselves. Two-hundred-fifty non-Anglo families in Tucson, Arizona, were interviewed. Respondents indicated they they differed in the degree to which they had knowledge of and practiced folk medical remedies. Holland did not provide evidence that the differences observed were statistically significant.

In contrast to studies that report continued adherence to folk beliefs and practices are the findings of Edgerton et al. (1970). In their research among Chicanos in East Los Angeles, they indicated that while curanderismo is present in the community, its importance has diminished greatly. They indicated that the preferred treatment resource of mental illness among this population is the general physician, and not the curandero.

Theoretical speculation on how and why curanderismo functions

Although there is inconclusive evidence, controversy over the prevalence and degree to which various groups of Chicanos adhere to curanderismo, the presence of curanderos is reaffirmed in almost every study reviewed here. A few authors attempt to set forth theories on why curanderismo continues to exist and what its function is in relation to the Chicano communities today. These theories will be summarized here.

Madsen's (1964) point ot of view is that folk medicine and illnesses among acculturated Chicanos functions as a mechanism to avoid or to relieve situations involving a conflict between Mexican and American values. He gives case examples of individuals, who in their attempts to take on the dominant Anglo culture ways, meet with conflict and fear.

The individual who has internalized values from both subcultures usually at some point becomes aware of painful cognitive dissonance. The individual's self-image loses its focus and decision-making becomes a matter of profound anxiety. The partly-acculturated Inglesado[1] finds identity with any recognized role in either subgroup almost impossible. He is scorned by the conservative Mexican-Americans and refused admission to Anglo society. Some Inglesados in this situation seek closer identity with Anglo culture through such means as conspicuous display of Anglo mannerisms or conversion to a Protestant church. Others seek to escape geographically and move to another state or to one of the larger cities in Texas. Others attempt to retreat into the conservative Mexican-American culture. Those who retreat are usually afflicted with a series of folk diseases. As Anglos are believed to be immune to such ailments, merely being afflicted by one is a means of cultural identification with la raza. To accept the diagnosis and to cooperate in the treatment are a declaration of acceptance of the conservative Mexican-American world view. The treatment involves the re-establishment of traditional roles and frequently some form of penance. Such treatments are nearly always conducted by curanderos. (Madsen, 1964, p. 433)

The cognitive dissonance theory has been used by Rosenthal and Siegel (1959) as a framework from which various hypotheses concerning the significance of folk beliefs and practices have been analyzed among traditional Chicano subcul-

---

[1]Inglesado is the term used to refer to a Chicano who is attempting to become Angloized; usually has negative connotations.

tures. The assumption is that magical beliefs and practices involve a cognitive component in that individuals may be aware that their techniques for coping with situations are not always consistent with what they know about the adequacy of these techniques. The general proposition as stated by Aberle (1957) is as follows:

The affirmation of values and the search for control where control is difficult have one thing in common to me: a state of tenson. Many but not all of these tensions involve conflict. They all involve some problem of discrepancy—of a gap between norm and performance, between wish and actuality, between desire to love wholly and feelings of hatred—and so on. It seems to me that both religion and magic attempt to cope with these tensions whether or not one chooses to regard this as their core function. (p. 9)

Rubel (1960) asserts that traditional concepts of health and disease contribute to the maintenance of Chicano social systems in Texas. He argues that mal ojo, susto, and mal puesto function to sustain some of the dominant values of Chicano culture by emphasizing maintenance of the solidarity of a small, bilateral family unit and by prescribing the appropriate role behaviors of males and females and of older and younger individuals.

Writing on the epidemiology of susto (soul loss), Rubel (1965) presents an epidemiological model that orders the descriptive

STATE OF HEALTH

1. Susceptibility to susto and other health conditions
2. Relative severity and chronicity of illness
3. Frequency of episodes

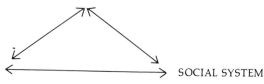

PERSONALITY SYSTEM ⟷ SOCIAL SYSTEM

1. Self-perception of relative success or failure in fulfilling social role expectations.
2. Individual's capacity to adapt to self-perceived inadequate role performances.

1. Society's sex specific and age specific role expectations.

data of this folk illness and in so doing offers a framework from which an analysis of similar phenomena can be attempted. The model is depicted on p. 276.

Underlying this model is the assumption that susto and possibly other folk illnesses are the product of the interaction between three open systems, each linked with the others. These systems are: (1) an individual's state of health, (2) his personality system, and (3) the social system of which he is a member (Rubel, 1964).

Rubel's theoretical framework is the most comprehensive one proposed as it encompasses and integrates the assumptions made by other authors reviewed here. His main hypothesis is "that susto illness in societies of Hispanic-America may be understood as a product of a complex interaction between an individual's state of health and the role expectations which his society provides, mediated by aspects of that individual's personality" (Rubel, 1964).

WHAT IS CURANDERISMO'S COMPARATIVE EFFECTIVENESS TO ANGLO PSYCHIATRIC TREATMENT?

Kiev (1968) examined in detail the specific aspects of curanderismo to clarify the therapeutic significance of its culture-bound elements. Using an anthropological technique, Kiev relied on a number of informants to gather ethnological information. He used the participant observor method with four native healers. He directly observed treatment techniques of the curanderos. In addition, he treated several Chicano patients with traditional psychotherapeutic techniques to determine the relative effectiveness of the two approaches.

In summarizing his findings, Kiev makes the following comparisons between curanderismo and psychotherapy. Curanderismo values the traditional absolute, faith and obedience, whereas dynamic psychotherapy strives for objectivity, impartiality, and a search for scientific evidence. Curanderismo questions specific techniques, philosophies, and goals of contemporary dynamic psychotherapy that may have developed more for their compatibility with the value system of Anglo culture than for any well-founded scientific

reason. Since Chicanos place great emphasis on safeguarding the inner worth and dignity of the individual *(dignidad de la persona)*, it seems reasonable that they would be reluctant to discuss their feelings and to participate in a therapeutic process that emphasizes objective nonmoralizing examination.

Kiev concludes that the examination of the material suggests that there are many similarities between curanderismo and contemporary psychotherapy and that many of the differences are not caused by scientific factors but by cultural ones. Finally, there is no evidence that dynamic psychotherapy is of more value than other forms of treatment such as curanderismo. In view of this, it is reasonable to speculate about the relative merits of dynamic psychotherapy and curanderismo for the treatment of psychiatric disorders of Chicanos.

Kiev presents the only direct comparative analysis of modern psychotherapy and curanderismo. Impressionistic data related in a number of other studies confirm the functional effectiveness of curanderos (Rubel, 1966; Madsen, 1964; Saunders, 1954). There are no carefully controlled studies to verify that curanderos are effective in producing positive therapeutic changes, but the work of transcultural psychiatry indicates that with most indigenous therapists, positive results are obtained by treatment procedures that are culturally relevant and significant (Torrey, 1970).

WHAT IS THE FUTURE ROLE FOR CURANDERISMO IN "MODERN MEDICINE"?

Although the present prevalence and intensity of curanderismo has not been adequately documented, it can be safely assumed that many Chicano subcultures maintain culturally specific beliefs, practices, and attitudes toward illness and health. This does not mean that they do not share in the dominant culture's attitudes of health and illness as well. Also, it does not mean that there is only one commonly held perspective for all Chicanos concerning illness and health. The group is too diverse to make such a broad generalization. Data that gives quantification of folk beliefs and practices is badly needed. Until such research is done, it is not possible to make any definitive statements regarding the differences in attitudes toward illness and health.

A number of studies indicate that the existence and belief in curanderismo does not necessarily preclude the acceptance of modern medical practices (Rubel, 1964; Martinez and Martin, 1966; Nall and Speilberg, 1967). This is an important finding as it is often assumed that traditional medical beliefs and practices are a hindrance to the use of modern medicine. It is easy to dismiss such beliefs as superstition and little attempt is made to understand or educate professional staffs of the value of such practices and beliefs. Some authors have suggested that underutilization of modern medical and psychiatric facilities can be attributed in part to the traditional medical staff's hostility, indifference, and ignorance of Chicanos' values regarding mental health and illness (Knoll, 1971; Kline, 1969; Karno, 1966). A number of studies that have set forth theoretical frameworks from which to analyze curanderismo and the reasons for its continued use have emphasized the functional aspect of such practices in terms of the socio-cultural environment of the Chicano (Rubel, 1964; Rosenthal and Siegel, 1959; Madsen, 1964).

There is documentation that Chicanos seek help from ethnic folk curers for relief of folk-defined illnesses and other less severe disorders (Clark, 1959; Creson, 1969; Saunders, 1954; Rubel, 1960; Madsen, 1964; Kiev, 1968). The use of this pattern of diagnosis and treatment does not appear to be used to the exclusion of modern medicine and cannot account for the numbers of mentally-ill Chicanos who are excluded from any formal mental illness statistical report (Edgerton et al., 1970).

Progress has been made in the health field in terms of increased sensitivity to obvious cultural differences such as language and the physical environment of community mental health facilities. Attempts at incorporating a Chicano cultural world view have not been tried. Many authors have advocated increased sensitivity to chicanismo in terms of increased awareness of cultural differences (Madsen, 1964; Kline, 1969; Saunders, 1954). While this

can be helpful, it does not maintain cultural democracy within the mental health area. In many cases, gaining Chicanos' acceptance of modern medicine has been at the expense of disrupting the community's own social organization and thus creating unnecessary tension. A more helpful position would be to attempt some compromise between the two cultures in which the essential values and autonomy of each is maintained and respected.

As a first step in this direction, some authors have recommended the use of traditional healers as paraprofessionals. For instance, Lubchansky et al. (1970) conducted a study to determine whether or not Puerto Rican Spiritualists hold distinct attitudes and cures toward mental illness. Based on the fact that Spiritualists offer a distinct belief system and treatment toward mental illnesses, and also on data that indicates that a large number of Puerto Ricans use the services of Spiritualists, they recommend that serious consideration be given to the use of these indigenous healers as paraprofessionals in the treatment of mental health. Lubchansky et al. (1970) see the professional attitudes and biases toward such healers as the main deterrent to this eventuality. They indicate that

To see the points of similarity as well as the points of contrast between the Spiritualists' methods and our own, we need to come to terms with a magical type of thinking that is alien to centuries of Western scientific striving. To a psychiatrist, the *concepts* of supernaturally-caused illness and supernatural cure are not only alien but unprofessional as well. The Spiritualist etiology of mental illness is so remote from our own as to be almost unacceptable. Yet, *in practice,* there are some similarities with professional psychiatric treatment.

In the study, the Star vignette technique, which portrays paranoid, schizophrenia, anxiety neurosis, alcoholism, compulsive-phobic behavior, and juvenile character disorders, was used to assess the attitudes and beliefs of Spiritualists toward mental illness and health. To determine the degree to which twenty Spiritualists held a set of attitudes about mental illness unique to them, a comparison was made between a cross section of forty Puerto Rican household heads and twenty Spanish-speaking community leaders. This comparison showed that the Spiritualists did perceive mental illness in a somewhat broader way than either the community leader group or the Puerto Rican household heads. Spiritualist treatment techniques were reinterpreted within a Freudian framework and seen to be effective.

Torrey (1969) presents a cogent argument for the use of indigenous therapists in formalized mental health services. He first presents indirect evidence that shows that patient expectations and the personal qualities of the therapist play major roles in psychotherapeutic change. Regarding patient expectations, he refers to the work of Jerome Frank and others, which indicates that, in general, "the therapist's power is based on the patient's perception of him as a source of help, and it tends to be greater the greater the patient's distress and his faith in the therapist's desire and ability to help him." Coupled with this, certain basic personality qualities seem to differentiate the successful therapist from the unsuccessful. Overall, three basic qualities are of crucial importance. These are: (1) accurate empathy, (2) nonpossessive warmth, and (3) genuineness. At this juncture, Torrey argues that the acquiring of knolwedge or intellectual training does not make a therapist. In the last analysis, it is what the individual can do when working with people in need of psychological guidance and help that determines success or failure.

The direct evidence presented by Torrey that describes the indigenous workers indicates that, with minimal training, they are often effective in producing positive therapeutic changes. He presents a good summary of the research done in transcultural psychiatry on indigenous healers and concludes that there are numerous examples that indicate that the community-sanctioned healer performs effective psychotherapy. He shows also that when the indigenous worker has been used in the formalized mental health services, his work has always been seen as useful and effective as compared with professional mental health personnel whose effectiveness in serving non-Anglo subcultures has been notoriously poor.

The author specifies and then refutes five possible obstacles to incorporating indigenous therapists within the formalized mental health services. These are:

1. Indigenous therapists include many quacks, charlatans, hysterical personalities, schizophrenics, and generally unstable personalities. This problem can be solved by instituting a careful selection process.

2. Techniques used by indigenous therapists are crude, primitive, often harmful, and occasionally fatal. The author feels that it would be possible to maintain the useful techniques employed by indigenous workers such as abreaction, suggestion, dream interpretation, hypnosis, confession, desensitization, and psychodrama while discarding the harmful techniques.

3. Training indigenous therapists will render them less effective. They must be left in their "natural state." The response to this criticism is that if this is true, then all present professional training programs for psychotherapists also must be destructive.

4. The goals of indigenous therapists are usually just symptom relief, not long-term personality change. At this point, no clear relationship has yet emerged between symptom relief, behavior change, and personality change. It is a complex and unresolved area.

5. Using indigenous therapists will threaten many people's jobs who are presently doing psychotherapy. There is currently a severe shortage of mental health professionals and the demand for mental health services is so great that there will be more than enough jobs to go around.

6. Psychotherapy is part of medicine and as such the people doing it should be at least professionally trained as therapists, if not as doctors. In response to this latter obstacle, Torrey indicates that:

> The evidence suggests, then, that we should not be apologetic when we use indigenous therapists; rather at this state of our knowledge, we should be apologetic when we fail to use them on a trial basis.

This chapter surveyed the practice of curanderismo as a method of folk psychiatry and community treatment. Many studies have demonstrated the ease with which traditional beliefs can exist alongside contemporary "scientific" notions of illness and health. The belief that traditional views interfered with acceptance of modern practices has lead to hostility, denigration, and rejection of both more traditional views and the individuals who hold them. It is clear that effective response to Chicano populations requires an acceptance and understanding of folk beliefs along with an integration of these beliefs into current mental health practice. There are obstacles; but they are by no means insurmountable.

REFERENCES

Clark, M. *Health in the Mexican-American culture.* Berkley: University of California Press, 1959.

Creson, D. L., McKinley, C., & Evans, R. Folk medicine in Mexican-American subculture. *Diseases of the Nervous System,* 1969, *30*(4), 264-266.

Dodson, R. Don Pedrito Jaramillo: The Curandero of Los Olmos. *Publications of Texas Folklore Society,* XXIV, Dallas: Southern Methodist University Press, 1951.

Edgerton, R. B., Karno, M., & Fernandez, I. Curanderismo in the metropolis: The diminishing role of folk-psychiatry among Los Angeles Mexican-Americans. *American Journal of Psychotherapy,* 1970, *24* (1), 124-134.

Foster, G. M. Relationships between Spanish and Spanish-American folk medicine. *Journal of American Folklore,* 1953, *66,* 201-217.

Holland, W. R. Mexican-American medical beliefs: Science or magic? *Arizona Medicine,* 1963, *20,* 89-101.

Karno, M. The enigma of ethnicity in a psychiatric clinic, *Arch. Gen. Psychiatry,* 1966, *14,* 516-520.

Karno, M. & Edgerton, R. B. Perception of mental illness in a Mexican-American community, *Archives of General Psychiatry,* Feb., 1969, *20,* 233-238.

Karno, M., & Morales, A. A community mental health service for Mexican-Americans in a metropolis. *Comprehensive Psychiatry,* 1971, *12* (2), 116-121.

Kiev, A. *Curanderismo: Mexican-American folk psychiatry,* New York: The Free Press, 1968.

Kiev, A. *Magic, faith, and healing: Studies in primitive psychiatry today,* New York: The Free Press, 1964.

Kline, L. Some factors in the psychiatric treatment of Spanish-Americans, *American Journal of Psychiatry,* 1969, *125* (12), 1674-1681.

Knoll, F. R. Casework services for Mexican-Americans, *Social Casework,* 1971, *52,* 279-284.

Lubchansky, I. Ergi, G., & Stokes, J. Puerto Rican Spiritualists view mental illness: The faith healer as a paraprofessional, *American Journal of Psychiatry,* 1970, *127*(3), 312-321.

Madsen, W. Value conflicts and folk psychiatry in South Texas. In Kiev, A. (Ed.), *Magic, faith, and healing,* New York: The Free Press, 1964, pp. 420-440.

Madsen, W. Anxiety and witchcraft in Mexican-American acculturation, *Anthropology Quarterly,* 1966, *39*(2), 110-127.

Martinez, C. & Martin, H. W. Folk diseases among urban Mexican-Americans, *Journal of the American Medical Association,* 1966, *2,* 161-164.

Nall, F. C., & Speilberg, J. Social and cultural factors in the responses of Mexican-Americans to medical treatment, *Journal of Health and Social Behavior,* 1967, *8*(4), 299-308.

Opler, M. K. (Ed.), *Culture and mental health,* New York: The Macmillan Company, 1959.

Padilla, E. The relationship between psychology and Chicanos: Failures and possibilities. In Wagner, N. N., & Haug, M. J. (Eds.), *Chicanos: Social and psychological perspectives.* St. Louis: The C. V. Mosby Company, 1971, pp. 286-294.

Padilla, A., & Ruiz, R. *Latino mental health: A review of literature,* DHEW Publication No. (HSM) 73-9143, 1973.

Philippus, M. J. Successful and unsuccessful approaches to mental health services for an urban Hispano-American population. *American Journal of Public Health,* 1971, *61*(4), 820-830.

Ramirez, M., III. The relationship of acculturation to educational achievement and psychological adjustment in Chicano children and adolescents: A review of the literature. *El Grito,* 1971, *4*(4), 21-28.

Rodriguez, R., & Rodriguez, G. L. Teresa Urrea: Her life as it affected the Mexican-U.S. frontier, *El Grito,* 1972, *4*(4), 48-68.

Romano-V, O. J. Charismatic medicine, folk healing, and folk sainthood. *American Anthropologist,* 1965, *67*(5), 1151-1173.

Rosenthal, T. L., Henderson, R. W., Hobson, A., & Hurt, M. Social strata and perception of magical and folk medical childcare, *Journal of Social Psychology,* 1969, *77*(1), 3-13.

Rosenthal, T. L., & Siegel, B. J. Magic and witchcraft: An interpretation from dissonance theory, *Southwest Journal of Anthropology,* 1959, *15,* 143-167.

Rubel, A. J., The epidemiology of a folk illness: *Susto* in Hispanic America, *Ethnology,* 1964, *3*(3), 268-283.

Rubel, A. J. Concepts of disease in Mexican-American culture, *American Anthropology,* 1960, *62,* 795-814.

Rubel, A. J. *Across the Tracks, Cultural Differences and Medical Care: The Case of the Spanish-Speaking People in the Southwest,* New York: Russell Sage Foundation, 1966.

Sanchez, A. The definers and the defined: A mental health issue, *El Grito,* Summer, 1971, *4*(4), 4-11.

Saunders, L. *Cultural difference and medical care,* New York: Russell Sage Foundation, 1954, pp. 141-173.

Saunders, L. Healing ways in the Spanish Southwest. In Jaco E. G. (Ed.), *Patients, physicians, and illness,* New York: The Free Press, 1958, pp. 189-206.

Schulman, S. Rural healthways in New Mexico, *Annals of the New York Academy of Sciences,* 1960, *84*(17), 950-958.

Torrey, E. F. The case for the indigenous therapists, *Archives of General Psychiatry,* 1969, *20*(3), 365-373.

Torrey, E. F. The irrelevancy of traditional mental health services for urban Mexican-Americans, Paper presented at the American Orthopsychiatry Association, San Francisco, California, March, 1970.

CHAPTER 27 THE RELATIONSHIP BETWEEN PSYCHOLOGY AND CHICANOS: FAILURES AND POSSIBILITIES

ELIGIO R. PADILLA

The 1969 annual convention of the American Psychological Association (APA) was the setting for several dramatic confrontations between the newly formed Black Student Psychological Association BSPA and the APA (Simpkins and Raphael, 1970). The first major confrontation occurred as the president of the APA was being introduced to present the annual presidential address. During the introduction the black students rose from the audience, walked on stage, and demanded to have their grievances heard. The convention agreed to hear their demands on the following day. The following morning the president of BSPA presented their demands, including five "areas of concern" that he said must be explored and developed if the APA is to deal effectively with the "problems of society." Specifically BSPA demanded that APA utilize its expertise and resources to research and develop programs in five areas of major concern to Black Americans:

. . . (1) the recruitment of Black students into psychology, (2) the recruitment of Black faculty members into psychology, (3) the gathering and dissemination of information concerning the availability of various sources of financial aid for Black students, (4) the design and provision of programs offering meaningful community experience for Black students in the field of psychology, (5) the research and development of terminal programs at all degree levels that would equip Black students with the tools necessary to function within the Black community.*

The response of the Council of Representatives was to morally commit APA to the five objectives presented by BSPA, to explore the most effective ways of meeting the objectives, and to actively seek the funds necessary to implement them. The Board of Directors then established the Commission for Accelerating Black Participation in Psychology (CABPP), composed of members of BSPA, ABP (Association of Black Psychologists), and APA, as its primary agency for implementing the intent of the Council of Representatives in its October statement. APA went so far as to initiate a drive for private contributions from its members to be used to develop programs recommended by CABPP.†

The dual purpose of this lengthy introduction is to serve both as an illustration

---

This article was prepared for the first edition of this book. It has not been published elsewhere.

---

*From Simpkins, G., and Raphael, P.: Black students, APA, and the challenge of change, American Psychologist, 1970, 25, xxi-xxvi.

†A summary of the response of APA to the BSPA demands, based on a statement prepared for the Council of Representatives by the Board of Directors, which appeared in the American Psychologist, 1970, 25(5), xxix-xxxi.

of what a profession can do at a national organizational level if it is willing to make a moral, social commitment for the betterment of an oppressed minority, and as a basis for contrast and comparison to demonstrate the long-standing and continued lack of response by psychology and other mental health professions to the needs of the Chicano population.

As a result of the 1969 confrontation between BSPA and APA a guarded, yet undeniable feeling of optimism has precipitated among certain black individuals and members of the APA that psychology may be entering a stage in its development where psychologists may be willing, as well as able, to have some kind of professional impact on the lives of black Americans in significant numbers. Unfortunately, for Chicanos to have similar hopes at this time is far removed from the realm of reasonable consideration.

When several psychologists wrote to the president of APA to ask why APA seeks funds for one particular disadvantaged minority group when there are others equally deserving of support, the president responded:

> . . . our Association does have an active and permanent Committee on Equality of Opportunity in Psychology which is concerned with a broad range of related problems. But because the Black groups are now well-organized and prepared to take responsibility for developing their own constructive action programs, the Board and Council have approved this special appeal. At the same time, the budget of the Committee on Equality of Opportunity has been increased and its charge and activities broadened.*

Thus, in less than a paragraph the moral responsibilities of psychologists to significantly increase the number of Chicanos trained in clinical psychology (a responsibility psychologists assumed, perhaps unwittingly, when the Council of Representatives made its commitment to blacks) has been neatly set aside to be forgotten . . . once again. APA has an "active" and permanent Committee on Equality of Oppor-

tunity in Psychology but even a cursory inspection of the results of their labor as it relates to Chicanos reveals a "broad range of related" failures.

A survey by Boxley and Wagner (1971) reveals that with 78.6% of all universities with APA and non-APA approved clinical training programs in the United States reporting there were *six* Chicano graduate students enrolled. To in any way suggest that the "active" Committee on Equality of Opportunity in Psychology has been successful in regard to the recruitment of Chicano students from a population approaching six million* is both ludicrous and an insult to the intelligence of concerned Chicanos and psychologists alike. Bayton and co-workers (1970) discuss some of the many problems associated with the sparse and uncoordinated efforts to recruit minority group students for careers in psychology. They outline the difficulties of attempting to motivate students in a "non-traditional" area of study where the professionals and scholars in that area have been (and, in regard to Chicanos, continue to be) insensitive to the problems of disadvantaged minority groups. One factor that is obvious is the lack of exposure to Chicano models who have attained even the semblance of success in psychology. It becomes increasingly obvious that a massive professional and financial effort must be inaugurated if these problems are to be overcome.

It is reasonable to conclude that the reason given by the president of APA to explain why APA seeks support for blacks only is precisely the reason why APA should seek support for Chicanos and other minority groups—these groups are not well organized and understandably so. How can Chicanos be expected to be "well organized and prepared to take responsibility for developing their own constructive action programs" when there are fewer than ten Chicano graduate students in clinical psychology in the entire nation? How can fewer than ten Chicanos hope to politically and morally pressure APA into committing itself professionally and financially to improve the status of their ethnic group, as

---

*From a memorandum to APA members from G. W. Albee, President of APA, which appeared in the American Psychologist, 1970, **25**(5), xxxii.

*The estimated population figures are from the Census Bureau in Seattle, Washington.

did BSPA so successfully at the Miami Beach convention? Chicanos are caught in an unpleasant bind—APA will not professionally and financially aid Chicanos until they are well organized, but Chicano graduate students will not increase significantly in number nor be well organized until they have the professional and financial support of APA. The responsibility of bringing about even the most trivial increases in the number of Chicano students in psychology will remain in the hands of the individual psychology departments. Judging from past performance, it is doubtful that their efforts will be of much significance to the Chicano community as a whole.

Even when the small number of Chicanos in graduate programs is taken into consideration, the opportunities of Chicanos to see a psychologist or other mental health professional who shares their cultural heritage are less than might be expected. There exists in a majority of training programs a sometimes subtle but more often an obvious emphasis on the training of individuals whose careers will be devoted mostly to research and teaching, rather than to a professional practice. Like most generalizations the above can be easily and justifiably criticized, but few can honestly say that there is no validity in this description of the current training situation, particularly in clinical psychology. Moreover, most departments contemplate no dramatic changes in the organization and direction of their training programs, because "the professional reward structure in psychology makes it very difficult for major changes to take place" (Bloom, 1969). There are, in fact, a few examples of a shift toward a more practitioner-oriented training model. For example, the University of Illinois has instituted a training program leading to a Doctor of Psychology Degree (Peterson, 1968), which has tentatively been accredited by the APA. However, most of these remain quite controversial and exceptional (Thelein and Ewing, 1970; Hunt, 1969; Hoch, Ross, and Winder, 1966).

It is a sad commentary that psychologists in their haste to receive accreditation from APA for their clinical programs have so rigidly adopted what the Shakow

Committee (1947) intended as a general recommendation for training programs. Is it possible that clinical psychology after only twenty-three years of official existence is justified in its inflexible attitudes toward the training of its professionals? Surely, such a position is untenable. Nevertheless, the maintenance of an adequate supply of academicians will remain indefinitely the first and foremost priority of most psychology programs.

A second major focal point of criticism in the training of psychologists deals with the narrow stratum of society with which most student psychologists come in contact. The survey by Boxley and Wagner (1971) showed that two thirds of the clinics associated in training with psychology departments that kept data on the race and socioeconomic level of the clients served were serving populations with 95% to 100% white clients. The remainder had a client distribution more in agreement with the general racial, ethnic, and socioeconomic population where the clinics were located. Counseling services related to colleges, the second major source of clerkship training, were highly geared (75%) to serve the white collegiate population because of the underrepresentation of Chicanos and other minority groups in American universities (Boxley and Wagner, 1971). The survey also revealed that a substantial majority (63%) dealt mainly with middle- and upper-class individuals.

Frank Beach, a leading comparative psychologist whose contributions extend beyond this discipline to all of psychology, has repeatedly sounded the warning that psychological theorizing is based on phylogenetic and empirical foundations that are narrow in the extreme. For those who are in agreement with Beach, the definition of psychology as "the study of a white rat and the college sophomore" is devoid of all humor (Beach, 1950). The effects of the highly restricted experiences of most graduate students often result in biased, explicit and implicit theories of human behavior with which the professional psychologists leave the university setting. How well is the recently graduated psychologist prepared to deal with individuals who come from different racial, ethnic, and socioeconomic groups and whose values, attitudes, and general life styles may be at great variance with his own? The current training situation is clearly unfair to the student and to his future clients who are underrepresented in the typical college population. "Professional psychologists are currently trained towards the ultimate goal of serving the psychological needs of the middle class" (Gordon, 1965).

What happens to an individual who is a member of a "visible minority group" when he seeks psychological or psychiatric assistance? If a person is well educated or wealthy, he will in most instances recieve some form of "insight" therapy; if he is poor, he will probably not see a psychologist or psychiatrist at all, but if he does, his treatment will most likely be short-term supportive psychotherapy or some form of physical treatment (Hollingshead and Redlich, 1958; Rosenthal and Frank, 1958; Kahn and associates, 1957; Schaffer and Myers, 1954). A minority group individual may find himself in the difficult position of trying to overcome what Schofield (1964) describes as the therapist's "Yavis syndrome," a common tendency of the therapist to differentially select clients who are successful, young, attractive, intelligent, well educated, verbal, and introspective. (The term "Yavis" comes from the first letters of young, attractive, etc.)

Similar observations were made by Yamamoto and colleagues (1968), who followed the progress of 594 patients seen at the Los Angeles County General Hospital Psychiatric Outpatient Clinic. This particular study differed from previous studies in that racial as well as socioeconomic differences wee considered. Chicanos and blacks were most often discharged or seen for minimal supportive psychotherapy. There is a clear indication that patients were treated differently depending on factors of ethnic group membership or race.

The most obvious reasons for the high dropout rate among Chicanos and other visible minority group members are economic. Insight therapies are expensive and time-consuming. However, even in free clinics individuals of lower socioeconomic status are less likely to be accepted for intensive treatment; if they are accepted, they will often be treated by the less experienced members of the staff and will discontinue treatment sooner than members of the Anglo middle, upper middle, and upper classes (Winkleman, 1965; Overall and Aranson, 1963; Brill and Storrow, 1960; Levinger, 1960; Schaffer and Myers, 1954). A study by Imber and co-authors (1955) showed that even when all patients were treated at a free clinic by similarly trained staff (at the senior resident level) the lower-class groups still showed the same significantly higher dropout rate.

There are several possible explanations for the higher dropout among Chicanos, blacks, and poor whites, even in situations where the service provided is free. For years it has been widely assumed that the underutilization of health and social services by the poor reflects some subjective inadequacy in the reluctant clients. Winkleman (1965) states:

> They [the poor] are people who want immediate gratifications and are not willing to postpone gratifications for future rewards. They are not goal directed. . . . There is an inability to anticipate the future and to understand the present in terms of the past.[*]

Haggstrom (1964) provides a similar opinion:

> Caught in the present, the poor do not plan very much. They meet their troubles and make their pleasures on a moment-to-moment basis; their schemes are short term . . . they go forward, but not forward to any preconceived place.[†]

In short, the poor are assumed not to be goal directed, unable to delay gratification, and not concerned with the past or with planning for the future. It is further assumed that the poor require an authoritarian attitude on the part of the therapist. According to this assumption, many drop out of psychotherapy because therapists refuse to give enough practical advice

---

[*]From Winkleman, N. W.: The Psychiatric Treatment of Lower Sociocultural Level Patients in a Union Medical Center. In Culture, Change, Mental Health and Poverty. J. C. Finney (ed.), University of Kentucky Press, Lexington, 1965.

[†]From Haggstrom, W. C. The Power of the Poor, M. F. Riessman, et al. (eds.), Mental Health of the Poor, New York: Free Press, 1964.

about how to solve their problems and how to run their lives (Prince, 1965; Hacker, 1964; Hollingshead and Redlich, 1958). The poor are believed to be accustomed to being told what to do; when the therapist resists, the poor individual may feel that he is wasting his time (Spiegal, 1964).

Schneiderman (1965) and Klein and Miller (1959) argue that the types of behavior considered above are adaptive in the light of the chronic poverty in which most of these people will spend all of their lives. For the chronically poor to consider the long range results of their actions may be irrelevant or decapacitating. In contrast the typical American is very much concerned about planning for his future, but this concern is supported by the firm conviction that the future will be better than the past. Most poor Chicanos cannot realistically be so optimistic.

Although Schneiderman (1965) and Klein and Miller (1959) attempt to explain the behavior of the poor in terms of adaptability, they nevertheless accept the assumptions that the poor do not plan for the future, are unable to defer gratification, and are culturally and medically deprived (Suchman, 1963; Rainwater, 1960; Lewis, 1959). However, there is evidence (Riessman, 1970) that with the advent of neighborhood-based services, staffed in part by community workers, the poor quickly come to utilize social, medical, family planning, and mental health services. It is interesting to note, for example, that most family planning clinics were grossly underutilized by poor people (Freedman and colleagues, 1959; Rainwater, 1960) until this service was reorganized and delivered in a humane, neighborhood-based fashion (Riessman, 1968). The demand for the service then grew rapidly (Polgar, 1966; Riessman, 1968). The community mental health movement, which was given a tremendous impetus by the late President Kennedy's Mental Health–Retardation Center Act, has touched the lives of a large and growing number of individuals. The current problem is not to persuade the poor to use the available services, but rather to find ways to meet the ever growing demands for these services.

One may be surprised to learn that mental health programs are not "new" to people of Mexican descent—the first hospitals for the mentally ill in North America were built in Mexico (Morales, 1970). However, mental health programs for Chicanos in the United States are a very new phenomenon. The first community mental health service with a bilingual staff was established in 1967 in East Los Angeles. The staff consisted at that time of four psychiatrists, four psychiatric social workers, three senior public health nurses, one community mental health psychologist, one community coordinator, one vocational rehabilitation counselor, and seven clerical people—with only one of these twenty-two unable to speak Spanish (Morales, 1970). Previously it had been assumed that the poor are generally nonverbal, or are verbal in different ways or situations from middle-class subjects (Bernstein, 1964; Riessman, 1964; Hollingshead and Redlich, 1958). Evidence from the East Los Angeles clinic indicates that this generalization does not necessarily hold true for poor Chicanos who are permitted and encouraged to enter into a dialogue where Spanish, English, or a combination of the two may be freely used by *both* the client and the therapist in order to enhance the meaningfulness of their communication (Morales, 1970). The importance of the staff's ability to speak both languages cannot be overemphasized. In East Los Angeles almost half of the Chicano population speak only or mainly Spanish (Karno and Edgerton, 1969). It now seems clear that the Chicano poor are quite capable of verbally expressing themselves in the most intensive "insight" therapy situation, if they are not forced to communicate in English, a language that may be partly or completely foreign to these individuals.

Unfortunately, the not insignificant success of the mental health movement does not mean that the federal government, and psychology and psychiatry as professions, are approaching a resolution to the complex problem of providing adequate mental health care for the poor and the entire population in general. Two reasons are evident for this pessimistic observation, the first of which applies most directly to the poor, but eventually affects all Americans. The first major problem deals with the financing of community mental health services. Morales (1970) summarizes the problems encountered in funding a community mental health center in an economically distressed area as follows:

The National Institute of Mental Health is authorized by the Community Mental Health Centers Act to provide federal funds for the establishment of community mental health centers in the areas of need.* Under the same Act, grants are made available to help pay the salaries of professional and technical personnel employed in community mental health centers. However, the funds are awarded on a decreasing percentage basis for the center's first fifty-one months of operation.* Grants may cover 75% of eligible staff costs the first fifteen months, decreasing to "0%" by the fifty-first month. A poor community such as East Los Angeles, with no financial-industrial resources, can hardly afford such a needed service. Affluent areas which are not as needy as East Los Angeles have been able to establish sixteen of these related programs throughout Los Angeles.†

Adequately financing mental health services in poverty stricken areas and throughout the rest of the country will be a pressing issue for many years to come. It is reasonable, however, to speculate that in time funding problems like the one cited above can be resolved. There are no current indications that the second problem—providing the manpower to meet the accelerating demand—will be solved in the foreseeable future.

As the supply of properly offered mental health services increases, the demand for these services increases even faster (Riessman, 1968). Albee (1967) flatly states that the mental health professions have made so many promises to so many groups in our country that it is beyond their wildest manpower dreams that they can provide these services. In 1968 he presented a sobering list of examples to illustrate this point. Labor unions are currently negotiating contracts for out-patient care for their members and families. The United Auto Workers union has succeeded in its efforts, and now two and one-half million UAW people are suddenly eligible for outpatient mental health care. Other labor unions will surely follow their lead. Under Medicare and Medicaid, an enormous new group of people are suddenly eligible for prepaid or insured mental health care. Under Title 19 of this law, millions who are defined as "medically indigent," along with their children, are eligible for outpatient psychiatric care and other mental health services. Compounding the manpower shortage even further is the goal of the National Institute of Mental Health to build 2,000 new comprehensive mental health centers by 1980. Albee (1968) pointedly asks:

How can the 2,000 [new] centers be staffed when two-thirds of our existing 2,000 psychiatric clinics are without a single full-time psychiatrist, and when little psychiatric care is available in at least one-third of our state hospitals? (National Committee against Mental Illness, 1966).*

He then darkly concludes:

All of the plans for increasing professional services for the aged, for the union members and their families, for the medically indigent, for the inner-city poor, and for all the others lining up for care—all of these programs are going to fail . . .*

The reason for the failure of these programs is simple. ". . . we do not have enough of the *kind* of manpower demanded by the disease model of mental disorders" (Albee, 1968). He also convincingly argues: "The explanatory model dictates the kind of professional manpower needed to staff the institution. This means a current and future need for non-existent medical and paramedical professionals." It has been the consensus of experts that the United States must produce 11,000 physicians a year if we are only to stay even with the population growth; at the present time only 7,500 are being trained (Bane, 1959). Physicians, and consequently psychiatrists, are going to be in

---

*This information was taken from a federal publication on the National Institute of Mental Health Support Programs, U.S. Department of Health, Education, and Welfare, Public Health Service, p. 9.

†From Morales, A.: Mental and public health issues: the case of the Mexican-Americans in Los Angeles, El Grito, Winter, 1970.

---

*From Albee, G. W. Conceptual models and manpower requirements in psychology, American Psychologist, 1968, **23**(5), 317-320.

even shorter supply, while the service demands sketched by Albee (1968) mushroom everywhere. The future available supply of clinical psychologists and social workers is at least as inadequate as the prospective supply of psychiatrists (Albee, 1967). As long as we continue to accept the disease model of mental disorder, the number of medical and paramedical people trained will fall drastically short of the figure demanded by the model and by the people seeking these services.

"While the concept of mental illness had a sort of temporary usefulness in counteracting the older explanations of sinfulness and taint, it is now a millstone around our necks" (Albee, 1964). The most compelling reason for the persistence of the disease model has been the absence of a viable alternative model. In the last twenty years, however, an explanatory model for disturbed behavior, often referred to as "social learning theory," has emerged from psychotherapy, experimental work in learning laboratories, social work, and cultural anthropology—to name but a few sources.

This theory argues that most disturbed behavior consists of learned operant anxiety-avoiding responses. The origins of the anxiety to be avoided are to be found in traumatic social interaction of infants and children with the parents or parent surrogates. Evidence to support this explanatory model is accumulating in the research literature.*

The illness model for disturbed behavior is supported by powerful societal forces that must be overcome if adequate care is to reach all socioeconomic strata of society. Psychology and the mental health profession are challenged to create their own institutional structure for developing methods for the delivery of service so that they can begin to elaborate this conceptual model of social learning theory, along with the language and intervention techniques that will eventually permit people with a bachelor's degree (or even less education) to be the line workers in the field of behavioral disorders.

The parallel with the field of education is evident. Intervention in the educational system is by bachelor's level teachers who are supported by more highly trained research workers from several fields. Only when institutions are built in which BA people can work with disturbed or retarded children and adults . . . will we begin to meet the demand.*

A study by Arnhoff and Denkins (1969) shows that a large majority of those questioned in the Clinical, School, and Counseling Division of the APA recognized a need and approved of the training of people with less than a Ph.D. to work in the clinical setting; but how to implement this could not be resolved. A possible solution calls for rejection of the disease model by psychologists, acceptance of some version of social learning theory, and concentrated effort to develop and refine the conceptual models and research underpinnings under which the new model would operate. Because of their training, psychologists more than any other professional have the expertise to undertake the tremendous task of developing a scientific system whose ultimate goal would be the maximization of human potential and which would be educational, and not medical, in nature.

The day may not be far off when psychological disorders will be treated not in hospitals or mental hygiene clinics but in comprehensive "learning centers," where clients will be considered not patients suffering from hidden psychic pathologies but responsible people who participate actively in developing their own potentialities.†

Unless the mental health professions accept this challenge and actively seek alternatives to the illness model, the manpower shortage in "mental health" will continue to get worse, with poor Chicanos and blacks suffering most, since middle-class affluence is growing and making the middle class capable of absorbing even more of the services of the professionals being trained. It is ironic that G. W. Albee, who has been somewhat insensitive to the need of producing more Chicano psychologists, has developed the outline of a plan which,

*From Albee, G. W.: Conceptual models and manpower requirements in psychology, American Psychologist, 1968, **23**(5), 317-320.

*From Albee, G. W.: Conceptual models and manpower requirements in psychology, American Psychologist, 1968, **23**(5), 317-320.

†From Bandura, A.: Behavioral psychotherapy, Scientific American, 1967, **216**(3), 78-86.

if put into effect, could eventually provide scientific, quality service to all Americans at a reasonable cost, regardless of racial, ethnic, or socioeconomic factors.

If the relationship between psychology as a profession and Chicanos is to improve significantly, psychologists are going to have to stop playing the illness game. The rules of the game are such that there will *never* be enough professional psychologists to provide care except to selected members of the middle and upper classes. It is urgent that psychologists begin to carefully consider the ideas of Albee and of others with similar plans to make psychology socially relevant. There can be no doubt that a change has got to come.

BIBLIOGRAPHY

Albee, G. W. A Declaration of Independence for Psychology. *The Ohio Psychologist,* June, 1964.

Albee, G. W. The relation of conceptual models to power needs. In E. Cowen, et al. (Eds.), *Emerging approaches to mental health problems.* New York: Appleton-Century-Crofts, 1967.

Albee, G. W. Conceptual models and manpower requirements in psychology. *American Psychologist,* 1968, *23*(5), 317-320.

Arnhoff, F. N., & Jenkins, J. W. Subdoctoral education in psychology: A study of issues and attitudes. *American Psychologist,* 1969, *24* (4), 436-443.

Bandura, A. Behavioral psychotherapy. *Scientific American,* 1967, *216*(3), 78-86.

Bane, J. Physicians for a growing America (U.S. Public Health Service Pub. no. 709), Washington, D.C., U.S. Government Printing Office, 1959.

Bayton, J. A., Roberts, S. O., & Williams, R. K. Minority groups and careers in psychology. *American Psychologist,* 1970, *25*(6), 504-510.

Beach, F. A. The Snark was a Boojum. *American Psychologist,* 1950, *5,* 115-124.

Bernstein, B. Social class, speech systems and psychotherapy. In F. Riessman, et al. (Eds.), *Mental health of the poor.* New York: The Free Press, 1964, pp. 194-204.

Bloom, B. L. Training the psychologist for a role in community change. *American Psychological Association Division of Community Psychology Newsletter,* 1969, *3*(3), 1.

Boxley, R., & Wagner, N. N. Clinical psychology training programs and minority groups: A survey, *Professional Psychology,* 1971, *2*(1), 75-81.

Brill, N. Q., & Storrow, H. A. Social class and psychiatric treatment. *Archives of General Psychiatry,* 1960, *3,* 340-344.

Freedman, R., Whelpton, P., & Campbell, A. Family planning, sterility, and population growth. New York: McGraw-Hill Book Co., 1959.

Gordon, J. Project cause: The federal anti-poverty program and some implications of subprofessional training. *American Psychologist,* 1965, *20,* 334-343.

Hacker, F. J. Epidemiological observations on psychiatric disturbances and psychotherapy. In J. C. Finney (Ed.), *Culture change, mental health, and poverty.* Lexington: University of Kentucky Press, 1965.

Haggstrom, W. C. The power of the poor. In F. Riessman, et al. (Eds.), *Mental health of the poor.* New York: The Free Press, 1964, pp. 205-222.

Hoch, E. L., Ross, A. O., & Winder, C. L. *Professional preparation of clinical psychologists.* Washington, D.C.: American Psychological Association, 1966.

Hollingshead, A., & Redlich, F. *Social class and mental illness.* New York: John Wiley & Sons, 1958.

Hunt, D. McV. Graduate training: Some dissents and suggestions. *The Clinical Psychologist,* 1969, *22,* 182-188.

Imber, S. D., Nach, E. H., Jr., & Stone, A. R. Social class and Duration of psychotherapy. *Journal of Clinical Psychology,* 1955, *11,* 281.

Kahn, R. L., Pollard, M., & Frank, M. Social factors in the selection of therapy in a voluntary hospital. *Journal of Hillside Hospital,* 1957, *6,* 216-228.

Karno, M., & Edgerton, R. B. Perception of mental illness in a Mexican-American community. *Archives of General Psychiatry,* 1969, *20,* 233-238 (Feb.).

Klein, W. F., & Miller, W. B. Implications of urban lower-class culture for social work. *Social Service Review,* September, 1959.

Levinger, G. Continuance in casework and other helping relationships: A review of current literature. *Social Work,* 1960, *5,* 40-51.

Lewis, O. *Five families: Mexican case studies in the culture of poverty.* New York: Basic Books, 1959.

Morales, A. Mental and public health issues: The case of the Mexican-Americans in Los Angeles. *El Grito,* Winter, 1970.

National Committee Against Mental Illness. *What are the facts about mental illness?* Washington, D.C., 1966.

Overall, B., & Aranson, H. Expectations of psychotherapy in patients of lower socioeconomic class. *American Journal of Orthopsychiatry,* 1963, *33,* 421-430.

Peterson, D. R. The Doctor of Psychology Program at the University of Illinois. *American Psychologist,* 1968, *23,* 511-516.

Polgar, S. United States: The PPFA mobile service project in New York City. *Studies in Family Planning,* 1966.

Prince, R. Psychotherapy and the chronically poor. In J. C. Finney (Ed.), *Culture, change, mental health and poverty.* Lexington: University of Kentucky Press, 1965.

Rainwater, L. *And the poor get children.* Chicago: Quadrangle Books, 1960.

Riessman, C. K. Birth control, culture and the poor. *American Journal of Orthopsychiatry,* 1968, *38,* 693-699.

Riessman, F. New models for treatment of low income groups. *Transaction,* January, 1964.

Rosenthal, D., & Frank, J. D. The fate of psychiatric outpatients assigned to psychotherapy. *Journal of Nervous and Mental Disease,* 1968, *127,* 330-343, (Oct.).

Schaffer, L., & Myers, D. K. Psychotherapy and social stratification. *Psychiatry,* 1954, *17,* 83-89.

Schneiderman, L. Social class, diagnosis and treatment. *American Journal of Orthopsychiatry,* 1965, *35,* 99-105.

Schofield, W. *Psychotherapy: The purchase of friendship.* Englewood Cliffs, N.J.: Prentice-Hall, 1964.

Shakow, D., Hilgard, E. R., Kelly, E. L., Luckey, B., Sanford, R. N., & Shaffer, R. N. Recommended training program in clinical psychology. *American Psychologist,* 1947, *2,* 539-558.

Simpkins, G., & Raphael, P.: Black students, APA, and the challenge of change, *American Psychologist,* 1970, *25*(5), xxi-xxvi.

Spiegal, J. P. Some cultural aspects of transference and counter transference. In F. Reissman, et al. (Eds.) *Mental health of the poor,* New York: The Free Press, 1964, pp. 303-320.

Suchman, E. *Sociology and the field of public health.* New York: Russell Sage, 1963.

Thelein, M. R., & Ewing, D. R. Roles, functions, and training in psychology: A survey of academic clinicians. *American Psychologist, 1970, 25*(6), 550-554.

Winkleman, N. W. The psychiatric treatment of lower sociocultural level patients in a union medical center. In J. C. Finney (Ed.), *Culture, Change, Mental Health and Poverty.* Lexington: University of Kentucky Press, 1965.

Yamamoto, J., James, Q. C., & Palley, N. Cultural problems in psychiatric therapy. *Archives of General Psychiatry,* 1968, *19,* 45-49.

CHAPTER 28 COMMUNITY MENTAL HEALTH AND THE CHICANO MOVEMENT

CERVANDO MARTINEZ

This paper presents a definition of the Chicano movement, with emphasis on those aspects of the movement that relate to the sociology and anthropology of Mexican-Americans. Some theoretical points of overlap and common interest between the Chicano movement and the community mental health movement are described, and some aspects of the Chicano movement that have implications for clinical practice are discussed.

The term *Chicano* will be used in this paper to refer to a Mexican-American who adopts a certain state of mind or ideological stance. Thus, not all Mexican-Americans belong to the Chicano movement; in fact, probably only a minority do. The term Chicano has been used to refer to all Mexican-Americans for about 50 years and has had a vulgar and somewhat pejorative connotation. Since its new usage refers to a set of beliefs, especially about one's identity as a Mexican-American, involvement in the Chicano movement can call forth strong and conflicting emotions. As will be described later, the Chicano movement presents a challenge of conscience to all Mexican-Americans including professionals.

If we accept that there exists such a thing as the Chicano movement—that is, a group of oppressed people loosely held together by shared political and ideological beliefs and acting toward some common goal—then it may also be said that belonging to this movement, even peripherally, has mental health implications for the individuals involved. This is especially so if a movement such as the Chicano or Womens' Liberation movement emphasizes increased self-awareness, pride in one's nature and background, autonomy from repressive institutions, and greater responsibility for one's destiny and actions. Participation in such a movement offers the opportunity for positive identity formation in adults as well as adolescents. Indeed, Erikson feels that just such allegiance to an ideology is a part of the normal process of identity formation.

The Chicano movement can provide the opportunity for healthy identity growth in Mexican-American young people with incompletely structured identity and in those with identity foreclosure such as has been described in black adolescents.[2] The Chicano movement can re-open the issue of identity in a Mexican-American and produce a crisis even in an adult, hopefully resulting in healthy resolution and growth. Likewise, other social movements that involve oppressed minorities can be viewed as part of a larger revolution in the sensi-

From Amer. J. Orthopsychiat. 43(4):595-601, July 1973. Copyright © 1973 The American Orthopsychiatric Association, Inc. Reproduced by permission.

Presented at the Southwest Regional Meeting of the American Orthopsychiatric Association. November, 1972, in Galveston, Texas.

291

bility and structure of human relationships in society. A common goal of these movements is to redefine social relationships between groups, be they black and white, men and women, homosexual and heterosexual, or Mexican-American and Anglo. The redefinition of these relationships will have effects, perhaps only transitory, but significant for the mental functioning of many people, even those not directly involved in the movement.

There can of course be negative and destructive emotional results from activity in a political movement. The release of anger long pent-up can precipitate decompensations in marginally adjusted individuals. Likewise, the buildup of hopes and aspirations can lead to depression and hopelessness in persons who over-invest in ideals and who despair over the mundane.

What exactly then is the Chicano movement? It is *not* an awakening of a sleeping minority, or a new assertiveness by a once passive population, or a political upsurge by a formerly apolitical people. On the contrary, it is simply a further extension and development in the political and intellectual history of Mexican-Americans. In fact, an integral part of the Chicano movement is the criticism it has fired at the stereotype of Mexican-Americans as passive, asleep, and inert.

Another important thread in the movement is its stand against cultural assimilation. Until recently most authorities felt that the road to economic happiness for Mexican-Americans would open as soon as they became assimilated into the American melting pot. This ideal of acculturation and assimilation was held by Mexican-Americans also. Here I am in the opening lines of a paper with H. Martin in 1966, "Acculturation and assimilation of persons of Mexican origin in the Southwest has been slowed . . . "[4] Emphasis is placed on acculturation and assimilation and then I go on to talk about the so called "quaint" aspects of the culture, the folk medical beliefs. The Chicano movement appears to be a force working against some types of acculturation by actively encouraging the continued use of Spanish and the retention of traditional habits and customs. We can no longer say that, like other ethnic groups, Mexican-Americans will

soon be assimilated and thus their problems will be over.

However, what most concerns us here has been the criticism, best articulated by Octavio Romano-V[5] in a series of articles in *El Grito,* of the sociological and anthropological notions about Mexican-Americans. The Mexican-American has been said to be content, present-oriented, resigned to his fate, and not interested in education as a means of getting ahead. This set of values was most famously ascribed to Mexican-Americans by the anthropologist Florence Kluckhohn in her book *Variations in Value Orientations,* but others have described the same thing. These traits are interpreted to be culturally transmitted and are defined as what keeps the Mexican-American from advancing in American society. These attributes and values are usually juxtaposed to what are considered middle-class American values of getting ahead, planning for the future, and striving for material success. Thus, the implication is that the culturally transmitted values of Mexican-Americans are contrary or opposite to middle-class American values. An equally pertinent criticism of these studies is that they were done among rural Mexican-Americans. Recent population studies have shown that at present 80% of Mexican-Americans are urban.[1] Romano-V adds that, by ignoring the political and economic factors (and facts) that have affected the Mexican-American, a cultural determinism replaces an economic determinism. This is to say that the Mexican-American *culture* is defined as a culture of poverty and as being inimical to the American dream. So if the Mexican-American will just get rid of his excess cultural baggage, he will get ahead in life.

However, Romano-V's criticism of this notion of a deprived (if not depraved) culture seems to me to be a part of a wider development. This is the radical economic and historical criticism of the entire culture of poverty theory. The culture of poverty thinking is as follows: The poor have different values and aspirations, they are fatalistic, live only for the present, and place little value on education and work. The radical critics say this isn't so. They maintain that the poor people they talk to have not developed a separate set of values but that they too are completely absorbed in the dominant wishes and myths of the American dream.

Thus two points are made: that Mexican-Americans share many values with other poor people and that the poor have values not too different from those of the middle class. They simply differ in their realistic assessment of whether they can achieve these same goals. This realistic assessment of their capabilities, instead of being viewed as a healthy adaptive attitude, has been called fatalism, contentment with their lot, and lack of concern, all implying pathology, differentness, and wrongness. It is this sort of stereotyping that leads people in positions of dominance and control to expect the stereotyped behavior and plan accordingly. But surely Mexican-Americans differ in some respects from other groups. They do indeed; however, the point is that they may differ in respects not previously noted and their difference must be seen in a sociocultural and economic context.

Romano-V[5] also points out that the negative stereotype of Mexican-Americans as ahistorical and unpolitical flies in the face of the fact of a long history of strikes (before the grape boycott), political organization, agitation, and pamphleteering. He makes the point that Mexican-Americans have been led to believe that their history was the same as the history of all Americans, a history in which they were invisible or villains. However, there is a Mexican-American history with heroes, heroines, and villains, but a unique history at that. This has various mental health implications in terms of a positive historically and culturally colored self image, and has led to the Chicano movement's emphasis on teaching of Mexican-American history, literature, and art in the public schools.

Another line of Chicano criticism[5] has been of the national character studies, such as those of Diaz-Guerrero and Octavio Paz. These studies have been of Mexicans and only indirectly of Mexican-Americans. Both of these men write from a psychoanalytic frame of reference, emphasizing the libidinal aspects of personality development. Their widely read studies present Mexican men and women

as hopelessly neurotic. The male is the famous *macho,* the woman is masochistic yet dominating and controlling. These views of the family roles and their underlying psychodynamics can be criticized for being out of date theoretically and not taking into account more recent developments in analytic theory. However, a more important fault is that they also contribute to the notion of the Mexican-American as containing some virulent psychopathogenic entity that keeps him down, be it his *machismo,* his dependency, or his entire culture. In fact, more recent studies[6] in Mexico have not found the extreme traits of machismo to be as prevalent as expected. Only about 11% of the males in an entire village demonstrated the extreme traits.

The implications to mental health workers of these attacks on stereotypes should be obvious. Chicano writers have called for a redefinition of what a normal Mexican-American is; needless to say, this calls for a redefinition of why and in what manner Mexican-Americans become mad. How we define normality determines how we define pathology. (The recent book, *Women and Madness,* by Phyllis Chesler seems to attempt to make just such a redefinition of madness in women, as did the earlier *Black Rage* for black people.)

Perhaps this use of stereotypes partly explains why epidemiological studies of mental illness in Mexican-Americans are such an enigma. They will not be discussed here. Hopefully, with this rethinking and redefining of the Mexican-American personality and family, a workable set of hypotheses will emerge that can be applied to the existing population studies.

This rethinking and redefining presents some perplexing problems. For example, a commonly encountered person in our clinic is a middle-aged Mexican-American man who breaks down into dependency, over-concern about his health, and depression following some stress. His history usually reveals a life of hard and demeaning work since childhood (and here I mean age five or six), usually in the migrant stream. There was, of course, no time for school, adolescence, young adulthood, or any of the other niceties. So now, in his early thirties or forties, he calls it quits. It is easy to discard the old stereotype of the passive Mexican with unfulfilled dependency needs and see that this man has already put in a lifetime of hard work and that his current response is, in a sense, understandable and adaptive. He has simply retired at a young age. He is now getting even, in his own way, with a society that does not provide its workers enough so that children don't have to work. But is this man "sick"? Do we prescribe chemicals or do we praise and congratulate him? I don't know the answer to these questions.

One pitfall that I hope the Chicano movement avoids as it promotes a reexamination of the Mexican-American experience is that of glorifying and romanticizing that experience. Related to this is the risk of developing a rigid dogmatism about what it means to be a Chicano.

The Chicano movement shares certain more specific concerns with the community mental health movement. Rubin[6] has pointed out that the development of community psychiatry can be understood "in terms of an historical convergence of two streams of ideas and actions: the mental hygiene movement and the quest for social justice." The Chicano movement shares the latter of these underpinnings, i.e., the quest for social justice, and, in the manner described previously, can also be seen as a movement with effects on the mental hygiene of the population. Community psychiatry emphasizes the early detection, treatment, and prevention of mental disorders by a mental health system serving a distinct population or catchment area. The Chicano movement calls upon Mexican-Americans to strengthen their sense of community (or barrio) and to make care-giving institutions responsive and responsible. Nay, it says that institutions that serve Mexican-Americans should be controlled and operated by Mexican-Americans even if the professionals to staff these are not yet available. Hence the call for greater use of paraprofessionals, and in some instances a dangerous antiprofessionalism.

Related to this is another area of potential difficulty: many professional and paraprofessional Mexican-American mental health workers are active in the Chicano movement. They are independent, competent, and aggressive in their work. Their clients, the emotionally disturbed, often have problems with low self-esteem and dependency. This situation contains the potential for harmful negative reactions from the mental health workers as they encounter the frustration of working with dependent and helpless individuals. In other words, working with someone who has a problem similar to one that has been overcome contains the potential for both empathy and angry rejection.

Another point of confluence between community psychiatry and the Chicano movement is crisis intervention theory. Just as a crisis theory has served as the link between the public health notion of primary prevention and its mental health application with troubled individuals, it can also form a bridge between the community mental health and Chicano movements. Crisis theory stresses responsiveness and availability of mental health workers for persons in crisis; the Chicano movement attempts to redefine and articulate the needs (including the health needs) of the community. Crisis theory emphasizes the potential for emotional growth present in the process of coping with a crisis of life; the Chicano movement confronts the Mexican-American with a crisis and offers a course for resolution. Likewise, the Chicano movement stresses that a mental health service should be prepared to deal with crises other than just the ones related to interpersonal or intrapsychic conflict. Unfortunately, this emphasis on the social and economic crises in life can lead some to the extreme position of denying intrapsychic conflict in the poor.

It does not have to be repeated that poor people and people from minority groups get spun off from mental health delivery systems, ending up in walk-in or medication clinics. Racism and other factors are involved. However, other questions arise, such as what system is best for delivery of mental health services to a specific Mexican-American population. Torrey[8] has said, and perhaps rightly so, that traditional mental health services are irrelevant to the needs of Mexican-Americans because of the lack of cultural and language congruence between therapist and client. But even given Mexican-American staff availability, what mental health system is best for Crystal City? San Antonio? Houston? Partly due to the impetus of the Chicano movement there is now demographic data being generated so that more specific programs and services can be planned. Some services, such as our Mental Health Field Project, are based on the storefront model first used in black and Puerto Rican ghettos. Other programs aim at bringing a bit of the community into the hospital or clinic, thus softening the impact of hospitalization or outpatient treatment. However, these are variations on old themes. It may well be that hospital-based services, unpopular as they now seem to be, are best suited for delivery of mental health services to Mexican-Americans.

Finally, I would like to offer some speculations about Mexican-American male homosexuals and then raise some questions about the therapy of Mexican-Americans. In several conversations with Chicano mental health workers, the following observations about a possible relationship between the Chicano movement and homosexuality in male Mexican-Americans have been made. These are speculations and nothing more. Several of the workers are in agreement that, during the past several years, the Mexican-American male homosexual has become more visible—in his overt behavior, in seeking help, and in the appearance of gay bars in the *barrio.* It is theorized that this increased visibility is just that and not necessarily an indication of more homosexuality. The larger society's change in its attitude toward homosexuals is of course largely responsible for this, but other forces within the Mexican-American community could also be partly responsible. One of these is the decline of the *barrio* gangs. It is theorized that the gangs served to keep male homosexuals underground by two mechanisms: by outright intimidation and harassment, and by providing a means by which latent homosexuals in the gang could channel their sadistic and sexual impulses. The Chicano movement, with its emphasis on helping one's own people in the *barrio,* led many maturing ex-gang members to return to the *barrio* to work with their old gangs by directing them into more socially acceptable activities, but thereby also weakening the gangs' authority and dominance. With dilution of the gangs' strength, their repressive and sublimative functions were also loosened, leading to the emergence of more overt homosexual behavior previously latent and to less fear of intimidation in already overt male homosexuals. No one seems to know enough about female Mexican-American homosexuals even to speculate.

As with most papers written by a physician, I will conclude with some words about treatment. We don't really know what is the therapeutic efficacy of our different modalities with Mexican-American psychiatric patients. For example, are Mexican-American patients more responsive to medication because of different culturally influenced expectations about pills, as Stenger[7] has suggested? Is it possible that some of the concepts of the therapeutic community run counter to established and not easily changed patterns in Mexican-Americans? Much of what a milieu does therapeutically is to change the values of its members, emphasizing openness of communication, egalitarianism, and blurring of staff-patient roles. Recognizing the previously discussed criticism of ethnic stereotypes, are there still some values that are too deeply ingrained to be changed? Or should they be changed? Is it necessary that these values of the therapeutic community be acquired in order for positive therapeutic change to occur? These questions need to be asked and some attempt made to seek answers to them. Thus, I hope that these thoughts will not only encourage others to look in a different way at the normative and psychopathological aspects of Mexican-Americans but also to question some basic therapeutic methods.

REFERENCES

1. Grebler, I., Moore, J., and Guzman, R. 1971. The Mexican-American People. Free Press, New York.
2. Hauser, S. 1971. Black and White Identity Formation. John Wiley, New York.
3. MacCobby, M. 1971. On Mexican national character. In Chicanos: Social and Psychological Perspectives. N. Wagner and M. Haug. eds. Mosby Co., St. Louis.
4. Martinez, C. and Martin, H. 1966. Folk diseases among urban Mexican Americans. JAMA 196(2).

5. Romano-V, O., ed. 1971, Voices: Readings from El Grito. Quinto Sol.

6. Rubin, B. 1971. Community psychiatry; an evolutionary change in medical psychology in the United States. Arch. Gen. Psychiat. 20:497-507.

7. Stenger, E. The Mexican-American: how his culture affects his mental health. Unpublished paper.

8. Torrey, E. 1970. Irrelevancy of traditional mental health services for urban Mexican-Americans. Papers presented at the annual meeting of the American Orthopsychiatric Association.

SELECTED BIBLIOGRAPHY

Acuña, R. *Occupied America: The Chicanos struggle towards liberation.* San Francisco: Canfield Press, 1972.

Acuña, who is Professor of Chicano Studies at California State University at Northridge writes of Chicano history from a Chicano point of view.

Cabrera, Y. A. *Emerging faces: The Mexican American.* Dubuque, Iowa: William C. Brown Company, Publishers, 1970.

An over-all view of the Mexican-American as a contemporary Chicano. Cabrera expresses his own particular orientation and responses to events as a Mexican-American. This is a good introduction to understanding Mexican-Americans. Easy reading.

Castañeda Shular, A., Ybarra-Fausto, T., & Sommers, J. *Literatura Chicana Texto y Contexto.* Englewood Cliffs, N.J.: Prentice-Hall, Inc., 1972.

A literary account of Chicano past and present. Expresses the human suffering and the Chicano spirit of endurance as well as the different aspects of Chicano lifestyle. This book is part of the emerging Chicano literature.

Duran, L. I., & Bernard, H. R., *Introduction to Chicano studies.* New York: Macmillan, Co., 1973.

An edited book of readings with a focus on historical articles.

El Grito. Quinto Sol Publications. P.O. Box 9275, Berkeley, California, 94709.

A journal of literary, historical, and psychological articles.

Grebler, I., Moore, J., & Guzman, R. *The Mexican-American people.* New York: The Free Press, 1970.

A comprehensive historical background on Mexican-Americans.

Kiev, A. *Curanderismo: Mexican-American folk psychiatry.* New York: The Free Press, 1968.

A psychological and anthropological look at folk techniques for dealing with emotional problems. Has much of a "community psychology" orientation.

McWilliams, C. *North from Mexico: The Spanish-speaking people of the United States.* New York: Greenwood Press, Inc., 1968.

Originally published in 1948. Far and away the most comprehensive study of the Spanish speakers of the United States Southwest, despite its age. Excellent historical background study of prejudice and racial relations. Details of Spanish influence in southwestern culture; labor struggles of the recent past.

Mathiessen, P. *Sal si puedes; Cesar Chavez and the New American Revolution.* New York: Random House, Inc., 1969.

A very readable portrait of Cesar Chavez and the grape strike. Cesar Chavez is the charismatic leader and advocate of nonviolence who began "La Causa," perhaps the greatest agricultural labor strike in the history of the U.S. This book gives an accurate and personal account of the San Joaquin Valley strike and the Chicanos who are struggling in "La Causa."

Nabokov P. *Tijerina and the Courthouse Raid.* Albuquerque; University of New Mexico, 1968.

Tijerina is the leader in New Mexico who has revitalized the fight over land rights. This book gives an account of Mexican-American history in New Mexico. Tijerina's personal history and present thoughts and strategy are examined.

Nava, J. *Viva La Raza!* New York: D. Van Nostrand Company, 1973.

A collection of historical documents highlighting some nearly forgotten aspects of the history of Mexican Americans.

Padilla, A. & Aranda, P. *Latino mental health: Bibliography and abstracts.* Rockville, Maryland: Alcohol, Drug Abuse and Mental Health Administration, 1974.

An extensive collection of books and articles on psychological and general mental health of Latinos. For sale by the Superintendent of Documents: U.S. Government Printing Office. Stock No. 1724-00316.

Parades, A. *With his pistol in his hand: A border ballad and its hero.* University of Texas Press, 1971.

A study of a ballad and a ballad hero. It is an account of the life of a man, of the way songs and legends grew up about his name, and of the people who produced the songs, the legends, and the man.

Rendon, A. *Chicano manifesto: The history and aspirations of the second largest minority in America.* New York: Collier-MacMillan International, Inc., 1971.

A comprehensive manifesto that gives an economic, philosophical, political, and spiritual history of the Chicano experience in America.

Romano-V., O. J. *El Espejo, The Mirror.* Berkeley: Quinto Sol Publications, Inc., 1969.

This book presents a number of contemporary Chicano writers. It gives a literary view of the thoughts and feelings of different Chicanos, and illustrates the diversity and complexity of the Chicano personality.

Simmens, E. *Pain and promise: The Chicano today.* New York: Mentor Book, 1972.

Thirty-two essays written by both Chicanos and Anglos. Considers the Chicano movement from many different points of view. The essays trace the history of Chicanos in this country, detail the forms of oppression they have faced, and describes the emerging Chicano movement.

Steiner, S. *La Raza, The Mexican-American.* New York: Harper & Row, Publishers, 1969.

A broad picture of Mexican-Americans supplying details of the political sophistication and cultural richness of Mexican-Americans. He gives an impressionistic history of the Mexican-American people.

Valdez, L., & Steiner, S. *Aztlan: An anthology of Mexican American literature.* New York: Vintage Books, 1972.

One of the current literary approaches to the Chicano experience. Valdez, Chicano playwright and founder of *El Teatro Campesino,* teaches Chicano studies at the University of California at Berkeley. Steiner is the author of *La Raza,* and other widely read books.

Womack, J. *Zapata and the Mexican Revolution.* New York: Alfred A. Knopf, Inc., 1969.

A very readable narrative history about Zapata and the Mexican Revolution. Provides a historical background on those Chicanos who are the descendants of some of the Mexican *campesinos* who began the struggle for freedom in Mexico.

INDEX